Class
Action

Doubleday

NEW YORK LONDON TORONTO
SYDNEY AUCKLAND

Class
Action

THE STORY OF LOIS JENSON AND THE LANDMARK CASE
THAT CHANGED SEXUAL HARASSMENT LAW

CLARA BINGHAM &
LAURA LEEDY GANSLER

PUBLISHED BY DOUBLEDAY
A division of Random House, Inc.
1540 Broadway, New York, New York 10036

DOUBLEDAY and the portrayal of an anchor with a dolphin are
trademarks of Doubleday, a division of Random House, Inc.

Book design by Gretchen Achilles

Library of Congress Cataloging-in-Publication Data

Bingham, Clara.
    Class action: the story of Lois Jenson and the case that changed sexual harassment
law / Clara Bingham and Laura Leedy Gansler.
        p. cm.
    1. Jenson, Lois—Trials, litigation, etc.   2. Eveleth Taconite Co.—Trials,
litigation, etc.   3. Women miners—Legal status, laws, etc.—Minnesota.   4. Sex
discrimination in employment—Law and legislation—Minnesota.   5. Sexual
harassment of women—Law and legislation—Minnesota.   6. Class actions (Civil
procedure)—Minnesota.   I. Gansler, Laura Leedy, 1958–   II. Title.
KF228.J464 B56 2002
331.4'133'0977677—dc21   2001058158

ISBN 0-385-49612-5

Printed in the United States of America
June 2002

FIRST EDITION

For Sam, Jamie, Will,
Henry, and Diana

Contents

PART THREE
The Verdicts
1996–1998

PART ONE

Close
to the Land,
Far From the
Law

1975–1987

CHAPTER ONE

The Mine

March 1975

It snowed all day and night on Sunday. By dawn, three feet of snow covered the Mesabi Iron Range. Lois Jenson warmed her delicate hands on her coffee mug as she looked out the window of her small house in Virginia, Minnesota. She glanced at the clock on the kitchen wall: 6:15. She drank the last of her coffee and set the mug in the sink. It was Monday, March 25, 1975, Lois's first day of work at Eveleth Mines. If she didn't want to be late, she had better give herself some extra time. The day shift started at 7:00 A.M. In this weather, it would not be a twenty-minute trip.

Luckily, her turquoise Ford Maverick rode high over the road, and though she had to inch along on Highway 37, she could clear most of the snow on the two-lane road, which cut a straight line through the austere landscape of aspen, birch, and jack pine. In the distance she could make out the three twenty-story stacks of the mine's Forbes Fairlane Plant, each mounting a tall white column of smoke in the bitter northern Minnesota sky.

At the town of Forbes she turned onto the long drive leading to the plant. Up ahead, a man flagged her down. She saw his pickup buried in a snow drift and when she discovered that he, too, was on his way to the plant, she gave him a ride. His name was Clarence Mattson. He told Lois he was an electrician and that he'd worked at Eveleth for ten years. He seemed like a decent guy, and he mentioned that the men were bellyaching about how, starting today, they had to behave themselves and clean up their language. He showed her where to park in the employee lot and where she should enter the enormous plant. The truth was, she felt relieved to be arriving at this place accompanied. The closer she got, the more it looked to her like a steel monster with tentacles jutting out from all sides. But, she thought, as she stepped out of the Maverick and into her new life as an iron miner, "If everyone's this friendly, I'm going to like this job."

As Lois and Mattson walked the fifty yards uphill to the main building, they were quickly joined by dozens of men. Most of them were streaming out of the building, dirty and tired after working the midnight shift; the rest were arriving to punch in for the day. Lois noticed that these guys were staring at her. She was twenty-seven years old, with shoulder-length wavy blond hair, blue eyes, and pale, clear skin—a Scandinavian beauty with a slender waist and an elegant long neck. She was used to feeling men's eyes upon her, but this time it was different. It felt as if the men had never seen a woman before.

Lois hurried into the trailer Mattson said was serving as the women's changing room while the mine built its four new female miners a permanent "dry"—a term left over from the days when miners worked deep underground, often in several feet of water. The "dry house" was where they changed into their clean clothes at the end of a shift. Because of the snow, Lois's three female colleagues hadn't made it to their first day of work, so she found herself alone in the small, barely heated room. The starkness of the quarters startled her: twelve steel lockers, a table, four chairs, and a shower, sink, and toilet stall, none of which worked on account of the cold. Waiting for her in the locker room was a white hard hat with a blue stripe and the name JENSON printed on the brim in block letters, a pair of men's size six Red Wing work boots, and clunky plastic protective glasses. In the unheated room, she changed into thermal underwear, a sweatshirt, a down vest, gray-and-blue striped coveralls she had bought the day before, the boots, plastic protective glasses, and hard hat. She stood in front of the mirror over the sink and burst out laughing—the person in the mirror looked like an auto mechanic, not a mother. Lois held her breath for a few seconds and walked out into the plant, where her first task was to go on a tour.

The Forbes Fairlane Plant evoked fear in a newcomer. Dominated by four cavernous buildings, the fine crusher, the surge, the concentrator, and the pellet plant, the facility sprawled over 2.3 million square feet—as if all 102 floors of New York's Empire State Building (2.1 million square feet) were spread end to end across the snowy Iron Range. That didn't even include the Thunderbird Mine, two open pits devouring 8,600 acres, from which spewed the iron ore–rich taconite rock that was mined. The plant operated 24 hours a day, 7 days a week, and consumed 70 megawatts of electricity per hour—about as much as the neighboring cities of Virginia, Eveleth, and Hibbing combined. The year the women started, the management of Eveleth Mines had ordered Forbes Fairlane's production capacity be expanded from 2.4 million tons of taconite pellets a year to 6 million tons. Everywhere she looked, Lois could see construction crews at work upgrading and enlarging the facilities.

Taconite rocks contain between 20 and 30 percent iron ore, a foreman explained to her. The taconite was blasted out of "the pit," as everyone called Thunderbird, which was located nine miles away, on the outskirts of the town of Eveleth. There, the boulders were loaded into trucks and brought to the pit's "primary crusher," where they were broken down to the size of footballs. A long line of railroad freight cars transported the rocks from the pit to the plant. The taconite was then carried by conveyor belt to the fine crusher—the first stop in a long, pulverizing process—where the rocks were ground into taconite gravel.

The crusher was outfitted with eighty-foot-high rock-crushing machines and a dizzying maze of conveyor belts. Before she could even take in the scene, Lois was gagging from the black dust that filled the air, like thick smoke in a crowded bar. She could barely distinguish one thunderous machine from another as she struggled to adjust her eyes to the haze. Sticky dust coated her exposed skin and hair, suffocating her. Even more disorienting was the noise. The crusher spoke in a giant, booming voice and the constant smashing of the rocks in the teeth of the machines made earplugs mandatory. Because the dust contained cancer-causing silica, the men also wore white paper masks over their mouths. The earplugs and the mask plunged Lois into a kind of isolation she had never experienced in a workplace before.

She was grateful for the relative peace of the concentrator, her next stop on the tour, until its foreman, John Maki, led her up to the building's catwalks. Unaccustomed to the weight of her work boots, Lois could barely lift her legs as she and Maki climbed higher. The clunky metatarsal guards on top of the boots kept catching as she stepped from one platform to another. Until now she had not known that she was afraid of heights. Skyscrapers in Minneapolis had never bothered her. But now she couldn't bring herself to walk to the edge of the grated catwalk and look straight down ten stories.

The first purpose of the concentrator was to grind the gravel to a sandlike consistency, using rod mills, which were large rolling tubes containing steel rods. Another set of revolving drums filled with magnets then separated the iron-bearing grains of ore, or "concentrate," from the waste rock, or "tailings." After passing through the crusher and the concentrator by way of a labyrinth of conveyor belts, the wet concentrate arrived at its final destination, the pellet plant.

The dirt here was overwhelming. The air, walls, and floors in the pellet plant were filled and coated with black soot the consistency of flour. Her every step left a footprint as she walked out of the service elevator on the top floor of the building and gazed down 100 feet at a panorama of revolving steel machines all lined up in rows like dryers in a monstrous Laundromat. These were the huge round rotating balling drums, churning and thundering so powerfully that they made her heart race. The balling drums rolled clockwise all day, shaping wet black concentrate into round, marble-sized pellets. Thousands of black pellets rolled inside the drums on the first floor of the pellet plant. They were then hardened in a 120-foot-long rotating kiln fired at 2,400 degrees. The end product was millions of smooth, heavy black pellets containing 65 percent iron ore, ready to be loaded onto train cars for the 60-mile trip to the Lake Superior ports of Duluth and Two Harbors. From there, the pellets were loaded onto huge freighters and shipped to steel mills in Chicago, Gary, Cleveland, and Pittsburgh.

The plant challenged Lois's basic assumptions about a workplace. With no sun and no air, it felt primitive, menacing. The workday would be regulated not by people but by huge, ferocious machines and literally tons of dirt. The size and might and violence of the place made Lois realize that she would have to toughen up. The job would demand more than physical strength, however. For although her coveralls, boots, hard hat, and protective glasses had effectively desexed her, everywhere the foremen took her, the miners stopped what they were doing, gathered together in small groups, and stared. She didn't know a man there, yet everyone seemed to know her.

In 1975, mining put food on the table for 12,300 families on the Mesabi Iron Range, and provided the foundation for the economy of all of northern Minnesota. Minnesotans call the thin, ore-rich seam that stretches 110 miles long and 1 to 4 miles wide from Grand Rapids in the west to Babbitt in the east "The Range." The region amounts to less than 2 percent of the landmass of Minnesota, yet it is the largest iron-ore deposit in the world. For the past century it has produced 30 percent of the world's and two thirds of America's iron ore. Blasted in furnaces into steel, the ore and taconite from the Mesabi's tiny strip of land has provided the raw material that built postindustrial America—its buildings and bridges; its railroads, cars, and military arsenal. Rangers, as they call themselves, pride themselves on working hard, drinking hard, and surviving hard times at the hands of the mine owners. They were used to fighting for themselves—strikes were their way to better wages and work safety. In 1975, the heavily unionized mines provided some of the highest-paying blue-collar jobs in America. Wages at Eveleth started at $5 an hour (the minimum wage was then $1.80 an hour), and included good health care and retirement benefits. But because this good life was threatened by layoffs or, worse, by permanent cut-backs, the miners lived with an engrained sense of job insecurity, hostile to any force that might displace them.

Up until the mid-seventies, the women on the Range who needed or wanted to work were store clerks, teachers, bank tellers, secretaries, and waitresses. Few of these jobs came with health care coverage or above-minimum-wage salaries. But in April of 1974, nine of the country's largest steel companies signed a "consent decree" with the Equal Employment Opportunity Commission (EEOC), the U.S. Department of Justice, and the Labor Department. The settlement forced the steel companies to hand over a historic $30 million in back pay to minority and women employees who had been discriminated against in the past. It also required the industry's mills and mines to provide 20 percent of its new jobs to women and racial minorities. Just like that, affirmative action had come to the Iron Range, and it set the stage for Lois Jenson and a handful of women desperate for a decent wage to walk into a place that had been forced by the federal government to hire them.

There is a saying about the Range: "Where the men are men and half the women are, too." But from the start, Lois was not like the other women at Eveleth Mines, or, for that matter, like most women on the Range. Feminine and ladylike, standing only five-foot-two and weighing a mere 105 pounds, Lois took pride in her appearance. She manicured her nails, wore perfume, and was known for her trademark scarves, artfully tied and color-coordinated with her outfits. The fact that she wore *outfits* set her apart. "In some ways I'm different from people around here," she said. "I always like to dress up. Even if I went out to Mugga's, our local place to dance, I would wear blue jeans with a dressy sweater and high heels."

She was different in other ways, too. She wrote poetry in notebooks that she carried with her. She exuded a sense of propriety that men, particularly those she turned down when they asked her to dance at Mugga's, took for conceit. She was a unique combination: stubborn but prissy, moral but flirtatious. She had a sense of herself that even her classmates at Babbitt High School had perceived. The quote they picked for her yearbook picture in 1966 read, "Don't dare me, I might surprise you."

Most people on the Range rarely drove the sixty miles south to Duluth, yet Lois had moved even farther downstate to Minneapolis/St. Paul after she graduated from high school, where she found work as a file clerk at an insurance company. She loved living in Minneapolis, loved how the people in the Cities were open-minded and well educated. But the Cities also brought her trouble. In 1967, a man she met at a party forced her to have sex with him in the backseat of a car. When she went to the police department to report the date rape, she watched as police interrogated another woman so cruelly that Lois walked out the door and never reported the crime. She became pregnant from the rape and bore a son, Gregory,* in January 1968. With nowhere else to go, Lois took the baby home and lived with her parents in Babbitt. When Greg was six months old, Lois left him in the care of her parents while she went to secretarial school in Minneapolis, making the 230-mile drive to Babbitt each weekend. After receiving a legal and medical secretarial degree, she took a secretarial job at an insurance company in Minneapolis and brought Greg to the Cities to live with her.

In 1969, Lois discovered that her high school sweetheart was back from Vietnam and living in Minneapolis. They fell in love. After a hard labor with Greg, Lois had been told by her doctor that she had a tilted

---

*Both Gregory's and his father's names have been changed.

uterus and could never get pregnant again, but in the winter of 1969, she discovered the doctor was wrong. She and James Larson had made plans to get married, but when Larson learned of her pregnancy, he broke off the relationship. At the hospital Lois decided to name the baby girl Tamara, then she put the child up for adoption. A week after giving the baby up, she visited her at a foster parent's home. The baby was covered in urine and had terrible diaper rash. Overcome with emotion, Lois changed her mind and demanded to keep her daughter. At age twenty-three, she found herself alone with two-year-old Greg and a new baby.

It seemed that her only choice now was to go home. She moved back to the Range, to the town of Virginia. There, at least, the cost of living was cheaper and she could be close to her parents, who lived forty-five minutes away in Babbitt. Her parents loved Greg, but strongly disapproved of Lois giving birth to a second child out of wedlock, and her mother refused to accept Tami as a member of the Jenson family. Nevertheless, her parents bought Lois a little house for $3,000 for which she paid them rent. Still, Lois and the kids were just barely getting by. Greg was teased often by other children in the neighborhood because he didn't have a father at home and his mother was on welfare. When Lois hired a twelve-year-old girl from across the street to baby-sit, the girl told her, "My parents said that you're on welfare so we're just getting our money back." At the Super One grocery store in town, Lois paid with food stamps, and people made comments like "She can afford to buy [expensive food] because she has food stamps." She felt humiliated.

Late one hot summer night in 1971, a tornado touched down in Virginia and changed her life. The wind picked up with horrifying speed, and through her living room window Lois could see the outlines of the funnel cloud in the distance. Her house did not have a basement. She had to seek shelter down the block at a neighbor's, but she couldn't safely carry both children at once. Faced with every mother's nightmare—a "Sophie's Choice" of choosing one child over the other—she instinctively picked up Tami first and ran down the block with the girl in her arms. Once Tami was safe, Lois ran back home through a torrent of flying branches and garbage and grabbed Greg. When the storm was over, she was shaken. She realized she couldn't take care of both children alone, that she could only offer them a life of poverty. Tami, Lois told herself, was still young enough to be accepted into a family who could give her more of a future. She decided again to put her up for adoption. This time, she said, "I signed the papers and didn't look back."

It was, as devastating experiences often are, also a galvanizing moment in her life. "When I gave her up, I promised her and myself that I wasn't going to waste my life," Lois said, and a week later she got a job with the credit union in Virginia, working as its teller, file clerk, and secretary. The job paid $1.80 an hour. Lois paid a neighbor $1 an hour to baby-sit Greg. Welfare and food stamps covered her medical and food expenses. For three and a half years she worked at the credit union earning an annual salary of $5,000. All the while, she cashed the paychecks for other Rangers, many of them larger than hers. At last, in 1975, she was told that she would get a 5 percent raise. However, 3 percent of the raise, her boss explained, would be put into a new pension fund for employees over age twenty-eight. Lois was nearly twenty-seven, making her effective raise 2 percent. This seemed grossly unfair to her, and she insisted that she deserved 5 percent, too. When her boss refused, Lois said, "Then I quit."

On her last day on the job, again about to join the ranks of unemployed single mothers, she confided her situation to a customer named Dayis Begich. Begich, who worked as a secretary at Eveleth Mines, reached into her purse and pulled out an application for a job at the mine. She told Lois that the mine had just hired four women laborers for the first time, but one of the women had failed her physical exam and there might be another opening. It had never occurred to Lois to work as a miner, but she vividly remembered women miners who worked for U.S. Steel, which had begun hiring women miners the year before, "coming in with these big checks." She also remembered feeling a little intimidated by these husky women. Not for the last time, she decided to swallow her misgivings. "I just wanted a job, frankly," she said.

On February 25, 1975, her twenty-seventh birthday, she sent in the application. The mine directed her to a clinic in Virginia where she received a physical—back X-ray, general health, hearing. The doctor also asked questions about her periods, and how long they lasted. "I thought it was so bizarre," she said. Lois had heard that women applicants would be subjected to pelvic exams to prove that they were not pregnant. But she later recalled, the clinic was so uncomfortable with the procedure that they wouldn't do the pelvic exam. "There was no interview, no reference check. They just needed four female bodies." When she got the job, she thought she had struck gold. She would be earning $5.50 an hour along with good medical benefits for herself and Greg. Working at the mine would be her ticket out of shame and poverty.

A few days later Lois drove out to the general office at the Forbes Fairlane Plant for an orientation session with the three other women— Priscilla Robich, Connie Saari, and Marcella Nelson. They were greeted by Milan Lolich, the supervisor of safety and training.

He looked Lois up and down. "You're too tiny, you're too feminine," he said. "The work is too hard, it's too dirty, it's too noisy."

She just stared at him, mystified. "I've got the job," she thought, "and he's trying to tell me not to take it."

Her own brother Duane, who had worked summers at the Reserve Mining Company in Babbitt, had also urged his pretty, well-mannered little sister not to take the job. "There were guys I worked with who, without the 'f'-word, were without a language. They couldn't express themselves," Duane told her. Reserve, he reminded her, had a reputation as one of the more civilized mines in the Range. Eveleth, on the other hand, was known in the area for its roughness, and for hiring miners not for their skills but because they knew somebody or were related to someone who already worked there. As a result, the mine's 750 laborers were a tightly knit group, with everyone into everyone else's business. Priscilla Robich, Connie Saari, and Marcella Nelson all had personal ties at the mine and understood its culture. But Lois did not. Until that day at orientation, she had never even visited her father at his job as a truck driver at Reserve mine.

Yet Joseph Jenson was all for his daughter working at the mine. College was a waste for girls, he believed. Why throw away good money on a girl who was only going to college to find a husband? He had no objection to his daughter working, however. This was her opportunity to make a good living and to get off welfare, he told her. Lois's mother disapproved of her daughter having two children out of wedlock and going on welfare, and Lois was painfully aware that her life's direction in recent years was antithetical to the straitlaced way she'd been raised. She saw the Eveleth job as her best chance for independence and respect. Although neither of her parents said anything to Lois at the time, she suspected that her parents thought the mine might be a place where Lois could meet someone. "They were always trying to find me a husband," said Lois.

Ironically, it was family status that got her and the other three women their jobs at Eveleth. Priscilla was a widow with four children to support, Connie was a divorced mother with one child, and Marcella was, like Lois, a single mother. "The fact that you are all heads of households will make it less traumatic for the men," Lolich told them. He added, with palpable displeasure, that the mine had been forced to hire the four women.

On her second day at work, Lois got her first taste of how some of the men really felt about her presence. She had been assigned to work in a long, low-slung building called the fine ore surge—the midway point between the crusher and the concentrator—reporting to the "Mexican feeder area" in the basement of the surge building. The gravity feeder took its name from the big bins, which resembled upside-down sombreros, into which the ground ore sludge was poured from a conveyor belt above.

Lois set to work in a ten-by-twelve-foot basement sump room with cement-block walls. Her job was to clean up the sludge that had fallen off a conveyor belt one story above. She soon discovered that the sludge was so thick that if she stepped in it, her boot would pull right off. As she began shoveling, a tall, heavyset man named Franklin Guye walked down a ramp into the room carrying a small portable crane on his shoulder. Neither looking at her nor breaking his stride he said, "You fucking women don't belong here. If you knew what was good for you, you'd go home where you belong."

Lois had expected that the men at Eveleth would condescend to her. Men she had worked with in office jobs in Minneapolis did as much. But nothing in her experience had prepared her for the vitriol that had just come out of Franklin Guye's mouth. As tears welled up in her eyes, she tried to buck herself up, saying, "I am going to be able to do this."

The next day she felt relieved when Priscilla Robich was assigned to work with her in Mexico. Their job was to clean under the big conveyor belt that carried black rocks into the feeder, then sweep the floor and dust the machinery. In the basement sump room, they had to heave shovels of wet sludge that had fallen on the floor into a hole in the wall above their heads. Lois's back, shoulder, and arm muscles were so sore during those first nights that she would make dinner for Greg and fall asleep by 7:00 P.M.

She had never performed heavy manual labor before, and after a few weeks, as her muscles began to strengthen, she found that she began to have just enough energy to come home and perform her second shift: clean the house, shop for groceries, and take care of her seven-year-old son. At the credit union Lois had felt a lot of pressure handling other people's money. If she got the numbers wrong in the till one day, she would have to pay back the difference out of her own pocket. Often she was swamped and stressed. Now she was discovering the satisfaction that can come with hard physical work, and she and Priscilla rooted each other on. One day as they were shoveling the floor Priscilla missed the hole in the wall above their heads and a shovel full of sludge fell on her face. The two women howled with laughter.

During their first weeks in Mexico, they were visited regularly by men in top management. The mine supervisors and some of the brass from Oglebay Norton, the Cleveland-based company that managed the mine, would descend into the sump room in their dark suits and ties and ask the women how they liked their jobs. What were they finding most difficult? Lois admitted that she was having trouble getting used to the heavy boots, but that otherwise she was happy. She and Priscilla kept Mexico spotless, and the mine's management told them that if they kept up the good work, more women would be hired. This made Lois uncomfortable. She had no interest in being a role model who would decide the future of other women in the mine. She and Priscilla were getting special attention and the other laborers resented it. "What are you trying to prove?" they would accuse her. "Are you trying to show us up?" At Eveleth Mines, earning the respect of management was an obstacle to earning the respect of the union brothers.

One day early on in her employment, Lois finished her tasks with time to spare. So she asked John Maki, the foreman who had taken her on the tour of the catwalks, for more work to do until the end of her shift. Maki's mood suddenly turned angry. He handed her a heavy three-inch-diameter rubberized high-pressure hose, told her to climb up to the top of an eight-foot ladder and clean the "brick room." But the hose was too short and Lois had to bend down to hold on to it. Maki turned on the water and told her he would be back in fifteen minutes.

Lois stood doubled over, holding on to the hose with one hand on the ladder. Fifteen minutes passed, then twenty, then thirty. Maki never came back. Just as she was going to have to either drop the hose from fatigue or fall off the ladder, someone turned off the water. After that she never asked for extra work.

"If it weren't for the good guys," she later recalled, "I wouldn't have lasted two days." A foreman named John Raffini had taken note of her willingness to work hard. One morning, Raffini said, "Whenever you join a crew, we'd like you to join ours." But as her brother Duane had predicted, the language her fellow miners used disgusted her. She had never used the word *fuck* herself, but it was a staple in the vocabulary of just about everyone she worked with. Lois found that if she let people know that it bothered her, they would lay it on thick.

In April, after she had been at work a few weeks, a miner named Paavo Kivisto approached and proceeded to tell Lois a dirty joke. Kivisto had an audience—a group of men huddled nearby to hear him tell his joke; then, as Kivisto produced a plastic penis and put it on his nose for a gag, the men looked on to see what Lois would do. Her face turned bright pink and she fled the room. A few weeks later, Lois heard that the guys were placing bets on how long the women would last. The longest any of the men gave them was nine months.

On payday, any concerns Lois had about the job disappeared. Every two weeks she received a $440 paycheck. She was now earning close to the same salary as her father. She worked a grueling schedule of ten days on, four days off, 7:00 A.M. to 3:00 P.M., but when she worked Sundays, she was paid time and a half. On working holidays, she was paid double time and a half. "I may be dirty, but I got money!" she thought as she proudly marched up to the credit union window she'd sat behind for three and a half years and cashed her checks.

Every payday she celebrated with Greg by taking him out to dinner at their favorite Chinese restaurant, Mr. Ju's. She bought him a bicycle and, for the first time in their lives, she was able to go into a store and buy new clothes for herself and her son. Knowing that layoffs and strikes could hit at any time, she saved as much as she could, but each payday she would treat herself to one special item—a new toaster, new cutlery, Tupperware. Most important, Lois could walk into the Super One and buy food with cash instead of food stamps. She could attend church without having to hear people snicker about her behind her back. She could hold her head high.

CHAPTER TWO

The Range

Summer 1975

Lois was wrestling with a three-inch-thick power hose on the floor of the concentrator one day in June when Chuck Killian walked by.

"You've got an audience," he said, a big smile on his face.

Killian was a foreman in the concentrator, where Lois had recently been transferred—"rotated" the miners said—after three months in Mexico with Priscilla Robich. Now Lois worked alone in this vast, gloomy building, the only woman among about fifty men. Once again her job was doing something the men did not like to do: clean—hosing the black dirt into piles, picking nuts and bolts off the floor, dusting handrails. "You women are so good at those cleaning jobs," Killian told her.

She turned around and sure enough, six men stood ten yards away, watching her handle the hose. She thought, "It's like they're still in high school." To Killian she said, "Would you tell them to go away?"

"It's your responsibility to tell them to leave you alone and go back to work," the foreman replied.

The scene repeated itself often during her first month in the concentrator. She would get a feeling that she was being watched, look over her shoulder, and find eight electricians gawking. Under her hat, safety glasses, and coveralls, "How can they even tell I'm a woman?" she thought to herself.

Killian's attitude—I'm here to work, not to protect you—was typical among the men at the mine, and Lois quickly learned not to expect any help from her superiors when it came to deflecting unwanted attention. John Maki even started joking about the phenomenon. "I always know where to find Lois. Just look for the hard hats," he said. "Like bees to honey."

But in Mexico, once the men got used to her presence, she found she could strike up friendships. Every morning at the panel, a narrow room where the controls for the concentrator were operated, and where workers got their assignments for the day, she and Priscilla and Connie Saari teased Lois's partner, Bruce Campbell, about his exploits of the night before: "So Bruce, did you get any last night?" Bruce, a good-natured ladies' man, gave as good as he got. Jocular teasing, Lois had decided, was harmless. But between dealing with the hostility and the sex jokes and learning the job, she also had decided not to date any men from work for at least a year. Not that she was blind. When a good-looking, well-built, olive-skinned maintenance mechanic named Gene Scaia shooed Paavo Kivisto away from her one day (it had become common knowledge that Lois was the woman a dirty joke would most mortify), she was relieved when he mentioned he was married. She and Gene became friends. Soon she began to rely on him as a protector.

In July, Lois was told it was time that she learned to "drive truck," meaning the eighty-five-ton dump trucks the plant used to transport tailings waste. On her first day, she came upon her instructor who seemed to be intently inspecting the lug nuts on one of truck's ten-foot-high wheels.

"Good morning," she said just as, to her disgust, he zipped up his fly. He had been urinating on the tire. Far from being embarrassed, the miner seized the moment to tell her about the time he pulled two tampons out of his wife, and to regale Lois with stories of deer having sex. Another instructor's hands shook and breath smelled of alcohol even at the beginning of the shift. The third instructor got a kick out of pulling Lois close to him every time someone came within sight of the truck.

Lois was worried that she would be pegged as a bad woman driver, but to her own surprise it turned out that she was adept at handling the vehicles. "Driving an eighty-five-ton truck is like driving an apartment building," she said. "There's no visibility on the right side, but everyone gets out of your way."

Not long after she'd earned her forty-hour certification Lois was summoned by the foreman, Bob Sametz, and told to go out to the trucks; Bob Raich was waiting for her out there. She already knew that Raich, the mine's director of personnel, was one of the most despised employees at Eveleth. A burly man with a flat-topped crew cut and thick, dark-rimmed glasses, he was, even by Range standards, "cocky and arrogant, a womanizer, a male chauvinist pig," one miner told Lois. Another chuckled over how Raich had found his desk and chair relocated to the men's bathroom the morning after he'd been dismissive of Doug Wilson, the plant's respected general manager. Most famous was the tale of how late one night Raich, who was known to frequent the bars, drove his car into a ditch. He called the plant and demanded that someone come and tow him out. Instead, the guys at Forbes Fairlane called the cops, gave them Raich's location and hoped that he would be arrested for driving under the influence.

Raich may have been mocked at the plant, but he had power there. He had worked at Eveleth ever since it opened in 1965 and had managed to ingratiate himself with the management in Cleveland. The day Lois met him he was standing beside the truck with a photographer sent by the company. Oglebay Norton needed a picture of a "lady truck driver" for its annual shareholders report, Raich said. Lois obliged and got into the truck and drove around for an hour while the photographer took pictures. The photograph that the company had picked was of her in her hard hat and dirty coveralls, bending over the truck's windshield as she washed it. She was later told that the company chose that pose instead of the shots of her driving because only in this one could they tell she was a woman.

A few months later, a foreman handed her a copy of the annual report. Instead of feeling proud, she felt like a token. From that day on, the men teased her about being Eveleth Mines' sex symbol.

In the hands of a miner worried about job security, the annual report must have seemed a bizarre document, with its portraits of Oglebay Norton chief executives past and present—smooth-faced men named Crispin, Courtney, and Frederick—dressed in bow ties and stiff white collars. Lois flipped through it, reading about the iron-ore empire that Earl W. Oglebay and David Z. Norton had built almost a century before, on the bad luck of six brothers from Duluth.

In 1890, prospectors Alfred and Cassius Merritt, sons of Lewis H. Merritt, a timber cruiser and one of the first settlers of Duluth, discovered soft red iron ore close to the earth's surface in the Mesabi Range. Previously, the Mesabi had been overlooked by geologists because its ore formations differed from those in other mines of the Lake Superior ore district. The Merritt's discovery sparked a rush for the "red gold," and by 1892, fifteen thousand prospectors had fanned out over the wilderness area previously populated only by bears, trees, and a few logging camps. Unlike the ore that had been mined in Michigan's Marquette Range in the 1840s and Minnesota's Vermilion Range in the 1880s, Mesabi ore did not require underground mining. Residue from glacial drift and a vast inland sea two billion years old had left deposits of soft high-grade ore in shallow pockets, some within ten feet of the earth's surface. The Merritt brothers soon learned that steam shovels could easily scoop the dusty red clay from the ground.

In partnership with four other brothers and one nephew, the Merritts (called "the seven men of iron") acquired a fifty-year lease on seventeen thousand acres of land from the state at the discount price of $141,000, broke ground at two mine sites in Mountain Iron, and began to build a railroad line to Duluth.

In October 1892, the first shipment of ore—4,245 tons—rumbled off the Range bound for the Lake Superior port of Duluth. Two years later, eleven mines on the Mesabi shipped more than 1.5 million tons of ore to steel mills in the East. But in the Panic of 1893, the bottom fell out of the iron and steel industry. The Merritts did not have enough capital to keep their mines and railroad operating, and they turned for help to the Standard Oil tycoon John D. Rockefeller.

Rockefeller had dabbled in mining in Wisconsin and saw a better opportunity in Minnesota. He loaned the Merritts the then unfathomable sum of $2 million. When they defaulted on the loan, they had to offer Rockefeller so much stock in their company, Lake Superior Consolidated Iron Mines, that they ultimately were forced to forfeit control to the oil baron. Rockefeller built the largest fleet of ore carriers on the Great Lakes and hired Oglebay, Norton and Company in Cleveland to manage his new ore empire of mines, railroads, and ore carriers.

Meanwhile, the industrialist Andrew Carnegie also had ventured into iron mining on the Mesabi so that he could provide his steel-blast furnaces with their own supply of cheap ore. In 1901, Rockefeller and Carnegie merged their mines and mills, creating United States Steel. The trust's holdings included 41 mines, 1,000 miles of railroad, a fleet of 112 ore-carrying vessels, and half the ore properties on the Mesabi. Wall Street financier John Pierpont Morgan masterminded the creation of what became the first billion-dollar corporation in America, controlling the biggest ore deposit in the world. The Mesabi soon became the engine that fueled the Age of Steel.

Iron ore from the region almost single-handedly built America's arsenal of ships, planes, tanks, bombs, and guns in both world wars. During World War II, the Mesabi shipped three billion tons of ore—fulfilling two thirds of the country's wartime needs. The Hull rust mine in Hibbing, once called the "iron capital of the world," alone supplied one fourth of all the iron ore consumed by the nation during the two world wars. The 535-foot-deep, 1,600-acre pit, called the "Grand Canyon of the North," was the biggest hole ever dug by man. But the demands of World War II drained the region of most of its soft, pure ore reserves, and by the early 1950s, several of the mines had shut down, decimating the local economy as the best-paying jobs dried up.

Bob Dylan (he was born Bob Zimmerman) grew up in Hibbing in the 1950s where his father and uncles owned a household appliance store. Dylan wrote about the desolation on the Range after the ore ran out in "North Country Blues":

> *Come gather 'round friends*
> *And I'll tell you a tale*
> *Of when the red iron pits ran plenty.*
> *But the cardboard filled windows*
> *And old men on the benches*
> *Tell you now that the whole town is empty . . .*
> *The summer is gone,*
> *The ground's turning cold,*
> *The stores one by one they're a-foldin'*
> *My children will go*
> *As soon as they grow.*
> *Well, there ain't nothing here now to hold them.*

Yet as early as 1913, an engineer named Edward W. Davis had begun experimenting on the low-grade ore rock called taconite, of which the Mesabi had a three-billion-ton reserve. While Rockefeller and Carnegie had discounted taconite as useless, Davis refused to give up on his hunch that it could be mined, and by the mid-fifties he had perfected the arduous process of making 65 percent ore-rich pellets from taconite.

Thanks to "Mr. Taconite," as he became known, the Range was

back in business. Defunct ore pits were converted to lakes while new craters were dug for extracting the hard black rock. Adjacent to the open pits, factories were built for manufacturing ore-rich pellets. Now the Range would not simply be digging up its iron ore, as it had in the past; it would process the ore as well. In 1955, the Reserve Mining Company opened the first taconite mine in the town of Babbitt and a plant in Silver Bay; two years later came the Erie Mining Company's taconite operation in Hoyt Lakes. And within days of Lois's high school graduation, on June 10, 1966, Vice President Hubert Humphrey, Minnesota's most revered politician, gave the keynote address at the dedication ceremony for Eveleth Mines' Forbes Fairlane Plant. Eveleth would be the third of seven taconite mines, and its opening marked the beginning of a new generation of mining on the Range.

Oglebay Norton was still in the business of managing mines and transporting ore. It managed Eveleth Mines, and owned 15 percent of the operation. Ford Motor Company held the other 85 percent, and the day the plant opened, Ford chairman Henry Ford II and Oglebay Norton president E. W. Sloane Jr. presided over the ceremony. Under a big white tent erected next to the plant, surrounded by 8,500 acres of swampland and forest, 800 civic leaders dined on barbecue flown in from Detroit. By the end of the 1970s the Iron Range employed 14,000 miners and exported 50 million tons of taconite pellets per year to steel mills in the East.

Doug Wilson remembers being in awe when he found himself sitting just a few rows behind Vice President Humphrey at the ceremony. Wilson was part of a group of engineers hired by Ford in 1963 to design the plant, and he and his colleagues located the operation in Forbes, halfway between the cities of Eveleth and Virginia, because it was close to the St. Louis River, which could provide a steady water supply. Oglebay Norton leased more than nine thousand acres of land from U.S. Steel for extracting taconite rock near Eveleth, nine miles away from Forbes. None of the other companies' mines were so far from their manufacturing plants, but at the time, said Wilson, "taconite looked like it was going to be so profitable that Ford didn't worry about the extra cost of moving the rocks from Eveleth to Forbes nine miles by train."

In the early days of the mine, employees felt as if they were part of the Ford Company family. "I could buy Ford cars on the same discount as a worker in the Dearborn, Michigan, plant," said Dan Schultz, who started working as an engineer in the plant in 1974. The mine's corporate image identified with Ford, and having only two owners made the decision-making process uncomplicated for local managers. But in 1974, Ford and Oglebay Norton decided to increase the capacity of the mine from 2.4 million tons of pellets a year to 6 million tons. To raise money for the two-year, $350 million expansion, Armco Steel Corporation and two Canadian companies—the Steel Company of Canada and Dominion Foundries and Steel—were brought in as corporate partners. The expansion changed the atmosphere at the mine. Between 1974 and 1976, 639 young and inexperienced employees came to work at the mine, and old-timers complained about the new arrivals' lackluster work ethic. Although management of Eveleth was still primarily Oglebay Norton's responsibility, there were now five owners, each with its own agenda. "We had no parents, no identity," said Schultz. Meanwhile, Oglebay Norton was having troubles of its own. On November 10, 1975, Oglebay Norton's flagship freighter, the 729-foot SS *Edmond Fitzgerald*, sank to the bottom of Lake Superior in a storm of 30-foot seas. The ship, with a crew of 29, was bound for Detroit, loaded with enough taconite pellets to build 7,500 cars. The disaster was later immortalized by Gordon Lightfoot's ballad, "The Wreck of the *Edmund Fitzgerald*."

Doug Wilson became the mine's general manager in 1977. After the expansion, he and the top management team traveled to Cleveland for meetings. "In the room would be representatives of the five owners, and each one had a lawyer and an accountant there to ask you questions like 'Why do you use so much shovel grease?' " Wilson said. "When Ford was the sole owner, it was much easier to get decisions made."

Once a month, the owners would fly in on their company jets to the small airport in Hibbing for a day of meetings at the mine. "They would swoop in like a flock of seagulls: make a lot of noise, eat all the food, and crap on you," said Schultz. "Our local management didn't have any authority, and Oglebay Norton had to be the mediator between the five owners for all of the budgeting and planning decisions. Cleveland didn't even have the power to make decisions." This led to common criticism on the Range by local businessmen and politicians that Oglebay Norton didn't have the same incentive to run a good company as some of the other single-owner mines, which were known for fostering better labor-management relations. The other problem that plagued Eveleth Mines was the nine-mile stretch between the pellet plant and the mine. When taconite prices plummeted in the early 1980s, Eveleth earned the dubious reputation for producing the most expensive pellets on the Range.

The Ojibwa tribe that first inhabited this northern reach of wilderness named the place Messabe—"red giant who slept in the earth." Until the Merritts' discovery of red gold in 1892, the area was a wooded wilderness dotted by swamps, lakes, and a few logging camps. By 1900, more than 23,000 people flooded the area; 20 years later, the Range's population had exploded to more than 100,000. Forests were burned and tree stumps removed to make way for towns that sprung up next to mines. Between 1892 and 1925, 175 towns were founded on the Mesabi. In the town of Hibbing three new buildings were built each week, as miners spilled out of hotels, boardinghouses, and mining camps, erected shantytowns, and settled in wherever they could. Sanitary conditions were primitive. People disposed of their sewage and garbage in open ditches. Cows and chickens wandered the streets freely. A reporter in 1908 described a street in Eveleth as "almost a solid row of large boarding, tenement and bath houses, with little or no open space between the buildings, nearly all overcrowded, with a number of home laundries in the block, and a row of cow sheds and much used privies on the high ground adjoining the alley." In 1909, ore was found underneath the town of Sparta near Eveleth, so the town was simply relocated to nearby Gilbert. This fate later befell the towns of Mesaba, Meadow, Adriatic, Leonidas, Spina, Belgrade, Elcore, and Hibbing.

In 1918, when ore was found under Hibbing's main street, the city was moved piece by piece over the course of thirty years. Bob Dylan sang about the upheaval in one of his Epitaphs:

(it was a dyin' town)
a train line cuts the ground
showin' where the fathers an' mothers
of me an' my friends had picked
up an' moved from
north Hibbing
t' south Hibbing
old north Hibbing . . .
deserted
already dead
with its old stone courthouse
decaying in the wind
long abandoned
windows crashed out
the breath of its broken walls
being smothered in clingin' moss

Hibbing made the most of this inconvenience by heavily taxing the mining companies. In 1923, the proceeds allowed the town to build a lavish $3.8 million high school and junior college—at the time, the most expensive in the nation. Mining money gilded all of the Range towns, which enjoyed the best schools and public works in the state. In some communities, the mines paid 99 percent of all taxes levied.

———

Utterly different from Minnesota's prairies, which were pioneered by families arriving in covered wagons, the Range was settled by men who arrived alone. Mostly they were poorly educated immigrants from Europe who came to dig the mines, build the railroads, log the forests, and send their earnings back home. Those men had tough lives and their ethic was passed on from generation to generation. The 1895 census showed that men outnumbered women on the Iron Range five to one. By 1900, the ratio had reached two to one. Not until 1930 would the gender ratio on the Iron Range draw even. Hospitals had no facilities for women. Saloons were the center of social life, prostitution and gambling thrived, and men got drunk on weekends and fought. Life in the early days was so hostile to women that one historian wrote: "It has been said that women often refused [high] wages of up to $5.00 a day [working in a boardinghouse] because of the crude remarks made to them when they arrived on the train from Duluth."

Much of Minnesota had already been pioneered by northern and western European immigrants who came to America as part of the migration wave of 1840–1890. By the time the Mesabi needed labor in the late 1800s, it was eastern and southern European immigrants who were flooding into New York, where they were met by mine scouts and put on trains to northern Minnesota. Because the bulk of the mining jobs could be filled by unskilled, non-English-speaking labor, the Iron Range soon became a melting pot of Old World languages and cultures. In 1910, twenty-five nationality groups could be found on the Iron Range. Finns, who fled to the United States to escape the Russification policy of Czar Nicholas II, represented 25 percent of the immigrant population. Slovenes and Italians were the next-largest group, followed by Swedes, Croatians, and Norwegians.

A hierarchy soon developed. Anglo-Saxons and Scandinavians, or "Whites," were hostile toward what they called the "Blacks," or southern Europeans. The new immigrants were taunted as "Finlanders," "Bohunks," and "Dagoes" and accused of living like pigs, working their wives like slaves, and being generally lazy. Hard-drinking "Black Finns" were considered troublemakers, while a separate group of "temperance Finns" was more socially acceptable. "Red Finns" were those who were socialists and union organizers.

People were divided among religious lines as well, with the Scandinavians worshiping in Lutheran churches, and the Italians, Slovenians, Croatians, and Slovaks founding Catholic churches. The Serbians and Greeks started their own Eastern Orthodox churches and the Finns were Unitarians. Self-segregation developed in many towns. Virginia had "Finn town," and Chisholm's Finnish neighborhoods were labeled "Pigtown" and "Finn Hell." Hibbing and Virginia considered themselves "white men's towns" because their population was predominantly northern European, while Chisholm and Eveleth were stigmatized as "Black" towns.

The rebirth of mining on the Range in the mid-fifties brought the Range's final wave of immigrants: Minnesota farmers from the southern and western part of the state, no longer able to make a living, were drawn to the region by the promise of good jobs in the mines. Locals derisively called the new arrivals "pack sackers," a term coined during boom times, when outsiders would arrive with their belongings on their backs to take jobs in the mines or work construction.

The Jenson family were a part of that pack-sacker wave, moving to Babbitt in 1956, when Lois was eight years old. Yet only two years before the town had been nothing but scenic woodland wilderness on the far northeastern tip of the Mesabi. In 1954, Reserve had built Babbitt from scratch and hired a thousand laborers to work in its mine. Almost thirteen hundred prefabricated houses were brought in on trailers, a school was established, and a sewer system was built.

Life in Babbitt stood in stark contrast to the Jenson's rural life in the small town of Ulen in northwestern Minnesota, where they grew their own vegetables, killed their own chickens, had no plumbing, and used wood-burning stoves to heat the Saturday bath water in a tin tub. When Lois, the youngest of four, was born in February 1948 in the middle of a snowstorm and the family's car was immobilized, Joseph Jenson hitched a hay wagon to a horse, put the baby in the wagon, and brought her home. In Babbitt, every family lived in identical prefab houses set on treeless streets; every father worked at the mine and earned the same salary. For the first time young Lois and her siblings—whose two sets of grandparents were both Norwegian—were exposed to people of Italian, Finnish, and Yugoslavian descent. In Ulen they'd attended a one-room schoolhouse; now they went to school with thirty children per class. The miners' earnings ensured that their wives did not have to work; so many children were soon born there that the young families became known as "Babbitt Rabbits."

Because it sprang up almost overnight, Babbitt was never considered by other Range communities to be a legitimate member of the Iron Range—only if your family had lived on the Range for three generations could you hope to be accepted as a local.

What the transplants gained in economic security and creature comforts they lost in family and community ties. On holidays, the Jensons would pile into the car and drive four and a half hours back to their hometown to visit grandparents, aunts, and uncles.

One cause powerfully united the diverse immigrant groups on the Range: their struggle against the management of the mines, dating back to when the Merritt brothers lost their company to John Rockefeller. Since then, mines on the Range have been owned by large out-of-state corporations and dominated by U.S. Steel. Absentee owners have been more concerned with meeting their tonnage requirements than answering the needs—and demands—of their workers. In July of 1907, the Western Federation of Miners organized a bitter strike, composed mostly of Finnish workers. The strikers demanded increased safety measures, an eight-hour day, and an end to the corrupt payment system, which depended on the number of railroad cars miners loaded every day. Mrs. Mary Harris "Mother" Jones, a senior member of the United

Mine Workers of America, traveled to the Range at the age of seventy to lead the strike. It lasted a month, ending when the mining companies imported as scabs Greeks, Italians, Croatians, Slovenes, and Montenegrins fresh off the boat. Finns were blacklisted by the mines for their roles in organizing the strike and had to find work in lumber camps or on farms. After it was over, the percentage of Finns who worked for the Oliver Mining Company, U.S. Steel's subsidiary, dropped from 18 to 8. Because of the blacklist, Finns became the poorest ethnic group on the Range for several generations. Making ends meet without a miner's paycheck was difficult in a place where the soil is rocky and the growing season short.

By 1916, the scabs became the strikers when the Industrial Workers of the World mobilized between fifteen thousand and twenty thousand miners to walk off the job. Living conditions, wages, and workplace safety were still substandard. Between 1906 and 1916, seven hundred men had been killed in the mines. Another female jawsmith, Elizabeth Gurley Flynn, or "Rebel Girl" as she was called, traveled on the back of a bakery truck from one end of the Range to the other speaking to large groups of striking miners. The strike lasted for three months and ended in defeat when the strikers ran out of money. They gained none of the points they fought for, but months later U.S. Steel raised all wages 10 percent. The Oliver Company, U.S. Steel's subsidiary, began to improve working conditions for its workers, but at the same time the company organized an elaborate internal spy network that identified and blacklisted union organizers. Not until passage of the National Labor Relations Act in 1935 did labor unions earn the right to bargain collectively. Known as the Wagner Act, it probably had more impact on life on the Iron Range than any other single piece of federal legislation, because the law gave real power to organized labor. Several mining companies signed contracts with unions in the late 1930s, but U.S. Steel didn't make an agreement with the United Steel Workers of America until 1943.

Since then, the United Steel Workers of America has held a powerful grip on the Iron Range. The unions, which dominate the political life of the region, are the backbone of Minnesota's liberal Democratic-Farmer-Labor Party, formed in 1944. The DFL, a merging of the Democratic Party with the noncommunist faction of the Scandinavian-influenced Farmer-Labor Party, became the home of Minnesota's greatest progressive politicians: Hubert Humphrey, Eugene McCarthy, Orville Freeman, and Walter Mondale. The pro-union, pro–welfare state party has always had a powerful base in blue-collar union communities like the Iron Range.

Over the course of the twentieth century, a strong Ranger provincialism evolved. On "da Range," people "speak Ranger." Said one local, "We drive truck, ride bike, go show, go Duluth." "Downstate" people call them "de-Ranged." Rangers don't care: They take pride in surviving the longest, coldest winters in the continental United States. They enjoy their reputation for being independent, hard-drinking, crude, opinionated, and insular. Colleges in Duluth and Minneapolis host alcohol-laden "Ranger Parties." The "Minnesota Nice" personality characterized in Garrison Keillor's *A Prairie Home Companion* does not apply here.

Much of what gives the Range its original character is the blending of the mores and lifestyles from the Old World. The Yugoslavs and Italians brought with them patriarchal, male-dominant societies. The Finns brought credit unions, food co-ops, and socialist political leanings. To this day, Rangers are more aware of their European roots than most second- and third-generation Americans. As late as the 1970s, intermarriage between Finns and Italians or Croatians and Swedes was frowned upon. At union meetings when a meal is served and grace is said, members can tell who their allies are by how they cross themselves. Serbians (whose names often end with "ich") cross themselves on the left first, then right. Slovenians (whose names usually end in "ik") cross from right to left. Arguments between people with Serbian-born parents and people of Croatian heritage broke out in bars and barber shops all over the Range during the Balkan war in 1999. Finnish saunas occupy backyards and garages, while Italian baci courts are carefully landscaped in others. Slovene batista pastries are sold at Range bakeries alongside Finnish lempia bread and Italian napoleons. Cornish meat pies, called "pasties," are favorites at church fund-raisers and school bake sales. Clubs and festivals feature Slavic button box accordion players and polka fests. Assimilation came slowly to the Range in part because it is so geographically isolated and because there has been little new blood since the 1920s.

It could be said that the Range's biggest contribution to U.S. culture is ice hockey. In a state where the high school hockey tournament is tantamount to a religious event, the Range is the Holy Land. Eveleth is the birthplace of American hockey, hosting the first game in 1902. The world's largest hockey stick (107 feet tall) hovers over the town's main street and the U.S. Hockey Hall of Fame is located in Eveleth on Hat Trick Avenue. Watching high school hockey is the main social event of the winter season on the Range, and the town of Hibbing, population 17,300, hosts an ice arena that seats 3,460. Eveleth has its own Eveleth Hockey Mothers' Association. Boys on the Range start in hockey leagues at age four.

Rangers are also avid curlers, snowmobilers, fishermen, ice fishermen, and hunters. They consider their personal playground the untouched wilderness of the Boundary Waters Canoe Area Wilderness—just a half-hour drive north with its 2,500 lakes and 1.1 million acres of forest populated with black bear, moose, and loons. The opening weekend for fishing walleye pike is a bigger holiday than the Fourth of July, and deer-hunting season rivals Christmas.

Practically every other storefront on the main street of any Range city is occupied by a bar, and it is not unusual for them to open at 8:00 A.M. to serve the men getting off the midnight shift. Owning a popular bar gives a Ranger clout in the community; each is its own fiefdom, and several local politicians-cum–tavern owners use them as their political power bases. Socializing on the Range takes place almost exclusively in these simple, wood-paneled rooms where food is served and children can be found playing pool and darts with their parents. On weekends, many families retreat to their "cabins," nestled on lakeshores just north of the Range. During hunting season, the men disappear into the woods to rustic hunting shacks that are often owned jointly by a group who try to keep the location secret from their wives. "Seven out of ten men will say they live here so they can hunt and fish," said one male Eveleth native.

Combine paternalistic Old World cultures and an economy based solely on mining with pastimes of drinking and hunting and you get a distinctly macho worldview. One woman Ranger explained the men this way: "Their buddies are first, then their sports, their wants and needs, and if there's any time left, well, the wife and family get it." A female graduate of Hibbing High School in the late seventies recalls walking through the "meat line" every morning on the way to school. "One hundred boys would line up on either side of the front entrance of the school and make comments about each girl's looks as we walked into the building."

"Females are there to be used and abused," said a Ranger male. "Take care of me, my kids, my family and don't bother me. I'm going fishing. Women are chattel." A classic Ranger bumper sticker reads: THE PERFECT WOMAN: A NYMPHOMANIAC WHO OWNS A LIQUOR STORE. One woman Ranger said, "We are twenty years behind the rest of the country."

The lack of industrial variety on the Range has always kept women economically, and therefore socially, powerless. The all-powerful mines with their frequent threats to lay off the workers, create a trickle-down effect. "The men are treated like second-class citizens by the mines, which just puts the women on an even lower rung on the ladder," a local psychologist said.

Few Ranger children leave home for other employment opportunities in bigger cities after high school. Why pay four years of college tuition to get a white-collar job that paid less than $20,000 a year, when at the mine a man could be earning $20,000 with full benefits just one year out of high school? After thirty years of service, a miner is entitled to a union pension that supports a retirement of fishing, hunting, and snowmobiling, next door to one of the most scenic wilderness areas in America. The Range has managed to survive cycle after cycle of boom and bust, and it still remains at its core a frontier culture. As the Minnesota saying goes, "You need a passport to get into the Range." But if you are accepted as a local, the Range can be a place rich with tradition and fun-loving people who live on good wages close to the land and far from the rules, restrictions, and laws of city life.

CHAPTER THREE

Hostilities

Fall 1975

As the summer of 1975 turned cold in early September, Rangers shut down their lakeside cabins and started spending weekends in town. Somewhere between the week when the birch trees shed their last bright-yellow leaves and the opening day of deer-hunting season, Lois and Gene Scaia started a romance. Their friendship had deepened that summer, and when he told her that he and his wife were separating, Lois decided to break her own rule against dating men at the plant during her first year.

She was drawn to Gene's personality. "He was one of the more out-going guys at the plant," she said. "He was a flirt, and would go out of his way to talk to me." He was handsome and charismatic and he helped Lois with her work. He cheered her on when she learned how to drive trucks, and shooed away the men who tried to embarrass Lois with a litany of dirty jokes. He did not swear, and he knew how to treat a woman. Gene started coming around her house after work. Then he asked her out to Sammy's Supper Club in Virginia—the nicest place in town, known for its good food, wine list, and dance bands. Lois discov-ered that Gene liked to dance, and he didn't get drunk. He was fun and engaging company, and she fell for him. Lois saw Gene as the best ex-ample of a knight in shining armor that the Iron Range had to offer. After their second date, Lois and Gene slept together. Lois had only been working at the mine for seven months.

The next workday, Gene asked her to join him for lunch in the concentrator lunchroom, across the hall from the women's dry. Usually Lois and the other women avoided the lunchroom because the men tended to tease them and use foul language. Instead, they preferred to eat with the other women in the new women's dry, which had been completed that summer. But with Gene there to protect her, Lois reasoned, the guys would be more respectful around her.

The large cinder-block lunchroom offered five rows of brown Formica-topped tables and metal folding chairs. Lunch fell between one whistle at 12 noon and another fifteen minutes later. The men barely had time to bolt the food in their lunch pails while trading the usual banter. Lois sat down with Gene and opened her lunch box. Inside, she had a sandwich, a soda pop, an orange, and a banana. She ate her food quickly, saving the fruit for last. No sooner had she peeled the banana and taken a bite than Gene started moaning.

"What else can you do with that mouth?" said Gene.

The room erupted into whoops and shouts. Lois quickly packed up the remains of her lunch and ran out the door to the dry.

After a few minutes, she collected herself and returned to her job. That day she had been assigned to cleaning the floors under rod mill number one with a high-pressure hose. She had to squat to protect her back from its weight. The cement floor was covered with a thick layer of black dust that Lois pushed into a pile with the force of the water from her hose.

Suddenly she felt a hand come between her legs from behind, and grab her crotch with such force that she fell forward onto the floor. Lois looked back and there was Gene, laughing triumphantly with a handful of thick, dark-brown grease held high over his head. Fifteen feet behind him stood five men, doubled over in laughter. By the time Lois registered what had just happened to her, they all took off running.

Again, she retreated to the dry. She examined the back of her yellow jeans in a mirror and saw a large hand print between her crotch and buttocks. All five fingers were clearly distinguishable. "I was crying big time," she later recalled. "I was mad and really hurt. Gene was someone I trusted and really liked." Connie Saari happened to be in the dry when Lois walked in. Saari had seen Lois and Scaia dancing together at Sammy's the previous Saturday night, and she knew that romances with men from work could backfire. When she saw the handprint on Lois's jeans, she guessed that Gene must have been the culprit.

Lois opened her locker looking for a change of clothes, only to remember that she had taken everything to the Laundromat the day before. She found a brown sweatshirt with a zipper and a hood and wrapped it around her waist, which did a pretty good job of hiding the handprint. She knew she couldn't stay in the dry long; her trips there were monitored by the foreman. It was 2:00 P.M.; one more hour to gut out before the shift was over. The plant was a gossip mill; inside of an hour, everyone would know what had happened to her.

Sure enough, when the three o'clock bell rang, more men than usual were loitering in the repair bay, where they reported in and out of work. Gene stood in the hallway surrounded by a group of his friends. Lois took a deep breath and walked down the hall.

As she walked out, she turned to Gene. "Well," she said in a loud voice, "at least you know which end—[her rear end]—is Italian!" Loud laughs echoed through the hallway. It was a small victory. Lois savored the laughter as she headed for the sanctuary of the dry.

She drove home, picked up the phone, and called her parents. "Dad, I want to quit. I'm not tough enough for this job."

"Can't you work one more year and save all your money?"

Joe Jenson was a stoic. He wanted Lois to make the best of it. He calmed her down and they hashed out her options. Ever since Greg's birth in 1968, Lois had depended on her parents. Greg lived with them in Babbitt for six months while Lois went to secretarial school in Minneapolis. Now that Lois finally had a good job and could support herself, her father didn't want her to throw it all away.

"Even if I could find another job," she admitted, "it would not pay a living wage and I'd have to go back on welfare to pay for health care, baby-sitting, and food." She hated welfare. Her benefits package at the mine was so good that it included eye, dental, and life insurance. She was home every day by 3:30 to take care of Greg. Her new paycheck had given her some self-respect and she was loath to give it up.

As she pondered her options, Lois convinced herself that she didn't want to be a quitter. She remembered the Oglebay Norton managers visiting her and Priscilla in Mexico and announcing that the two women were being held up as examples. She felt that she had a right to work at the mine.

One mid-November afternoon when most of the miners had disappeared to the woods to hunt deer, Gene knocked on the door to Lois's house. She had not spoken to him in a month. Hoping that he had an apology in mind, Lois let him in. He sat on her couch and explained that he wanted to call a truce. He said that he had told his friends at work that he had slept with her, but no one would believe him. "So the guys put me up to a dare." He had no choice but to respond. "It was just a joke, Lois. You should get a sense of humor." Gene wanted to pick up where they had left off the night at Sammy's Supper Club.

"I can't do that," said Lois. "Don't you understand that you completely betrayed and humiliated me?" Lois demanded an apology, but Gene refused. Lois asked him to leave.

The next day at work, Lois found herself crying for no reason. A week later, on November 24, a dizzy spell came over her. She reported her problem to Chuck Killian, the foreman. Killian sat her down in the foreman's office, a white trailer house perched in the middle of the concentrator. She still felt too dizzy to get up, so Killian walked her down a flight of stairs to the first-aid room. When she reached the bottom step, she fainted. He called an ambulance and Lois was taken to the Virginia Regional Medical Center. The emergency room doctor there could find nothing wrong and sent her home.

That month marked the beginning of a change for the worse in Lois's health. Whereas she'd rarely been sick before, she now often caught colds. For the first time in her life she had trouble keeping her weight down. She avoided Gene at work, and if he came near her when she had a hose in her hand she would turn it on him. Gene retaliated by standing around the hallways waiting for her; when she passed by, he'd stick his finger out of his fly. But Gene wasn't her only problem. Other men apparently felt free to take liberties with her. In late December, she found herself alone in the elevator with the concentrator foreman, Bob Sametz. He tried to kiss her. Lois pushed him away and ran out the elevator door. She tried to avoid another foreman named Nick Senich who peppered every sentence with "fuck," and liked to ask the guys in his crew whenever she was around, "Did you eat at the Y last night?" When Lois came near Senich, he'd lift a hand to her face and try to pinch her cheeks.

Yet she noticed that as soon as these men bothered her, other men would treat her nicely. It was as if the good guys wanted to make up for the bad behavior. In December, members of her crew hung a sign across the repair bay hall that said, MERRY CHRISTMAS LOIS. On Valentine's Day, another sign in the repair bay said, LOIS, WE LOVE YOU. STAY WITH US?

Late one day in February, on her way to lunch break, she noticed Gene and Paavo Kivisto laughing and walking quickly away from the area in which she had been working. The looks on their faces made her uneasy. She ate lunch in the dry and went back to work. In between the control panel and the foreman's office, she could see something hanging from a beam next to a row of rotating ball mills. As she got closer she was confronted at eye level with a round piece of thick pink rubber, about twelve inches in diameter. A slit had been cut in the middle, and another piece of rubber was pushed out of the hole. Primitive-looking strands of hair were drawn around the slit in black pen. On top of the mock vagina read the words: "Lois's Cunt."

Lois ripped the thing off its wire suspension and marched up the stairs to the rod mill deck where Gene worked. She threw it in his face.

"*This* is not funny!"

"I didn't have anything to do with it," he said, throwing the contraption on the floor. Lois picked it up and threw it in a big bin filled with scrap metal.

In a blind rage, she stomped back to the dry. Sobbing, she asked herself, "What am I doing that's causing this?" Three other women had started work when she did—they weren't having her caliber of problems. Connie Saari, tall and stocky, teased relentlessly about her large breasts, nevertheless had a tougher attitude: she just taunted the men back. Priscilla Robich, smaller than Lois, was in her forties and didn't think twice about looking a foreman in the eye and calling him an asshole or a male chauvinist pig. Marcella Nelson had the best protection of all: Her brother was a foreman at the plant.

"I've just got to find a way to stay away from all the jerks," Lois told herself. "Then work won't be so bad." Giving up the paycheck, which grew every year, thanks to the union, was just too hard to do. She resolved to try to make it work. She began to layer her clothes—and the men teased her about her armor. Her weight shot up from 105 to 112 to 148, but instead of turning the men off, they now said things like "You must be in love because you're getting fat." She was careful about which men she smiled at. It was exhausting, trying to gauge how a gesture or word might be misinterpreted. Her back hurt all the time, her blood pressure shot up, and she had anxiety attacks. She began missing days of work and a doctor prescribed tranquilizers to help her sleep.

Meanwhile, Lois was turning into the Blanche Dubois of Eveleth Mines. Her obvious discomfort with bad language and off-color jokes were like catnip in the mine. The female miners viewed her as an object lesson in what not to do, said Diane Hodge, an attractive brunette who went to work at the plant in February 1977. Diane, a flirtatious twenty-two-year-old party-girl to Lois's prissy moralist, secretly admired the older woman. When she had her own frightening encounter with a supervisor, Lois was one of the two women she went to for advice. "She wasn't afraid, if somebody swore, to say, 'Please don't say that in front of me,' " Diane said. "I'd never have the guts to say that." Women like her who were born and bred on the Range, she said, "didn't know enough to know the men's behavior was offensive or to know it was belittling. Our own brothers, our own neighbors, all our lives said the same things the guys at work said. That's the way it is. But Lois isn't *from* here."

"The thing Lois did wrong was she cried and broke down in front of the guys. We learned, don't ever let them see you cry, because we saw what happened to her when she did."

All the hourly laborers at Eveleth Mines were members of the United Steelworkers Local 6860. It came with the job. Union dues—3 percent of the miners' gross earnings—were automatically deducted from their paychecks every two weeks. Lois joined the union when she went to work at Eveleth and attended meetings where the union oath was passed around to every person on pieces of paper. At the end of a meeting each piece of paper was taken back so that the oath would not be leaked. It said no union member should ever rat on another union brother. It read in part, "Union members have to defend on all occasions to the extent of your ability the members of the organization. . . . I will never knowingly wrong a member or see a member wronged." To be a squealer was to betray the entire union movement, tantamount to becoming a company spy. Lois took this to mean that reporting a union brother, no matter what his behavior, would bring certain shame down on her.

The oath was a holdover from the 1920s when mining companies hired spies to ferret out union organizers and communists. By the mid-seventies the oath had become an us-versus-them creed: Anything the company did was bad; anything a union man did was good. The ethic virtually disabled the union from disciplining its own members.

"Back in 1975, women were treated as a novelty," said one male miner. But by 1977, thirty-three women were working at Eveleth Mines, and the us-versus-them dynamic was expanding to include the women among the ranks of *them*. Lois had hoped that there would be safety in numbers. Instead, things got worse for all the female miners.

Michele Mesich was born and raised in the town of Virginia. She graduated from Virginia's Roosevelt High School in 1975, but had no interest in going to college. Built like a fire plug, with a feisty personality and quick wit, she lived with her parents and worked at a nursing home, and then as a short-order cook and waitress at the Chestnut Café in Virginia. In September 1976, her uncle, who worked at Eveleth, told her that the mine was hiring women. "Anything would be better than flipping hamburgers," Michele decided. She sent in an application. When she interviewed with Milan Lolich, he told her that she probably wouldn't get the job because she was too short—five-foot-one—and because she wasn't a "hardship case." Michele told Lolich that she was living at home with her parents. "I don't want to go to college, and I need to make more money. Why isn't that a hardship case? At least give me the opportunity to try," she told Lolich. "Fire me if I can't do the job."

To her surprise, he hired her, and she started work on October 4, 1976. Mesich was nineteen years old. She worked shifts in the pellet plant and gradually got to know Lois during brief meetings at shift change, and even though Lois mostly kept to herself, the two women became best friends. On Lois's thirty-third birthday, Michele stuffed her friend's locker with helium-filled balloons. Lois wrote her a thank-you note in the form of a rhyming poem.

> *Pink, is the fairness I see in you.*
> *Yellow, the warmth that always shines thru.*
>
> *Red, is your wit, quick and keen.*
> *Blue, is the wish for your every dream.*
>
> *Green, is the growth I've seen since we've met.*
> *Colored balloons for my best friend yet.*
>
> *These are the things I see in you.*
> *Good heart, good mind and hot air too!*

Thanks for the effort on "33"
Remember soon, it will be thee!

In her second week of work, Michele got her own first hint of unwelcome attention. A friend on her crew told her there was graffiti about her in the men's bathroom. Without hesitation, Michele walked in. On the door inside one of the stalls, she spotted a large pen drawing of a naked woman with her legs spread. Underneath were the words: "Michele M. likes to be eaten here." Disgusted and embarrassed, Michele took a scrub brush to the picture and cleaned it off the door.

She convinced herself that it had been a onetime thing. For the most part, Michele got along well with the men on her crew. She became the only woman at the plant who drove the big steel cats, front-end loaders, and bulldozers. She joined the guys for beer-drinking parties after work at bars, or during warm weather by the banks of the St. Louis River. Sometimes she would get in amiable hose fights with the workers. But one day, the joking came to an end. She had been at the mine for about three months when some men on her crew presented her with a foot-long dildo that they had crafted for her out of "whitmore," an industrial grease as thick as clay, used to lubricate the ball bearings beneath the kiln. Michele didn't think the dildo was funny, threw it back at the men, and shouted a streak of obscenities at them.

Soon afterward, a miner named Don Cummings threw a pair of work gloves at her crotch. Michele told him that if he bothered her again, she would punch his face. Soon afterward, she found "Michele M. is a slut" and "Michele M. eats pussy" written on the walls of the concentrator bin where they both worked. Like Lois, she, too, had trouble with Nick Senich. If Michele had the bad luck of standing near the foreman, he would pull her close to him, rub up against her breasts, and pinch her face. "Michele, you getting any?" he asked her. She finally got him to stop when she said, "I don't think my father would like what you're doing to me."

Michele's father in fact opposed women working in the mines. The only advice he gave her when she first started working at Eveleth was to remember that she was replaceable. "Take care of yourself," he told her, "because the company won't." So she joined the union leadership, because she thought it would be a good way to protect herself, both from the rank and file and from the company.

The same month that Michele started at Eveleth, Judy Jarvela began working there, assigned to the pit—the Thunderbird Mine, nine miles out from the plant, on the edge of the city of Eveleth. Some of the miners stationed there drove trucks that hauled the taconite rock, some blasted the rock with explosives, and some worked in one of the two crushers.

Judy was thirty-five, the mother of three high school–age children. She was five-foot-two, 120 pounds, and so reticent that she'd only learned to drive three years before. Her brother and brother-in-law both worked at Eveleth, and they had helped her get this job because her family was on the brink of poverty. Judy's husband, Bill, had worked at a DuPont plant in the town of Biwabik, which made chemicals used in blasting deep holes into the veins of hard taconite. In May 1976, Bill was training a worker who forgot to shut off one of the valves in the plant, leaking a poisonous chemical, Monomethylamine. Bill ran into the room to shut off the valve and inhaled the gas, a mixture of ammonia and acid. Within seconds, he couldn't walk straight. Irreparable damage had been done to the nerve endings in his brain and he never worked a day after the accident. His salary continued for six months, after which he received small stipends from workman's compensation and Social Security disability, but it wasn't enough to support the family. Judy's prior job, packaging potting soil at the Power O Peat plant in Central Lakes, had suited her quiet demeanor but earned only $2.10 an hour. At the mine, she would be making $5.89 an hour, with good benefits for Bill, the kids, and her. It would just cover their expenses.

Judy's first job at the pit was cleaning up the dirt that came off the conveyor belts in the north crusher. "Everyone at work asked me what in the world I was doing there," Judy recalled. "I spent a huge amount of time explaining that I was there because my husband couldn't work and that I didn't think I was taking another man's job. I kept pretty much to myself. I tried to stay out of everybody's way. I did all the cleaning, and there weren't too many other people that cared to do the cleaning, so I was pretty much alone." She ate lunch alone and tried to talk to as few people as possible. "I was just there to earn the paycheck, and the more I kept busy, the faster time went." It wasn't long before her hard work earned her respect, and her coworkers treated her well. But all that changed a month later.

Vernon Niedermeier was the service truck driver on crew B. It was his job to drive workers to their stations at either the north or south pit. His job allowed him to be anywhere during the shift and rarely did he let Judy out of his sight. He sat down next to her at lunch, and followed her around at work—"Just observing, just watching, just making me feel uncomfortable because he was watching me wherever I went." The other men on the crew noticed Niedermeier's obsession and were worried about Judy's safety. Some of them even complained to the foreman. "No one liked him," said Jim Ravnikar, a maintenance mechanic. "He was creepy." Judy told Niedermeier that she was happily married and asked him to stay away from her.

Then the phone calls started. While Judy was at work, a man called her house brazenly talking to Bill and the kids. "Tell your mother to meet me at a bar after work for a drink," he said to her daughter. When the calls wouldn't stop, Bill paid a visit to Niedermeier, whom he suspected of making the calls, at his house in the outskirts of Hibbing.

Small, wiry, and gentle, Bill knocked on Niedermeier's door early one morning and introduced himself as Judy's husband. "I want to talk to you," he told the stunned Niedermeier. "Why don't we go have a cup of coffee at Hardees?" Niedermeier didn't want to go to Hardees, but invited Bill into his house for coffee. At the kitchen table, Bill confronted the truck driver about the phone calls; Niedermeier said he didn't know what he was talking about. But Bill recognized his voice. As he got up to leave he looked Niedermeier in the eye. "If you ever call my house again," he said, "I'm going to call the cops on you."

The next day Niedermeier found Judy in the lunchroom, grabbed her by the lapel, pulled her into the hallway, and yelled at her for accusing him of making the crank phone calls. Mavie Maki watched the confrontation from the lunchroom. A second-generation Finn whose husband had retired after a life of working in the mines, she, too, had started at the mine in 1976. She was fifty-two, not so far from retirement age herself, but she needed the extra income to raise her two young granddaughters, who had lived with her and her husband since their infancy. When Mavie saw Niedermeier pull Judy out of the lunchroom, she remembered something. A month earlier, while she'd been scrubbing a toilet in the women's dry, she heard a noise behind her. When she looked into the dry she saw Vern Niedermeier with his hand in Judy's locker. He stammered that he had come to check if the water pipes were leaking. Mavie hadn't thought twice about the incident, until today. After he let Judy go, Mavie approached her and told her about the time she found Neidermeier in her locker.

In January 1977, three months after Judy started working at Eveleth, she told her foreman that she would like to be switched off Niedermeier's crew. But even when she started working on crew C, Niedermeier still waited for her outside the women's dry on her way in and out at shift change. He loitered near her bus. Judy didn't complain to management because she didn't think she had the right to. "I felt like I was working with all these men and I just had to cope with it. I just had to deal with it the best I could, and my way of dealing with it was to try to get away from it. When I got out of my car at the bottom of the long stairs, I left myself there on the pavement. It was another person who walked up the stairs. I had to be more stiff and just try to be inside myself because I always knew Mr. Neidermeier would be standing up there. Every day he was there on the corner to watch and leer when I walked into the dry."

In August, she transferred to a higher-paying job as a conveyor attendant loading the trains with ore from an underground tunnel. In addition to better pay, the job meant that she wouldn't have to drive trucks, which scared her, and she wouldn't have to work outside in the twenty-below-zero temperatures. She worked with only one other person in an isolated area, which allowed her to avoid Niedermeier's gaze. But her new coworker turned out to be an alcoholic, always drinking on the job. A year later, Judy bid on a job that was one step above her position as conveyor attendant. She got it—and another raise. She was pleased to discover that she'd be working with Mavie loading trains with taconite rocks in the north crusher. She was distressed, however, when she learned the new job would put her back on crew B with Niedermeier. Judy talked it over with her husband and decided to take the job, because she and Mavie would be working alone in a glass booth operating the valves that loaded a long train with rocks. She figured no one could approach without her seeing him.

One day about a month before she took the new job, Judy opened her locker in the dry and noticed some kind of goo on her shirt. She lifted the shirt out of the locker and smelled an unmistakable odor. Someone had ejaculated on her shirt. Judy was so shocked and embarrassed that she didn't tell anyone—not Bill, not even Mavie. A few weeks later, she returned to her locker and there it was again—a gob of semen on her clothing. Again Judy kept quiet about it, but she was scared. She felt certain that she knew who had done this.

A week later, she opened her locker at the end of a shift and reached inside for her yellow sweater. When the sweater was just over her head, she felt a wet spot that smelled strongly of fresh semen. Judy ripped off the sweater and showed it to Mavie who was standing next to her.

"Look at this!" Judy said, furious. "This takes the cake!"

Mavie didn't understand what she was so angry about.

"Smell the sweater," said Judy.

Mavie took a sniff. "Oh, my gosh."

"I've had it!" Judy yelled. "This is the third time he's done this. I can't take this anymore."

The two women went directly to the office of their foreman, Bill Jackson. Judy thrust the sweater in his face. Jackson asked her what the problem was. Judy told him to smell the sweater. "Oh, I don't believe it," said Jackson, clearly disgusted. Judy said she was sure that Vern Niedermeier had done it, and this was the third time it had happened. Mavie added that she had caught Niedermeier opening Judy's locker. Jackson said he would look into it. But weeks later, no one in management had investigated the incident; Niedermeier was still driving the service truck.

A few months after the women reported Niedermeier to Bill Jackson, Jackson approached Mavie in the lunchroom. He put his arm around her and asked her if she would go out on a date with him Saturday night to Clark's Lounge. "I'm married, Bill. I'm a grandmother," she said. After Jackson's proposition, the two women lost any hope that he would do anything. Word about Judy Jarvela's sweater traveled quickly. Dennis Frazier, who had just started at the mine as a security guard, heard that a foreman had called the office and asked the guards to investigate the incident. They were directed to find the culprit and to watch the women's lockers so that it did not happen again. A report was written up, but it was buried. No one followed up.

Frazier had grown up on a farm in Iowa and had been a prison guard. He was shocked by the cavalier attitude toward rules at the mine. Drinking and stealing were common, consequences rare.

When Frazier first started work at the mine, he was put in the parking lot to control traffic during shift change. He was surprised when half of the people who passed him in their cars gave him the finger. "I thought, this wouldn't even happen to me if I was in prison. At least the prisoners know that they have to try to get along with the staff."

The semen-on-the-sweater story soon became popular mine gossip. Marcy Halberg was sitting in the pellet plant lunchroom in the winter of 1976 when she heard it. She was twenty-three and had been working at the mine since August. As she sat alone eating her lunch, she overheard a group of men laughing about how a guy at the pit jerked off on the clothing of one of the female employees in the women's dry. Marcy's heart sank. "I wanted to shrink in a corner and figure out how to make myself invisible so that something like that wouldn't happen to me. Intimidation doesn't even come close to how I felt. It was pure fear."

Marcy grew up only fifteen miles from the Forbes plant in a small farming town called Cherry. She came from a long line of Finnish miners on the Iron Range. Her grandfather was blacklisted from the mines because he was a communist and a union organizer. He headed the local chapter of the Communist Party and had ten children. One of those children was Gus Hall, who became the leader of the United States Communist Party from 1959 to 1999. He also ran for president four times. Marcy had fond memories of her worldly "Uncle Gus." Imprisoned in Leavenworth Federal Penitentiary for eight years during the McCarthy era in the fifties, Hall eventually settled in Yonkers, New York. He took his niece to the World's Fair and the Statue of Liberty and spoiled her with dresses from Lord & Taylor.

Several of Marcy's uncles worked in the mines, but her father had declared that he had no faith in the mining system because of its history of corruption and discrimination against Finns. Instead, he eked out a living running a store in Cherry, selling lumber, and raising Arabian horses. Yet when Eveleth started hiring women, it was Marcy's father who pushed her to apply for a job. He didn't want his daughter to be a bartender, which was what she was doing when the call went out in the summer of 1976 that the mine was hiring more women. Marcy was living in a trailer on her parents' farm and having a hard time making ends meet. "I handed in the application and figured, fat chance—a lot of women I knew wanted a job at the mine because of the pay. I was only twenty-three years old. When they called, Dad made me come to the store before the interview to make sure my hair was in pigtails and that I wasn't wearing any makeup."

"They don't want no floosies out there," he said.

Like Judy, Marcy's first job at Eveleth was at the pit. She trained on heavy trucks on the midnight shift. If she wanted to work at the mine, she was told, she'd better learn how to drive trucks at night. After a month, she bid on a safer job as a sampler in the lab at the plant. As a rule, whenever a position became open at the mine, it was posted and whoever applied for the job with highest seniority would automatically get the first chance to take the job on a trial basis for fifteen shifts. The lab was considered a good place for women to work: It was inside and did not require heavy manual labor or machine operation. The congenial crew in the lab included a handful of women, and they all socialized together after work, bar-hopping, bowling, playing baseball, and skiing.

In her job as a sampler, Marcy pushed a cart around the concentrator, pellet plant, and crusher, collecting samples of the taconite in its various stages of production. She then took them directly to the lab to be tested for their ore purity. One day as she was pushing her cart around the plant she could hear herself being paged over the loudspeaker. Marcy walked over to the nearest gray phone on the wall and picked it up. The person on the other line said, "I can't hear you, try the other ear." Marcy held the receiver to her other ear and realized that the earpiece was slathered in grease. Three men hiding nearby emerged laughing, their arms holding their bellies. Quick to have a laugh, Marcy thought the joke was almost as funny as the men did, even as she picked gobs of the heavy black stuff from her hair.

In January 1977 she discovered she was pregnant by her live-in boyfriend, Pat Steele, who did not work at the mine. After her first prenatal doctor's visit, she went to see the director of personnel, Bob Raich, and asked that her company medical insurance cover the costs of her pregnancy. Raich told her that the men's girlfriends weren't covered for prenatal visits, so she couldn't be covered because she was not married. Marcy puzzled over this reasoning. *She* was pregnant and *she* was the person who worked at the mine and earned her own health insurance. She was not a miner's girlfriend; she was a miner.

An incredulous Raich asked Marcy, "You aren't planning to come back to work after you have your baby are you?"

"Yes, I am," she said.

"What kind of mother are you?" he said. "A good mother would never come back to work in a place like this."

Marcy refused to pay the doctor's bills, throwing each in the trash. Eventually, the company paid them.

When her son Travis was born, Marcy was able to take a few weeks off after his birth only because there happened to be a strike at the same time. After it was over, her parents agreed to take care of the baby so she could go back to work. She married Pat, an electrician, but he had trouble keeping a steady job. More than ever, Marcy felt she had no choice but to keep her job at the mine. It was no longer a question of working there for a year or two to save enough money to buy a car. Now she had to support her child.

The lab required a grueling schedule of seven afternoons on, two days off; seven days on, two days off; seven midnights on, four days off. Marcy wanted a job that was straight days so she could come home in the afternoons to be with Travis, and soon one came available, though it was as an oiler on an all-male crew.

Oilers were responsible for keeping the machinery all over the plant lubricated. The work required tasks like crawling under the huge, burning hot kiln that fired the taconite pellets and dumping a five-hundred-pound drum of oil on its ball bearings. Marcy was able to get the job because no one else wanted it. The oilers were not happy about the prospect of working with a woman. Two young oilers were assigned the job of training Marcy. They made it clear to her that they didn't want her on their crew and hazed her by taking her up on high catwalks to do a job and getting her lost. The head oiler asked Marcy to oil an overhead crane, which required standing on a narrow ladder at a perilous height.

Marcy never again saw anyone else do that job. The young oilers later told her that the head oiler had said, "Get rid of her in the first fifteen shifts."

She buckled under the hostility. She would go to the dry during breaks and cry. Another woman noticed how distressed Marcy was and reported it to her boss, Jim Walker. Walker called in Marcy, and several men on the crew and gave them a lecture. He said that Marcy had every right to be on the job and that they should not be so hard on her. Walker finished the meeting with a suggestion to Marcy that she "toughen up." As they left his office, the guys turned to her and said, "So, you tattletale? What did you do that for?"

Marcy took her foreman's advice. She stopped crying. She swore at every chance. Once when Walker heard her unleash a particularly harsh torrent of obscenities, he said, "Marcy, I told you to toughen up but I didn't mean that much!" When a foreman named LeRoy Stish waved a dildo he'd named "Big Red" in Marcy's face, she ignored it. When a man dropped his pants near the sidewalk as she walked toward the entrance to the women's dry and whistled at her, Marcy just kept on walking.

Although Marcy liked to flirt, and enjoyed the company of men, her style at work was more like Lois and Judy's—she kept her head down and her body covered. So she found herself fascinated by the arrival of Kathy O'Brien. One night at 11:00 P.M., the end of the afternoon shift, about twenty women were changing out of their sooty, black work clothes, washing their hands in the round "bird bath" fountain in the middle of the locker room, and showering in one of the two shower stalls. A radio that sat on top of a counter next to a battered yellow refrigerator blared rock music. Most women had two or three lockers to themselves in which they stored their boots, coats, and street clothes. Each locker was each woman's territory; family photos of husbands, boyfriends, daughters, or sons with hockey sticks in their hands were taped inside and out. On a counter next to the refrigerator sat a large tub of Mary Kay facial moisturizer that everyone shared. One of the "gals" doubled as a Mary Kay saleswoman. In the middle of the room, a pile of dog-eared women's magazines—*Cosmo, Redbook, Ladies' Home Journal, Reader's Digest*—sat on a brown Formica-topped kitchen table that seated six.

A two-foot-square mirror hung on the white cinder-block wall next to the refrigerator. Marcy walked out of the shower, one towel wrapped around her body, and another around her head, and caught her first glimpse of Kathy O'Brien, who was standing in front of the mirror carefully applying her makeup. Marcy, who rarely dressed in fancier clothes than tennis shoes, blue jeans, and a sweater, noticed that Kathy was wearing tight gold lamé stretch pants and platform sandals. To a farm girl like Marcy, Kathy was exotic. She was tall, slim, with large breasts that she liked to show off in tight clothes. Kathy sang in a country-western band, acted in local theater groups, wrote poetry, and considered herself a diamond in the rough—more cultured, sophisticated, and sexier than the crude, Northwoods women miners. "She was like the character Opal on 'All My Children,'" said Marcy. "There she was at eleven P.M. prancing down the walkway to the parking lot wearing gold stretch leggings, and platform heels. She was going out to Good Fellas, dancing. It was the funniest-looking thing. I'll never forget it."

Yet Kathy was as much of a farm girl as Marcy. She'd spent most of her childhood working on her grandparents' dairy farm in the northern Minnesota town of Black Duck. She was one of seven children, and her father, a miner and sailor in the merchant marines, left the family when Kathy was five years old. At sixteen, Kathy gave birth to twin girls; two years later she had a boy. She married the father of her three children but divorced him after he started hitting her. She found herself working sixteen-hour days in two waitressing jobs, which left her no time to be with her kids and very little money to pay their bills. Like every other woman in the dry, Kathy had taken the job at the mine because she needed the money. As much as she enjoyed the company of men and was wise to the ways of Iron Rangers, Kathy's initiation at the mine was as rough as Marcy and Lois's.

She started as a laborer, cleaning the crusher in the south pit. Three weeks into the job, Kathy entered the cramped lunchroom and crossed paths with a man named Frank Lipka. Lipka made sure he had a sizable audience before shouting. "Hey Kathy, do you fuck on the job?"

"Kiss my ass!" Kathy said, and walked away.

At the next break a few hours later, Kathy heard her name being paged over the public address system. She went to the box in the lunchroom that contained the intercom, or gray phone. When she opened the box, a bat flew out into her face. The bat-in-the-phone was a common prank at the mine; Kathy, who was afraid of bats, let out a loud scream. As she sat on one of the lunch tables to calm herself, Frank Lipka approached. He said, "I'll show you what will really scare you." Then he twisted Kathy's nose between the knuckles of his middle and index fingers. He held on. Blood streamed down her coveralls. She threatened to kick him in the testicles if he didn't stop. He grabbed her feet and flipped her backwards off the table. She knocked her head against the wall.

Kathy ran into the men's bathroom (there were no women's bathrooms at this time) and saw the blood in the mirror. She thought, "I can't handle this." Too upset to go back to work, Kathy waited in the bathroom until quitting time. But by the time the miners began pouring out of the crusher and into buses waiting to take them back to the main office, she had figured out how to retaliate.

Kathy stood at the head of the stairs, brandishing a heavy iron shovel. She let everyone pass by until Lipka appeared.

"Come on, you son of a bitch!" She shouted at him. "It's your turn!"

Someone called the superintendent. Two pickup trucks appeared on the scene. Lipka was ushered into one, Kathy into the other. The superintendent, Don Olin, asked her what had happened. Kathy refused to tell; she was afraid she would not be admitted into the union if she ratted on a union brother. As an employee working at the mine for less than a month, she was in the early stages of joining the union. She told her foreman to ask Lipka what had happened. No one asked Lipka any questions, but the next day he was moved to a different crew. After that, Kathy brought a screwdriver to work. On a grinder in the plant's machine shop, she filed the tip to a sharp point. Every day for the next nine years, she carried it in her boot.

Of all the women hired at Eveleth in the period between 1975 and 1977, Kathy O'Brien received some of the most brutal treatment from the men. She worked in the pit for a year and a half before anyone said anything civil to her. One truck driver left notes in her cab describing explicit sexual acts he'd like to commit with her, and followed her home in his car every day. Another miner frequently hit her in the arm and called her names like bitch, cunt, and whore. After a few weeks of this, Kathy one day slugged him in the face as hard as she could. He never bothered her again.

She started driving two-hundred-ton trucks and then graduated to driving steel Cat "dozers" that rolled on chain treads like army tanks. She drove her dozer around the vast moonscape of the "pit" where armies of massive vehicles greedily picked up tons of boulders with their claws. The process of digging, lifting, and carting layer after layer of taconite from a crater five miles wide seemed to Kathy like toys digging in a big sand box. She felt relatively safe, even powerful, in the cab of a giant truck, and it was one of the highest-paying jobs at the mine.

Not unlike Lois, however, Kathy's health began to falter the longer she worked at the pit. Dehydration, not stress, was the initial culprit. When she was assigned to work in the tailings dump, there was a scarcity of portable toilets. The men climbed down from their two-story-high vehicles, faced the tires, and relieved themselves. Kathy knew she couldn't trust anyone to let her do this in peace. When she complained to her sister's husband, a union official named Stan Daniels, he said, "If you want to work like a man, you got to learn to piss like a man, and if you can't, go home and bake bread."

Her only option was to wait until lunch break, when a truck would pick up her crew and take them to the crusher, where there was a bathroom. So she stopped drinking water in the morning. But sometimes lunch breaks were held out at the pit, and she would have to wait for eight hours to use a toilet. As summer approached and the days got hotter, Kathy suffered abdominal pains, bladder infections, and began urinating blood. By the end of the summer, she was hospitalized for three days with severe dehydration. Her doctors told her that she must drink water at work. She resorted to using the radio in her Cat to ask for the delivery of a port-a-potty or a ride to the crusher. But the radio calls were heard by all six hundred people working in the pit, and Kathy's requests were soon answered with meowing sounds and taunts of "Does Kathy gotta go pee-pee?" On days when she menstruated, she bled through her blue jeans. While riding the bus back to the main office at the end of the day, she tried to cover up her pants by tying a jacket around her waist, but her disguise did not work and the men taunted her with fish jokes.

She was proud and too much of a hothead to let herself become the laughingstock of the pit, and she stopped asking for rides to the bathroom. The bladder infections continued, progressing eventually to a severe kidney infection.

One night after work Kathy went for a drink at Mugga's with another miner, Audrey Daniels, who was divorced from Stan Daniels's brother. The two women ordered a round of drinks. The music called for a slow dance, and a man with a crew cut asked Kathy out onto the floor. He told her he worked for Sears. After dancing for a few minutes, the man started to caress her breasts and buttocks. She shoved him away, saying, "You're old enough to be my grandfather! If you want to embarrass someone, do it on your own time, not mine." As she walked off the dance floor, the man grabbed her arm, spun her around and said, "Do you know who you're talking to?"

"No, not really," said Kathy.

"Do you like your job at Eveleth?" the man asked. "Because if you don't you should just quit."

Kathy left the bar immediately. As she and Audrey climbed into her car, Audrey told her that she had just danced with Bob Raich.

For a long time the women at Eveleth didn't share their troubles with one another. The company put the women on different crews so they rarely worked together, and therefore did not have much time to talk. Plus, they all sensed the pressure to get along. "You just toughed it out and didn't talk or you'd get labeled a troublemaker," Michele Mesich recalled. Kathy O'Brien was exhibit A as to what happened when you fought back. "We were always being told that we were taking away a man's job, so we didn't want to do anything to jeopardize the job."

The escalating animosity among the men had two major effects on the women. First, the decent guys on the workforce now felt peer pressure to curtail kind gestures toward the female workers. "If I walked into a room with four or five guys sitting on chairs and a guy got up and gave me his chair," recalled miner Diane Hodge, "one guy would say, 'What are you giving her your chair for? Are you fucking her?' In order to be nice to a woman you had to be fucking her." Even men who were openly supportive of the women felt resentment. "The company asked me if I would work midnights for Lois because she had a nine-year-old child. I said, hell no!" said one miner who was respectful to his female coworkers. It was the same with Audrey Daniels. "I had a day-shift job and they asked me to trade jobs with her so she wouldn't have to do shift work. I said no." Conversely, the women learned that although caring for a sick child was not an acceptable excuse for staying home, a hangover was. "They all had drinking problems. They could relate to it," said Marcy. "But 'My kid is sick,' they couldn't relate to that. Their wives took care of their kids."

More disturbing, the anger brewing in the men was creating an imperative to up the ante. Before women worked at Eveleth, crude graffiti had seldom appeared on the walls of the plant. Now, graphic pictures and words proliferated, posters and calendars of nude women were hung in plain sight, almost like badges of honor among the men. Verbal teasing became physical contact that more and more became violent. In February 1977, one threat turned criminal.

In bed in her house in Virginia, Lois awoke at 3:00 A.M. when she heard her front door creak open. She always locked the door, but that night she had forgotten. She lay frozen in terror as she watched the shadow of a man walk by her bedroom door and into her son's room. The man then entered her room. He was stocky, and she saw the outline of his body against her doorway. As he stood over the edge of her bed, Lois lunged for the light switch on the wall behind him. The man grabbed her.

"Get the hell out of here!" she shouted. To her surprise, he immediately walked out of the house. Lois ran to the door and locked it. A few minutes later, there was a knock at the front door. Through it a man's voice begged her not to call the police. Lois didn't. "They'd never believe me," she decided. "I didn't even get a look at him."

A few days later, a truck driver named John Jagunich pushed past her at work. To Lois's surprise, he wheeled around and kicked the wall behind him with his boot. He was stocky, with shoulder-length hair. She remembered the day a week before when she had a gallstone attack at work and Bruce Campbell drove her home in her car. Jagunich followed in the company's service truck so he could drive Campbell back to work. Lois, in a fair amount of pain, had not paid much attention to the truck driver, except that she noticed he had long hair. Now she realized that Jagunich was the man who had broken into her house that night.

Lois decided to tell the other women what had happened because she wanted to warn them about Jagunich. She told her story to a group in the dry during shift change. Audrey Daniels spoke up. The same thing had happened to her. She had gotten sick at work and Jagunich drove her home; then, a few nights later, he broke into her trailer. "I got a loaded little twenty-five-automatic pistol out of the closet," Daniels told the women in the dry. "I put on my house coat and walked out of my bedroom. There he was, standing in my living room. I walked slowly toward the lamp and turned it on. He said 'Hi Audrey,' and I said, 'Get out of here.' I kept one hand on the gun in my pocket, and he left."

"Let's report him," urged Lois. Audrey was too scared to report it. Audrey decided instead to take her security into her own hands. She began to carry the automatic in her car. Sometimes she would even hide it in her bra at work.

"Screw the union oath," Lois thought. John Jagunich had crossed a line. Greg's safety was at stake.

Lois walked into John Maki's office and told him the story. Maki seemed mildly concerned and instructed her to tell him if Jagunich bothered her again. That same day, Lois saw Jagunich in the finisher area underneath the balling drums where she was working—far from his actual work area. She told Maki and he sent her to his superior, Tom Erspamer, the mine Superintendent.

Nervously, she sat down with Erspamer and another high-level manager, Corky Krollman. She told them the story about Jagunich breaking into her house. After listening politely to her story, Erspamer told Lois that what happened off company property was not his responsibility. Lois said that Jagunich found out where she lived because of his job as a service truck driver. "At least you could transfer him to a different job," she said. "I'm worried that he might do it again. He did the same thing to Audrey Daniels." But Erspamer and Krollman made no promises. "If he hurts someone, the mine might be liable," warned Lois. Erspamer was unimpressed. Years later, Erspamer denied that Lois reported this incident to him.

CHAPTER FOUR

No Name for It

1980

By 1980, Diane Hodge had been working at Eveleth Mines for three years. She was now twenty-five years old, a single divorcée with no children, and she considered her crew her family. She baked lasagna and cookies for them, gave them birthday cards, went on ski trips, and bowled with them. After work she joined the guys at bars in Virginia and Eveleth to shoot pool and drink beer. Diane, an attractive brunette, liked to be liked. She grew up in Hibbing with five brothers, and was adept at being one of the boys. She spent her childhood roughhousing, building tree forts, and uttering four-letter words with great enthusiasm. When a foreman walked up to her and said, "Diane, there's a bunch of guys down at the maintenance bay that wanna start a gang bang, why don't you go down there?" She replied, "I'm a little tired from the gang bang last night. Why don't you call your wife?"

Whenever the foreman on her crew was sick or on vacation, Willie Johnson, a senior member of the crew, would take his place. Diane, who got along with everyone, was friendly with him, too. Diane had dated two young, handsome miners at the plant, neither of them on her crew. But Willie mistakenly believed Diane was sleeping with several of the men on the crew, and he let Diane know that he felt gypped that he was not getting his share.

"That's what the mentality was," Diane later explained. "If you got along with somebody, you must be screwing them. If you were seen walking or talking to the same guy two or three times, you must be screwing him." (Diane and her brother Myles Fontaine often ate lunch together. Soon, rumors spread that they were having an affair—no one knew they were brother and sister because they did not share the same last name.) Some rumors about various women were based, to an extent, on the truth. Many of the women who worked at the mine dated, slept with, and even married miners. Like any normal woman in her twenties, Diane liked to date and have fun; she simply wasn't interested in Willie, who was almost twice her age.

The first time he made a move on her, she was asleep. It was the 4:00 A.M. lunch break during midnight shift. She and five other crew members were in the crusher control panel, where Willie worked. The control panel was a small mobile home placed in the middle of the deafening crusher building. Two walls of the dark, dingy trailer were covered with knobs and gauges that controlled the thundering taconite rock crushers outside. In the loudest of all the loud buildings in the plant, this was the only place where workers could find some quiet, make a cup of coffee, and sit down. Diane sat down for the twenty-minute break and immediately fell asleep. When the break ended, a coworker woke her up. She went back to work with her friend George Anderson, who told her that while she had slept, Willie Johnson crawled between her legs and pretended to perform cunnilingus.

"You guys just stood there and let him?" she asked, extremely hurt. "None of you did anything to stop him?"

"What am I supposed to do about it?" George replied sheepishly. "I can't hit him. I'll lose my job."

George Anderson's response was typical of many of the men at the plant. "The men didn't stick up for the women because it wasn't our responsibility," one miner admitted. Plus, Willie was in charge of the control panel and had the ability through the flip of a switch to make people's jobs miserable. He could stop conveyor belts, plug up chutes, and cause spills that could take hours to clean up. Not having the courage to confront Willie about what just happened, Diane went back to her job of cleaning and adjusting the water levels in the dust collectors.

Diane was at home the second time Willie approached her. One morning, just after she had woken up from having worked late the night before, Willie knocked on her door. He said he always came to Hibbing to buy his meat at the F&D Market and that he thought he'd stop in for coffee. Diane walked to the kitchen to put on a pot, and suddenly Willie grabbed her waist from behind. "I snatched him by the belt loop of his pants, shoved him out the door, and slammed it in his face," she said.

The third time Willie made a move on Diane she was sitting in a chair in the control panel, watching some electricians install a new instrument board. "Willie came up from behind me and grabbed both my breasts in front of three or four electricians. I slapped him in the face and walked out." Another time in the control panel, Willie "took his false teeth out and threw them at my crotch."

When Willie took charge of the crew as step-up foreman, things got worse for Diane. He made a habit of taking her off her regular dust-collector job and sending her to the end of Conveyor Belt Two. The walk to the end of the longest belt in the plant was the length of six city blocks. The belt was encased in a thin metal box that extended 150 yards out from the crusher building, with a galley wide enough for only one person to walk. At the end of the chute, the belt dumped its load of rocks through a large hole onto a ten-story-high pile of rocks, called the coarse ore surge. The rocks were then delivered by another underground conveyor belt back into the crusher to be smashed into smaller pieces.

Taking the surreal walk out to the end of Belt Two in the dark of the midnight shift unsettled Diane. One night she realized, to her horror, that Willie had followed her. They were far from the sight or sound of another human being. "Willie came out there and tried to kiss me. Scared the shit out of me. I mean I was way out on this long belt. I was afraid he was going to throw me out that hole and cover me with rocks. Who'd ever find me out there?" The next time Willie sent her to the end of Belt Two and followed her, Diane lost what little restraint she had maintained.

"Willie," she said, "think about it. What would a twenty-five-year-old girl want with a fat old man like you?"

Willie stopped making passes at Diane after that comment. Mysteriously, the water that fed Diane's dust collectors tended to shut off for no reason, causing the machines to overheat and break down. "I'd get hollered at by the maintenance foreman for burning up the dust collector. And I knew I wasn't doing it." Diane traced footsteps in the fine layer of ground dust from the dust collector to the control panel, proving what she already knew: Willie was sabotaging her work.

Diane stopped coming to work on the days he worked as step-up foreman. "I told the general foremen in the main office that from now on, when he's step-up foreman I'm not comin' to work because he puts me out on that Belt Two and scares me out there." She also asked them to move Willie to a new crew. They refused. Diane asked the dust collector attendants on other crews if they would switch crews with her but no one would—no one else wanted to be on Willie's crew either. Diane began to miss days of work, in one case an entire week. "I was hanging myself. I couldn't come to work, but if I missed work, I was gonna lose my job."

At 5:15 on the morning of June 25, 1980, Willie found Diane sleeping on a bed of rags in a remote part of the crusher. Instead of turning her in to one of the foremen, who were likely to levy a minor punishment, Willie called a security guard, who was required to write up a report of the infraction.

The normal punishment for sleeping on the job was five days. Diane got thirty days off without pay, because of her bad record of absenteeism. Diane felt the punishment was unfairly harsh, since her absenteeism was due to the company's refusal to separate her from Willie.

Diane heard through the grapevine that Willie had been bragging, "I told her I was going to fuck her, one way or another."

Diane called Lois—whom she barely knew but respected. Lois listened to Diane's story and told her that she had to fight to get her thirty-day punishment reduced, and that she must tell the company the history of Willie Johnson's actions. But Diane did not want to turn in a union brother. She feared she would be stigmatized as a snitch, which would make her life at work impossible. Indeed, Stan Daniels, the union president, urged Diane not to reveal Willie's name because it would mean breaking her union oath.

"You *have* to tell them Willie's name," Lois countered. "This case is above the oath. They know who he is anyway. What he has done is beyond the scope of decency. Plus, your job is on the line." But they both knew that there was a double standard at the mine. While Willie could turn Diane in without serious repercussions, she could not do the same.

"Why doesn't this union thing go both ways?" Diane asked Lois. They agreed that there was one person in the union to whom Diane could try to appeal.

Patricia Doyle Kosmach was the most powerful woman at the mine. She stood five-feet eight-inches tall and weighed an imposing 225 pounds. She had a head of thick curly red hair, a bellowing voice, and a hot temper that she attributed to her 100 percent Irish blood. Born and raised in the town of Virginia, Minnesota, Pat started working in the mine in January of 1976 at the age of thirty-nine. Before applying for the job, Pat had met Bob Raich by chance at the bar in Virginia's Coats Hotel. She told Raich that she heard Eveleth Mines was hiring women and she would like to apply for a job. Raich told her that she could only get a job at the mine if she learned how to "stand up and piss like a man." Pat, who was no shrinking violet, applied for the job anyway.

She was living on the edge of poverty working two jobs and barely making her bills and supporting her five children. In 1967, she had left her alcoholic husband after discovering that he was sleeping with her best friend. It was an unusual act of independence for 1967, particularly on the Range, where divorce was rare and socially unacceptable. Pat's children's ages ranged from two to ten, and she had to find a way to support them on her own. They lived in the basement of their half-finished house, because Pat and her husband had been in the midst of building the house when he moved out. Pat took on waitressing jobs. "We were poor," recalls Pat's oldest daughter Bobbie Musto. "You only went to the dentist when you were dying, and there often was no heat in the house. I remember getting dressed in the morning in front of an open stove. There was just no money. Bills didn't get paid. The house had to be taped and stapled together."

The day Pat learned she'd gotten the job at Eveleth Mines—with a $5.89-an-hour starting salary and benefits—was a happy day in the Kosmach household. "It was huge. We had a celebration," said Bobbie. Working at the mine meant dental care, consistent heat in the winter, new clothes, and a mint-condition trailer home. "That was coming up in the world. The furniture even matched the drapes. There was money for the first time."

Pat's commitment to the union movement and her authoritative personality landed her in a place where no woman had been before—the senior membership of the Steel Worker's Local 6860. Her Irish humor and charisma made her a kind of modern-day Mother Jones. She served on the local's twelve-member executive board, the civil rights committee, and the Iron Range Labor Assembly, which set policy for all the unions on the Range. Michele Mesich, editor of the union newsletter, the *Steel Scope*, was the only other woman who was active in the union. As chairman of the human services committee, Pat specialized in convincing people who had substance abuse or mental health problems to get help and keep their jobs. Pat had a reputation at work for dragging men to Alcoholics Anonymous meetings, sending women with bruises on their faces to Range Mental Health, and keeping everyone's secrets. She was both opinionated and nurturing. To nineteen-year-old Michele,

Pat was a "second mother." Diane Hodge also looked up to Pat, but like some of the other women, she was also wary of Pat's intrusive manner.

"She was head of human resources and she knew their secrets and their problems and she expected them to shape up," Michele said. "She was outspoken, sharp-tongued, and she valued her own opinion."

People knew her for her self-help aphorisms: "You have to get your own head on straight before you try to straighten out anyone else," and "All the money in the world won't make you happy," or "You have to make yourself happy, no one else can do it for you." A self-avowed feminist, Pat made a point of taking care of the women at the mine. She was ten to fifteen years older than most of them. "She was a mom," said miner Joan Hunholz. "She tucked us under her wing. If you were having marital problems, she'd always take you aside and talk to you." Joan spent the night at Pat's several times when she needed to get out of her own house.

Pat lived next door to her daughter in the woods two miles outside of Eveleth. She decorated her three-bedroom trailer with owls of every kind—stuffed animals, pillows, pictures, figurines. "Owls were just her thing," said one friend. Friends dropped by frequently. A pot of coffee brewed on the stove while Pat, wearing her signature blue jeans and denim shirt, and chain-smoking Kents, listened and handed out advice.

Every September she attended union school with all the other Iron Range Steelworker locals at a nearby nine-hole golf resort. Pat roomed with her friend Jeanne Aho, who worked at Minntac, a taconite mine outside of Virginia. They took classes on unionism, stewardship, collective bargaining, and they would party. Pat loved everything about union life. "It was a social thing," recalled Aho. Pat also traveled with the union to St. Paul for conferences or to lobby the legislature. The top union leaders in Local 6860, Stan Daniels and Sam Ricker, were Pat's good friends. "She was one of the guys," her daughter Bobbie said.

Jeanne Aho first met Pat at a solidarity rally in 1977 when all 14,500 Iron Range miners walked off the job for 138 days. Aho listened to Pat give a rousing speech about sticking together as union members and as Iron Rangers. Aho was so inspired that she introduced herself to Pat and they soon became friends.

By the 1980s, when her children were grown, Pat channeled all the energy it had taken to raise and care for four girls and a boy into her job on the union's human resources committee. Her clout in the union, and her significant physical presence, generated a certain respect among the male miners. Furthermore, Pat did not hesitate to use her power to try to help women who were being harassed. Not that it helped. Michele asked Pat to help her after Don Cummings threw his gloves at her crotch.

"Don," Pat said when she found him in the lunchroom, "it's come to my attention that you threw gloves in Michele Mesich's lap and said 'You're lucky it's not my hands.' You can't do that, Don. You simply can't do it." Red in the face, Cummings shouted, "That little bitch is saying that? I'll throw her in the fucking bins."

Pat tried to intervene when Judy Jarvela, who had moved from the pit to the plant, was being relentlessly propositioned by a man on her crew named Gene New. Judy had complained about New to her foreman, LeRoy Stish. Stish assured Judy that New was going to quit soon and advised her to stay out in the open and avoid working alone.

Unsatisfied, Judy took her complaint to Stish's superiors, the general managers in the main office. She told them she wanted New moved off her crew. The managers said that it was New's crew, too, and he had just as much right to stay on it as she did. If she didn't want to work with him, she could switch.

Judy turned to Pat for help. Pat talked to Stish, and Stish told her he would discuss the problem with his supervisor. No one ever disciplined New. Even Joan Hunholz, Diane's friend and a tough one-of-the-boys kind of woman, complained to Pat when her foreman, Jerry Benz, began making sexual comments and touching her. His favorite trick was to touch her breast pocket where she kept her cigarettes and say "Be careful, Joanie, don't lose your cigarettes." Once again Pat tried, but also made no headway with Benz.

She confided to Stan Daniels, the union president, about the women's problems and Daniels assured her he'd take care of them. Pat was one of his most trusted deputies. He called her his "left arm." Pat kept Daniels, who conducted his job like a turn-of-the-century political boss, informed. But when it came to disciplining people like Cummings or New, Daniels did not return her loyalty. His opinion was that it was not his job to discipline union members; it was his job to "protect them from discipline." The union, he would later say, "never disciplined anybody." That dirty work, he said, was up to the company.

Lois kept her distance from Pat. In temperament and background, they were about as different as any two women at the mine. Most of their contact had been through Michele Mesich. Lois found Pat to be brash, a bragger, and very controlling. Pat, who had never been on the receiving end of a manicure, thought Lois was a fluff, the kind of woman who used her feminine charm, enjoyed the attention of men, and liked to flirt.

Their differences aside, Lois knew that Pat was the only person who could help Diane fight Willie. With Pat's help and Lois's support, Diane took her case further than any of the other women had ever done before, because, as Lois had pointed out, her job was indeed on the line. Not only was the thirty-day suspension a financial burden Diane could not afford, but the severe punishment sent a clear message that she was "on the loading dock." One more infraction and she could be fired. Diane knew that reducing the penalty would be the only way she could prevent that from happening.

In August of 1980, Diane filed a grievance through the union asking for twenty-five days of back pay. The union and the company then held three hearings in August and September in front of a neutral member of the Iron Ore Industry Board of Arbitration. Pat attended the meetings with several other union officials and management representatives. She and Stan Daniels had figured out how to fight Diane's fight without turning her into a tattletale on her union brother. They argued that she had missed work because she was being bothered by a step-up foreman. They did not use Willie's name, but identified him as the only step-up foreman on Diane's crew. It was obvious to everyone in the room who Pat and the union were talking about.

In a twisted set of reasoning, the management representatives at the hearings claimed that although they had been told about the problems between Diane and Willie, they could not take action because Diane refused to reveal the harasser's name. But the real reason Diane's complaints were not taken seriously was revealed in the middle of a conversation between a union official named R. E. Thomas and Bob Raich. "Well you know R. E.," said Raich, "Diane is loose."

On October 23, 1980, four months after Willie Johnson had turned her in, the arbitration board awarded Diane fifteen days of back pay. The report said that because Diane still refused to reveal the name of the man who harassed her, she would have to accept ten days of her suspension for excessive absenteeism. Despite this last rebuke, the decision was largely a win for Diane. The report added that her "sexual harassment claim" was the "mitigating factor" that got her back the fifteen days' pay. The report would later become significant, as it was the first official piece of evidence that sexual harassment had occurred at Eveleth Mines.

That Christmas of 1980, two months after Diane's arbitration report, Lois decided to organize a party for the women miners. "There was a lot of frustration," she said. "The girls were coming into the dry in tears, throwing their hard hats. The tension was getting bad." Lois wanted the women to have a chance to talk and get to know each other. Being on different shifts and different crews made it hard for the group to bond. "The whole point was to have no men around." Lois wanted everyone to have fun together, and start to trust each other enough to talk about the problems they were having at work.

Eighteen women, including Marcy Steele, Pat Kosmach, Diane Hodge, Joan Hunholz, and Michele Mesich filled two tables at the Lantern, a restaurant on Route 53 between Forbes and Virginia. It was a solid turn out. For the most part, the conversation kept to lighthearted subjects, jokes about men, talk of children and families. But occasionally some of the women mentioned the problems they were having at work. "We were so embarrassed" to go into details, said Lois, "that we all talked in vague terms. The problem was, there was no name for it."

At the time of their Christmas dinner, the legal concept known as sexual harassment was only five years old. In 1975, a forty-four-year-old university secretary named Carmita Wood quit working for a Cornell physicist after the stress of his repeated sexual advances made her physically ill. When Wood filed for unemployment compensation claiming that it was not her fault that she could no longer work, her case was discovered by Lin Farley, who taught a course at Cornell about women being forced to leave their jobs to avoid their boss's unwanted sexual advances. Farley and two of her colleagues coined the term *sexual harassment* to describe the phenomenon. That spring, she accompanied Wood to a feminist "speak out" in Ithaca, where the term *sexual harassment* found its first public airing. Later that same year, the New York City Commission on Human Rights, chaired by Eleanor Holmes Norton, held hearings on the topic of women in the workplace. Lin Farley was asked to testify. When the *New York Times* ran an article about the hearings, titled "Women Begin to Speak Out Against Sexual Harassment at Work," the term entered the national lexicon for the first time.

The *Times* article tapped a vein, and Farley and her colleagues were flooded with reports of women across the country who were experiencing problems similar to Carmita Wood's. But if the sociology of sexual harassment was developing rapidly, the law was still in its nascence. When victims of sexual harassment sought legal redress or protection, lawyers, lacking a legal framework and precedent, tended to frame it in unemployment insurance or workman's compensation claims.

Gradually, however, courts were recognizing sexual harassment as a form of sex discrimination under Title VII of the Civil Rights Act of 1964. Title VII prohibits employers from discriminating against workers on the basis of race, religion, color, national origin, or sex. The Civil Rights Act was designed to fight discrimination against African-Americans, and originally gender was not among the categories of discrimination.

The act was a controversial and contentious piece of legislation. Virginia congressman Howard Smith, the leader of the southern conservatives who opposed the bill, tacked on what he disparagingly called the "sex" amendment, prohibiting discrimination on the basis of sex. Smith, who was in his eighties, assumed that making employment discrimination against women a federal violation would be so unpopular that it would sink the bill. In his floor speech, which was nothing short of burlesque, he said the purpose of the amendment was to set aright the "imbalance of spinsters." Smith and his allies miscalculated. The Civil Rights Act, along with the "sex" amendment, passed. But the haphazard addition of gender to the bill meant that there was very little legislative history—floor debate and committee reports—that would shed light on what Congress intended the scope of the amendment to be.

The interpretation of Title VII's intentions, when it came to protecting the civil rights of female workers, was left to the courts. Prior to 1975, little case law was produced on the question of what constituted gender discrimination. The *Times* article increased awareness of the problem, which in turn led to more litigation on the subject. In 1976, two courts rejected the proposition that sexual harassment could be a form of gender discrimination under Title VII. But that same year, the U.S. District Court in Washington, D.C., became the first federal court to hold otherwise in *Williams v. Saxbe.*

In that case, a woman named Diane Williams was fired from her job with the community relations department of the U.S. Department of Justice after she refused her supervisor's sexual advances. She claimed that this was a violation of Title VII, because she had been denied equal employment opportunities. If she had been a man, she argued, her boss would never have propositioned her. It was her turning down the proposition that led to her firing, she said. In this scenario, being a woman was her liability, and that was illegal under the Civil Rights Act. The defendants—the attorney general of the United States and the Department of Justice—argued that she had not been fired because she was a woman, which would be a violation of Title VII, but because she refused to have sex with her employer. That, they argued, might have happened to a man or a woman, depending on to whom the advances were made. They also argued that Williams had not been fired because of a policy or formal action of the department, but because of an "isolated personal incident which should not be the concern of courts and was not the concern of Congress in enacting Title VII."

In a watershed decision, the court rejected the defendants' arguments. The court found that, in firing Williams for refusing to have sex with him, the supervisor had imposed a condition of employment on Williams that he did not impose on other workers, and that he did so because she was a woman. Therefore, the court reasoned it was a violation of Title VII, which, thanks to Congressman Smith, prohibits the discriminatory imposition of conditions of employment on workers due to their gender.

That precedent stuck, and by 1977 three federal courts of appeals and a number of district courts had held that sexual harassment could be a form of sex discrimination under Title VII. All of the cases involved situations in which a male supervisor or coworker made unwanted sexual advances to a particular female employee or conditioned employment on the granting of sexual favors.

Two years later, Catherine MacKinnon, then a young law professor at the University of Michigan, published a treatise called *Sexual Harassment of the Working Woman*. In it, MacKinnon made the novel assertion that "quid pro quo" harassment, meaning "this for that," which she referred to as "put out or get out," was not the only form of sexual harassment that violated Title VII. She argued that subjecting women to a hostile work environment, including repeated exposure to sexually offensive or denigrating material, as a condition of employment could also constitute a violation of Title VII.

Although courts did not immediately embrace MacKinnon's theory, it gained currency when in 1980 the Equal Employment Opportunity Commission (EEOC) issued federal guidelines on sexual harassment in the workplace that incorporated both the "quid pro quo" and "hostile work environment" theories. The guidelines were issued in November, less than a month after Diane Hodge's arbitration report, but they had no binding legal force. Still, they immediately became a benchmark for courts and employers in sorting out what conduct violated Title VII. They stated simply that:

> *Unwelcome sexual advances, requests for sexual favors, and other verbal or physical conduct of a sexual nature constitute sexual harassment when (1) submission to such conduct is made either explicitly or implicitly a condition of an individual's employment, (2) submission to or rejection of such conduct by an individual is used as the basis for employment decisions affecting such individual, or (3) such conduct has the purpose or effect of unreasonably interfering with an individual's work performance or creating an intimidating, hostile, or offensive working environment.*

While these guidelines were not exactly front-page news in most American communities, by 1980 a revolution was taking place in the American workforce. More than twelve million women had flooded into the workplace since 1970, accounting for 42.6 percent of employed Americans and 60 percent of the labor force expansion in the 1970s.

Also in 1980, sexual harassment was addressed in a way more palatable to the masses in the movie *Nine to Five*, starring Jane Fonda, Dolly Parton, and Lily Tomlin. The film, which depicted the sexual harassment of three secretaries by their male boss, was a comedic-revenge fantasy. Lois and Michele saw the movie when it was released on video. Sitting around Lois's apartment, drinking sodas and eating cheese and crackers, Lois and Michele thought the movie was hilarious. When Tomlin, Fonda, and Parton manage to string their boss up to the ceiling,

Michele said, "Holy buckets! It's great that the gals got revenge." But they thought that what happened to the women in the movie was mild in comparison to what they experienced every day at work. Lois wondered if it was because the women in the movie were secretaries in the low-paying "pink-collar ghetto," while she and the other women miners were doing men's work for men's wages. They were threatening to a man in the way a female secretary would never be.

By the winter of 1981, Lois had been working in the electrical department as a lightbulb changer for two and a half years. Her health and weight had stabilized, and she looked forward to occasional strikes and layoffs during that time because they provided her with weeks, and sometimes months, off work. She used this downtime to collect herself emotionally and spend time with Greg. The money in the electrical department was better and the day-shift hours more regular.

But the job was high profile. It took her all over the plant, exposing her to many more people than she had met on her other jobs at Eveleth. Every day Lois filled a big box full of three-hundred-watt incandescent bulbs, long fluorescent tube lights, and small, powerful halogen and mercury bulbs. She swung the box over her shoulder by affixing a thick rope to either end and canvassed the fifteen acres of interior space that made up the Fairlane plant. She shimmied up pipes, climbed catwalks, and replaced burned-out bulbs. It didn't take long for the men she encountered on her route to say things like "Nice box. I'd like to get into that box," accompanied by a suggestive gesture.

Lois soon learned how to fend off some of the unwanted attention. When a miner repeatedly pinched her, she surprised herself by actually swinging a fist at him. When an electrician stopped her in the office and stared blatantly at her breasts and crotch, "I saw it as a challenge and did the same thing to him. He didn't like it." When increasingly lewd pin-ups started appearing on the wall near her lightbulb shelf, she tore them down. After new ones continued to go up, Lois cut a bra and panties out of a piece of paper and taped them over the woman's body.

She had less luck dealing with the intentions of Eugene Perpruner, or "Prunes" as he was called around the plant. Perpruner, a big lumbering man who had a reputation around the mine for not being the "sharpest knife in the drawer," would not let Lois out of his sight. When coworkers noticed that Prunes seemed to have a crush on Lois, they egged him on. "Jenson and Perpruner fucked here" and "Lois Jenson gives head" started appearing on the walls of the Motor Control Centers that Lois and Prunes had to clean. People made comments like "Hey, what do you two do in those dark rooms?"

Lois managed to keep enough distance from Prunes without alienating him, and he never physically came on to her. But the delicate balance was wrecked when Mrs. Perpruner called Lois and complained that her husband talked about his coworker all the time at home and compared her, unfavorably, to Lois. She also called Lois's supervisor, Jim Thomas, and complained that Perpruner was spending too much time with Lois on the job. Thomas ordered Perpruner and Lois to work separately on all jobs. His directive enraged Perpruner, who cornered Thomas in the elevator, picked him up by the neck, and threatened to kill him. For the next few months, Perpruner continued to follow Lois around at work to the point of frightening her. Hoping to avoid him, Lois switched out of the electrical department, but after fifteen shifts in the concentrator with foreman John Maki, who said he did not want a woman working on his crew, Lois returned to the electrical department.

The reaction of Perpruner's wife was typical of many of the wives whose husbands worked at Eveleth Mines; they were suspicious and jealous of the women who worked with their husbands. Several times Lois had seen men from her crew shopping at the Super One with their spouses. Instead of greeting her, they quickly turned away before she could say hello. Marcy Steele, Joan Hunholz, and Diane Hodge, all attractive women, were picketing with a group of men from the union during the 1977 strike when a local TV camera crew showed up to film the strike. The men, Marcy said, "scattered like flies." Later, one of them told her that they did not want their wives to see them on television with the women they worked with. "We told them you're all fat and ugly," he said. The wives took to calling the women who worked at the mines "mining sluts" and "mining whores."

One morning in the winter of 1981, Lois walked into the electrical department at 7:00 A.M. and noticed that a group of men were loitering around looking like they were waiting for something to happen. One of the electricians said to Lois, "Looks like somebody left something for you." Lois looked at her lightbulb shelf and next to a stack of incandescent bulbs rested an eight-inch-long replica of a penis that had been attached to the edge of the shelf and was sticking straight out into the room. It was sculpted, with a disturbing amount of detail, out of a dense gray-green clay the miners called "bear poop," a material electricians used to waterproof hot wires.

When Lois found herself in the women's dry in tears for what seemed like the twentieth time since she'd started working at Eveleth, she decided to do something constructive. She knew she was not the only one getting such treatment. Lewd graffiti about the other women covered the walls of the plant. Diane had confided in Lois about Willie Johnson, Marcy had talked to her about her problem with the other oilers, and Lois had witnessed Jerry Benz feeling Joan Hunholz's breasts while pretending to fish a pack of cigarettes out her shirt pocket. "We were having discussions every day in the dry. Things were getting worse and worse," Lois said. She also knew that complaining to the foremen did not work. Management had shown no interest in disciplining the men. That left, in Lois's mind, only one place for the women to go: the union.

Why didn't she go to Pat, who was not only a power in the union but also a woman who had been fighting this fight long before Lois made her first official move? For reasons Lois wasn't completely conscious of—the passive-aggressive side to her personality perhaps played a role in her decision—she did not go directly to Pat for guidance. The two were both born leaders, but their methods were like night and day, and consequently, they didn't much like each other. Instead, Lois approached Stan Daniels.

"Stan, I think the women need their own committee within the union," she said, and explained that the women were having problems they did not feel comfortable discussing with the men in the union. She thought a committee within the union would be a place where the women could talk confidentially, and then go to the union officers for help. It would provide a way of dealing with the harassment without breaching the union oath by involving management. "If we don't get this under control," Lois told him, "it's going to turn into a huge problem."

"It's okay with me, just make sure you clear it with Pat first," he said. With some trepidation, Lois approached Pat the next day at shift change in the dry and floated her idea. Before Lois could finish, Pat abruptly said, "Nope. It's just going to be a big gossip session."

Lois tried to reason with Pat, but "she was like a rock. She wouldn't budge." Lois's heart sank. "I knew the other women wouldn't go along with it if Pat wouldn't go along with it because Pat was our voice in the union." Without Pat's blessing, Lois's idea for the women's committee was dead in the water. Lois was so angry at Pat for destroying what she thought was the women's only chance of resolving their problems that she found herself avoiding Pat and resenting her. "It was a huge block for the two of us," said Lois.

The conflict was part personality conflict, part power struggle. "Pat wanted to have everything under her control," recalled Michele. "She didn't think we needed a committee because it would cause more friction between the men and the women than there was already." Pat still had not given up the hope of using her influence as an insider in the union leadership to help the women. But before long, these two very different women would find themselves thrown together over a much bigger cause.

CHAPTER FIVE

The Letters

December 1981

December 31, 1981, was the kind of winter night on the Iron Range when the mercury disappeared into the bottom of the thermometer—twenty below at dinnertime and dropping. But it was New Year's Eve and Lois had a date with a man from the mine who, to her surprise, seemed to want to treat her like a lady.

She had met Dan Plesche two weeks earlier at a union Christmas party at the armory in Eveleth. Michele had dragged her friend to the party—a beery, door-prize kind of an evening that Lois usually took pains to avoid. He was a coal loader in the concentrator whom Michele knew. When they first met, Lois noticed that he wore a hairpiece, tight polyester pants, and held a drink in each hand. "He was stuck in the seventies," she said.

Lois's idea of a good night out was Mugga's. The bar was in Eveleth overlooking Highway 53, and it drew the Range's more sophisticated partiers: singles in their late twenties and early thirties who liked to mingle and dance to the live country-western bands that played there almost every night. She had managed to keep her weight down, she looked slim and beautiful; heads turned when she entered a room. Blue eye shadow accented her pale blue eyes, and a delicate gold chain adorned her neck. She wore her trademark dressy sweater, high heels, and blue jeans. "I ended up setting a trend because they didn't know anyone who dressed that way," she later said. She drank Amaretto on the rocks with a splash of Coke and limited herself to two. "After two I switch to grapefruit juice," she explained to the puzzled Rangers in Mugga's, who tended to drink beer all evening. Michele admired Lois's sophisticated tastes and took to ordering Amaretto, too. "But," she laughed, "I ordered mine straight up."

In Mugga's, Lois was in her element. "She was a good dancer, she remembered people's names, and she was very sociable," said Michele, who often accompanied her to the bar. Lois considered swing dancing to country music her main form of exercise, and she took pride in her ability on the dance floor. Although she was not friends with the men she danced with regularly, they regarded each other with mutual appreciation.

When Dan Plesche spotted Lois at Mugga's, he walked right over and asked her out. "I told him no," she said. For one thing, he was twenty-five years old and she was thirty-three. And then there was the hairpiece. But the biggest strike against him was that he worked at the mine.

It had been almost seven years since she had been out with Gene Scaia and two years since she'd been on a date with anyone at all. Her work environment was having an effect on her desire to meet men. "I didn't want to be with men off the job. I had my fill of attention at work." Still, Lois could not help but be flattered by Dan's persistence. He told Lois that he had his eye on her ever since his first day of work in October 1976, when she took him and a group of new employees on a tour of the plant.

As they sat and talked at a table with eight of their coworkers, Plesche asked her out to dinner. Then he asked again. And again. He asked six times in all that night.

"No. I'm not interested. I'm not dating," Lois said. But Plesche's abject adoration got to be funny, even charming, and Lois finally relented.

On New Year's Eve, he took her to dinner at a nice restaurant in the small town of Tower, where they were not likely to run into anyone from the mine. Dan told funny jokes all through dinner, even on himself, and made Lois laugh. When she told him that he did not need his toupee, instead of getting angry or hurt he agreed to pitch it. Unlike most of the Ranger men she had dated, he did not drink much or swear. Lois liked his laugh.

By the time he drove her home after dinner, the temperature was forty below zero. Dan stopped his car outside of her house so they could talk, but when he tried to start it up again, it was dead from the cold. Lois could not get her car to turn over either, so Dan slept on her couch. Lois was impressed that he behaved himself.

After that night, he became a regular visitor at Lois and Greg's little white clapboard house on Twelfth Avenue South, in Virginia. Before long, their relationship started to get intimate, but this time Lois was adamant that no one at the plant know about it. Dan, trying hard to win her over, agreed. For three months the two dated clandestinely, settling into a happy domesticity. He shopped for groceries and helped with the cooking and cleaning. They played Scrabble and Monopoly, and he taught Lois how to golf. Most important, Dan was nice to Greg. "He knew the only way to get me was by winning Greg over first," Lois said. Dan lived on a lake and began taking Greg canoeing, fishing, biking, and hunting.

Up until this time, Lois had always felt able to guide Greg. But now her sweet little boy had sprouted into a tall, handsome, confused teenager. At age twelve, a neighbor had given Greg whiskey and he had come home drunk. At thirteen, he was getting into minor scrapes at school. Now, at fourteen, he needed a male role model. Restrictions of time and money kept Greg out of the Iron Range's male ritual—ice hockey—where he might have found a mentor. "All these years I had not married, we could do fine without a man. But when Greg became a teenager, I panicked. I was terrified I couldn't do this alone." A man in the house would be good for both of them, she thought.

One day in April, Dan called Lois on the phone at work. He was in the coal loading area, she was in the electrical shop. To the racket of coal being dumped onto a conveyor belt in the background, he asked her to marry him.

She was taken by surprise. "What? We've never even discussed this before." Lois could hear the guys Dan worked with in the background and knew they were eavesdropping. "Let's talk about it when we get home." Greg begged his mother to accept. Lois said yes. Soon she and Dan had picked out a diamond solitaire engagement ring. Rather than suffer through the big wedding that Dan's overbearing mother was busy planning, they flew to Las Vegas to elope.

"Looking back," Lois said, "that was the first sign of trouble." On the flight to Vegas, Dan drank heavily. His personality changed, he became argumentative, even belligerent. He did not have a drink after that, and was his usual attentive self to Lois, which calmed her down. But when Dan went to the casino and lost most of the money they had brought with them, she got worried all over again. For the next three days, they put off getting married until it was practically time to board the plane. Finally, the couple walked into a little wedding chapel, picked their music and flowers, said their vows, and signed their license. They walked out married. "I felt empty and a little sad, and so did he. It was so cheap." It was July 24, 1982. Lois was thirty-four. Twice a mother, she was a married woman for the first time in her life.

Lois sold the house in Virginia where she and Greg had lived for eleven years for $18,000. They moved into Dan's big cedar A-frame house on the banks of Swan Lake in the town of Pengilly—an inconveniently long drive to work, but a step up in luxury. The house was still under construction, and Lois put the money from the sale of her house into helping Dan finish the A-frame. They also worked together, wiring the house themselves, framing in the closets, prepping for Sheetrock. Lois's father gave them an old furnace.

At work, she discovered the flip side of machismo. Now that she was married and belonged to another guy, most of the men refrained from making passes and rude remarks. Instead, in the morning, her fellow electrical workers would ask her the same question they routinely asked each other: "Did you get lucky?" They still commented constantly on her clothes, her makeup, and her hair. But the tone was less sexual and more paternal.

The benefits of being Dan Plesche's wife were limited to work, however, because at home he started drinking heavily. He would often toss back the first beer at a bar early in the morning after midnight shift and continue to drink all weekend. He would yell at Lois and Greg. Dan never hit either of them, but he scared Lois when he came home loaded. "When he stayed out, I stayed on guard because he would come home at three A.M. and threaten Greg." When she discovered that he owed $5,000 in back taxes, she thought, "Who is this man? He's not the man I thought I married."

On April 28, 1983, just after the drywall had been put up and they were ready to paint, a fire gutted the house. The only thing left standing was the front-door frame and a safe. They lost everything—wedding presents, furniture, clothes, family photos. Dan, Lois, and Greg moved into a trailer, parked next to the burned-out house, that had no plumbing or electricity. Soon after the fire, Lois caught Dan secretly depositing the checks from the insurance company into his father's bank account. Dan became increasingly distant, and his drinking grew worse.

That spring Lois sat at the kitchen table in the dingy trailer, staring at Greg's ninth-grade school photograph. "I have never seen such a sad kid," she thought. In all of his previous school photos, Greg always looked happy. This year was different. Greg's gaze was downcast, a sad, distant look in his blue eyes.

The photograph was her wake-up call. Nineteen eighty-two had been a hard year for Greg. Lois started shift work that year and was only home at odd hours and rarely got weekends off. When she first started working at the mine, Greg was seven and proud of her. Lois knew that the women miners were called lesbians and whores, and that Greg had to suffer people calling her names at school, but he kept it to himself. When Lois's schedule permitted, she would pick Greg up after school and drive him home. In the afternoon after school, Greg stood on the side of Highway 169 in Nashwalk, a town near Pengilly, and waited for Lois to pick him up. But one afternoon, her mind in another place, Lois drove by him, leaving him standing alone on the highway.

Lois put the photo down and decided that she and Greg had to get out of the trailer and out of the marriage.

In June, they moved into an apartment in Mountain Iron; in September, she filed for divorce and Dan did not contest it. They agreed that he would have the land and what was left of the house; she would take the insurance money that covered the cost of the house's contents. On October 19, 1983, the divorce was final. Lois and Dan had been married for sixteen months.

The day of her court hearing she asked her boss, Bob Radosevich, the general foreman in the electrical department, not to tell anyone where she was. Lois had a friendly, respectful relationship with Radosevich. She shared her poetry with him, and they both were photography buffs and critiqued each other's pictures. She hoped that he would help her keep her secret. The next morning, as Lois copied blueprints on a big ammonia machine in the electrical shop, Steve Povroznik popped his head in the door and said that he had heard she was divorcing. Her heart sank. If he knew, everyone knew.

Steve Povroznik was a short, skinny, thirty-three-year-old senior engineer who buttoned his old flannel shirts to the neck and his sleeves at the wrist. He wore his jeans high-water style and he walked in a slouch, with his head down. Steve earned about $40,000 a year—an enormous sum in the Range at that time—but did not like to spend money, so he lived with his mother and drove a beat-up Horizon. He did not have many friends and was roundly considered a nerd, but he fancied himself a pop psychologist and was known around the electrical shop for offering guys advice about women. This was ironic, because Steve also had a reputation for having little luck with women. In fact, as far as anyone could tell, he had never had a long-term, serious relationship.

Lois first met him in 1981 when he trained her to copy blueprints. Despite his awkward manner, Lois was friendly towards him—at least he did not swear like so many of the other men. One day early that year, when they were both working in the Motor Control Center, Steve told Lois he was afraid he was about to be fired. Lois tried to console him.

"Steve, don't worry, you're not going to get fired," she said, smiling at him and patting him on the shoulder. When she did so, he physically recoiled; he seemed shocked that she'd touched him. Lois was a warm person. Every once in a while she would touch someone's arm when she spoke to him or her. She did not mean anything by it. But this time, she immediately sensed that Steve had misinterpreted her.

"He acted like I'd offended him," Lois said. "I never touched him again after that."

A year later what she'd taken for revulsion had turned into something else. Shortly after she and Dan got engaged in April 1982, Steve asked her out. Lois told him that she was getting married. Steve pouted and acted like a spurned lover. It was truly bizarre, Lois thought, because they had barely spoken since their conversation about his job fears. Then it got even more bizarre when, in May, Lois was again cleaning the Motor Control Center when Steve walked in and put his car keys in her hand. "Your birthday present is in my car," he said. "Go and get it."

Lois did not know how to respond. "Steve, my birthday is in February," she said. "Besides, I can't leave my job right now, in the middle of the shift." Steve stormed out of the room.

In February 1983 he sent a birthday card to her at the house in Pengilly. Lois thought, "How stupid and inappropriate," and tossed the card out because she did not want Dan to see it. By this time, she realized that Steve was romantically interested in her, but she was a married woman, he knew it, and that was that. Or so she thought.

Now, on the day after Lois's divorce, Steve wanted to be the first to come to her rescue. He told Lois that he had taken some psychology courses in college and would be glad to counsel Lois on her marriage.

Lois, a look of disbelief on her face, said, "We don't need counseling, and I don't think it would be appropriate anyway."

But Steve persisted. "Then what are you going to do with your life?"

"I'm getting on with my life. I'm giving my ex two years to straighten up his act."

Lois hoped this would persuade Steve to back off, but he only intensified his efforts. He frequently stopped her in the halls to offer his services as marriage counselor and when that failed, he told Lois he had a book about relationships, *One on One*, which he wanted her to read. Lois told him she was not interested but as she was leaving work, he pressed the book into her hands and walked away. She returned it the following day.

On Thanksgiving weekend Steve sat down and began to write her a letter. It took him three days to finish, and by the time he was through the document filled twenty-eight pages on both sides of the ruled, white paper. Lois came home from work on November 31 and found a thick business-sized envelope in her mailbox. She opened it and started to read Steve's cramped handwriting.

The first six pages of the letter were a treatise on six types of love Ludus, Pragma, Storge, Mania, Eros, and Agape. "Agape, patient, dutiful and altruistic type of love . . . is my style, the one that fits me best. I call it the mature love." He transcribed a long poem about Agape love, which he kept on his wall at home: "To love another is to refuse to force one's own feelings and desires unto him (her). It is to give him (her) freedom—not as a duty, but as a delight out of respect and humility. . . ."

Then he described what he wanted in a woman. "Let me speak from personal experience and share with you my 'ideal woman.' I am totally infatuated by long, long, long hair. My sister calls it the 'straight and stringy' type of style. I prefer blond hair but I had all types of colors. But it must be long and straight. I like girls as tall as myself, flat and skinny, my sister says, and that is what turns me on [or] in my terminology trips my trigger. But unfortunately, this type of lady tends to be very insecure, very moody and very destructive to me. The end result—I am totally crushed in the end." Lois had blond hair, but it was not long and straight.

After three pages on the pitfalls of divorce, the never-married Steve Povroznik pontificated on marriage for another six pages—how passion lags after the birth of a child, how important it is to learn how to fight, and how to communicate. Then he wrote:

> *Let's digress a little right here and let me back track. I want to make a few points that have been bothering me. First, let me go back to the summer (1981). . . . At that point you seemed to me to be in your shell, like a clam closing his shell. I decided sometime during that Fall to see if I could break you out of that shell. So I tried to be very discreet and gave you a Valentine. Very low pressure, very unaggressive. No pressure at all as I wanted to be friends. Shortly after, you started dating and I was pleased that perhaps I was successful. . . . I had no way of knowing that I was in the way as I was under the assumption we could still be friends. And then at the time in May, you punished me for being nice. I was shocked and crushed! I felt really bad! I don't want you to feel ANY guilt at all about this as it is over and done with. Anyway, at that point I wrote you off 100% as I couldn't understand what kind of a person could get her kicks out of punishing someone for being nice. Of course, if you had only said something I would have understood. But you didn't and anyway I wrote you off. . . . Still I did feel badly for quite a while and I want you to know that so you don't do it again. Don't feel guilty about it, it is over and done with. Just please don't punish me for being nice! That's all I ask! And it was your loss as I had intended to bring along my guitar and play a series of songs and sing to you. And that you can't buy or sell in any store! . . . Probably just as well—it probably would have blown your mind anyway. A guitar is a lethal weapon with women. It usually blows*

their minds. . . . I don't like being liked or loved for my guitar and not for me the person. Very destructive.

Steve wrote, "Do you still want to stay friends with me? I doubt if I will see much of you anymore at work. Things are piling up all around and I will have to pick up more of the drafting work which will tie me up. I will be office bound for a while. It's pretty much up to you. . . . If you want to do something I am open to suggestions. Pick a role for me to play and we'll discuss it." He signed the letter, "With Love, Steve."

Lois put the letter down. She felt sick. Steve had serious emotional problems and he was distorting her words. What had she done to encourage him to write such a letter? He seemed to believe that they were close friends, had a history, a past together, but it was not true. He said he wanted to be friends, but clearly he wanted much more than that. Lois's sister Marilyn dropped by the apartment just as Lois finished reading the letter. She handed it to Marilyn, who sat down on the couch and read the whole thing. "Oh God, this guy needs help," she said. "He has no business getting in your face like this." Marilyn, a married mother of two and a bank manager, lived a forty-five-minute drive away in Babbitt. She always worried about her sister's bad luck with men. "The unstable ones tended to be drawn to her," Marilyn noted.

The next day, Lois confronted Steve in the electrical shop. "Don't write me, and don't call me anymore," she said. But he would not listen. He said, "How can I tell you what's going on if I can't call or write you?" Lois, who hated being mean and had trouble being direct, managed to stand her ground in a firm but polite way.

A few days later, Steve did just what she had asked him not to. He called Lois at home.

"I told you not to call me," Lois said.

"But I never know when you're joking."

"I'm not joking," she said, and hung up. Steve called back again. This time he asked Lois how she liked his letter.

Lois, in a rare moment of bluntness, replied, "I hated your letter."

As though he had not heard her, Steve replied that he wanted to give her a Christmas present. She asked him please not to and hung up again.

A week later, Steve sent Lois a Christmas card. He called her at home and begged her to allow him to give her a Christmas present. He promised it would just be something little, something he was also giving each of his three sisters.

It was so much harder for Lois to say "No" to Steve than to say "Yes." In a bar, if a stranger asked her to dance, she could say no. Yet when it came to someone she knew, she had always found it almost impossible to be direct. She marveled at how her friend Michele could just tell someone who was bothering her to fuck off. But Lois dreaded hurting other people's feelings—even people at the plant who had hurt her—and to avoid doing that, she took the path of least resistance in conversation. She liked to be someone people could confide in and seek advice from, and she somehow felt that if she were more direct and blunt, she would lose that role. Because of this, she gave into Steve's cajoling. It was a huge mistake.

"Okay, but it has to be cheap—no more than five dollars, and it cannot be personal, and if it is, you're getting it back immediately." She also told him not to expect a present from her in return.

When his present arrived in the mail, it was a pair of high-quality, $100 thermal underwear. The next day, Lois returned the underwear to Steve, telling him that she could not accept such an expensive present from him.

He took back the present but was undeterred. He called her at home and asked her to go for an ice cream sundae. Sharply, she refused.

Steve whined, "What could be wrong with something as innocent as getting an ice cream together?" He pouted and persisted until he irritated Lois so much that she blurted, "My son is fourteen years old, and if he acted the way you are acting, I would spank him!"

Later, when she reflected on this conversation, she realized that the spanking comment was a blunder. "Boy, did he get a lot of mileage out of that!" She had unconsciously used a sexually provocative image, and it gave Steve just the opening he was looking for. But at the time, she saw nothing suggestive in her behavior. Steve responded by writing a sixteen-page letter. He chastised her for returning his gift:

> *I really thought my present was very practical. I use mine all the time. I have a full set too. . . . I want you to know I was both mad at you and hurt by you the other day. But it passed. However, it made me very cautious of you. . . . I told you, I have a ton of emotion. I didn't want to come right out and say—I love you—I tried to avoid that. I feel comfortable with that, yes I do love you in my own way, in many ways I thought you could read between the lines. I guess everything has to be spelled out for you. So that will make you most uncomfortable. So why did you seem so warm and open before? That really confused me. I thought you were safe. You really turned on me, refused to even let me buy you a sundae, really now, that was childish. . . . I was quite mad at you and quite hurt because I didn't expect any rejections. I simply can not take rejections. You really stirred up a lot of hurtful emotions. . . .*
>
> *So—why are you so afraid of me? Yes, I do have lots of emotion, I guess that could scare you. . . . If you push me away it will hurt. I'm not prepared for it. It isn't in my script of how I had planned this thing to work out. So PLEASE—Don't push me away. Or you'll pull me down. . . . I will do anything, yes anything, to avoid being pushed away. . . .*

Steve described the "intimate" friendship that he had pictured in his "script." He would make Lois happy, they would spend lots of time together. At the same time, there would be "no pressure." He told her that she could call the shots, but he also said he could not handle rejection.

> *I want you to know I can't turn off my feelings like flipping a switch. That is impossible. And maybe you are uncomfortable*

with that. . . . My biggest pleasure I have is my guitar and that I can sing really nice. Except that I expect you to be a mature lady and not rip off my clothes when I finish. Should I ever get the chance to play to you. . . . If ever you really want to experience a really touching time, let me know. I'd be happy to play for you on my own turf of course. I have to be comfortable with the situation, to be totally in control. Right now you are totally in control. I don't like it at all. . . .

I will do anything you say. Whether in your words—you want to spank me or not. But I want you to know that if you pull out that 14 year old little girl on me I will SPANK YOU. . . . But I do want very much to be friends. I believe it will be mutually beneficial. And if you want to distance me then I want to stay in touch probably by calling. I still think you are a very special lady. . . . By spending time with you, I can get control of these emotions that I am experiencing. Because your time is very valuable, it is quality time. Life is so short it is a shame. It gets wasted. If you tell me my timing is off, well, it took me 4 years to get this far, I guess a few more won't hurt to wait, provided that is OK? I'm really in no hurry. . . .

This letter scared Lois. She did not know what to do or how to respond. A similar one arrived on Christmas eve. A few days later, Steve called. Lois tried to reason with him, explaining that she did not want the kind of friendship he wanted, and that she hoped he could find another woman who could make him happy. She also asked him again to stop calling and writing. A fifth letter arrived the next day, apologizing and rehashing their telephone conversation. On January 4, 1984, he wrote Lois a sixth letter. On January 8, came the seventh, in which for the first time, he blamed her for his loss of control. He accused her of being a "toucher," based on the time three years ago when he confided in her about his job and she had placed her hand on his shoulder to comfort him.

On January 9 and 10 she received two more letters. She was afraid to even open them. She would have been even more frightened had she known that during those two days in January, Steve had written another dozen letters to her, which he burned before sending.

Lois was looking forward to a two-week January vacation in Nevada with Greg and her parents. On Friday, her last day of work before she left, she brought the two unopened letters to work to give back to Steve, but when she noticed that he was acting strange—snickering and giggling like a little kid who knew a secret no one else knew—she thought she should read the letters. She read the last one first. It was an interoffice memo dated January 9, 1984, to Dan Schultz proposing that Lois be promoted to the job of drafting electrical drawings. The two-page, typed memo explained that because of layoffs and restructuring in the electrical department, a backlog was growing of electrical drawings that needed updating. Steve argued that the company was losing as much as $100,000 a month because of the lack of proper electrical documentation. He proposed "Electrician Helper" Lois Jenson for the job because she had already been trained in how to do field documentation. Hiring her would be four times cheaper than hiring an electrician for the job, he said, not to mention the fact that a new electrician would take time to get up to speed and Lois would not.

He admitted that it was a salaried position and Lois was not a salaried worker, which made for an irregular employment situation. But he argued that hiring Lois would not simply save money, "It is life or death," he wrote. "Without field documentation we will reach a time when the problem will not get fixed," leading surely, he reasoned, to electrical accidents.

What he failed to mention in the memo was that giving Lois the job would bring her under his direct supervision. On the top of the first page of his letter to her, Povroznik had scribbled, "Lois, don't show this to anyone. As you see the battle has begun. I hope this will be my penance for the letter at Christmas. Wish me luck."

By the time Lois read the memo, Dan Schultz, the maintenance superintendent who was Steve's boss, had already seen the proposal. There had been a lot of new construction at the plant since 1978, and up-to-date electrical drawings, called schematics, were needed so that when machinery broke down it could be fixed easily and quickly. If the schematics were out of date, it could take six hours to fix a clogged filter, shutting down the whole plant and costing the company thousands of dollars, and it was true, accidents had occurred. The problem was that the electrical department was short-staffed because of a rash of layoffs. In 1983, the bottom dropped out of the steel industry, and the number of employees at Eveleth had plummeted from 1,450 in 1981 to 723 in 1983.

"The last thing we could do is hire a new engineer when we were laying people off," Schultz said. "And if we put a union person on salary, they could be out of a job in six months [if they got laid off] with no union protection." By hiring Lois to do drawings, which was a salaried job, yet keeping her on the hourly (unionized) payroll, Schultz could fill a necessary position with someone who was trained and already on staff. It was a convenient, if slightly unorthodox, proposal.

After two years in the electricians' department Lois had begun to learn how to trace wires and label them. She would take home the prints and type up labels for each wire because, as a union member, she was not permitted to go into the main office to use a typewriter. She would go to the pellet plant and the concentrator and trace the lines, looking for hot wires. She brought colored pencils to work and would get on her stomach and draw the wires onto the blueprints. "It's just common sense. Electricity has a mind of its own. All you have to do is give it a safe path." Although her title was electrician's helper, she was doing much more advanced work. Lois had begun to love this job and she was good at it.

Schultz was confident that Lois could do the job. He had known her since her days as a teller at the credit union, when he made his car payments to her every month. He thought she was a diligent, hard worker. He appreciated having her in the office because "she was a personable, attractive, nice lady." He also thought she was honest and trustworthy.

Schultz knew that Lois had taken a course at Mesabi Junior College in basic electronics and drafting, and that her role as an electrician's helper had already expanded beyond its usual job description of changing lightbulbs and cleaning Motor Control Centers.

Similarly, Schultz appreciated Steve's meticulous, detailed, and accurate work. But something about the tone of the memo troubled him. He thought that Steve had overdramatized the "life and death" situation. He also thought the memo was oddly emotional, even desperate-sounding. Anyway, the budget for the year had already been approved and there was no money for a new draftsman, union or salaried. Schultz told Povroznik no.

When Lois finished reading the memo, she was furious. She did not know that Schultz had already turned down Steve's request. But she did know that she did not want any job with Steve as her direct superior. She found him and told him that she did not want, and did not deserve, the job. "Straighten this out before I get back from vacation," she told him.

That night, Steve called Lois at home and offered to drive her to the airport in Minneapolis the next day. She told him she was angry with him for submitting her name for the drafting job, and that she believed his motives were personal. He denied it, arguing that he needed her help, and that she was the only one who knew the plans well enough to fill in. In a rush to finish her packing, she told him they would discuss it when she returned.

Lois went to Nevada believing Steve's proposal would fizzle. She was confident Dan Schultz would never agree to give her the job; she simply was not qualified for it. Yet she was tense for the entire two weeks in Boulder City. She dreaded going back to work.

Her anxiety was justified. When she returned to work on Monday, January 30, she had the electrician's helper job. Steve had badgered Schultz into approving the drafting position. Lois was informed by one of the foremen that she would now be a clerk/draftsman and that Steve would oversee her work. To compensate for the fact that she was not a full-fledged electrician, she was assigned a coworker, an electrician named Mark Lakenen who would oversee Lois's drawings, help her with the fieldwork, and answer her questions.

Mark, a mild-mannered man who had a wife and children, had been called back from a second layoff to take the new drafting job. Steve and Schultz made it clear to Lois that if she did not accept the job, Lakenen would have no job to be called back to do; she *was* his job. Lois liked Mark and she did not want him to lose work. And if word got out that she was responsible for him being out of a job, there would be one more reason for her coworkers to pick on her. Finally, but not insignificantly, she loved the work. Against her better judgment, Lois talked herself into taking the position.

She hoped she could make it work by avoiding contact with Steve as much as possible. But he did not take well to being avoided. He wanted constant communication with Lois. In February, he sent her a tape recorder, two audiocassettes, and a note explaining that she should listen to the "educational" tapes that he had made for her. Lois was afraid to listen to them; she knew that they had nothing to do with education. She put them in a brown bag and asked Mark to put the bag on Steve's desk. The next day, February 13, a Valentine package was waiting for Lois in her mailbox at home. She did not open it. In the morning, she asked Lakenen to return the package to Steve. Once again, Mark obliged.

Minutes later, just before the nine o'clock break, Steve stormed into Lois's area in the electrical shop. He looked furious. He demanded that she come to his office. Warily, she followed him. Steve tried to close the door, but Lois blocked it. On the verge of tears, he ripped open the package of tapes. "If you had only listened to these, you would understand what a good person I am and what kind of relationship we can have," he said. Lois tried to explain that she had told him over and over again that she was not interested.

Then Steve opened the Valentine. It was a wood plaque engraved with a romantic sentiment. "You didn't take this," he said, his voice rising. "You didn't even open it! See what I wrote to you here." He ranted that none of this fit into his script of how their relationship should be. Lois told him that he needed counseling, and that he was out of control. Steve leaned across his desk. "Slap me!" he begged. Lois refused.

"What you are doing right now qualifies as sexual harassment," she said. "If you don't stop, I'm going to turn you in."

At that point, Steve's manner changed. He demanded that she give back all the letters he had written her. Lois, realizing that she might need them to prove a complaint, refused. From across the desk, he grabbed one of her wrists, walked around the desk and grabbed her other wrist, and forced her into a chair. He held both of her wrists in one hand, kneeled down on the floor, and started rubbing her knees and the backs of her legs with his free hand. As Lois struggled to break away, he said, "I like to wrestle like this with my sisters."

Lois got one hand free, kicked him, and pulled her other hand free. She kept them in front of her face, moving them rapidly so that he could not catch them. He stood at the door, blocking her, so she dug her nails into his forearm as hard as she could, and he let her go. But when she walked out of the room, Steve slapped her on the rear end.

Lois got back to her desk and sat down. She was in shock. Mark, who was in their office, wanted to know what was going on. She told him, but asked him not to tell anyone. Mark told Lois that when he returned the Valentine, Steve said "That bitch" and had run out of his office. At that point Lois could have reported the incident to her boss, Dan Schultz, but she knew that Schultz relied heavily on Steve and she assumed that the chances of him believing her side of the story over Steve's were remote.

The next day Steve came to Lois's office to talk to her. Lakenen was also in the room. Steve and Lois talked for an hour. Lois, who for the past four years had been scanning every periodical she could find for information about sexual discrimination in the workplace, had developed a rudimentary understanding of harassment. She told Steve that she considered what had happened in his office to be sexual harassment. He said he was baffled that what he had considered a "misunderstanding" could be construed as sexual harassment. But Steve took her seriously and immediately started looking for another job, calling his old employer and other mines in the area, to no avail. He believed that if Lois showed his letters to the company, Oglebay Norton would most certainly use them as an excuse to lay him off.

For the next few months, Steve steered clear of Lois, providing what work direction and corrections that needed to be made to Mark, who, beginning to resent the role of middleman in a melodrama, passed the information on to Lois. In April, Steve heard from Schultz that Lois was doing such a good job that he was considering giving her a permanent salaried position. K. D. Nault, the maintenance superintendent, said that Lois and Mark's drawings of the concentrator and crusher were so good that the company was able to eliminate the job of one of the electricians who worked in the area. Steve had been right—Lois and Mark were saving the company money. Nault told Steve that if there were ever a salaried opening, he would like to consider Lois for the job.

In mid-July 1984, Mark was sent to the pit for a week to work as a fill-in foreman, leaving Lois alone in their office in the electrical shop. For the next two weeks, Steve came on strong. He confronted Lois for three days running, and each conversation was about the same thing: He wanted his letters back. Again and again, Lois refused. "They are my only protection," she said. On July 17, Lois made a note on a piece of scrap paper. On the bottom of the page, she wrote, *Please God Help Me.*

On July 20, Steve approached Lois for the sixth time. He had a piece of paper in his hand, and he told her that the company had asked him to write up his budget for 1985, and that he needed Lois's help. She told him that his budget was none of her business, and to leave her alone.

"But I need your help with the wording," said Steve.

"Please leave me alone. Remember, you are salaried, and I'm hourly."

"No, you don't understand. What I need from you is terminology to help me determine my choice. I need to know what our relationship will be."

Steve showed Lois a sheet of paper that had several items listed. The first four were: "computer," "drafting machine," "draftsman," "engineering aid or clerk." There were dollar figures after each line item. He explained that he needed to know what their relationship would be so that he could decide whether or not to put Lois in his annual budget.

Slowly, Lois realized that Steve was telling her that her job security hinged on whether she was willing to have a romantic or sexual relationship with him. She slumped in her chair, and started to cry. Taken aback by her reaction, Steve apologized, and kneeled on the floor next to Lois to try to conceal from anyone passing by that she was crying. When an electrician walked into the room to ask Steve a question, Steve asked him to leave. Lois, in tears, told Steve, "I don't care what you do."

Michele Mesich had begun to worry about the effect Steve's badgering was having on Lois. Before the letters, Michele and Lois had been constant companions. They liked to go out dancing or on photography trips in the woods. But now, Michele noticed, Lois was afraid to go out of the house. When Michele visited her, the curtains were always drawn. Michele had relied on Lois to be the fun, outgoing one, but now she could hardly get Lois to leave her apartment.

Even though Steve had apologized on July 20, he continued to press the issue of their "relationship" and the letters with Lois. On August 5, Lois looked at the schedule and noticed that Mark was going on vacation. Up until now, Lois had been reluctant to report the situation with Steve to management. She had tried to handle the problem privately, with the help of Mark Lakenen, but in fact, she had just made matters worse. Now that Mark's absence was about to leave her alone on the job with Steve for two weeks, she realized that the time to talk to someone official about her problem was long overdue.

She approached Dan Harp, a union officer who worked in the electrical department, and told him about her problems with Steve. "I want him to leave me alone," she told Harp. "Please just get him to leave me alone." Harp was sympathetic, but suggested that he talk to Steve first before taking any steps to wage an official complaint.

A few days later, Harp took Steve aside and told him that Lois had complained about his behavior. Harp reported to Lois that Steve had admitted that there was a problem, and even admitted that the more he tried to resolve the problem, the worse things got between them. Harp assured Lois that everything was settled, and Steve would leave her alone from now on. But the next afternoon, Steve talked to Dan Harp and said that he wanted Harp to ask Lois for the letters back.

Figuring that if Lois had reported him to Harp there was no telling to whom she would talk next, Steve, in a panic, drove out to Dan Schultz's big red clapboard house on the edge of the woods in Virginia. It was Saturday, August 11, and Schultz, who had just come home late the night before from a two-week family vacation in Canada, was not happy to see Steve at his door. He could tell that his employee was highly agitated. Schultz told him to drive him into town to pick up his car at the mechanic, and they could talk.

On the way, Steve told Schultz that he was afraid that Lois Jenson might file a sexual harassment claim against him. Steve gave Schultz a brief history of his relationship with Lois. He told Schultz that he had written several letters to Lois between November 1983 and January 1984, the point of which, he insisted, was to provide Lois with counseling on her recent divorce. He admitted that they had had an emotional confrontation in February when she would not accept a Valentine's Day card from him, which ended with Steve slapping Lois on the rear end.

Schultz told Steve that he should have told him about these problems sooner and that he should avoid any further contact with Lois. The easy solution to Steve's problem was to do what should have been done three months ago—reassign Lois out of the electrical department. Earlier in the year, there had been departmental discussions about the need to eliminate Lois's electrician's helper job in order to save an electrician's slot. Lois had been slated to leave three months ago, but Schultz had been temporarily transferred to another department before he could execute the plan. Now, it was obviously the thing to do. But her departure could not be viewed as retaliation. It also had to be done smoothly.

Schultz told Steve not to worry and implored him not to make any "hasty moves." He would iron things out with Lois. Anyway, Schultz said, he knew that Lois had had problems with other men at the mine, including Eugene Perpruner, her lightbulb-changing partner, and that she had written a friendship poem to Bob Radosevich. In other words, it was not all Steve's fault. Schultz also thought to himself that Povroznik was just the kind of guy who would misinterpret Lois's warmth. "She was especially outgoing and warm to people. The bad news is it got her in trouble because it could be read as flirtatious to the wrong people," Schultz said years later.

The following Monday, Lois came to work as usual at 7:00 A.M., only to find her chair, drafting table, supplies, notes, reference books, and prints gone. One drafting table, which Lakenen had been using, remained in the office. Lois discovered that Steve had come to work an hour early, put her table in storage, and put all of her drawings and supplies in his office.

Furious, she found Dan Harp and reported what had happened. Then she called Steve and demanded to know what was going on. He walked over to Lois's office and told her that he removed her table and drawings because Lakenen would not be coming back to work and people had been complaining that the small room was so crowded that they could not get proper access to the files. Lois did not believe him.

That morning, when Dan Schultz came to work, he blew up at Steve. Steve had done precisely what Schultz had asked him not to do: He had confronted Lois and changed the status quo of her job. His actions were clearly a form of retaliation against Lois and killed any prospects of resolving this problem quietly and privately.

Word of the conflict in the electrical department spread quickly. Schultz heard from Bob Raich and Eugene Gilmore, the director of industrial relations for Oglebay Norton, that they were not happy to learn that Lois was doing "management" work. Schultz was in trouble both for letting Lois do a nonunion job and for failing to prevent trouble between Lois and Steve. In an attempt to quickly clean up the mess and cover his own back, Schultz told Lois that her job would be ending on Friday. He said that since her job was supposed to end in May, and since Lakenen would be working as a fill-in foreman most of the time and Lois would have no supervisor, she should finish the drawings she was working on by the end of the week. Then she would be demoted, or as he put it diplomatically, "given the opportunity to bid out of the shop."

Lois told Schultz about her problems with Steve and that she had documentation of his advances. Steve needed counseling, she said. Schultz admitted that Steve considered himself such a good counselor that it got him into trouble. But he asked Lois to keep the problem quiet. "Steve's a good engineer," he told her. "I would hate to lose him."

For Lois this was the last straw.

Up until now, her contact with the union, through her conversations with Dan Harp, had been unofficial. She photocopied all eight of Steve's letters, ninety-three pages total, typed up a nine-page report explaining the history of her trouble with him, and gave the whole package to Clarence Cadeau, the most senior union officer in the electrical office. Cadeau was also a grievance officer. Lois told Cadeau that she wanted to file an official union grievance against Steve for sexual harassment. It was the first time in nine years of working at Eveleth Mines that Lois filed a complaint against a coworker. One of the reasons she felt that it was possible was that Steve Povroznik was not a union member. He was the enemy—he was management.

Although the union was usually eager to file grievances against salaried employees, this time, Cadeau hesitated. He arranged a meeting with union and management officials to see if the dispute could be resolved unofficially. The meeting took place on Friday, August 17, in the conference room of the General Office, a small building near the plant that housed senior management offices. The meeting lasted from 9:30 A.M.

until noon. Representing Lois were four union officials: Cadeau, Harp, Sam Ricker, the union vice president, and Pat Kosmach. Lois sat on one side of an oval table, with Pat Kosmach on her right and Clarence Cadeau on her left. Dan Schultz and Jay Henningsgard, the vice president for personnel, sat across from them on the other side of the table. Henningsgard's boss, Bob Raich, was on vacation.

Lois's hands shook as she related the entire history of her encounters with Steve, from his first Valentine's Day card in 1982 to the scuffle in his office, to the clearing of her desk six months later. On the brink of tears, she spoke about the phone calls, the letters, the gifts, and the endless conversations at work.

Pat was Lois's most vocal supporter. She said angrily that this was not the first case of sexual harassment that had come to her attention. In fact, it was the third one in two and a half months. "Something has to be done about this," she demanded. Pat would not mention names, but she said the other two incidents were between two union members and were handled inside the union and without the company's involvement. Lois assumed that Pat was talking about Judy Jarvela and Marcy Steele. Lois marveled at how Pat commanded the attention and respect of the men in the room. She also could not help but think that if Pat had agreed to having a women's committee three years ago, they might not be sitting in this room today. But whatever lingering hurt feelings Lois had about Pat's rebuff quickly dissolved as Pat came to Lois's defense in the meeting.

Ricker and Cadeau made it clear that removing Lois from her job would be viewed as retaliation. Lois wanted to continue with her job, they said, and only under the condition that she not have to work with Steve Povroznik. The union officers also demanded that the company set up a policy on sexual harassment for their employees.

Jay Henningsgard listened thoughtfully to Lois's story. Henningsgard, who was not from the Iron Range, had had some experience with sexual harassment complaints in his previous jobs in Duluth, and realized that the company might have some exposure on Lois's claim. When

Lois finished, he said that the company was committed to investigating and correcting any sexual harassment complaints. Henningsgard and Schultz agreed to keep Lois in her current job, drawing the filter area, until she was finished, which would be sometime in October. They also agreed to transfer Povroznik from the plant to the pit.

Lois left the meeting with a feeling of optimism, and relief that she would not have to go through with an official union grievance. A week later, nothing had happened. Lois had not been transferred, but neither had Steve. Lois and Clarence Cadeau met with Schultz to find out what was going on. Schultz asked for more time, explaining that he was in the process of writing up a report and set of recommendations for Raich.

In fact, Schultz was struggling with his report. On the one hand, he believed Lois had an argument, now that he had heard the story from her point of view. But on the other hand, he liked Steve, even felt protective of him, and thought that Lois was probably responsible for at least some of what had happened. Schultz gave Steve the courtesy of letting him read an early draft of his report. "Steve was very upset after reading the report. He knew it was incriminating to him," Schultz said. Schultz quickly scanned a few of Steve's letters—how could he be so stupid, Schultz wondered—but in the end, his eight-page memo soft-peddled Steve's behavior. In response to Steve's complaining, Schultz tacked on a new conclusion: "It is the writer's opinion that we ended up with a major confrontation due to Lois misunderstanding Steve's intentions. We have had two previous situations where she had apparently encouraged a male employee, either deliberately or not, and then used threats of harassment charges to turn him away." The two other men Schultz claimed Lois "encouraged" were Eugene Perpruner and a pellet plant employee whose name Schultz did not even know but had heard of secondhand. "To be blunt," Schultz admitted years later, "Steve probably deserved worse than that, but the point was to get the facts down and not to persecute anybody."

Despite the suggestion that Lois was at least partly responsible for what had happened, Schultz attached a cover memo recommending that his report be placed in Steve's personnel file, and that the engineer be required to get some counseling. Schultz also recommended that Steve, who he said had used "bad judgment," be instructed to avoid all contact with Lois and that no disciplinary or retaliatory action be taken against Lois. Finally, Schultz recommended that "training will be provided to salaried personnel regarding the company's policy against discrimination and sexual harassment and to explain what might be construed as such." The recommendations reflected the agreement reached between the union, Lois, and Henningsgard with the exception of transferring Steve. "Lois never asked for Steve's head on a platter," Schultz said later. "No one asked for him to be publicly humiliated. She was not looking for blood."

Schultz's report was waiting for Raich when he returned from vacation the following week. Before Raich even finished reading it, he called Schultz into his office. "Where'd you get all these ideas?" Raich wanted to know. When he got to Schultz's last recommendation about training and the company's sexual harassment policy, Raich seemed incredulous. "What makes you think we're going to do that?"

Two days later, Raich came to Schultz's office with a new version of the cover memo that Raich's secretary had typed up. It was still addressed to Raich from Schultz. But now, instead of five recommendations for resolving the matter, there were only two: "Mr. Povroznik has been specifically instructed to avoid further contact with Ms. Jenson. He was also instructed not to make any further attempts to retrieve the letters he had written her between November 1983 and January 1984. Mr. Povroznik has volunteered to go for counseling with a psychiatrist in Duluth and follow any recommended treatment." Raich's version said nothing about a company sexual harassment policy, one of the union's key requests.

Raich leaned over Schultz, who was sitting at his desk, handed him a pen and said, "Here, sign it." The revised memo and Schultz's report were sent to Cleveland. "I was basically neutered at that point," Schultz said. "Management's perspective was: You don't air your dirty laundry, you bury it." Schultz felt compromised by the revised memo because it did not make good on the agreement that he had made with Lois and the union. When Henningsgard asked Raich about the sexual harassment training, Raich waived him off. He told Henningsgard that the Jenson-Povroznik problem would be handled by senior Oglebay Norton management in Cleveland from now on.

Raich implied that the company was concerned that if it adopted any kind of sexual harassment policy, it would be viewed as an admission of fault. Henningsgard thought that was shortsighted; he believed their best protection was to institute a harassment policy immediately. If training was needed, then the company should provide it. To Henningsgard and Schultz, it seemed a small price to pay to resolve the problem with Lois. They both knew that the environment at Eveleth could use some cleaning up.

But their recommendations fell on deaf ears. The entire matter was now in the hands of Raich, a man who clearly did not think women should work in the mine in the first place. He was not interested in a sexual harassment policy, or in any form of training. Nor, apparently, were his superiors in Cleveland.

As the promised changes failed to materialize, Lois began to show more serious signs of stress. She clenched her jaw all day and developed an ulcer. At home, she jumped when the phone or doorbell rang. She was afraid to answer the door. She relied on Greg, who was now sixteen, to take care of her. She told him that under no circumstances should he allow anyone in the apartment that he did not know. When they drove together, she told Greg to watch the cars behind them in case they were being followed. She had trouble sleeping at night. In four months her weight climbed from 119 to 165. Her apartment was a pigsty. To relieve the stress she felt at work, she would come home and eat a large pizza in one sitting. At work, she ate candy bars all day. One night, Lois was watching an HBO comedy show on television and she laughed out loud at a joke. Greg raced into the room. "What's wrong?" he asked. Greg had not heard his mother laugh in so long that he didn't think it was normal. "That's when I decided to go into counseling," she said.

Lois called Range Mental Health and asked to see a female therapist. The therapist, Judith Burke, noted immediately that Lois was suffering from severe stress. Burke was also so alarmed by Lois's situation with Steve, particularly the obsessive, rambling letters, that she recommended that Lois consult Donovan Frank, the prosecuting attorney for St. Louis County. Lois met with Frank a few days later. Frank was sympathetic, but told her that he could not do anything to help her because Steve had not committed any crime.

Frustrated, Lois went to the public library to look for legal information about sexual harassment. The only thing she could find was a small manila folder that contained articles about sexual abuse. On August 25, 1984, Lois typed a short diary entry about her visit to the library:

> *Found nothing. It amazes me that through the years women have kept so silent, but think it should not amaze me, for I have done the same. Since it is against the law. In fact this is not an isolated case but merely that we do not go public. One thought comes to mind. How many violent crimes have emanated from women trying to handle harassment themselves? After all most companies have no set policy until it becomes a necessity and that means that a woman has tried everything she could first and then went to the company. . . .*

Her discovery in the library lead Lois to an epiphany. If she did not speak up, who would?

On September 17, Cadeau showed Lois the memo from Raich informing him that Steve Povroznik had been instructed to have no further personal contact with her, and that he would seek professional counseling. There was no mention of a transfer or a sexual harassment policy. Raich signed off with, "We believe that action should resolve the problem. Thank you for your cooperation on this matter."

Lois could not believe her eyes. She refused to continue to be supervised by Steve and concluded that she had no choice but to go forward and file a union grievance against him. Lois had hoped that it would not come to this. The purpose of the meeting she and the union had with management was to reach an agreement and avoid putting her complaint on paper and involving the state chapter of the United Steel Workers.

Lois talked to Michele, who was also a union grievance officer. Michele had attended a seminar at union school the year before on the subject of filing sexual harassment grievances. The female instructor explained what sexual harassment was, gave a legal case history, demonstrated how to file a grievance, and explained that the union was responsible for educating its membership about sexual harassment.

"Hey, this is what it is!" Michele thought to herself during the class. It was a revelation. The behavior she assumed she had to accept in order to do a man's job was actually illegal.

Michele told Lois that the union had a duty to protect her, and that she had a basis for her grievance. She also told Lois that she was afraid to file the grievance herself. They agreed that it would be better if Clarence Cadeau, who had more experience and who had been involved in the initial meeting with management, filed the formal complaint. Michele was confident that Clarence and the other union officers would support Lois. Union etiquette had prevented Diane Hodge from naming Willie Johnson in her complaint, and without a name, the union had refused to go to bat for Diane. But Steve, a salaried employee, was an acceptable union target.

When Michele and Lois asked Clarence to file a grievance on Lois's behalf, he told them that he did not know how to file a sexual harassment grievance. Michele reminded him that they had just been taught how at union school. When Clarence continued to say that he did not know the procedures for filing a sexual harassment claim, Michele gave him the telephone number of the instructor of the seminar, which she had kept in case she ever needed it. Pat Kosmach also pestered Clarence and Stan Daniels about filing Lois's grievance. Eventually, Stan Daniels told Lois, "If you want to file a grievance, you write it, and I'll sign it." So Lois typed two simple sentences on the union form and handed it to Stan Daniels.

"I feel that Eveleth Mines and Steve Povroznik, in violation of my Civil Rights, have been sexually harassing me. I ask the Company to take immediate action on this issue, and allow me to continue in my present job."

Stan's and Clarence's reticence did not inspire confidence in Lois; she wanted to know what other alternatives she had. In late September, without telling anyone, Lois called the Minnesota Department of Human Rights in St. Paul. The woman she spoke to patiently answered her questions about how the department processed, investigated, and prosecuted sexual harassment complaints. Could she change her mind and drop out after making a complaint, if she wanted? The Department of Human Rights employee assured her that she could drop the charges at any time in the process. Lois described her history with Steve Povroznik. The woman told Lois that it sounded like she had a valid complaint and that she would send her the forms to fill out. Lois had ten days to send them back.

Meanwhile, at work, rumors were tearing through the plant about her union grievance. Some of the guys teased her; others told her that they did not believe Steve had harassed her. The foremen, who were all salaried workers, shunned her, averting their gaze whenever she passed by. Even Mark Lakenen stopped talking to her. Pat and Michele checked in with Lois every day to give her updates on what was going on in the union, and who was saying what.

On October 1, Clarence Cadeau told Lois that Raich claimed she was known to touch men, and that her behavior got her into trouble. When Lois heard this, she demanded to meet with Raich herself. The next day, Lois walked into Raich's office with Clarence and Sam Ricker by her side. She carried a briefcase full of documentation in hopes of being taken seriously. When she sat down in the chair across from Raich's desk, Lois immediately knew she had made a mistake in coming.

"Dan Schultz has mentioned that you were frequently touching the men at work," Lois remembered Raich saying at the beginning of the meeting.

"First of all, this is just not true. It is a fabricated statement," she responded. "And second of all, if this is such a big problem, why hasn't it been mentioned to me before?" Sam Ricker jumped to Lois's defense and told Raich that it was not fair for the company to blame her. It was also unfair, Ricker added, that she still had to work under Steve Povroznik's supervision.

Raich all but dismissed Lois's complaint apparently believing that Lois did not have a case. It dawned on her that the entire nightmare of Steve Povroznik's behavior was now being twisted to look like it was her fault, and if it was her word against theirs, she would never win. "They didn't want to ruin his reputation," she said, "so they thought they'd ruin mine."

Lois handed Raich her union grievance. The third page of the report contained a typed list of seven demands. Lois showed them to Raich. She wanted Steve transferred or dismissed, she wanted to see Schultz's report, she wanted her stress-related health problems to be covered under workman's compensation, she wanted to stay in her current job, and she wanted the company to implement an educational program on sexual harassment. Raich read the list, ripped the third page out of Lois's complaint, dated it, and did not give it back. He told her that he wanted Stan Daniels to present the complaint to the company instead of her.

Rattled by Raich's hostility, Lois said something she had not planned to. She told him that she had contacted the Minnesota Department of Human Rights. Raich snapped. "What's your lawyer's name?"

"You don't need to know that information."

"Then when they call us, we won't give them anything." He called her bluff.

"Well, I don't have a lawyer yet, but I have an appointment to see one."

"You should make an appointment at Range Mental Health instead."

Lois left the meeting in tears.

The forms from the Minnesota Department of Human Rights had arrived in the mail the week before. That left Lois two days to decide if she wanted to fill them out. Her meeting with Raich confirmed her fear that the company was ready to fight. She knew that taking outside action would be the only way to protect herself from being fired. Lois was terrified of taking this next step, but her simple request that the company post a sexual harassment policy and that she not have to work for Steve had escalated into a fight for her job and for principle before she even knew how it had happened.

On October 3, she asked Pat and Michele to come to her house after work to discuss her options. Lois taped the conversation because she wanted a record of where Pat stood—whether or not Pat would support her move to file with the state, and what Pat and Michele thought she should ask for in her complaint. Lois also wanted to find out what Pat knew about what was going on behind the scenes. Lois soon discovered that Pat was solidly in her camp. "The company does not understand what sexual harassment is, what it entails," Pat told her.

Lois showed the two women the Human Rights Department forms. "Start at the beginning" was Pat's advice. "Start with two years ago when you can show how he worked it over a period of time."

Pat urged Lois not just to follow through with her complaint with the state, but also to consult a private attorney and consider a civil action against the company. "You have to get some professional legal advice at this point," said Pat. "Go for the gusto. They are playing with your mind right now." If Lois did not follow through with her grievance, Pat worried that it would send the wrong message. "By their inaction they [the company] have shown the rest of the women and the guys out there that they can get away with happy horseshit."

"Listen to the gals—the gals are the victims and they don't understand what sexual harassment is either," Michele said.

"They don't understand that some guy can't call them every name in the book," replied Pat. "Women have to be made to understand that when a guy starts it, she has to tell him right from point one, 'No way, get out of my face, I'm not tolerating this type of action.' If she lets it slide and never tells him, she is as guilty as he is."

Pat promised to take Lois's union grievance all the way to union headquarters in Pittsburgh, if necessary, and to make sure it got to arbitration. She encouraged Lois to be ambitious about asking for what she wanted—be it job stability or better benefits. "I think that you probably won't get rich and you probably won't own the company, but I think you can give them a real sock in the shorts. We'll see a lot of hunched over superintendents out there," she said. "In my opinion, it's time. The company has dragged their feet and if you don't do anything, if you don't put the pressure on, they're gonna keep on dragging. . . . I've been a fighter all my life. I had to learn the hard way. Don't let anybody shit on you because if they do it once, they will do it again."

After Pat and Michele went home, Lois sat down at her desk and started writing. It took her ten hours to write just three pages. She said in the letter that the company had "been trying to discredit my story by saying I led S.P. on by touching him and that I was headed for further problems." She also reported that in her meeting with Raich, he told her that "Dan Schultz made a comment to the effect that he has been aware that I was especially active in touching the men I work with for the last two years. (This is interesting because not only was I married at the time but I was also spending most of my working hours isolated from anyone doing clerical and print work.) Lois signed the letter and added: a P.S. "I feel that this job will be pulled at any time now."

She mailed her package to the Department of Human Rights on her way to work the next morning, October 5, 1984. As she punched her time card, she heard that Steve had quit. All of the mines on the Range were laying off 50 percent of their workforce at the time, yet Steve had landed a job at National Steel. "The rumor was that they had found him another job," she said. Later that day, Stan Daniels filed Lois's union grievance, number 177-84, with Raich and Henningsgard.

One week later Lois walked out to her car in the parking lot at the end of her shift and found that all four of her tires were flat. They had been slashed.

CHAPTER SIX

The State

Winter 1987

On the morning of January 21, 1987, the temperature hovered just below zero as Helen Rubenstein started her four-hour drive from the Cities to the Range to meet Lois Jenson. A month earlier, Rubenstein's boss at the Minnesota Attorney General's Office had dropped a thick folder on her desk. Here, he announced, was just the right case for his idealistic new lawyer.

Rubenstein followed the chronology of events: first the state, after an initial investigation, determined "probable cause" for Lois Jenson's sexual harassment charge, filed twenty-seven months earlier. Then the conciliation process began. The state requested that the mine institute a sexual harassment policy and pay $6,000 in punitive damages and $5,000 for mental anguish to Lois Jenson. In return, the company would not have to admit liability. Oglebay Norton agreed to put a sexual harassment policy on the books, but refused to pay Lois any money, beyond her counseling expenses. Because she still had a job at the mine, and Povroznik did not, the company argued that Lois had no right to claim restitution for damages or mental anguish. Lois refused to accept Oglebay Norton's offer, even though she feared she could be fired any minute. The company would not change its position, and the case was transferred to the Attorney General's Office, where it languished in bureaucratic limbo until, more than two years after it was filed, the case arrived on Rubenstein's desk ready for litigation.

The young lawyer could not believe her luck. This was the kind of case that had first attracted her to the law. Just three years out of law school, the thirty-eight-year-old Rubenstein was a veteran of the women's liberation movement. As an undergraduate at George Washington University from 1968 to 1972, she had thrown herself into the women's and antiwar movements in Washington, D.C. Her life had changed after attending a "consciousness raising" meeting in a friend's kitchen. Soon she found herself marching in protests, working for a radical feminist publication called *Off Our Backs*, and selling books in a community bookshop on Dupont Circle.

After graduating, Rubenstein moved to Minneapolis, which she found alive with grassroots activism. There were strong community organizations, and a large chapter of the National Organization for Women. Rubenstein spent ten years as an activist, working at places like the Twin Cities Women's Union and the Women's School, which offered courses designed to empower women, such as women's literature, car repair, and karate. In 1981 she entered William Mitchell Law School hoping to become a civil rights lawyer.

As Rubenstein saw it, Lois Jenson's plight was as obvious as racial desegregation—it was about integrating the workforce. The discrimination Jenson suffered at Eveleth Mines presented a basic right-to-work case for women. Rubenstein had some familiarity with the Iron Range. In 1984 she had worked as the junior lawyer on a case up there. A teacher named Mary Silvestri had sued her employer, the Chisholm School District, because she had been sexually harassed and assaulted by a fellow teacher. Because of her lawsuit, Silvestri was fired. When she went to court, the administrative law judge ruled in her favor and awarded her $22,000 in damages. Silvestri returned to work the following year only to face more harassment from her peers in retaliation for her disloyalty. In 1986 she was fired again. Silvestri appealed the low judgment, and in a second trial, an advisory jury awarded her $800,000, but the judge threw it out. Silvestri wound up demoralized. Her experience gave Rubenstein a grim picture of the way women were treated in the insular Iron Range communities. Rubenstein would also never forget the school district's aggressive lawyer who grilled Silvestri mercilessly on the stand. He was from Duluth, and his name was Ray Erickson.

Route 35 took Rubenstein through the outskirts of Minneapolis's affluent suburbs and north into farm country, past small towns that looked like Garrison Keillor's mythical Lake Wobegon, "the little town that time forgot." After two-and-a-half solid hours of heartland, Route 35 dead-ended on the banks of Lake Superior at the port city of Duluth. The city climbed a steep hillside overlooking the ice-covered inland sea. Grain elevators towered at lake's edge. Massive iron docks jutted out into white ice, row after blackened row, waiting to load barges with tons of taconite at the first thaw of spring. The gateway to the Iron Range, Duluth still served as headquarters to the iron-ore industry.

North of Duluth, on Highway 53, snow flurries began to fall. Rubenstein passed a gas station, a bait shop, then nothing but snow-covered birch and pine trees and the occasional semi with logs strapped from axle to axle. Fifty-five miles out of Duluth, Rubenstein spotted a tall yellow water tower in the distance. The name "Eveleth" was painted in red on the cistern. A green sign on the right side of the highway announced that she had entered the town of Eveleth, "pop. 5,042." To the left of the highway, on an adjacent road called Hat Trick Avenue, Helen saw a motorcycle and snowmobile dealership and two bars advertising that night's bands on tall billboards. Then two large boxy buildings came into view: a Holiday Inn and the U.S. Hockey Hall of Fame, a national shrine that the town of Eveleth was proud to host. For with its tiny population, Eveleth had produced more professional championship players and done more for the growth and development of the sport than any other comparable community south of the Canadian border. The town called itself "The Capital of American Hockey."

Four miles west of Eveleth, with only 1,934 residents, Gilbert proper consisted of three treeless blocks lined with more than a dozen bars, a liquor store, a grocery store, and a restaurant. Side streets bore names like Louisiana, New York, and Florida. Fifty state flags fluttered from a median on Broadway looking like a distant outpost of New York's Avenue of the Americas. At the end of town stood a big brown wooden building that housed an ice rink.

Lois's directions were precise, and soon Rubenstein's car climbed a steep hill at the top of which stood the Summit View Estates, Lois's two-story red-brick apartment building complex. From the parking lot Rubenstein could see the Forbes Fairlane Plant erecting its colonnade of three smoke pillars into the big northern sky.

Lois, dressed in blue jeans and a holiday-themed sweatshirt, opened the door and greeted Rubenstein with a handshake and a hug. As the two women sat at the kitchen table, Rubenstein looked around Lois's two-bedroom apartment and found it a cozy antidote to the bleakness of the Range. Pots of ferns hung in the windows and dried flowers filled vases around the living room. There were angels everywhere: porcelain angels, crystal angels, wooden angels—seraphs alighting on coffee tables, angels winging over side tables and windowsills. Even the soap in the bathroom soap dish was an angel. There were also self-help tapes, such as *Speak for Yourself—Totally Conquer Stress* and books like *What Every Woman Should Know About Men* by Joyce Brothers and *A Woman's Reality: An Emerging Female System in a White Male Society* by Ann Wilson Schaef. On the coffee table Rubenstein spotted a pile of magazines: *Ms, New Woman, Psychology Today.*

While the attorney sized up the plaintiff's apartment, the plaintiff was sizing up her counsel. Rubenstein stood only five feet tall, had short-cropped brown hair, wore wire-rimmed glasses, and looked ten years younger than her age—thirty-eight, the same as Lois. Lois wondered to herself, "How is anyone going to take this tiny little girl seriously?" She could have asked the same question of herself. But once they started talking, Lois recognized Rubenstein's sharp mind. Better still, Lois was overjoyed to find that Rubenstein was enthusiastic about the case. Here, finally, after two years on her own, Lois had help. To have a real live lawyer from the state's Attorney General's Office sitting in her own living room listening, and taking her seriously, was a dream come true.

Lois summarized her travails at the mine: Franklin Guye's remark on her first day of work, Scaia's crotch grab, John Jagunich's break-in, the rubber vagina, the dildo, Steve Povroznik. She explained that two months after Steve Povroznik's resignation, in November of 1984, her job at the electrical department was eliminated and she was transferred to crew four in the concentrator. Lois had only been in her new job for two months when Bob Sametz, the operating foreman of the concentrator, pulled her on his lap in front of her crew and jokingly tried to spank her. The taunts, Lois told Helen, had eased, but they had not ended. Lois worried about the safety of her job.

Then she told Rubenstein about the other women: Diane Hodge's problems with Willie Johnson, Michele Mesich's with Don Cummings, Judy Jarvela's with Vern Niedermeier, Marcy Steele being hazed as a new oiler. As the episodes mounted, Rubenstein suddenly thought, "This is bigger than a single discrimination case."

Perhaps, she suggested, the case should be brought as a class action on behalf of all the female workers at Eveleth. Rubenstein did not know whether a sexual harassment case could be brought as a class action; she only knew that Lois had described a much bigger problem and potentially a much bigger case than her claim against Steve Povroznik.

Lois liked the idea. She knew she did not stand a chance taking on Eveleth Mines and Oglebay Norton alone. Not only would there be safety in numbers, but there would be a better chance of actually changing the system at the mine for all of the women if they joined together as a class.

The next day, Rubenstein met with Lois and three other women at Diane Hodge's house in Hibbing. More than half of the women invited had not come. Lois introduced Helen to the small group: Pat Kosmach, Michele Mesich, and Diane. Everyone else had called in with last-minute excuses—sick baby-sitters, shift changes, long grocery lists.

The small group sat in a circle. One by one, the women told Rubenstein their stories. They all spoke of the graffiti, the pin-ups, the pinches, the dildos, the stalking. Rubenstein was stunned by the depth of the harassment, and by how much shame and humiliation the women carried with them. With her experienced feminist eye, Rubenstein could clearly see that these women were the real thing—foot soldiers in a war she and her big-city sisters had been fighting for fifteen years.

Rubenstein told the women that she was convinced that Lois's case against the mine could qualify as a class action. In the deafening silence that followed, Rubenstein asked Diane, Pat, and Michele to decide then and there whether they "wanted in or out."

Diane, who had been laid off since 1983, hedged. She would have to speak to her husband first.

Pat looked panicked. On a social and political level, she had more to lose than Lois. The union had been Pat's life, and she had respect as an influential insider among the men both in the union and in management. The union only halfheartedly supported Lois's grievance, but Pat held out hope that she could convince its leadership to see the company as a common enemy of both the women and the men. Even so, Pat knew that spearheading a class action lawsuit against the mine would have grave repercussions. Four of Pat's five children lived in the Eveleth area, and Pat worried that they might suffer social ostracism from her lawsuit against the mine. She would not commit.

Michele had been laid off since 1984. She looked around the small circle of women and said, "I'll do it for Lois."

"No," said Lois, "do it for yourself."

Michele paused for a minute. "Then I'll do it," she said.

The next morning, Diane told Lois that she would not join. Diane thrived on being liked and popular at work, and joining the case was bound to be an unpopular move with the men and the women when she returned from layoff. What's more, Diane's girlfriends at the mine were steering clear of the case.

In high school terms, the women at the mine divided along a split that might be characterized as the cool girls (Diane, Joan, and Jan) against the library committee (Michele, Pat, and Lois). Even Marcy Steele, who was friendly with everyone, shied away from the case. Joan Hunholz led the pack of Diane's friends. Joan, suspicious and reserved, disliked Lois and disapproved of the case. Jan Wollin Friend was tough and coarse. Both Jan and Joan had no interest in admitting that they were victims. They were committed to toughing it out on the job and getting along. Diane had decided to follow her friends, play it safe, and stay out of trouble with her employer.

One week after the meeting with Rubenstein, Pat Kosmach called Lois. She announced that she would join the class. As devoted as Pat was to the union, she had become disillusioned by its lack of response to the sexual harassment problems that Pat had presented to them. Even though she had not personally suffered as much sexual harassment as many of the other women, Pat told Lois, "I'd be a downright hypocrite if I don't join the suit." What she had never told Lois was that on her first day at Eveleth Mines, in 1976, she had heard the jokes about how Gene Scaia had grabbed Lois's crotch—the story had bothered her conscience from day one. Pat had finally accepted that no amount of persuasion on her part could change the system from within. Lois could not believe her ears. For the first time, she and Pat were on the same team.

"Pat knew that if she joined the case it would get worse before it got better, and it was hard enough already," recalled Pat's best friend, Jeanne Aho. "She knew it was the right thing to do and that Lois was right. Pat knew that two people saying 'Yes this did happen,' had more power than one."

———

Two months later, on March 26, 1987, Lois received a fat manila envelope in the mail from the Attorney General's Office. Inside, she found a cover letter addressed to her listing the contents of the package:

1) Complaint

2) Complainant's Request for Disclosure of Witnesses and Production of Statements

3) Notice and Order for Hearing

4) Notice of Appearance

5) Notes of Dan Harp and report by Dan Schultz

Lois read through the twelve-page complaint in which most of her troubles, and those of Michele and Pat, were listed in neat, numbered, short declarative paragraphs. Lois and Michele's stories, combined with Pat Kosmach's report that as head of the union's civil rights committee she had been informed by women at the mine of twelve incidents of sex discrimination and sexual harassment at Eveleth Mines, made for powerful reading. Rubenstein asked that a sexual harassment policy be installed and that $6,000 in punitive damages be paid to all the women who would qualify for the class.

When she got to paragraph six on the last page—"Pay to the State a civil penalty of one million dollars ($1,000,000)"—Lois shook her head. Nowhere near that kind of money had ever been on the table before. With the threat of a class action and a million-dollar penalty, Lois realized that the stakes had shot up significantly. Rubenstein had tacked the million-dollar penalty onto the complaint to get the attention of the mine.

She got it. Heads turned when Rubenstein's complaint landed on Oglebay Norton's conference table during contract negotiations with the union. To the union's delight, the negotiations were temporarily put on hold. The company was driving a hard bargain, and Stan Daniels needed to buy as much time as he could. Oglebay Norton had threatened to shut down the mine if Local 6860 did not agree to an 8 percent wage reduction. Ever since 1982, the Iron Range, as well as the nation, had slid into an economic recession. Domestic ore could not compete with cheap foreign imports, and in the depressed economy consumers had less need for steel. In 1979, at the height of the industry's boom cycle, the Range had produced 56 million tons of taconite pellets. By 1982, pellet production had dropped to 23 million tons. In the late 1970s, a bystander on the sidewalk of any Range city could tell when it was shift change because the streets were clogged with cars. But the workforce in all seven mines on the Range had dropped from 14,022 in 1979 to 5,935 in 1984. The streets in the mid-1980s were now empty at shift change.

At Eveleth Mines, attrition was high. In 1980, 1,425 employees worked at the mine. But in 1982, the mine shut down an entire line of production, cutting the workforce in half. In August 1983, Eveleth shut down completely for eight weeks. By the end of 1983, a paltry 723 remained—702 miners had vanished as if into a pit. Eveleth Mines had an additional problem: It was the least efficient of all the mines on the Range. Its labor and railroad costs were the highest, and it expended the second largest amount of energy per ton of taconite pellets.

With so few jobs to go around, hostility at the mine increased toward the women who had enough seniority to keep their jobs. Joe Begich, a state legislator representing the Eveleth area at the time, remembers that in the mid-eighties, when the economy started to hurt, "people complained that if there weren't so many women in the mines, there'd be more jobs." At Eveleth Mines, Bob Raich grew incensed during the layoffs. He repeatedly complained to his personal secretary, Kathy Tessier, that women were taking jobs away from men, and that they could not pull their weight in the positions they held. Almost like a mantra, Tessier heard Raich repeat the adage, "Women belong at home, barefoot and pregnant." Three months later, when Tessier herself was fired, Raich told her that he eliminated her position because her husband had a good job and she did not need her pension.

When Raich saw Lois's state complaint, he turned to his colleague Milan Lolich and said, "Lois is getting what she asked for."

Lolich, supervisor for safety and training, replied, "What do women expect when they come to work in the mines?"

In Cleveland, Oglebay Norton stood its ground. It had been two and a half years since Lois had filed her union grievance, and the company insisted on putting the complaint process on hold pending the first discrimination charge from the Human Rights Department in November of 1985. When the union brought Lois's grievance up in meetings, the company raised the same question: "What really is the contractual issue here?" Sexual harassment was not in the union contract; therefore, it could not be held up to a known standard. The union did little to counter that argument. The relationship between union and management was like that of opposing football teams. "You play all day long as hard as you can and then go out for a beer afterward," explained Jay Henningsgard, the mine's supervisor of labor relations. "Most of the union grievances were easy to resolve. You just pay the overtime, or something like that. There was no principle involved."

But Lois's grievance was about principle. When Henningsgard raised the issue with Eugene Gilmore, Oglebay's director of industrial relations, and Henningsgard's contact in Cleveland, Gilmore replied that he believed Lois did not have a case. Gilmore believed that since Lois's job had not been eliminated, she had no legitimate sexual harassment claim. So the company "dug in its heels," said Henningsgard.

In fact, Gilmore's understanding of the law of sexual harassment was outdated. Since the EEOC guidelines were published in 1980, a more expansive definition of sexual harassment started percolating its way through the courts. In 1986, the U.S. Supreme Court heard a case in which a woman named Michelle Vinson claimed that a supervisor at the bank where she worked routinely demanded that she have sex with him as a condition of her keeping her job. She initially refused but gave in when he told her that he would fire her if she did not comply. She claimed that when she tried to end the relationship, he raped her on several occasions. She also claimed that she then reported these transgressions to a senior bank official, but he did nothing. The bank denied it had any knowledge of the conduct, and argued it was not liable because it was outside the scope of the supervisor's job description. The trial court agreed with the bank, and said that the relationship was voluntary because Michelle Vinson was free to quit her job.

Meritor Savings Bank v. Vinson reached the Supreme Court, and on June 19, 1986, the Court declared not only that sexual harassment can constitute sex discrimination, but that it can be based either on a quid pro quo or a hostile work environment theory. The Court also held that employers could be liable for sexual harassment of either kind if they did not take meaningful and concrete steps to prevent it, such as instituting a sexual harassment policy and disciplining employees who harass other workers. The Court did not say specifically what employers must do to avoid liability, but it did say that merely adopting a policy or procedure was not enough if the company did not actively implement it.

The Court's decision in *Meritor* confirmed much of the EEOC guidelines and made an employer's responsibilities regarding sexual harassment clearer. But it left open a number of other questions. One of the most important was what kind of evidence was relevant to show whether or not conduct was "unwelcome." The Supreme Court concluded that evidence about the way a plaintiff dressed and whether she discussed sexual fantasies at work could be admitted, if the trial judge deemed such evidence to be relevant. Some women's rights advocates expressed concern at the time that these cases could end up like rape cases, where the victim is put on trial. Generally, though, the *Meritor* case was considered to be a major victory for women in the workplace.

Jay Henningsgard believed the company was being dangerously

shortsighted, both in failing to address Lois's union grievance and the state's complaint, and in failing to take action to prevent further instances of sexual harassment. It therefore fell to Henningsgard to work up language that would address the issue for the new labor contract, which would take another three months to ratify. Henningsgard's experience in the personnel departments of four Duluth companies had given him some familiarity with basic corporate sexual harassment policies. He inserted four sentences of boilerplate language into the company's labor contract. It now stated that sexual harassment was considered discrimination and the company would take "corrective action as appropriate." As much as Raich and the honchos in Cleveland wanted to avoid the subject, Henningsgard convinced them that they had to have a sexual harassment policy, as vague and bland as this was, on the books.

Henningsgard's additions to the contract were significant more for what they excluded than for what they included. The new contract did not define sexual harassment, it did not provide training, and it did not name a point person to handle complaints. It did not define a punishment for harassers. It just simply stated for the first time in the mine's history that sexual harassment was against company policy.

By March of 1987, Lois had been working with crew four in the concentrator for over two years and she had developed an easy camaraderie with her colleagues. For the first time since she started work at the mine, Lois felt supported by and comfortable with the men on her crew. It had been more than two years since Povroznik left the mine, and her emotional and physical health had stabilized. Lois's weight, which often mirrored her well-being, dropped down to 112.

In July of 1985, Lois and Greg had moved from their apartment in Mountain Iron twenty-five minutes east to Gilbert. Their new apartment's reduced rent of $300 a month was a welcome savings because of frequent layoffs. But two other reasons beyond cheaper rent motivated the move, which took them out of Greg's school district, forcing him to switch high schools his senior year. First, Greg had a serious girlfriend who lived in Gilbert. Second, a woman named Ruth Johnson, who was a friend of Steve Povroznik's mother, lived in their Mountain Iron apartment building. In May of 1985, Ruth made a scene in the hallway of the building where Lois stood with a friend, by recounting the tawdry stories Steve's mother had told her about Lois. Ever since her confrontation with Ruth, Lois felt uncomfortable when they crossed paths. Feeling surrounded by enemies, Lois decided that it was time to move.

In June of 1986, Greg graduated from high school and enlisted in the navy. Lois was relieved that despite the traumas of her job, Greg had managed to reach this important accomplishment in life—high school graduation. When stress at work got particularly bad, Lois told herself that she could not quit working at the mine before Greg's graduation. Lois thought that getting a job in a different part of the state and uprooting Greg in the middle of high school would be too disruptive for her son. Greg had grown into a sensitive, shy, well-meaning young man who treated women with respect. But Greg's plans hit a snag the summer after graduation. Before joining the navy, Greg went to work with Lois's brother on Labor Day weekend cutting down trees for a farmer in Fargo, North Dakota, where a large tree accidentally fell and crushed his leg. It took months to recuperate from the injury and cost Greg his chance of being in the military. Instead, Greg halfheartedly attended technical college in Hibbing.

With Greg grown and largely independent, Lois had more time to make friends of her own. The "lifesavers" for Lois on crew four in the concentrator were Kent Erickson and Dwight Davis. Kent Erickson grew up in Minneapolis, and was not a Ranger. Divorced with three daughters, Erickson relied on Lois for advice, and affectionately called her "Scruff." Dwight Davis operated the panel, where all the controls for the concentrator were housed. Lois worked just outside the panel room on the deck. Davis was tall, muscular, and gruff. He was so strong that one day, when Lois was cleaning a large tub and could not get out, Davis leaned over the high walls and yanked her out with one swift pull. "He was very loyal and had a strong sense of right from wrong," said Lois. Lois worked a few Christmas shifts with crew four. "We cooked dinners out there. I would bring the turkey and they would barbecue, or sometimes we would cook in the kitchen at the main office."

Inside the concentrator, the noise was so loud that the workers on a team had to touch each other to communicate. "I don't think being touchy is my style," said Lois. "That was the company twist—that I was 'touchy.'" As far as Lois could tell, the company's only evidence was the one time she touched Steve Povroznik in 1981. "Besides," Lois recalled, "on certain jobs like grinding mill helper, if I had to clear a maintenance man away, you can yell and no one could hear—once I pulled a pants leg to get a guy off the mill. I think I can remember every time I touched a guy, whether it was on his hand, or his arm. But the guys all the time were doing stuff like tapping your shoulder on one side, and then they'd be on the other side laughing. Or they'd come up behind you and buckle your knees, or pinch you, or grab your waist, or tap your butt. It was always something."

"No one had a problem with Lois on the crew," said Dwight Davis years later. "She was never flirtatious or touchy feely."

The day after she received the attorney general's sexual harassment complaint in the mail, Lois brought a copy of the twelve-page document to work. She let everyone on her crew read it so that they could see that their names were not mentioned. But even Kent and Dwight avoided talking to her for eight days following the filing of her complaint. Davis would later admit that the complaint made a lot of people nervous. "They didn't know if they could say anything or do anything" without being accused of sexual harassment.

Pat Kosmach was so afraid of her crew's response to the complaint that, as a peace offering, she made them a batch of her famous "funeral bars"—brownies filled with caramel, oatmeal, chocolate, and nuts, which she usually took to wakes. "Pat realized that filing the lawsuit was a big undertaking, and she was scared," said her friend Jeanne Aho. Pat became paranoid. She told Aho that she was worried that she could end up like Karen Silkwood and get run off the road at night. "She would always tell me, 'Things can happen.' "

Word of the state complaint buzzed through the mine. Lois instantly noticed the change. People stood together in groups giving her dirty looks, people avoided talking to her. Pat was also shunned. Rumors flew that forty men were named on a list and that many of them would be fired. Lois, Michele, and Pat had given Rubenstein a list of names of men whom were both witnesses and perpetrators of sexual harassment. Then followed a McCarthy-like episode, when Stan Daniels walked around the mine with the list, buttonholing groups of men and saying, "You're named, you're named, and you're named."

The complaint could not have come at a tougher time economically. Suing a crippled company hardly inspired support from the mine's employees. "The guys were scared about the plant closing and losing our jobs," recalled Eveleth Mines mechanic Jim Ravnikar. "For a while we were afraid to talk to the women because we could be accused of sexual harassment." At the time of Lois's complaint, Ravnikar admitted that out of some seven hundred miners on the job, about thirty of them were "bad guys—creepy, perverted—chauvinists who hated having women there and who spent a lot of time harassing them."

By declining to fire the creeps, Ravnikar noted, the company and the union, by default, jeopardized all the other miners. Jim Ravnikar's wife at the time, Lorrie, worried that the sexual harassment claim would force her family onto the welfare roles. Lorrie recalled that when Jim had been laid off in the mid-eighties, "We were on food stamps, it was scary. I was worried about him losing his job. I had a child and didn't want to work." Lorrie heard through the grapevine that the women were only out to get money. Add two and two together, and the reality of the complaint for the average Eveleth miner equaled job loss.

Pat pestered Helen Rubenstein and Lois to get coverage of the complaint in the local newspapers. She thought publicity would give her and Lois protection. Lois disagreed. She wanted to keep the complaint as quiet as possible and let it work its way through the legal process. She feared that public attention would make their lives even harder at the mine. Naturally impatient, the slow pace of the legal process drove Pat crazy. She knew that Lois had already waited two and a half years to get this far, and she didn't want to have to wait another two years to see any progress. She was afraid of retaliation and of being fired. She was also afraid that the longer the process dragged out, the uglier life in the community would get for her and her family. Publicity would be a way, she thought, of speeding up the process and forcing the company's hand.

When Lois and Pat talked to Rubenstein about this, Rubenstein said that she had been told that the public relations people in the Minnesota Human Rights Department had declined to issue a pro forma press release about the complaint. Rubenstein told them that if they wanted to get the word out about their case, they would have to drop flyers from an airplane. On March 11, two weeks before the complaint was filed, Doug Johnson, a state senator from the Iron Range, had introduced a budget-cutting package. Along with a long list of items, the bill included the wholesale elimination of Rubenstein's Human Rights Department—cutting twenty-nine jobs and saving $1.75 million. Then, on April 13, Senator Johnson and Governor Rudy Perpich, the son of a Croatian miner and Minnesota's first governor from the Iron Range, held a meeting in St. Paul with the Oglebay Norton top brass to talk about reducing railroad and electricity rates. Regardless of whether there was any connection between the lawsuit and Johnson's budget-cutting proposal, it was clear to both Rubenstein and Lois that neither union-loyal Democrats nor corporate-friendly Republicans in St. Paul wanted to touch the case.

In a last-ditch effort to avoid alienating the rank and file, Lois mustered the courage to go to the next union meeting and explain her complaint. Lois held out some hope that Stan Daniels might be sympathetic. Two years earlier, Daniels had gone out of his way to set up a meeting for Lois with a union lawyer who advised Lois to ask the company to settle for no less than $15,000. This meeting, and subsequent conversations Lois had had with Daniels, led her to believe that there was some chance the union might back the women.

Lois's goal was to get the union to agree to allow the men to testify about their union brothers without the threat of being blackballed. She knew she had no chance of doing this unless she put an end to the rumors about men being fired or punished for past offenses. "You're crazy," Pat told Lois. As strong and willful as she was, Pat admitted that she would never have the guts to stand up in front of all those men and talk about sexual harassment. "The men had a right to know that the complaint won't jeopardize their jobs," Lois argued. Despite Pat's pleas, there was something in Lois—maybe a combination of naïveté, stubbornness, and a loose screw—that led her to the front of the room in the Clinton Town Hall on April 21, 1987.

Union meetings were held on the third Tuesday night of every month. Most months, only the first two rows of seats of the hall were filled. But on this day, with contract negotiations in full swing, between 150 and 200 men packed the room. Pat and Lois sat together in a middle row. Franklin Guye and Gene Scaia sat in the back row. Lois had heard that the two men wanted the union to back them in a countersuit against her.

When business concerning the contract negotiations concluded, Lois asked Stan Daniels for the floor. She walked down the center aisle and stood in front of the head tables where the union officers sat facing the crowd. She had brought seven copies of the complaint with her and spread them out on a table for everyone to read. Then she started talking. Lois had carefully scripted a speech, but she was too nervous to look at it. The only other time she had ever spoken in public was at the Credit Union's annual children's program where she introduced the clowns. Now, she was almost blind with fear. Most of the faces in the crowd were a blur, and she worried that she would be booed down. Lois held a copy of the complaint over her head and said, "You have every right to know what's in this complaint and to know that of the forty people listed, some are witnesses, some have knowledge, and some are perpetrators." After she finished her first sentence, the room fell silent.

Encouraged, Lois kept talking. "It is time to put the rumors to rest. I do not apologize for the complaint's content. We are not after anyone's jobs. This is not retaliation. All we want is to get a sexual harassment policy. The complaint puts the responsibility where it belongs, in the company's lap, while still trying to protect the union and its union brothers and sisters. . . . This was not an easy decision, but one I stand by nonetheless." When Lois finished, no one asked questions. In complete silence, she walked back to her seat.

The meeting adjourned. To Lois's surprise, her friend and carpool companion, Dave Gulon, came up to her and said, "Boy, you've got balls. It's about time you did this." Another friend, Claude Carter, read the complaint and gave Lois some words of encouragement. Most of the copies of the complaint went untouched because the men didn't want to be seen reading it. Herb Larson, a union official, presented Lois with a draft of the new sexual harassment language Jay Henningsgard had written for the union contract. "Here, look what we got for you," he said triumphantly. Larson seemed to think the language was just what Lois wanted. Lois read the four sentences, shook her head, and told Larson that the words were not much more than a cover-up. But Lois did go home that night with some hope that the union might come through. Just maybe, she thought, the animosity the union members held toward the company during these times of budget cuts and layoffs would translate into the union helping her proceed with her case instead of blocking it.

On July 22, 1987, Helen Rubenstein turned her car onto the long driveway to the Fairlane plant. She passed two miles of flat swampland before she could see the massive black factory looming ahead of her. The day before Rubenstein arrived, Bob Raich stood at the doorway to Milan

Lolich's office chatting about Rubenstein's upcoming visit. Raich's secretary overheard him complaining that not only was the lawyer from the Attorney General's Office a Jew, but she was also a goddamned woman.

On the day of Rubenstein's tour, Lois worked the morning shift, driving a tailings truck. The tour was scheduled for 3:00 P.M., when the morning shift changed to afternoon. But the mine's lawyer, Rubenstein's old nemesis Ray Erickson, and Bob Raich kept Rubenstein and her assistant waiting for an hour and a half. Rubenstein presumed that they were trying to shake Lois. When Rubenstein met Raich and Erickson, she noticed their dismissive attitude toward her and felt distinctly like an outsider. As the tour began, Lois popped out of the women's dry and joined the group. When Raich saw Lois, his face turned bright red—he looked as if he were going to explode. Erickson, sensing a disaster, intervened and politely introduced himself to Lois. Raich announced that Rubenstein could not take photographs because they might reveal trade secrets. She would also be restricted from viewing certain areas of the plant because she might divulge information to their competitors. Lois had seen Russian and Japanese tour groups pass through the plant taking snapshots of themselves in front of trucks and ball mills; she knew the restriction was a ruse. She had also seen the maintenance crews hard at work the previous week painting over graffiti.

Lois, Rubenstein, and her assistant, Jackie, moved from the crusher to the concentrator to the pellet plant quickly with Erickson and Raich huffing and puffing behind them, trying to keep up. Ever since filing the complaint, Lois, at Rubenstein's suggestion, had been snapping clandestine photographs of the most sexually explicit graffiti. She also started keeping detailed notes—almost like a daily diary—in a green six-by-nine-inch spiral notebook that Rubenstein told her to label "work product," so that it would be protected under lawyer-client privilege. To Lois's great relief, most of the things she told Rubenstein about were still visible.

First stop was the crusher. Raich walked into the building and pointed out the freshly painted walls. He pushed the elevator button and explained that the company had recently installed stainless-steel panels in order to prevent graffiti. But when the elevator doors opened, the word *cunts* stared the group in the face. It was scratched in ten-inch-tall letters on the stainless-steel interior elevator wall. Raich hurried to stand in front of the graffiti.

As they walked through a tunnel leading to the Mexico building, the group found "I eat cuntz and lots of it" scrawled in large white letters along the black walls. On the wall of the tunnel between the crusher and the concentrator no one could miss a primitive sketch of a man sticking his finger up the anus of a bent-over woman. Raich's eyes lit on the drawing at the same time as Helen Rubenstein's; it was not very large, he said, and besides, he couldn't be expected to catch *everything*. They walked into the foreman's office in the concentrator and found a nudie calendar hanging from the file cabinet and a pin-up of a naked woman on the foreman's desk, pressed under a piece of Plexiglas. Erickson quickly whisked the group out of the room.

Outside the women's dry, the bulletin board still contained a photograph of the back side of a female fitness instructor who had her legs apart doing jumping jacks. Someone had drawn a large penis pushing between her open legs. After viewing the graffiti, Rubenstein turned to Jackie, who was busy scribbling notes, and said, "Be prepared, you may have to testify that you saw this stuff."

"But . . . I can't say these words out loud on the stand," said Jackie.

With each new discovery, Raich's fury increased. The pellet plant proved to be the only building on the tour with clean walls because the foreman there had actually followed Raich's orders, whereas the foremen in the crusher and the concentrator had defied him. Rubenstein had been warned about the content of the mine's graffiti, but she was not prepared for the arrogance of the mine's management. Even the threat of a $1 million fine had not scared them into cleaning up their act. The tour drove home the point to Rubenstein that the mine just didn't care. "Their attitude was, What is *she* going to do to *us*?" Helen recalled.

Two days after Rubenstein's tour, Pat Kosmach came to work on a Saturday morning. LeRoy Stish, the concentrator foreman, walked up to her in a fit of laughter. Kosmach knew Stish better than she would have liked. Stish had a big metal locker in his foreman's office in which he stored supplies. On the inside door of his locker he taped a large poster of a nude woman lying on her back, legs apart, spreading her labia with her fingers. Stish liked to make fun of Pat in front of the whole crew; he'd open his locker door and say "Don't look, girls!" When Pat first saw the poster she suggested that Stish take it home and pin it up on the wall of his living room so his wife and daughter could enjoy it as much as he did. The poster remained in place after the filing of the state complaint. Stish told Pat that the company couldn't force him to take it down.

Pat therefore wasn't surprised, that Saturday in July, when Stish said that the guys were doing some retaliating of their own. He suggested that she take a look at the company bulletin board. Pat strolled down the hallway past the lunchroom and the women's dry. The company bulletin board was a locked glass case that housed shift schedules, crew lists, and job postings. But today, the bulletin board also contained a sign that read:

SEXUAL HARASSMENT
IN THIS AREA
WILL NOT BE REPORTED
HOWEVER, IT WILL BE
GRADED

That same Monday night, Lois worked the midnight shift driving a 120-ton dump truck filled with tailings up a long, zigzagging road. As she pulled the truck away from a conveyor belt in a narrow drive-through "pocket," Lois hit the side of the building. The accident bent two pieces of sheet metal on the side of the pocket. It was Lois's first accident in twelve years that caused structural damage. Tom Dostal, the pellet plant superintendent, gave her a one-day suspension.

Lois used the day off to work on the lawsuit. The case was now in her thoughts every moment. Lois helped Rubenstein by trying to recruit salaried women who worked in clerk positions. She crept around the plant taking pictures, tearing down posters and pin-ups to use as evidence for the case. She also met with local representatives of the Mine Safety and Health Administration to discuss the possibility of integrating sexual harassment into MSHA's safety and health training. The stress of her divided life, and the continued shunning by her coworkers began to diminish Lois's job performance and her health. In August she was hospitalized for flu symptoms. She developed a bladder infection and back problems. She hyperventilated so much at work that her arms became numb. A doctor prescribed tranquilizers, and she began making regular visits to a chiropractor in Hibbing.

Meanwhile, the case was beginning to affect Helen Rubenstein as well. She had received some early encouragement from administrative law judge, John Lunde, who was receptive to her idea of broadening the case to include other women at Eveleth Mines. But Ray Erickson, a partner at the Duluth law firm of Hanft, Fride, O'Brien, Harries, Swelbar & Burns, was a determined and tough adversary. From her experience in the *Silvestri* case and another disability case in Eveleth in which he had represented the other side, Rubenstein knew Erickson to be politically savvy, arrogant, and vicious in court. Erickson also had a team of lawyers and assistants helping him.

By contrast, Rubenstein's boss, Richard Varco, required his staff of attorneys to work on their own. Varco gave Rubenstein free rein to try the case as a class, but he did not give her much direction, and she felt overpowered by Erickson and his team. Although she was not being pressured to pull out of the case, she was also not being given the resources she needed to fight it. The AG's Office was habitually understaffed and underfunded, and only in top-priority cases, such as those against the tobacco companies, would a team of lawyers be assigned to one case. Erickson infuriated Rubenstein with his relentless attempts to set up legal roadblocks at every turn. He made routine procedural steps, such as turning over documents and scheduling depositions, into major skirmishes that had to be resolved by Judge Lunde. Erickson even sent Rubenstein illegible copies of company documents, forcing her to go back to him to ask for clean copies, and causing more delays. Rubenstein had never encountered a lawyer with Erickson's willingness to wage war. After just a few months, Rubenstein had a severe case of battle fatigue.

In late August, she called Lois and asked her whether she was sure that she wanted her to continue working on the case. A bit perplexed, Lois said that of course she wanted Helen to stay with the case. But did Helen still want to keep up the fight? Rubenstein assured Lois that she felt strongly about the suit and was dedicated to pursuing it. But back in the Cities, Andrea Kircher, whose office was next to Rubenstein's, noticed that Helen was suffering under the strain of fighting Erickson. All of the lawyers at the AG's Office had heavy caseloads—sometimes carrying as many as ten cases at a time. But Andrea could tell that Rubenstein's troubles with the Jenson case were clearly exceptional. "I was on my own," recalled Rubenstein. "No one was going to stop me, but no one was going to help me either. I felt I couldn't do it anymore."

In early October 1987, she saw a posting for a job opening in the antitrust division. After much soul searching, Rubenstein decided she wanted out. She applied for the new job and her transfer was granted.

Rubenstein felt guilty for abandoning Lois and Pat. She drove up to the Range and met Lois for dinner at the Coats Hotel in Virginia on October 16, 1987—just ten months after their first meeting. She told Lois that she had been transferred and had no choice but to leave the case. Rubenstein left out the small detail that she herself had requested the transfer. Even so, Lois had a feeling that she was not getting the whole story. A lateral transfer for no apparent reason just didn't make sense. She could tell that Rubenstein felt guilty and wanted to know why Helen hadn't fought the transfer. Rubenstein assured Lois that she would stay in touch with her and keep close tabs on the case. But she also advised Lois to pester the Attorney General's Office herself and make sure the case didn't fall through the cracks.

Helen Rubenstein had been the first person to believe in the case, the first to take it seriously. With Rubenstein out, Lois felt despondent. She had been fighting the mine for exactly three years. Now she would have to start all over again from scratch.

PART TWO

Rough Justice

1988–1995

CHAPTER SEVEN

Civil Action

Winter 1988

It was inevitable that the Jenson case would fall through the cracks. Lois heard nothing from the Attorney General's Office. November came and went. So did December. Lois assumed that the state would do its job, so she didn't pester them. But as time passed she began to think about alternatives. In October of 1987, while sitting in the waiting room at Range Mental Health, where she had begun to make regular visits to Claire Bell, a new psychologist, Lois came across an article in a local business magazine called *Corporate Report Minnesota*.

It was about a woman named Carol Flowers, a Kmart employee who worked in the store's appliance department in Blaine, Minnesota. Her boss had flicked his tongue at her to suggest cunnilingus, made comments about her breasts, and professed to want to have sex with her. Flowers had sued the company for sexual harassment and won a jury award of $800,000 in damages and a $2.45 million civil penalty—the largest ever paid in a sexual harassment case. To Lois, Flowers's story had a familiar ring. The only difference was that Flowers's experiences were milder than Lois's. Also, Flowers was represented by a private attorney. "If she sued over a remark," Lois said to herself, "why can't we sue over much worse things?"

On December 6, 1987, Lois was laid off for a month—something that happened frequently during these times at Eveleth Mines. The time off allowed her to focus again on the case and her attitude changed from hopeless to determined. She started with the Yellow Pages and called every last attorney in the Iron Range cities. Some told her they would not touch a mining company. One attorney in Hibbing who was known for taking on mining companies told her that after he tried an age-discrimination case involving Reserve Mine in Hibbing, it had broken his firm. The case took eleven years and, as the attorney told it to Lois, the "mine beat us up." He just couldn't afford to take on a case like that again.

At least he returned her call. Many of the Iron Range lawyers never did.

Lois went to the library and photocopied the listings for attorneys in the Duluth and Minneapolis/St. Paul Yellow Pages. When that led to still more rejections, she called the Minnesota Bar Association and got some suggestions. In all she called fifty lawyers. No one would take her case.

Lois returned to work on January 3, 1988. Four days later, she called Rubenstein's boss, Richard Varco. When Varco told Lois that he had yet to reassign her case, Lois broke down. "Do you know what it's like to work in this place day after day with this thing pending, knowing that nothing is being done?" In desperation, Lois called Helen Rubenstein. Helen gave Lois the names of four lawyers whom she knew specialized in employment discrimination cases. One of those lawyers was a man named Paul Sprenger.

Not surprisingly, by the time Lois called the offices of Sprenger & Associates, she was not the least bit optimistic. She was put through to a woman named Cheree Norris, a legal assistant and case screener, who was at least kind enough to hear her out. Norris made no promises but asked Lois to send more information about her case in writing. For the first time since Helen Rubenstein took the case, Lois felt that someone was actually listening to her.

A week later, on February 23, 1988, Lois and Pat dressed in their best slacks and jackets and made the 190-mile drive south on Interstate 35 to the Twin Cities. Sprenger wanted to meet with them in his law offices.

"We were so busy talking we missed the exit ramp," Lois said. Frankly, what they saw when they pulled into the parking lot disappointed them. Sprenger & Associates was housed not in a steel-and-glass skyscraper downtown, where most of the big Twin Cities firms are housed, but in a small, unprepossessing building on Ridgewood Avenue, a quiet residential street near Lowry Hill. "How good can a lawyer be who works out of a place like this?" Lois wondered.

Yet as they waited in the lobby, decorated in contemporary and primitive art, the telephone at the receptionist's desk rang off the hook, and the entire place seemed full of activity and energy.

Cheree Norris greeted the women and ushered them into a small conference room. In a moment, a man appeared and introduced himself. A former track star, Paul Sprenger, at forty-seven, was still trim and compact, with dark brown eyes and a tweedy, absentminded professor style of dress. "Paul asked some questions. I was surprised that he was so young-looking. He was quite handsome. And I kind of think I went, Oh God, don't go there," Lois recalled. Most important, she said, "He wasn't intimidating." In fact, his voice was so low and soft and even halting that he sometimes seemed on the verge of running out of the energy or interest necessary to finish his thought.

It was probably good that Lois did not know much about Sprenger. Because she might have been even more nervous had she realized that this casual man who worked out of an odd little office was one of the most successful and sought-after plaintiff employment discrimination lawyers in the country. A decade earlier, Sprenger had been an insurance lawyer defending corporate clients against lawsuits and working in one of those glass-and-steel skyscrapers. By 1988, he estimated that he had sued almost every major company in the city.

Paul Sprenger was born September 8, 1940 in Stillwater, Minnesota, a pretty town on the St. Croix River. His father served in the navy, causing the family to move around constantly. By the time he was in high school, his father was overseas much of the time, and he and his mother and younger brother were living at a navy base in Grosse Ile, Michigan. The Sprengers were not destitute, but poor enough that Paul was one of the children invited to the Rotary Club's annual dinner for disadvantaged youth. The point of the dinners was not so much to feed the children as to expose them to a formal social setting and, by extension, another way of life.

Sprenger was a standout in high school, both academically and athletically. He played on the varsity football team when he was only a freshman and later became captain. But his real love was track. A record-setting pole vaulter, he landed a partial track scholarship to the University of Michigan in 1958. He also received additional money in the form of a scholarship from the local chapter of the Volunteer Firefighters. "My coach didn't tell me about the scholarship until right before I left for college," Sprenger recalled with a laugh. "He was afraid I'd spend it."

He was the first person in his family to go to college. His mother was thrilled; his father was not. "He would tease me, call me 'the professor.' He wanted me to go into the navy, like he had, and like my brother would."

Sprenger sensed that he would not be happy in such a regimented world, though he was secretly skeptical about whether he could handle college. But the coach of the Michigan track team told him that if he could read and write and pole vault, he would get through. He ended up doing much better than that. He got good grades, joined a fraternity, and worked in the dining hall to put himself through school. He was hyperconscious of the fact that many of his classmates were living a different lifestyle. "I remember there were guys there who did not have to work, who drove around in convertibles." Sprenger was thinking only of getting through school and settling down—that was what people of his background did. The day after his twenty-first birthday, at the beginning of his senior year, Sprenger married his college sweetheart.

As graduation approached in June of 1962, he debated what to do next. He knew he did not want to punch a clock, he wanted a profession. He thought about business school, but ultimately chose law school because it seemed more interesting. Although the civil rights movement was gaining ground, he was not radical. He did, however, have a particular interest in the rights of man, and a particular aversion to what he considered unfair treatment. He remembered that guards at Grosse Ile Naval Station would sometimes give him special privileges because he lived there and knew them, letting him swim after hours or return to base after curfew. "It was fun, but it also probably undermined my sense of authority. I realized that there was one way things were supposed to be and another way that some guys could do things. It struck me then that the flip side to privilege is discrimination." Yet Sprenger's early exposure to classmates from wealth and privilege had also instilled in him a desire for financial security, and it would be years before he could see the way to reconcile these two poles of his life.

He applied to and was accepted by the University of Michigan's law school, one of the best in the country. When he graduated, he went to work for the corporate defense firm of Johnson & Sands. For the next seven years he did insurance defense work, traveling throughout Minnesota and the upper Midwest trying cases for insurance companies and large institutions at a rate of about one a week. The cases ran the gamut from slip-and-fall claims to auto accidents to product liability cases. It was invaluable experience for a trial lawyer—many litigators try only one or two cases in an entire year, if that. His trial skills and courtroom instincts, his sense of how to play a particular judge, how a jury was leaning, were honed in this period of his life. But while Sprenger was becoming a seasoned trial lawyer, he was beginning to get bored.

The catalyst in his professional life was a woman named Willie Doll Partee. Willie Doll was the daughter of a former slave who was suing the state of Wisconsin to collect a small inheritance a distant relative had left to her. Sprenger was asked to take on the case. "She was a fantastic witness," Sprenger recalled. "She raised one hand, she said 'Praise the Lord,' she talked about being baptized in a little creek and growing up in a dirt-floor shack. And the judge wrote a fantastic opinion about the State of Wisconsin keeping better records on dairy cows than on black people." It was Sprenger's epiphany.

For financial reasons, Sprenger continued to work for Johnson & Sands, but he wasn't getting the same satisfaction he got from representing Willie Doll—a real person as opposed to the "assistant to the assistant to the assistant" he typically was working for in corporate law cases. At the same time, he knew the Willie Dolls of the world were usually plaintiffs, and he knew that representing plaintiffs was a lot riskier financially than representing corporate defendants. In terms of stability, corporate defendants were the best kind of client: They paid by the hour whether or not you won.

Plaintiffs, on the other hand, usually wanted you to represent them on a contingency fee basis: You only got paid if you won, in which case you would get a percentage of the award. Then there was the problem of getting clients in the first place. Would-be plaintiffs were a dime a dozen, but good ones, credible people with legitimate claims, were harder to find. Even when you had a good client with a strong case, defendants, especially corporate or insured defendants, could more easily afford the out-of-pocket expenses of litigation than plaintiffs' lawyers could. Experienced defense lawyers, usually with the resources of a large law firm behind them, could drive up the costs of a case so high that the plaintiff's lawyer would have to yell "Uncle" first, and accept a settlement that would pay his bills but might be far less than the plaintiff would have been awarded by a jury.

Given all the downsides of leaving the security of an insurance defense practice, Sprenger was not ready to make any drastic moves. But he did begin to keep his eye out for other cases that might engage him the way Willie Doll's had and that could pay the bills to boot.

Then one day in 1973 he was contacted by the local chapter of the National Organization for Women to see if he would be interested in representing a group of women who worked for 3M Company, a Minnesota giant. The women claimed they had been discriminated against in all aspects of their work because of their gender, including recruitment, hiring, training, job assignments, pay, and discharge. Although he had never done a civil rights case before, Sprenger took the case. Later, Sprenger speculated that NOW approached him because of some publicity he had received in an antitrust class action for a local liquor retail association. "It was an amazing set of facts. In the hiring process, it turned out the applications were even color-coded: blue for men, pink for girls." As he dug deeper, Sprenger also realized that there were other problems beside gender bias at 3M, and he later amended the complaint to expand the case to include racial discrimination against black employees.

The 3M case was to be the first of many employment discrimination class actions that he would bring under Title VII of the Civil Rights Act of 1964—and in fact, was the first Title VII class action in the Eighth Circuit, the federal jurisdiction that includes Minnesota. When the case ultimately settled in 1977, Sprenger's take was around $800,000.

But even before the 3M case wound down, the thirty-five-year-old lawyer was beginning to make a name for himself in the area of employment discrimination law. "It didn't take much," he later conceded. "In the seventies in Minnesota, there just weren't too many lawyers doing employment discrimination class actions on a contingency basis." In 1975, he received a phone call from a temporary assistant professor in chemistry at the University of Minnesota named Shyamala Rajender. Rajender had been passed over for a tenure-track position, and she believed it was because she was a woman. She also believed that the university routinely denied tenure-track positions to qualified female employees. Sprenger took Rajender's case and filed it as a class action on behalf of hundreds of female faculty members.

In 1977, while *Rajender v. University of Minnesota* was still pending, Sprenger decided that he was ready to leave Johnson & Sands to start his own firm. He and two other lawyers from the firm rented space in the same building, hired an elderly bookkeeper out of retirement to keep track of things, and opened shop as Sprenger, Olson & Shutes, P.A. They would do some civil rights work on contingency, but their main source of revenue would come from clients paying them on an hourly basis.

The next year, the University of Minnesota agreed to a groundbreaking settlement in the Rajender case, paying Sprenger's client $100,000. In addition, the university set up an affirmative action program for female employees and agreed to a process for resolving the claims of the other women in the class. The university's affirmative action policy soon became a model for others across the country, and the Rajender case was celebrated in legal circles as a milestone in employment-discrimination litigation in higher education.

But Sprenger still had not been paid for his work on the case. Title VII is one of many federal statutes that provide that courts may award attorneys' fees in successful cases. In the settlement, the university had agreed to pay "reasonable attorneys' fees," though it did not specify an amount. That decision was left to Judge Miles Lord, the judge assigned to the case. In July 1982, Judge Lord issued his award: a breathtaking $1.4 million to Sprenger, Olson & Shutes, and $500,000 to Johnson & Sands for the work that Sprenger did on the case while he was still with the firm. The award set a record for the highest attorneys' fees ever awarded in an employment discrimination case against an academic institution. Judge Lord arrived at the figure by tripling both firms' usual rates, explaining that such significant fees were necessary to deter discrimination and to encourage plaintiffs' lawyers to take discrimination cases.

The university called the award unreasonable and vowed to appeal. A few months later, Sprenger and the university came to an agreement: Sprenger would accept $1,175,000 to be paid immediately, rather than the higher amount over time. Likewise, Johnson & Sands would accept $300,000 under the same conditions.

After the Rajender case, Sprenger's phone started ringing with calls from people seeking representation in employment discrimination and Title VII cases. "It began to occur to me," Sprenger said later, "that I might be able to make a living just bringing employment discrimination class actions." It would be risky, because the cases were primarily contingency fee–based class actions that often took years to resolve. But Sprenger was coming to understand that he thrived on risk.

Most lawyers love knowing their upside and downside. They might not be able to do better than their hourly rate, but then again, they can't do worse. But for Sprenger, the idea of working for an hourly rate was depressing. It reminded him of the clock-punching that used to control his father's life. He wanted not to be able to see around the bend. In fact, he became itchy with boredom if he could see too far ahead.

By now, Sprenger was able to afford a taste of the lifestyle he had admired from afar in his youth. He and his wife, Judith, had two daughters and a son, a comfortable house in Minneapolis, a condo on Captiva Island, Florida, and, the pièce de résistance, a fifty-six-foot sailboat christened *Class Action*. In 1980, Sprenger, Olson & Shutes were doing well enough to look for new office space. Sprenger had an intense dislike of high-rises. "I don't like waiting for elevators," he explained. He looked around for an alternative. When he found the house on Ridgewood Avenue, he knew it was just right.

Sprenger's next big case was a race discrimination class action against Burlington Northern Railroad Company and thirteen railroad workers unions. The lead plaintiffs were two former railroad workers, William McBride and William Butler, who claimed that the company had forced them out of their jobs because of their race. The class action ultimately included several thousand employees.

Burlington Northern was represented by Steptoe & Johnson, a white-shoe Washington, D.C., firm. The lead Steptoe partner on the case was Tom Powers, a former head of the Equal Employment Opportunity Commission. After some initial legal skirmishing, Sprenger and the Steptoe lawyers negotiated a progressive settlement, which called for Burlington Northern and its codefendants to pay $10 million in back pay to the former workers, and for the company to hire five thousand blacks over the next six years, at a cost of approximately $40 million. Like the Rajender case, the Burlington Northern settlement became a milestone in employment discrimination cases, and cemented Sprenger's reputation as a top-flight advocate for Title VII plaintiffs.

But the case also made Sprenger realize that while employment discrimination class actions could be profitable, it was too risky for the firm to have too many eggs in one basket. For five months, the vast majority of the firm's time had been tied up in the case. They spent more than $2 million on out-of-pocket expenses, including expert testimony and statistical research, and that did not even include the value of their own time. They had to use their line of credit to keep afloat. So even though, as part of the settlement, they were ultimately awarded attorneys' fees of $1.8 million in addition to their out-of-pocket expenses, Sprenger realized that the strategy of focusing all of the firm's resources on one case was untenable.

Shortly after the case wrapped up, Sprenger, Olson & Shutes closed its doors. The stress of handling one big case at a time, with great financial outlay and the threat of debt, had taken its toll on Sprenger's two partners, both of whom announced that they wanted to do something else with their lives. But Sprenger was determined to find a way to make it work. This time around he realized that he would need a big war chest. He remembered the words of Judge Lord, who had once said that class action litigation is "not for the weak, and it's not for the poor."

The plan Sprenger came up with to develop and maintain a big war chest was somewhat counterintuitive, like driving into a skid or swimming with an undertow. If he could not afford to handle one big class action at a time, he would radically expand his class action operations to handle ten, twelve, however many he could staff. That way, instead of relying on billable hours for the influx of cash necessary to sustain his contingency fee cases, they could finance each other.

The Burlington Northern case also changed his life in another way. At a discovery meeting with the Steptoe lawyers in the spring of 1983, Sprenger, whose marriage to Judith was breaking up, could not help but notice the elegant blond Steptoe partner assisting Tom Powers. Her name was Jane Lang, and she noticed Sprenger, too. "I tell her she fell in love with me at first sight," he chuckled years later.

As the case got closer to trial, Lang became the lead negotiator for Steptoe in settlement talks with Sprenger. It came down to the wire. "We had a trial date for a Monday morning at ten. In the wee hours of Monday morning I thought that we agreed to settle. . . . Jane was in a downtown hotel, we had a lot of phone conversations, in the morning we went to the judge and told him we had agreed to settle and we outlined the terms." But even then, there was a lot of work to do. "We had to turn a simple agreement in principle into a seventy-five-page injunction." That required meetings "in Chicago, Minneapolis, Washington." Paul later conceded that perhaps they met in person more than was absolutely necessary.

On the surface, Sprenger and Lang were an odd match. Lang was the glamorous, sophisticated daughter of wealthy New York businessman philanthropist Eugene Lang, founder of the I Have a Dream Foundation. She was raised in New York City, had a passion for the performing arts, and was an intellectual. She was also a champion of the underdog. She went to Swarthmore College and excelled academically. When she graduated in 1967, she decided to go to law school. She enrolled at the University of Pennsylvania, one of only eight women in her class.

Lang clerked for Steptoe & Johnson during the summer of her third year in law school, and joined the firm as an associate when she graduated in 1970. She became the firm's first female partner in 1977, and was asked to serve in the Carter administration as general counsel of the Department of Housing and Urban Development. She returned to Steptoe in 1981. In 1968 while in law school, she had married Tom McGrew, a lawyer with the firm Arnold & Porter, and they had two children together. By 1984, the marriage ended although Jane and Tom remained friends and lived only a block away from each other. In 1986, feeling a need to make a change, she left the 185-lawyer firm to start her own five-lawyer practice that she housed in an elegant 1891 brick and sandstone town house just north of Dupont Circle at 1614 20th Street.

By 1987, Lang and Sprenger were working together on several cases, although they still had separate firms. Sprenger opened a D.C. branch office of his firm in Jane's building so he could spend more time with her. Their different personality styles—her East Coast edge, his midwestern reserve—and their talents—she was the writer and negotiator, while he was the litigator and strategist—complemented each other. Like Tracy and Hepburn in *Adam's Rib*, Sprenger and Lang were an intelligent, idealistic, and powerful team.

That year, they jointly filed a hostile-environment sexual harassment case against a General Electric facility outside Washington, D.C., that operated top-secret government contracts. "It was the most dismal situation," recalled Lang. "The head of the office was sleeping with two women who worked there and was harassing others." Although Sprenger had tried other types of gender discrimination cases, the G.E. case was both Sprenger and Lang's first sexual harassment case. For Lang, at least, it was a bitter experience. The trial lasted through two weeks of grueling, emotional, explicit testimony. Although G.E. was found liable for maintaining the environment that allowed the abuse to occur, no damages were awarded because, at the time, Title VII did not provide for damages based on emotional distress in sex discrimination cases.

Sprenger was undeterred, but Lang was scarred by the toll the case took on both her client and on herself. "The case was bruising and devastating to everyone involved," said Lang. "There are no winners in sexual harassment litigation. I never wanted to try a sexual harassment case again as a litigator. When women approach me, I offer to help them settle, but I send them to other counsel if they want to litigate."

By 1988, Paul Sprenger was listed in *The Best Lawyers in America*, and Sprenger & Associates was receiving upwards of a hundred calls a week from people with employment discrimination claims. Sprenger hired Cheree Norris to handle initial intake. Working out of the Minneapolis office, Norris would screen calls and letters, and pass the promising ones on to Sprenger. He would review the information and either tell Norris to send a letter declining to take the case, or, if he were interested, to ask for more information. Over time, Sprenger had developed a rough set of criteria for determining whether or not to take a case. First, the case had to be a potential class action. Second, there had to be some possibility of a significant monetary recovery. Third, the claimant had to be credible and have reasonable expectations of how much money their case was worth. "It also helps if there is something about it that I find interesting or challenging." Soon, Sprenger & Associates was rejecting about 95 percent of the requests it received for representation.

By the time that Lois Jenson and Pat Kosmach arrived at Sprenger & Associates' offices, Sprenger was predisposed to take the case. He had read the case file from the state and was impressed by the severity of the sexual harassment Lois had endured and the stubborn approach the company took to the issue. He also thought the case was a natural class action because the environment of the mine was so clearly hostile to all the women who worked there. Helen Rubenstein had called him to see if he might be interested, and what she told him added to his sense that it was a good case. Sprenger assumed that the Attorney General's Office's slow uptake on the case had to do with politics. Ray Erickson's firm had close ties to the mining industry, and so did Governor Rudy Perpich. The attorney general at the time was Hubert H. Humphrey III. "Skip Humphrey was young, weaker than his father. He was not about to stand up to pressure," Sprenger surmised.

But before he agreed, there were things Sprenger needed to see for himself. "The most important was what kind of plaintiffs I thought they would make. A lot of whether a person wins or loses at trial has to do with how appealing they are." Would they be credible? Sympathetic? Greedy? Would working with them be easy or hard? Some clients had strong claims, but they were not sympathetic to the jury or judge. Some were so emotionally disturbed that they would weaken their own case. Sprenger was reserving judgment on the Jenson case until he could assess Lois and Pat in person.

After a few moments in the conference room, Sprenger was encouraged. As a package deal, the two women were promising clients. Lois was personable and attractive, she seemed to have a good memory, and her story was compelling. But Sprenger knew there was a chance that a judge would take a look at the letters Steve Povroznik sent to Lois and fall into the "he said, she said" trap. "Her specific complaints about him could have been characterized by a judge as 'she was egging him on.' "

"Pat offset that. She seemed intelligent and articulate, and levelheaded. Real salt of the earth. Whatever she said, a judge would believe it." Sprenger was also impressed that Pat was a union official. He thought her insider status would give her credibility, and attract more women to join the class.

Then Sprenger asked the two women a question that he often asked prospective clients. What were they in it for? What did they want out of suing?

"If you have someone with a $50,000 case who wants a million dollars, then you know you're not going to be able to make them happy," Sprenger later explained.

So when Lois replied, "I want to make sure that other women who work in the mine do not have to go through what I went through. I want a policy," Sprenger was relieved. "As for money," Lois continued. "You're the one who knows about these kinds of cases, I'll leave that up to you."

Lois had passed his test.

"It struck me as perfect because, after all, the law said that if the defendant adopted a sexual harassment policy it was off the hook," Sprenger said later. "All along, I saw this case as being about getting a good sexual harassment policy in place. I actually did not think, at the time, that it was worth a lot of money. I definitely did not see it as a multimillion-dollar case, because at that point the women still had their jobs."

But even though he did not see it as a big dollar case, Sprenger did think it should be relatively easy to get the company to agree to adopt a progressive, comprehensive policy, and to pay some modest amount of damages. "Anybody in their right mind would want to settle this," he told Lois and Pat. He thought to himself that he could easily wrap it up inside of two years.

Sprenger's interest in the case lay not in recouping huge fees—if the case settled as quickly and for as little money as he expected, the case would not make him rich—but in seeing whether it could be brought as a class action. He had tried the G.E. case, an individual sexual harassment case, but he had never tried a sexual harassment class action. As far as he knew, nobody else had either. But because the women were looking for a sexual harassment policy that would affect all the women working in the mine as well, it seemed to him to be "a natural class action."

He told the women he would take the case. "There's only one problem, we need more people. In a class case you need a representative group of plaintiffs. So we need someone who works in the pit."

Sprenger noticed that this suggestion made Lois straighten her posture in a defensive gesture. Her attitude, he recalled, was "This is my case."

But Pat chimed in, "I've heard a few tough stories out of the pit. I think I can help you find a gal over there who would join us."

Sprenger explained his fee structure and gave them both copies of his retainer agreement—Sprenger & Associates would bear the cost of the trial, and in return would take 33 percent of any monetary relief. Each plaintiff was required to pay the firm $50 a month for twenty-four months. Sprenger said the reason for the fee was to keep the plaintiffs committed to the case. Lois thought the fee arrangement was fair. Most of all she couldn't believe she had a lawyer.

Before letting him know that they would retain Sprenger, however, Lois said she would need more information about his qualifications. Sprenger told her about some of the cases he had tried, and Cheree Norris gave Lois and Pat an article about Sprenger's practice that had just been published in the Minneapolis *Star Tribune*.

Keeping their cool, Lois and Pat thanked Sprenger, and told him they would get back to him soon. But once they were outside the building and safely down the street, they let out whoops of excitement and danced up and down, hugging each other. On the drive home, they stopped in Hinckley for something to eat, and began to go through the materials Sprenger had given them, including the *Star Tribune* article. When they read the sentence "Paul Sprenger has carved an unusual niche in the legal profession and a reputation as one of the nation's leading attorneys in large job-discrimination suits . . ." they became concerned that Sprenger might change his mind before they got to Eveleth. "He must think I'm a total twit! We're such small-town girls," said Lois. But Sprenger did not change his mind, and when they got home, Lois and Pat signed the retainer agreements Sprenger had given them and mailed them immediately.

Sprenger assigned the Jenson case to Jean Boler, a tall, soft-spoken young lawyer who had just joined the firm from the Human Rights Division of the Attorney General's Office. Jean's first step in March 1988 was to inform the Attorney General's Office that Sprenger & Associates was now representing Lois and the other women. The transfer of the case to Sprenger & Associates was not good news to the mine and its lawyers. They were aware of Sprenger & Associates' reputation and preferred to keep the case tied up in the administrative process, where the combination of Attorney General's Office's workload and Erickson's delaying tactics could keep things bogged down indefinitely. Erickson immediately filed an objection to the dismissal of the administrative action on the grounds that it would be prejudicial to his client. There was no basis for his objection, since the statute under which Lois's complaint had been filed very clearly states that a party to an administrative complaint can terminate the administrative proceeding and initiate a private action at any time before an evidentiary hearing is held.

Even though Erickson had been advised that Lois had new counsel, he sent papers and filings directly to Lois and the other women. After several months of this, Boler called Erickson to ask him to stop. "It is a violation of professional ethics to communicate directly with an adverse party whom you know to be represented by a lawyer," she said later. The call did not go well. "He was arrogant and dismissive, saying that if Lois could be bothered by such a minor thing, he could tell what the allegations in the complaint were based on, and that she was prone to overreacting." It was Boler's first communication with Erickson, and it set a negative and combative tone for all future contact. "But he did stop," Boler said.

Sprenger and Boler planned to file the claim under both federal and Minnesota state law. Although *Meritor* and the other precedent-setting sexual harassment decisions were based on Title VII, the Civil Rights Act only allowed for monetary awards for lost wages, other out-of-pocket losses, and injunctive relief. Damages for pain and suffering, including emotional distress, were not available under the federal statute. This meant that Lois and Pat's damages claims—and therefore, the pressure they could bring on the mine—would be miniscule under federal law, since neither of them had lost their job as a result of the harassment they had suffered. Minnesota state law, however, had no such limitation on damages, but the state law was less developed in terms of theory and precedent. Sprenger also believed that federal courtrooms tended to be more neutral than local ones. He had tried enough cases on the Iron Range when he worked for Johnson & Sands to know that outsiders, particularly big-city lawyers suing one of the largest employers in the area, could not expect to be welcomed with opened arms. Fortunately, Federal Rules of Civil Procedure allow plaintiffs to join state and federal claims together in federal court when the claims are similar, so Sprenger and Boler did not have to choose between state and federal law.

By bundling multiple claims together, the damages would be much higher, which would put more pressure on the company to take the case seriously. From a strategic point of view, a class action was more likely than an individual case to get the attention of the senior management of the sued company. In Sprenger's experience, lower-level managers tended to have a more personal view of employment cases—they often felt they needed to vindicate themselves or their subordinates at all costs. That attitude often led to irrational decision-making, a willingness to pursue a case to trial when a reasonable settlement could have been easily reached at the outset. Senior management, on the other hand, tended to take a more dispassionate approach, looking at a case from a purely economic point of view. Once cases reached the board of directors, reasonable settlements were much more likely.

Of course, larger settlements meant that potential attorneys' fees would be much higher as well. The truth was that Sprenger could not afford to take a case that would require a significant investment of time and money unless it was a class action in federal court. By providing plaintiffs' lawyers with enough incentive to take a case, class actions allow people who otherwise could not afford a lawyer to protect their rights.

When Lois and Pat went to see Sprenger, there had never been a sexual harassment class action in federal court. Quid pro quo harassment, by its nature, tended to give rise only to individual claims. Only the rare megalomaniac would demand the same sexual favors from multiple women at the same time and promise them all the same rewards.

But as Catherine MacKinnon had argued in her 1979 paper, a sexually hostile work environment could theoretically affect more than one woman. Still, the conventional wisdom was that incidents of sexual harassment, even those that could give rise to a hostile work environment, are too individualized, too personal, to ever be brought as a class action.

Whether a case can be brought as a class action depends on

whether it meets certain standards that, for federal cases, are spelled out in the Federal Rules of Civil Procedure. A judge makes that determination after a hearing in which each side argues for and against the class. To authorize a class action, the judge must find that:

1) The claims of the potential class members share common questions of law or fact.

2) The claims of the named plaintiffs are typical of the claims of the other potential class members.

3) There are enough plaintiffs to make a single case judicially efficient.

4) The named plaintiffs can adequately and vigorously represent the interests of the class.

Helen Rubenstein had always assumed that the case would be brought as a class action, and at the time Jean Boler had called Andrea Kircher, Kircher was working on a class action complaint. But the rules for bringing a class action in federal court are much more stringent than they are in an administrative proceeding, where the Federal Rules of Civil Procedure do not apply. When Sprenger took the case, he instinctively thought it would make a good class action, and the more he studied it, the more certain he became. If Lois and Pat had experienced a sexually hostile work environment, other women at Eveleth likely had, too.

Back at home, Lois bought a fuchsia-colored folder and put the *Star Tribune* article about Sprenger in it. She also copied the Kmart article and six other articles about developments in sexual harassment law that she clipped from the local newspapers, *U.S. News & World Report*, and *Newsweek*. Lois called a battered women's shelter in Minneapolis and asked them to send her material on sexual harassment, which she placed in her folder: "The Myths and Facts of Sexual Harassment: What

You Need to Know." On a plain sheet of paper, Lois copied by hand the EEOC's 1980 sexual harassment guidelines, which also went into the folder. She placed the folder, along with a stack of Sprenger's business cards, in her locker in the women's dry. Armed with her folder, she was ready to wage her new campaign to educate the women about sexual harassment and convince them to join the class.

Lois and Pat were now the only official plaintiffs in the case. Michele Mesich had dropped out. When she originally joined the case in 1987, she had been laid off since 1984 and didn't have to worry about retaliation. In her time off from work, Mesich got a degree in graphic arts at the technical college in Eveleth. In July of 1987, she moved to the Twin Cities where she found work in the file room for a color separator press. Mesich earned $6 an hour at the press—half her hourly salary at the mine. Soon after she moved to the Cities, Mesich received a notice from the mine that she could go back to work. She didn't reply. "I figured it wasn't going to be fun," recalled Mesich. "Lois was having a hard time. I thought, no thank you." Mesich also said no thank you to joining the civil action with Sprenger. She had a ten-year-old daughter, was strapped for cash, and didn't think she could afford Sprenger's $50-a-month retainer fee. She also worried that the lawsuit would jeopardize her current job. "No one likes an employee who sues their boss," she said. But Michele tried to provide moral support to Lois by keeping in close touch with her by phone and making regular visits to the Range.

Pat and Lois argued over who else to recruit. Pat did not want to include women who slept around or had alcohol or drug problems. Lois thought they had no right to make that determination. Besides, Lois argued, ruling out those three factors would cut out most of the women at the mine. Both Pat and Lois worried that Kathy O'Brien Anderson could potentially hurt their cause more than help. Kathy, who worked in the pit, had just married George Anderson, a foreman at the plant. They met when Kathy was briefly transferred to the plant and worked on George's crew in the crusher. Together they owned the Maco News in Virginia, which sold gourmet coffee beans and magazines, some of them pornographic. Andrea Kircher had asked Kathy to join the state's class action against Lois and Pat's wishes. Kathy was a drama queen, and Lois and Pat were afraid that even though the truth about what had happened to Kathy was bad enough, she might be tempted to embellish it even more. "Pat thought Kathy was a flake," said Jeanne Aho, Pat's best friend. Before Kathy married George Anderson in 1988, she had been "pretty busy" with other men, according to Lois. Sexy, flamboyant, Kathy courted trouble. Now that Kathy's name was on the state case, Lois changed her mind and thought she should be asked to join their civil action. Pat did not.

"I don't feel I have to baby-sit Kathy O'Brien," Pat told Lois over the phone. "I don't like her in the first place, I don't trust her in the second."

"I've had to do plenty of baby-sitting through this," Lois replied. "The important thing to remember is our class certification. At this point, we need anybody and everybody who qualifies. I'll try to call her myself."

Pat and Lois's partnership, which had strengthened over the past year and a half, was buckling under the pressure. They didn't start out as friends, but in the face of a common enemy they had bonded. Mostly, their relationship was about business. They did not socialize together, and they worked different shifts, so they rarely overlapped at the plant. But they talked on the phone every day, plotting, strategizing, and just venting. "Pat tried real hard to be a friend to Lois, even though Lois bugged her," Jeanne Aho recalled. Lois, on the other hand, never felt that she could trust Pat, and became paranoid that Pat was giving information about the case to the union. In a June 27, 1988, diary entry, Lois wrote: "I wonder if Pat's been doing something in the background. I wish we could trust each other. I know she's up to something, and I don't know what, she has been from the start. All I want is for the plans to go through as a class."

Meanwhile, Sprenger asked Lois to write a detailed chronology of her experiences at Eveleth Mines. On May 20, Lois sent a twenty-seven-page single-spaced typed document to Sprenger. The project took ten days of hard concentration and willpower. Before she could start writing, Lois cleaned up her apartment, gathered all of her old desk-top calendars, medical bills, letters, notes, and receipts, and sat on the floor and got to work. *On Feb. 25, 1975, I filled out an application for Eveleth Mines,* the chronology began. She then recounted every incident of sexual harassment that she could remember. Digging up every detail about Scaia, Perpruner, and Povroznik was painful and emotional, causing her to have nightmares and unexpected crying jags. But Lois's memory was sharp as a tack. "My mind was a database," she said. Each time she finished writing, Lois would fanatically clean up her notes and put everything away in a drawer. Then she would take a vacuum cleaner and scrub brush to her already clean apartment as if the toxic information she had just written down had contaminated her living space.

The same day she sent her chronology to Sprenger Lois received a strange phone call from a policeman who lived nearby in Gilbert. He said that he was looking for a Tami Jenson. "I was so taken aback that I said, 'There's no Tami here,' and hung up." Then Lois got concerned that maybe something had happened to the daughter, Tami, whom she had put up for adoption in 1971. She called the policeman back and asked why he was looking for Tami Jenson. He said that an insurance company she had filed a claim with didn't have her address. "That's when I realized that Eveleth had hired him as a private eye. It just didn't make sense. If they were her insurance company, they'd have her address."

Two months later, in late July, Lois put together another document for the lawyers. Sprenger told Lois that he had to know everything about her life, because if he didn't he wouldn't be able to defend her against the defense lawyer's attacks. Lois wrote seven pages of what she titled "Soap Time," in her legible, schoolgirl script. Lois didn't waste time getting to the point. The letter began:

> *Graduated June '66. Moved to Mpls and worked as a file clerk for Harry S. Newman at New Hampshire Ins. Co.*
> *May '67 I was raped, by a friend of a friend while I was leav-*

ing a party. It's hard for me to put this on paper so if you need more details you'll have to let me know. I did go to the police to report it—I sat on a bench for over an hour at the sexual assault/robbery unit. Two officers were interviewing a woman who [had been] badly beaten and raped. They were so horrible to her—I left.

August '67 I had to quit my job because I was pregnant. . . . When I was five months pregnant I tried to commit suicide— didn't work. I'm still here!

The true story of Greg's paternity was Lois's deepest secret. *Greg does not know the full truth about his father and he will not!!!!!* Lois wrote the lawyers. Lois said that the rape was a "difficult" experience, but she had always felt that the attack was about the man's anger and had nothing to do with her personally.

It's hard not to take such a personal attack personally, but I have never blamed men in general because of the act of one person. On a comparative note, Steve Povroznik did more damage because of the focus and personal aim and the relentlessness of his attempts. With no sex involved.

Lois told the story of her second pregnancy—a mistake with a childhood friend to whom she was engaged. Spooked by the news of her pregnancy, the fiancé, a sergeant in the marines who had also just come home from Vietnam, broke up with Lois. Before Tami was born, Lois found out that he had married another girl whom he had gotten pregnant. Lois recounted her tortured decision to put Tami up for adoption: *I am still sure that I did the right thing for all of us.*

She wrote about her dating habits.

When I did date on a more serious level—I usually waited 6 mo. or so before another more serious relationship. That's not neces-

sarily saying I dated someone for 6 mo. before—but I didn't change sexual partners quickly. I think '76 would be the only exception. And if problems developed I saw the doctor and usually stopped seeing that individual after telling them. I'm letting you know that I am not a saint by any means. . . .

Mr. Sprenger you have an idea now of what I am all about. I'm not afraid to tell the truth or to face my past . . . as painful as all of this is to relive and share with strangers, I pray something good will come out of it.

Sprenger was sanguine when he read about the skeletons in Lois's closet. He knew that when the time came for depositions and a trial, it would be his job to minimize Lois's past. "It had happened almost twenty years ago," he said. He stored the letter away and didn't look at it again until it was time to prepare for Lois's first deposition.

CHAPTER EIGHT

The Petition

August 1988

On August 15, 1988, Paul Sprenger filed *Lois E. Jenson and Patricia S. Kosmach v. Eveleth Taconite Co.* in the U.S. District Court for the District of Minnesota. The complaint alleged that the plaintiffs, Lois Jenson and Patricia Kosmach, had been subjected to sexual harassment and discrimination at Eveleth Mines, and their coworkers and supervisors "created and condoned" a work environment that was "hostile to all women employees." The complaint also alleged that the company discriminated on the basis of gender in hiring and promoting its workers.

The complaint asked that the case be certified as a class action, with Lois and Pat as the lead plaintiffs and Sprenger & Associates as class counsel. It asked the court to enjoin Oglebay Norton from future violations of Title VII, and require the company to adopt an anti–sexual harassment policy.

Two weeks later, the company filed its answer. Oglebay Norton admitted that it was a corporation doing business as Eveleth Mines, and that Lois and Pat worked there. It denied everything else.

The company also claimed that even if there was occasional use of "slang language and suggestive conduct," the company had a practice of "immediately investigating and correcting sexual harassment."

Buried in paragraph fifteen, the company stated that "to the extent that any of the plaintiffs have been damaged or otherwise injured, . . . the same was caused by the acts or conduct of said plaintiffs. . . ." In other words, it never happened; and if it did, they brought it on themselves.

Two days after Sprenger filed the civil suit, a reporter for the Duluth *News Tribune* called Lois at home, catching her off-guard. "I'm sorry, I can't talk to you. Please call my attorney," she told them, and hung up. The next morning, August 18, 1988, the *News Tribune* ran a headline on page A2: "Women Charge Harassment in Suit Against Company." The article identified Lois and Pat as the women who were filing the action "in behalf of all the company's female employees, past and present."

The other six major iron mines on the Range took note of the suit. Soon after it was filed, they swiftly established company sexual harassment policies and complaint procedures so that they could inoculate themselves from being sued.

At Eveleth, however, the reaction to the news that Lois and Pat had filed a class action civil lawsuit against the company was immediate and brutal. Two days after the article ran, while Lois worked the midnight shift with crew four in the concentrator, she saw the article tacked to a bulletin board in the hallway at work. Someone had scrawled a word on the clipping: *cunt*. From then on, whenever Lois and Pat walked into a room, conversation stopped. Wherever they went, they were met with hostile stares. Lois and Pat, however, were not the only ones who were given the cold shoulder; many of the men believed that all the women were involved.

One day not long after the suit was filed, a large group of workers waited for the elevator on the ground floor of the concentrator at shift change. Kathy Anderson was among those in front. Kathy hadn't even joined the lawsuit yet, but there were rumors that she was planning to. "The elevator came down and Kathy got in alone and everybody stood there," remembers Diane Hodge. "And all these guys were in front of me, I couldn't get past these guys anyway. They all just stood there and watched the elevator doors shut, and she went up. I was so embarrassed for her I thought, she must be *dying* in there." It was one of the most painful moments Diane had witnessed at work. It also made her afraid. "It was like, Oh no, I'm not dealing with this. I just wanted to be left alone, you know?" Diane made a mental note: If that is what happened to women who were suspected of joining the lawsuit, then it was something she did not want to happen to her.

"In 1988, when the suit was filed, a lot of the guys more or less shied away from Lois. They wouldn't go on the elevator with her," recalled one male miner. "I didn't stop talking to Lois, and most of the guys would come up to me and say, 'Aren't you afraid you'll get involved in the case?'"

"Anyone who had anything to do with me was shunned," Lois recalled. "My crew paid a dear price for associating with me. If I was seen walking down the hall, no one would come up to me except my crew, and it pissed a lot of people off. I watched everything I did, knowing it was being interpreted."

In June of 1988, the mine reactivated its second pellet plant production line, bringing its capacity to the highest level it had been in six years. In July and August, Joan Hunholz, Marcy Steele, Diane Hodge, and Jan Friend, and a half-dozen other women came back to work after being laid off for three to five years. During the layoff everyone had taken low-paying odd jobs to try to make ends meet. Diane and Marcy had even started a house cleaning service. But by 1988, the women were broke and needed their jobs back. From the point of view of job security—or insecurity—Lois's lawsuit could not have been more ill-timed.

The publication of the Duluth *News Tribune* article turned the women's dry from a sanctuary to a battleground. Joan Hunholz and Jan Friend, who had never been friends of Lois's, led the forces against the lawsuit. Marcy Steele tried to stay neutral. The other women, after much cajoling and confusion, fell into line behind one of the three factions. Lois and Pat knew they were up against heavy artillery. Jan Friend advertised her take-no-prisoners style on her locker where she posted a picture of a vulture. It was captioned: "I'm 51% sweetheart, 49% bitch, don't push it." Jan was angry and foul-mouthed. Joan Hunholz was calculating and cunning. The Mickey Mouse tattoo on her left hand between her thumb and index finger sent a deceptively cute message about her personality. Joan hung an air freshener on the front of her locker with a picture of a Chippendale male stripper in swimming trunks.

The stickers, posters, and pictures the women put on their lockers in the dry were their calling cards. Marcy Steele had a goofy sense of humor and a soft, easygoing manner. The sign on her locker read, "If your job is getting you down, don't worry be happy." Diane Hodge's locker poster said, "Do not disturb, I'm already disturbed enough." Denise Vesel, a tall, muscular woman who spent most of her time outside of work on the backseat of her husband's Harley-Davidson, had a bumper sticker on her locker that said, "If you don't like what you see, lower your expectations." Vesel had a tattoo of the Pink Panther on her left forearm and a large three-headed eagle on her right shoulder. In 1977, she spent the night in jail for punching a policeman who pulled her over for drunk driving.

Before the publication of the Duluth *News Tribune* story, several of the women miners seemed on the brink of joining the lawsuit. Lois had kept her folder with the articles about sexual harassment in her locker. During breaks she held tutorials on sexual harassment for anyone who would listen. On July 27, 1988, Lois wrote in her journal:

> *Diane seemed upset. I told her to just be herself. We discussed at length what harassment meant. Denise Vesel seems sure she wants to go with it. Marcy is undecided but will be a witness. They are forever talking about it but are afraid. Gave Denise article about Sprenger and his phone number.*

The negative reaction of the men following news of the lawsuit put a temporary halt to Lois's campaign. Marcy found herself in the uncomfortable position of arbiter. "I was caught between two camps. I was more pro-Lois, but I didn't have the guts to join her. The way I saw it, everyone wanted to be liked and popular. It was a high school scenario."

At dawn on August 27, after working the midnight shift, Lois came home to a ringing telephone. Marcy Steele had bad news. After hanging up the phone, Lois wrote in her diary:

1) *Joan Hunholz circulated a petition among the girls against our complaint. I do not know wording at this time.*

2) *Joan told all the girls, anyone who joins will lose their jobs.*

3) *Steve Grahavic will not get in elevators with women because of this.*

4) *Jan, Diane, Denise, Loretta, Marge, Percy, Michelle, and Joan have signed it. Marcy and Marcella Nelson had not at this point. Joan had treated her with contempt. They weren't going to talk to her. She felt pressured.*

5) *They plan to post it, send it to the* Duluth News *and attorney and company.*

Lois did not know what to do. At Marcy's urging, she called Jean Boler at home to tell her about the petition and find out what could be done. Boler told her that there was nothing they could do. What she did not tell Lois was that the petition had the potential to kill the class. "If a group of women who are in the prospective class say they want no part of it, that alone could be enough to prevent the judge from certifying a class," she said later.

Lois and Pat decided that "we would say nothing," said Lois. "Our game plan was to be as neutral and calm as possible on the outside. But inside, we were a wreck." At this stage, all Lois and Pat had was each other; most of the women had stopped talking to them. "We could open up to each other and vent, but we could also burn each other out," said Lois.

On September 10, 1988, two weeks after Lois's conversation with Marcy, Lois reported to work at 11:00 P.M. for the midnight shift. She walked into the dry, glanced at the bulletin board, and spotted a piece of white paper with a long column of signatures on it. Lois stepped up closer and read:

PETITION
Petition against the
HARRASSMENT/DISCRIMINATION LAW SUIT:
at EVELETH MINES

We the undersigned, do not believe, that the law suit filed by Lois Jenson; Gilbert, and Pat Kosmach; Eveleth, are in the best interests of all the females workers employed at Eveleth Mines. We do not agree with or support the Law Suit.

We, here in sign, petitioning against the Law Suit:
Joan Hunholz
Janice Friend
Denise Vesel
Marjorie Tolbert
J. M. Zdrasky
Deborah Sersha
Priscilla Robich
Loretta Hendrickson
Diane Hodge
Michelle Naughton
Evelyn Cadeau

Lois walked out of the dry and found a second copy of the petition on the lunchroom bulletin board. Then she spotted another one under glass on the company bulletin board. At least Marcy had not signed it. In all, she counted seven petitions. She even discovered one surrounded by pin-ups on the wall in the truck shop. She carefully folded one copy of the petition and tucked it in her pocket to send to Boler. The others she left in place. Lois returned to the truck shop at lunch break with her camera, and took a picture of the petition posted there, surrounded by pornographic pin-ups. What a slap in the face to Joan, thought Lois. It proved that no matter what they did, the women still couldn't get respect.

When she got home from work at dawn, Lois called Michele Mesich in the Cities for moral support. "That petition just about killed her," said Michele. "The women wouldn't talk to Lois, they ignored her. They were worse than the men. You'd think they would stick together. The guys did."

Pat understood why the women signed the petition. She knew they were afraid for their jobs, that they did it out of pure fear. Even so, it was painful for her, too. "I was totally ostracized," Pat said. "[People who] over the years had always said hi, a friendly hi, no longer knew me or saw me."

Lois could never bring herself to confront any of the women who signed the petition, and as a result, her anger began to chip away at her spirit and confidence.

The next day, September 11, Lois reported to work as a grinding mill helper in the concentrator. Her responsibilities included checking the densities and temperature of the hot black sludge, or "concentrate," that fed the ball mills and rod mills. That day, the rod mills were down and being worked on by a dozen maintenance men. As Lois walked up to the second deck where the rod mills were being fixed, she noticed that the soot-black walls were covered with the words *fuck the women* and *fuck you cunts* written in white chalk. Where there was not enough room, the writers settled for "FTW." The maintenance men pretended Lois was not there.

Lois began to go about her business, checking oil pressures, temperatures, and the belts that fed the mills. When she came to the number two rod mill, she noticed a rope that was draped over a hose hook about chest high. It was knotted like a noose. For a moment, Lois imagined that it was meant to be a message to her, but she quickly dismissed the idea as mere paranoia and went back to work.

She went to the other side of the concentrator to take samples. When she returned a few minutes later, the rope had been moved. It was now draping over the edge of a ball bucket, about eye level, where she could not help but see it. "When I first saw it, even though it scared me, I wasn't going to jump to conclusions," Lois said. "When I saw it a second time and it was put right where I couldn't miss it, I knew it was intended for me. I was absolutely shaken and terrified. I was stiff, shaking, telling myself 'you have to stay in control.' I didn't leave. I had to do my job."

Despite Lois's complaints, the noose stayed where it was for several more days. Slowly, her fear turned into anger. She wanted to take a picture of it to send to Boler, but there were always too many people around.

In September of 1988, as the reverberations of the lawsuit and the petition shook the mine, Bob Klasnya started his job as the mine's administrator of records and benefits. He reported to the director of personnel, Bob Raich. Klasnya, a thoughtful man, tall and lanky, graduated from Hibbing High in 1957. He promptly left the Iron Range for college in Minneapolis, and except for the occasional holiday, never looked back. In 1988, Klasnya, the only child of a U.S. Steel miner, had to move back to Hibbing to take care of his ailing father. He left behind a life in Seattle where he had worked as the director of employee relations at Rainier Pacific Bank. Out of work, and with more than fifteen years of personnel relations experience under his belt, Klasnya asked his childhood acquaintance Bob Raich for a job. Klasnya was clearly overqualified. Rainier Bank had 5,000 employees. The mine had 643.

Rainier also had a sexual harassment policy and a complaint procedure. Sixty percent of the bank's workforce was comprised of women, but there were very few incidents or complaints. "Once you have a policy in place and a grievance procedure internally, it's pretty hard to bring a sexual harassment suit," observed Klasnya. At Eveleth, "we had nothing." Even though he had grown up on the Iron Range, Klasnya had been away long enough to be struck by the way the men treated the women at the mine. "A large group of people were very antiwomen, and they said a lot of crude things about the women. Their general argument was that the women had it good and they shouldn't complain. What do they expect, working in a man's job?"

Every morning at 7:30, Klasnya and Raich met at the parking lot of Suburban Lanes bowling alley on Route 37 to carpool to work. On the daily eighteen-mile drive, Raich would often tell Klasnya that the biggest mistake he ever made was hiring women. Raich complained that the women had no business working in the mine, their stories were made up, and Lois was a troublemaker. Klasnya took note of Raich's opinions. "His beliefs were very deep and very backward," Klasnya later recalled.

Late in the fall, Stan Daniels asked Raich to submit a settlement proposal to Oglebay Norton. Daniels suggested that the company offer to institute a formal sexual harassment policy, and to pay Pat and Lois a total of $5,000. Raich later told Klasnya that he submitted the proposal to management in Cleveland, and the response had been "fuck 'em." Raich and the other local managers took that as a directive, and it became their official attitude toward the litigation.

Klasnya was concerned by the company's and Raich's approach, if only because he thought the company was exposing itself to potentially significant liability. The management in Cleveland "knew nothing about the conditions in the mine." They would fly into Hibbing in their corporate jet, where Klasnya would pick them up and drive them to Forbes. There, they would spend the day in the conference room at the general office discussing tonnage, capital improvements, and the budget. "Sometimes there would be a superficial plant tour—they would drive around and look inside one of the buildings," said Klasnya.

A few months after the suit was filed a representative from Ford, one of the mine's co-owners, came to the mine for a board meeting. He stopped by Klasyna's office after the meeting to ask about the sexual harassment suit. He said that Ford had a sexual harassment policy, and he would be happy to have his personnel people help Eveleth draft a policy of its own. When he reiterated his offer to Raich, Raich said, "We don't have a problem. We don't need a policy on sexual harassment." The man from Ford just shrugged his shoulders and said, "Well, I offered."

After this visit, Klasnya realized that urging settlement would not be in his best interest. Raich had worked at the mine since 1965, and knew nothing else. "As Oglebay Norton began preparing for their defense," recalled Klasnya, "Bill Ruf the VP for personnel and industrial relations, was on the phone every afternoon with Raich. His position was the women don't have a case, and we're going to fight it." Any attempts Klasnya made to try to explain sexual harassment to him and others in the office fell on deaf ears. Klasnya resolved that his job would be to do whatever he could to protect the company from liability.

The opening salvos in the discovery battle in the *Jenson* case came with both sides lobbing interrogatories and requests for documents at each other. The week after Christmas, Boler sent Lois the company's first request for documents and information from her, along with an explanatory letter. The company asked for all documents in her possession or control relating to her employment at Eveleth, her grievance, her administrative complaint, her claims against the company, and her monetary demands. They also asked for all of her medical records, as well as all documents that might become evidence in the lawsuit, and all documents that might touch on the lawsuit in any way. The company also sent a fifteen-page interrogatory that included a staggeringly broad range of questions: every place she had ever lived, gone to school, or worked; every criminal or other legal action she had ever been involved with; every person who had any knowledge about her claims, or who might be called as a witness, and why; every specific fact relating to her claims; every action of the company that gave rise to her claims, including every incident of sexual harassment; and every fact that supported her claim for damages and other relief.

Two questions at the end hinted that the company planned to base its defense on a blame-the-victim, nuts-and-sluts strategy. Question 41 stated: "If you have ever uttered a swear word or made an obscene gesture while on a job site owned by the Defendants, . . . state in specific detail each and every such utterance and/or describe in specific details the gesture made." Lois answered that she seldom used the word *fuck*. *On the few occasions I have used it, it has been in front of my crew in the last two-year period. And when I say it they know that I have been pushed to the max.*

Question 42 stated: "If you have ever engaged in any affectional [*sic*] conduct while on a job site owned by any of the defendants, including but not limited to kissing, touching or embracing, describe in specific detail the nature of the conduct, state the date and locations of the conduct, and identify all persons involved and all persons witnessing same." Lois answered, *I have not touched, hugged or kissed anyone on company property, including my husband with two exceptions: Wayne Hill's retirement party—a kiss on the cheek, and when Charles Novak retired—a hug.*

On January 1, 1989, Paul Sprenger and Jane Lang made their professional partnership official. Sprenger & Associates became Sprenger & Lang. The new firm was seeking discovery of its own: requests for Eveleth Mine's hiring and promotion records and applicant files; interrogatories regarding hiring and promotion practices, sexual harassment complaints, and human resources policies and procedures.

While Lois worked on the answers to the interrogatories, Pat took time off from work. A year earlier, Pat had twisted her ankle and it never healed. She visited chiropractors, massage therapists, and several doctors on the Iron Range, but no one could help her. The problems with her ankle started to move up into her leg. Pat wasn't in severe pain, but her leg was shrinking and she walked with a limp. On January 8, 1989, after testing negative for a spinal tumor, silent diabetes, and multiple sclerosis, doctors at the University of Minnesota Hospital in Minneapolis told Pat that she had Lou Gehrig's disease, or amyotrophic lateral sclerosis (ALS).

Pat's doctors explained that the disease causes the degeneration of the motor nerves. When the muscles stop receiving impulses from the nerves they atrophy, causing loss of all motor control and eventually the ability to breathe or swallow. Fifty percent of all ALS patients die within eighteen months, only 20 percent survive for five years after they are diagnosed. The doctors gave Pat one to three years to live.

Pat took the news with her usual wisdom and humor. "The night she found out what was wrong with her she said, 'You gotta be careful of what you wish for, because I said that I just wanted to live long enough to get you all on your feet,'" recalls Pat's daughter Bobbie. Pat's only son, Robbie, had just announced that he was getting married, and Brenda was getting a much-needed divorce. All five of her children were adults and self-sufficient.

One of Pat's daughters called Jeanne Aho that night to tell her about the diagnosis. Jeanne told her boyfriend, who went to an Elk's Club meeting a few nights later and told Michelle Naughton's husband about Pat's disease. Michelle had signed the petition against the lawsuit and was no friend of Pat Kosmach's. The next morning, January 24, 1989, when Lois walked into the dry, she still did not know anything about Pat's ALS. The first thing that came out of Michelle Naughton's mouth was the news that Pat had Lou Gehrig's disease. *I was so angry*, Lois wrote in her diary. *I know Pat wanted Jeannie to keep it quiet, but Jeannie's boyfriend told Shelly's husband and before the first half hour the whole plant knew.*

"I felt terrible," said Aho. "Pat wanted to be able to tell people in her own time. I never would have told Michelle myself—there was so much animosity there."

When Lois finished work, she drove straight over to Pat's trailer. She told Pat that she would respect whatever decision Pat made about continuing the lawsuit, and that she would understand if she chose to drop out of the case and concentrate on her health. Pat said that she was determined to stay with the case; she just hoped that the trial would start soon enough so she could walk into the courtroom on her own without having to use a wheelchair. Lois left Pat's trailer thinking, "She's a gutsy lady." At Pat's request, Lois went home and called Michele Mesich, and the lawyers to give them the bad news.

On January 29, 1989, Lois wrote in her diary: *For my eyes only! Today Jeff Nelson was making remarks about the collection for Patty. "The bitch is suing us and we are supposed to give her money. It's nothing that a good f— wouldn't cure."*

In addition to conducting discovery, Sprenger and Boler were considering whether to amend the complaint to add two additional elements. First, they decided that they needed to have at least one more lead plaintiff—one who worked in the pit. They were concerned that the judge might decide that Lois and Pat were not adequate representatives of a class that included employees who worked in the pit, since they themselves never had. In addition, Boler believed that the women in the pit had it even worse in a lot of ways, and that it was important to be able to show what was going on there. If the class did not include women in the pit, all the evidence might not be allowed to come in at trial.

They focused their attention on Kathy Anderson, who worked in the pit driving heavy machinery. Pat and Lois were still skeptical of including her. But Lois and Pat could not deny that her stories—being punched by Frank Lipka and being stranded with no bathroom in the pit—certainly merited legal action. "I tried to tell Paul that there were some people who should probably come into the case later," said Lois. "But he wouldn't listen because they wanted bodies for the class. No one would listen to me because they thought I was backstabbing."

Sprenger was a little skeptical of Kathy, too, but for a different reason. Stan Daniels was married to Kathy's sister. Sprenger worried that she might be close to him. But Boler was convinced that they needed to add her in order to be able to tell the whole story of what was happening at Eveleth Mines. Boler called Kathy on the phone, and later met with her in person, to see if she wanted to put her name on the complaint. When Boler first approached Kathy, she said, "You mean sue them for everything they did to me? Sure." Boler also discovered that Kathy hated her brother-in-law, and felt no conflict of interest joining the case on Stan Daniels's account. Also, Kathy's husband, George, did not object to Kathy's participation in the lawsuit.

They also decided that they had to amend the complaint to make the union a party to the case. Lois and Pat's claims were not against the union, or even against any individual employees or union members. Their claims were against the company. But one of the things they were asking the court to do was to order the company to adopt an anti–sexual harassment policy and a meaningful process for addressing specific incidents of sexual harassment.

Sprenger was troubled by a recent case in the Eighth Circuit in which the court had denied class certification in an employment discrimination case because the employees' union had not been made a party to the case. The court's reason was that the employees were suing for relief that included changes in corporate hiring, employment, and disciplinary practices, which might require modifications to the collective bargaining agreement between the union and the company. Therefore, the court held that if the union were not a party to the case, the court could not order the union to make the necessary changes to the agreement.

Sprenger realized that the same could be said of his case. He knew that naming the union as a defendant was risky. Even if it would only be what is called a "nonaligned party" or a "relief defendant," meaning that it was not charged with liability or fault, that distinction might be lost on the union members. All they would know is that they were being sued by the women. Sprenger knew that once the union members believed that the women were suing them, as opposed to the company, all hell would break loose. Northern Minnesota was, after all, union country. Suing the union, even for technical reasons, would be viewed a lot differently from suing the company. But Sprenger knew the judge might easily conclude that the case could not go forward without the union.

Sprenger decided to try to persuade the union to join the plaintiffs.

"I called Richard Kaspari, the union's lawyer at the time, to see if they could get the union to come in as a nonaligned party, or even as a plaintiff. I knew Kaspari from other cases, and I knew he would understand the situation." Sprenger explained to Kaspari that the women needed to have the union be a part of the suit one way or another, but they would prefer not to name it as a defendant. They were not seeking any finding by the court that the union had been at fault in any way, and they were not seeking any money from the union. Besides, he said, these women were union members. Pat Kosmach was a union official. It would be natural for the union to want to take their side. At the very least, Sprenger said, the union should want to be neutral. Kaspari called back to say that he had consulted with his client, and the union had refused to participate voluntarily. "I think Kaspari was sympathetic, but he was stymied by his clients," said Sprenger.

On February 8, 1989, six months after Sprenger had first filed suit, he filed the amended complaint. It had been almost a full year since he had met Lois and Pat. The complaint included Kathy Anderson as a plaintiff and the union as defendant. Although the latter change was necessary from a legal perspective, from a personal perspective it would prove to be fateful for the women. Now they were taking on not just the management of the company, somewhere in Cleveland, but the most powerful organization on the Iron Range and, by extension, every single laborer at Eveleth Mines. "Naming the union pushed the union and the company into bed together, when they usually have a very antagonistic relationship," said Bob Klasnya.

It was particularly painful for Pat Kosmach. "It was horrifying to Pat when we filed suit against the union," said Michele Mesich. "The union oath said you don't turn in your union brother or sister. Pat truly, honestly lived, breathed, and believed that everything the union did was right."

A few weeks after the amended complaint was filed, Lois invited all the hourly female miners and a handful of salaried women at Eveleth to a meeting to discuss the case. Sprenger, Lang, and Boler would be at her apartment on the evening of February 27. On February 15, Lois sent out a typed form letter that read in part:

No matter what your feelings are regarding these proceedings, they will have an effect on you. We do care and therefore urge you to come to this meeting and ask questions. Nothing will be assumed by your attendance and if you wish privacy, we will make those arrangements.

Gloria Husby, an accounting clerk, received Lois's letter and knew she was holding a stick of dynamite. Gloria's boss, the comptroller, told her and the other women who worked in the accounting department, "Don't even think about going to those meetings. Someone is going to watch everyone who goes in there." For Gloria and the other salaried women, joining Lois's lawsuit was riskier than it was for the laborers, because they did not have union protection. Management had full leeway when it came to firing salaried employees.

A few weeks after the meeting, Gloria ran into Lois at the Virginia public library. Gloria was afraid to be seen in public with Lois, but she tentatively approached Lois who told her about the lawsuit. Gloria whispered, "I want you to know how much we're supporting you." When Lois asked why she and the other salaried women wouldn't join the suit, she said, "They have told us that if we join, we'll lose our jobs. Oh, the things I could tell you that have happened to us. We're behind you one hundred percent. None of us is brave enough to join."

Lois handed Gloria Paul Sprenger's card. She tucked it in her pocket and walked away as quickly as possible. Gloria kept the card in her wallet for years, but never called him.

Paul Sprenger and Jane Lang attended the meeting in Lois's apartment in Gilbert, where from the terrace you could see the Fairlane plant pluming smoke on the horizon. By 8:00 P.M., Pat, Kathy, Marcella Nelson, and two salaried workers named Sharon Rossi and Jeanie

Desnosier had arrived. But after another thirty minutes no one else had shown up. All day, Lois had fielded last-minute cancellations. Jan said she had to go to the bank. Joan said she was going shopping. Marcy said she had to go to her aunt's wake. Later, Marcy confided in Lois that "as long as the guys know we aren't participating in the suit, we're okay." Lois was bitterly disappointed.

Determined to sign up more women, Lois tacked a glowing newspaper profile of Paul Sprenger to the bulletin board in the dry along with his business card. The next morning, Sprenger's press photograph had grown a mustache, beard, and devil horns. The following week, his card was gone. Undeterred, Lois put a new card up. Later, Joan arrived in the women's dry, fuming about "these fucking people who sue for everything." She muttered that it was no wonder insurance rates were so high. Later, when Lois heard her complaining about something Bob Raich had done, Lois yelled back at her, "Join the suit!"

A perpetual "should I, shouldn't I" debate seesawed among the women. Lois started taking detailed notes of conversations that she overheard or took part in. She would work a full shift at the plant, then go home and write notes about what went on that day. She filled a green spiral notebook with scraps of paper on which she had jotted down dialogue at work. Once every few weeks, she would write long letters to the lawyers reporting on the soap opera of events at the mine.

Four days after the meeting with the lawyers, Marcy Steele said that she would agree to give a deposition about what went on at the mine, but she still did not want to be part of the suit. Three days later she changed her mind:

> 3/3/89 Marcy asked for sheet back, does not want involvement—information about certain men, what she knew about the guys that could be used in the lawsuit. Stish "Big Red," "threatened to hit me. I told him to go ahead, I'll join Lois's suit. I'll be rich. He said, no you won't, you'll be dead. He repeated it twice." It was only a joke, but it scared her.

On April 17, 1989, Lois chronicled the following scene in the dry:

Diane and Denise have been fighting. Denise has been calling Diane a F— C—, etc. . . . on and off the job.

Joan: "Women shouldn't be putting other women down. We have to take it from the men but we don't need it from other women."

Stan snubbing me, won't say hi etc. . . .

Meanwhile, Lois's relationship with Pat was strained. At home all day, Pat was depressed and slowly losing control of more and more of her muscles. Lois visited Pat regularly. Pat's weak condition drained Lois of all her energy. "It had a huge effect on me," she said. Lois wrote to Lang in her letter that Pat's impatience with the slowness of the legal process was magnified because of her ALS. Delays were a life and death issue now for Pat, not just a casual frustration. *How do I keep her jets cooled?* Lois wrote Lang.

How do I tell her that she is important to this and yet tell her to be patient. We all want it settled but not at the point of settling for less. This is what we fought for. Now, it's a new game plan for her and the old one for me. I feel so cold when I now hear, at a very precise time, "Did I tell you that my symptoms are going into the other leg or arms?" And it's always timed just right. In my eyes, right or wrong, she is getting to me. . . . I have determined to not talk to Pat unless something comes up that must be shared.

Lois, in her new custom of turning her lawyers into personal confidants, allowed at the end of the letter that she wished Pat could be as happy as she. *I'm in a situation (at least personally) where I'm the happiest I've been in years.* For almost a year, Lois had been dating a man named Joe Bjergo. She had not been romantically involved since her

1983 divorce from Plesche. At forty, with no more responsibilities for the twenty-year-old Greg, who had a serious girlfriend and worked odd jobs while living in Hibbing and attending the community college there, Lois was free and healthy enough to kick up her heels. "JoeB" had his own custom-car-painting business, collected old cars, and lived in Minneapolis. They met at Mugga's at a birthday party for a female bartender who was a mutual friend. As she later described their meeting, it was "click, click, click." Their bartender friend gave Joe a lecture on how to treat Lois, which got them off to a good start. "He came up here to hunt. We'd go fishing together. He'd take me out on his motorcycle or convertible, and we'd go dancing. He showed respect and attention to me when we were out." JoeB also took Lois on glamorous vacations. He flew her to Cabo San Lucas, Mexico—it was the first time Lois had seen the ocean. On Lois's birthday they drove to Boulder City, Nevada, together. "Every time I had to come home from vacation, I'd cry like a baby," she said. "He got me through a lot."

Lois was in love, but her dogged pursuit of the case had become an obsession that was testing not only her friends and family, but her lawyers and Joe, too. "If a person only talks about one thing, you get pretty tired of hearing about the same thing," said her sister Marilyn. "No matter what the topic of conversation was, Lois would always come back to the lawsuit." But Lois, convinced that she was right, believed that everyone else would share her indignation and come to see the case as she did. Her holier-than-thou attitude rubbed some of the women the wrong way. On April 4, 1989, Lois wrote in her diary: *Jan, Joan, Diane, and Denise were having a fight—Jan looked at me and said, "Don't you sometimes feel that people think that you are a self-righteous bitch?"*

CHAPTER NINE

Men Under Oath

Spring 1989

In May 1989, the men got the chance to tell their side of the story. Sprenger & Lang started taking depositions from salaried supervisors in the mine, working their way up to the senior management in Cleveland. Sprenger and Boler were both swamped with other cases that spring, so Sprenger sent Becky Troth, a young associate, to Duluth to take the depositions of LeRoy Stish, Nick Senich, and Milan Lolich. Richard Leighton, Erickson's associate, represented the company.

Stish, a foreman in the fine crusher when Judy Jarvela worked there, confirmed that Judy had complained to him about being stalked by Gene New. He claimed to have told his supervisor about it. A little while later, he checked with Judy to see if Gene had stopped following her around. She said he had, so Stish figured the problem had been taken care of. He never spoke directly to New, even though he was New's immediate supervisor. Stish also confirmed that someone had been ejaculating in Judy's locker. He thought it was inappropriate, but never took any steps to find out who had done it, or to prevent it from happening again. He explained that he was a union member, and that it was management's—not his—responsibility to handle disciplinary problems.

Troth brought out a series of pictures that Lois had taken at work.

One by one, she placed them on the table and asked Stish if he had seen them at work. The first one was a picture of a man with his face crammed into a woman's crotch. Stish had not seen that one. Then came a picture of an obese woman, with the caption "AIDS prevention week poster girl." No. Then a picture of a naked woman with the caption "Nice pussy." No. Then a picture of a naked woman stretched out, with a penis drawn underneath her. No. Then a poster advertising a bare-breasted stripper. That one, Stish admitted, he had seen.

As Stish glanced at each picture, Troth was aware of the fact that she was the only woman in the room. Even the court reporter was male. At first, she felt uncomfortable and self-conscious. Then it dawned on her that, in fact, the men—all of them—were even more uncomfortable than she was. Stish squirmed slightly in his chair, and his answers contracted to monosyllables. "Good," she thought. "At least they can still be embarrassed by this stuff."

Then Troth showed him grainy black-and-white photographs that Lois had taken of graffiti, and read the words out loud. "I think this picture says something like, 'I eat cocks and lots of it.' " The words hung in the air for a moment. Then Leighton, who appeared to be feeling as uncomfortable as Stish, said, "I object to counsel's testimony. The exhibit speaks for itself."

The next picture, which had been found in the crusher, was of a topless woman. When Troth put it down, she said, "Since Mr. Leighton doesn't like my characterizations of the pictures, what is that picture, Mr. Stish?"

"Outline."

"Of what?"

"Woman's body."

"Nude woman's body?"

"Not necessarily."

"Mr. Stish?"

"She could have clothes on."

"Is the top portion nude?"

"I don't know."

"Mr. Stish, you can see nipples on that picture, can't you?"

"Some clothes you can see through," Stish said defiantly.

Later, Stish recalled that in July 1987, John Niemi told him to paint over all of the graffiti in his area. Because supervisors did not paint walls, he told the painting crew to take care of it. Stish also said that a few months after that, he had opened his own locker in front of Pat Kosmach and Evelyn Cadeau, in order to give them supplies. On the inside door, in plain sight, there was a poster of a naked woman with her legs spread, touching herself. Stish explained that it was not his poster: It had been there when he was assigned the locker. He did not take it down because it was not his. He left it there when he was assigned another locker a few years later. For all he knew, it was still there.

Then Troth asked him whether he had told Marcy Steele that if she joined Lois's lawsuit she would be dead.

"No, I don't think so, no."

After Troth reminded him about the penalties for perjury, he became less certain.

"But if she said it happened, it may have happened?" Troth asked.

"It's possible."

The next morning, it was Nick Senich's turn. Senich, a maintenance foreman in the concentrator, had been a miner since he was discharged from the army in 1946. He had worked for Eveleth since 1965. Senich's definition of sexual harassment was "beating up a woman or continually pestering her." He said that in his view, it was not sexual harassment if a supervisor told an employee that he would give her a better job if she dated him. He admitted that a week before the deposition, Raich had called him down to talk about the deposition. Raich told him that he had been "charged" in the lawsuit.

"Did he tell you what the charges were?"

"Well, about pinching the girls on the cheek, which I've been doing for how many years? Even babies I pinch on the cheek. I don't do it to hurt them. And I was supposed to have said something to Mrs. Anderson that I don't recall I ever said." Senich denied ever seeing any of the particular exhibits that Troth showed him. He also said the company routinely "took care of" graffiti right away.

Senich did admit to joking with the men on his crew about oral sex.

"When you were at work you'd often ask the men if they'd eaten at the Y last night?"

"Yes, I'm not going to lie to you. I have. That was a standing joke out there with all the young guys."

"And you'd say that in front of the women?"

"I never recall saying it in front of any women. But I've said it to the guys, a lot of the young kids."

"What did you mean by that comment?"

"It was just a joke, really, is what it was."

"And what did you mean when you asked if they'd eaten at the Y?"

"What did I mean by it? Just wanted to see what their reaction was . . ."

"You were not asking them if they'd eaten at the YMCA, were you?"

"No, I didn't ask them that."

"And then what did you mean when you asked, did you eat at the Y last night?"

"What do you mean, what did I ask? I asked if you ever eat pussy. Is that what you want to know? That's what I asked them, yes. More than once I asked those kids that, but it's a standing joke out there with everybody."

"And you would say that when there were women around?"

"They might have been. I don't know. I said it so damned often."

Senich was defensive about using the word *cunt* as well.

"Is that language you use?"

"Everyday language out there. I'm not the only one. Maybe ninety percent of the guys use it at one time or another."

Troth realized that Senich, like many of the men there, simply did not understand that his behavior might be offensive to women. When Troth circled back and asked Senich whether he had ever pinched Lois's cheeks, he replied:

"I've pinched the cheeks of a lot of women, girls, out there. I pinch them at the bar every day."

"And you hugged Lois Jenson?"

"If you call putting an arm around her. I've never put my arms around her and squeezed her or made passes at her."

"Lois has told you she didn't like it, didn't she?"

"I can't recall, really. She might have."

"Didn't she tell you that?"

"I'm not the only one that's ever put arms around her. I seen other people do it, too. . . . If that is harassment, cripe."

Senich admitted that he may have asked Kathy Anderson whether her then fiancé George Anderson "ate pussy," but he said it was said in "a joking manner." When asked whether anyone had told him that that kind of language was inappropriate in the workplace, he said, "Never heard anyone bitch about it ever."

When Troth asked Senich whether any of his supervisors had ever told him to stop swearing, he recalled that Corky Krollman, who was Senich's supervisor for a time, told him on several occasions, " 'Senich, clean up your fucking act.' "

With that, Leighton's head fell to the table.

In the *Meritor* case, in which the Supreme Court first recognized that the existence of a hostile work environment could be a form of sex discrimination, the Court had made clear that a company could be liable for a hostile work environment if it had not adopted and implemented an anti–sexual harassment policy. Up until now, most of Sprenger & Lang's discovery had focused on what had happened in the mine. Now it was time to try to find out what the company had known about what was going on at the mine, and what, if anything, it had tried to do about it.

The first step was to depose in Cleveland members of Oglebay Norton's senior management who were responsible for managing Eveleth Mines. Paul Sprenger and Jane Lang liked to depose CEOs and other senior management themselves—chieftain to chieftain. But Sprenger was swamped, so even though Lang had tried to avoid the nitty-gritty of sexual harassment cases ever since the G.E. case, she agreed to go to Cleveland in June 1989. She started with William Ruf, Oglebay's vice president of industrial relations and personnel, who was accompanied by Erickson. Ruf explained that he set the company's general EEOC policy statements, but that the responsibility for enforcing those policies and responding to employee complaints belongs to the company's top EEOC person. At the time of the deposition, it was Paul Gorman. Ruf was also responsible for negotiating the company's labor agreements. Ruf explained that Bob Raich and his subordinate Milan Lolich were responsible for hiring bargaining unit, or union, laborers. He had no direct involvement with hiring beneath management level.

When Lang asked Ruf what Oglebay Norton's policy was toward sexual harassment he replied, "We are against it." But he admitted that the policy had never been communicated to Eveleth Mines or any other subsidiary, even though the company was concerned that there might be sexual harassment of its female employees when it began hiring women in the mining operations. Ruf explained that he did not think a formal written policy was necessary, because "to me it was common sense."

Ruf admitted that the company was aware that there had been complaints about sexual harassment from time to time at Eveleth, but "I did not feel [they] were cases where women were being discriminated against. It was the use of sexual overtones or things of that nature—*Playboy* pictures on the wall, for instance, those kinds of things that the women found objectionable, but I don't think they were directed at sexual harassment or at trying to prevent them from being promoted." Ruf said he toured the Eveleth sites on average twice a year. Lang asked if he saw photographs "of a sexual nature" on the walls or bulletin boards during those tours.

"If you say that *Playboy* is sexual in nature, yes." But, he added, there was no problem with that kind of thing "unless they were objected to by somebody." But when Lang showed him the exhibits that Troth had shown to the other men, Ruf seemed genuinely surprised. He said that if he had seen them, he would have "personally" taken them down, and agreed that someone in authority should have done so.

"And why is that, sir?" Lang asked.

"Well, they are crude, objectionable, I can't . . . I don't know how many words you want me to put to them, but they are totally tasteless."

"Do you believe that they constitute sexual harassment?"

"Yes," Ruf admitted.

The next day, Lang deposed Robert Thomas Green, Oglebay Norton's vice president of Iron Ore Operations. The fifty-two-year-old Green was typical of Oglebay Norton senior management: He had never lived on the Range. He had grown up in Ohio, where he attended a private prep school before going on to Amherst College in Massachusetts.

Like Ruf and Gilmore, Green took the position that he had been unaware that there was a problem with sexually explicit materials and language at Eveleth. Although he toured the mines once or twice a year, he focused on production and costs, and did not have any direct contact with the laborers. He had not seen any inappropriate pictures or calendars, but admitted that, before the lawsuit was filed, he was not looking for them. He did say that on a visit to Eveleth a month earlier, having been made aware of the case, he noticed "a calendar of a gal. Being aware of this, I mentioned that I thought that was inappropriate. . . . She wasn't naked or anything, but it was other than in proper taste."

Bemused, Lang replied, "Well, I am glad your consciousness has been raised, sir." Green said, "Well, it has been," whereupon Erickson strenuously objected and demanded that the comment be stricken from the record.

When Lang showed the photo exhibits, Green said that he had never seen them.

"Is the posting of such pictures in offices of foremen compatible with Oglebay Norton Company's policy of equal employment opportunity?" Lang asked.

"You see," Green replied, "I don't know of our policy with respect to that. I am just talking about common decency."

A hint of class bias seeped through much of Green's testimony, as it did through that of other senior management. From their pristine, no-frills headquarters, they seemed to view what happened in the mines with paternalistic detachment. While the exhibits they were shown offended their social sensibilities, they viewed the fact that they were displayed in the mines as inappropriate departures from "proper taste" and "common decency," rather than a potential violation of employees' civil rights.

The same theme was echoed by Richard Harmon, another vice president, who was deposed a year later. After showing Harmon a number of the pictures and graffiti that had been found in the mines, Lang asked: "Is it your view that it is appropriate to display that on the property?"

"Oglebay Norton in Cleveland likes to maintain the sophistication of a corporate headquarters and not a working office . . . I, for example, have pictures of airplanes on my wall, and I have never seen at Eveleth a picture of an airplane."

"Well," Lang said, "I think that you are safe in this lawsuit, then, Mr. Harmon."

A few weeks after Lang returned from Cleveland, Troth returned to Duluth to depose Leon Erickson.* Erickson, a concentrator operating foreman, was openly contemptuous of the women and their sensitivity to the sexually explicit materials in the mine. But by being direct and frank about his attitudes toward the women and the lawsuit, he also offered one of the most revealing glimpses into the attitude of many of the men at the mine. At one point in the deposition he testified that he had had a picture of a topless woman in his locker. He put it up after he had been told by his supervisors to remove sexually explicit pictures following the filing of Lois's lawsuit.

---

*No relation to Ray Erickson or Kent Erickson.

"Did you think that putting it up would violate the company policy against sexual harassment?"

"How does a picture violate company policy on sexual harassment? . . . They had no business in my locker anyway in the first place."

"Who had no business in your locker?"

"Lois."

"So, how did you know that Lois was in your locker?"

"I never said she was in my locker. I said my door was possibly open and she possibly had seen it."

"Why do you think she may have seen it?"

"All the employees go in and out of that office, steady. I'm sure her little eyeballs seen it."

When asked what the men thought of being told to take down other calendars on the walls of the foremen's office, he said, "Everybody thought it was stupid."

"Why did they think it was stupid?"

"If they didn't want to look at them, what the hell did they come down to the office for."

"Who?"

"The women. They're the ones raising all the hell, ain't they?"

Later he admitted that the women frequently had to come into the foreman's office to have work orders signed, or to get gloves or other equipment.

Leon Erickson was also openly defiant about his belief that women simply did not belong in the mines. When he was asked if he had ever heard any of the men at Eveleth express that belief, he replied that "I'd say it myself. For myself, I wouldn't want my wife working there."

"Why?"

"It's dirty. It's filthy. . . . A woman can't handle it."

On January 16, 1990, Lois wrote a letter to Jane Lang that included background information about more of the mine's foremen whom the attorneys were preparing to depose. At the end of her letter, Lois made an ominously prescient remark: "I do wonder about the long-term effects of all the stress. I do wonder what it would be like when all is said and done. I wonder what it would be like to work for a place that I trust (to a point), I can respect (to a point), I wonder what I am (at 42) capable of."

In her gut, Lois feared that the worst was yet to come. Her deposition with Ray Erickson was scheduled for June 1990. It would be the first time she would testify under oath for a legal battle she had been fighting for five years. It was the company's first official opportunity to question Lois and probe her credibility. She began to get anxious as early as a year before she actually sat for the deposition. She felt sure Ray Erickson would fight dirty, probing into the painful parts of her past. The anxiety about the looming deposition made Lois question herself. Maybe she did deserve the harassment. Maybe she really was a self-righteous bitch, as Jan Friend had said.

She felt her resolve cracking. Lois spent several sessions talking about the deposition with her therapist Claire Bell, whom she had begun to see regularly in June 1989. Bell tried to prepare Lois for the deposition by telling her that she should think about every skeleton in her closet. "They are going to be rattling," Bell warned. Jean Boler met with Lois and Pat a week before the deposition—Lois was scheduled for June 6, Pat for June 7—and gave them some basic legal pointers: "Don't guess, don't offer information, don't give away anything, don't lie."

Paul Sprenger knew that Ray Erickson would use the opportunity of his first deposition with Lois to try to intimidate her into dropping the case. On June 6, 1990, Sprenger, who had been spending a considerable amount of time in D.C. working on other cases, made a point of flying in from Washington to be at the deposition at 9:00 A.M. "Depositions," Sprenger said later, "are the toughest place to protect a client because there isn't a trial judge in the room to tell the lawyers to behave themselves."

When Lois, Sprenger, and Boler arrived at the Hanft, Fride, O'Brien's offices on 1000 First Bank Place in Duluth, they were shown into a large conference room with a view of Lake Superior and the massive industrial infrastructure supporting the ore docks and barges. The only person in the room was the court reporter. Erickson made them wait for half an hour, then entered nonchalantly and introduced himself. He had the look of a former quarterback; tall and heavyset with broad shoulders, a full head of sandy-brown hair and a thickset jaw.

They went on the record. Erickson asked Lois a few biographical questions: when and where she had been born, when she graduated from high school, her job history. Then he asked her how many children she had, and their names and birth dates.

"And who is Greg's father?" Erickson asked next. Sprenger objected to the question on the grounds of relevance, and requested that the portion of the deposition pertaining to Greg's father be sealed so that it did not become part of the public record.

"I can't agree to seal a record sight unseen," said Erickson.

"I just don't want any chance that this information becomes a public record," Sprenger responded. The two lawyers argued for more than half an hour about how the information about Greg's conception would be handled. Finally, Erickson granted Sprenger's request that the information be sealed. But the questions continued. Lois told the story of her rape, visiting the police station afterward and walking out, discovering that she was pregnant, working as a nanny for a family who hired her through Lutheran Social Services, and Greg's birth. Lois answered Erickson's questions politely and efficiently with "Yes sir" and "No sir."

Erickson wanted to know if Lois had confronted her rapist. Lois said that she did, two to three weeks after the rape.

"Well, did he tell you in any way, shape, or form that you had enticed him through the incident?"

"He did not blame me for the incident at all, sir."

Erickson wanted to know Lois's exact words. "What did you tell him?"

"I don't really know how to respond to that. At this—in—" Lois fumbled. Her voice started to crack.

Sprenger objected. "I think this may be becoming repetitive and argumentative."

"I don't need the coaching either, counsel," snapped Erickson.

Erickson asked more obvious questions. Then he came to Tamara's birth. When did Lois learn that she was pregnant? Who was her doctor? The same doctor who delivered Greg? Lois explained that after Greg's birth, her doctor told her that she would never be able to conceive again because she had a tilted uterus. He had not prescribed birth control. The second pregnancy, which was with an old childhood friend to whom Lois was engaged, was an unwanted surprise. The fiancé claimed that it was not his child because he had never gotten anyone pregnant before, and he left Lois.

"I notice from your medical records that . . . in 1970 you took an overdose of drugs. Is this approximately the time in which that occurred?"

Again, Sprenger asked for the record to be sealed. Erickson refused.

"Have you, on any occasion, taken an overdose of drugs?" Erickson asked again.

"Yes sir, I did take an overdose of drugs."

"When was it?"

"It was when I was five months pregnant with Greg."

Erickson wanted to know every detail. Where was Lois? What was the drug? Who was her doctor? Which hospital did she go to? Why did she do it?

"I believe, sir, that when I took the overdose I was so angry that I don't know that I knew my intent."

"I'm not asking intent. I'm asking did you know that you were taking more pills than had been prescribed to you?" Erickson wanted to know exactly how many pills of phenobarbital Lois took. What was the prescription? Was there a warning label on the bottle?

"Presumably you took the pills because you didn't want to live any longer. Is that fair to say?"

"That's very straightforward."

"Being straightforward, is it true?"

"Yes sir, that is very true."

"And your intent at that time was to commit not only your own suicide, but that of your child that you were carrying at the time; is that true?"

For a moment, Lois could not speak. Sprenger objected.

Finally, Lois said, "I really don't know how to respond to that. I don't know how to respond to that question, sir."

Erickson didn't let go.

"It's true, is it not, that in taking the overdose, you understood that it would also terminate Greg's life?"

"No sir, it is not true that I took Greg's life into consideration."

"Why didn't you take Greg's life into consideration?"

"At the time of my overdose, I don't believe I was considering the fetus inside me."

"You were considering your own circumstances; is that true?"

"I was considering my anger and my own circumstances."

The worst was over, but they still had a long way to go. Lois waded through the rest of the deposition in a fog. She had just been accused of attempted murder. She answered questions about Tami's birth and her decision to put her up for adoption. He asked her if she had suffered bouts of depression. Then Erickson switched to the subject of her language at work. Had Lois ever said the word *fuck*? She admitted that she had, out of anger, on two or three occasions. She described each in detail. Then he asked her about other women's language at work. Had Diane Hodge ever said it? Had Jan Friend ever said it? What about Michele Mesich? Did Greg ever say it? In her home?

Finally, he asked her about her mental health. When was the last time she had seen a therapist? When was she last admitted to the hospital for stress? Was she currently depressed?

Suddenly, the five-hour ordeal was over. Erickson stood up and strode out of the room. He had not really obtained any information that he did not already have. But he had achieved a strategic victory. He had planted the seeds for the time-tested nuts-and-sluts defense, implying that she was more a victim of her own mistakes and weaknesses than of illegal harassment by the men at the mine. By questioning her use of foul language and that of other women in the mine, he implied that she, and they, were as crude and offensive as the men with whom they worked. And by ending on the note of her mental health history, he had left the impression that she was emotionally and mentally unstable. Most important, Erickson had given Lois a preview of the trial ahead. It was as though he were saying, "This is what you are going to get. Do you really want more?"

After they left the room, Lois was quiet. "I felt like a house had been dropped on my head," she said later. Even Sprenger, who was used to tough depositions, was furious. "Ray Erickson is on my top ten list of assholes," he said later. Lois was so tense as she drove home from Duluth that she could hear her bones cracking. Tears streamed down her cheeks, then stopped, then started again, then intensified, all beyond her control. By the time she pulled into the parking lot of her apartment building she was sobbing and shaking. "I felt horrible because I knew that if I wanted the other women to join the suit, Erickson would do the same to them."

"Lois's first deposition probably marks when it began to get rough for her because the reality started setting in of what this lawsuit meant," said Claire Bell. "The interrogation was intrusive, the questioning was degrading—it was violating." Like many people, Lois had submerged her feelings about the traumas in her past. Now she was forced to face them all at once. "Just think of every painful thing that has happened in your life," said Bell. "And imagine it being brought up by an adverse attorney in some sterile boardroom."

That night, Joe called. Pat called a little later. Lois didn't return their calls. For three days, she didn't talk to anyone. Finally, she called Jane Lang, whose empathy she had come to rely on. Lois apologized to Lang. "I feel like I flunked my whole life," she told the lawyer. Lang tried to think of the right words to comfort her, but she felt helpless. This was why she hated sexual harassment suits so much—they were so painful for the women involved, and at that time there was really nothing the lawyers could do about it.

The second deposition took place six weeks later, on July 20, 1990. This time, Lois had a better idea of what to expect, and so she was even more nervous. The deposition lasted a total of nine hours and twenty minutes. Erickson started out by asking her about the women's petition against Lois and Pat's suit. Why had the women signed it? Didn't it mean that they disagreed with her suit? Lois held her ground, explaining that the women had signed the petition out of fear, to protect themselves from retaliation. He questioned her about the details of her experiences that formed the basis of her complaint. Already, many of the events Lois had to recall had taken place ten, even fifteen years earlier. In such cases, the goal of the defense lawyer is to try to pin a witness down to as much detail as possible, in the hopes that some details of the witness's testimony at trial will differ slightly from what she said in her deposition. Any discrepancy, no matter how minor, can undermine a witness's credibility at trial.

But now it was Erickson's turn to see what he was up against. Lois possessed a remarkable memory. She had also been keeping a diary of events at work since 1987. She calmly and clearly recounted what had happened to her and to other women at Eveleth Mines. She described conversations she had had, supplying details about when and where they had taken place. When shown exhibits of pornographic pictures and graffiti, she could say exactly when and where she had seen them at the mine. It was the first time that she was able to describe her experiences in her own words, on the record.

In June and July of 1990, Erickson traveled to Eveleth to depose Pat Kosmach twice for a total of eight hours. Weakened and in her wheelchair, Kosmach managed a feisty response to most of Erickson's aggressive questioning. He grilled her on everything she knew about Lois and the other women's sexual harassment experiences, as well as her own. At one point near the end of the second deposition, Pat started to get tired and had trouble answering one of Erickson's questions about her out-of-pocket expenses. "If you're not able to do that, then it is really a waste of my time and your time," snapped Erickson.

After Lois's second deposition, Sprenger and Lang flew to Cleveland to discuss settlement with senior Oglebay Norton officials, including their general counsel. Ray Erickson was also present. "It was a very cordial and professional meeting," Lang recalled. "We talked substantively about settlement." Sprenger and Lang were offering to settle the case in exchange for an agreement on the part of Oglebay Norton to adopt a sexual harassment policy, as well as damages of approximately $465,000, plus $210,000 in attorneys' fees and costs.

The company did not make a counterdemand on the spot, but agreed to consider their offer. "We left feeling very optimistic about the prospects for settlement," said Lang. When they returned to Minneapolis, they sent the company a letter formalizing their offer. The letter included specific proposals for an anti–sexual harassment policy and an employee training program. When several weeks had gone by and there had been no response, they again wrote to the company, urging more settlement talks. Again, there was no response.

In the meantime, discovery continued, and Sprenger & Lang's costs and fees continued to rise. Kathy and Pat were deposed, as well as more of the men who worked in the mine. Medical records were gathered, prepared, and turned over. Fresh rounds of document requests were issued and responded to. In October 1990, Jean Boler went to Eveleth Mines to review personnel documents as part of the discovery process. She brought along Ed Bakke, a former accountant in his mid-sixties, who knew his way around documents. Paul Sprenger had hired Bakke to work for the firm as a bookkeeper and trained him to be a legal assistant. The goal of Boler's visit to the mine was to try to establish a pattern of discriminatory hiring.

The walls in the general office where Boler and Bakke worked were thin, and Boler realized that she could hear everything that was going on in the room next door. She heard a woman come into the room to bring her two male bosses some time cards. "The men all started making comments, sexual comments to her," Boler recalled. When the woman left the room "the men continued to talk about her in that way." Then all of a sudden, the men stopped talking, as though they remembered that Boler was next door.

By November they still had not received a response to the settlement offer. Sprenger could only surmise that someone higher up in the company had overridden those who favored a reasonable settlement. It confounded Sprenger, whose experience taught him that senior management typically was able to dispassionately make decisions on the basis of the overall best interests of the company. Clearly, the best thing for Eveleth, and Oglebay Norton, would be to settle this case as cheaply and as quickly as possible. The women's demands were relatively modest, and even though they had risen since the $210,000 figure included in the offer in June, attorneys' fees were still fairly low. This was the golden moment to settle the case on terms that would actually benefit the company without costing them a significant amount of money.

But the company's silence in response to their offer of settlement told Sprenger that someone at Oglebay Norton was not acting dispassionately at all. Sprenger recognized the signs of irrational decision-making: the plaintiffs' lawyer's worst nightmare.

CHAPTER TEN

Certification

Spring 1991

Half a foot of old gray snow covered the ground on March 12, 1991, when Diane Hodge and Joan Hunholz walked into the red-brick union hall in Forbes. Stan Daniels had asked them and two other women, Michelle Naughton and Deborah Sersha, to leave work an hour early and come to a meeting with the union's lawyer. A month before, Stan learned that a date had been set for the class certification hearing: May 13, 1991. The news that the lawsuit was going to trial with the union named as a defendant had pushed Stan into action.

In the meeting room along with Stan were two lawyers named Higbee and Erickson. Diane thought at the time that they both worked for the union. Only months later would she discover that Ray Erickson represented Oglebay Norton. Stan sat the women down and explained that Lois, Pat, and Kathy Anderson were suing the union for all of its money. He said that there was no reason for the lawsuit to go to court. He knew that all of the women wanted a sexual harassment policy, and the union and the company had a proposal for them. A committee could be formed consisting of women miners, including the women in the room, and they would be given the authority to put a policy in place. "There is no reason why we can't all work together," Stan assured them. Cooperating, he explained, would also entail testifying in court on behalf of the union. All four women agreed to testify.

Stan then presented the women with highlighted sections of Lois and Pat's depositions. "Those were the sections they wanted us to say didn't happen," Diane recalled. Stan also told them that if they were asked about graffiti and dirty pictures, they should answer according to what they saw in 1991, now that the plant's walls had been cleaned up. Diane said Stan assured the women that Lois, Pat, and Kathy were suing only because of pin-ups, dirty jokes, and graffiti—the stuff anyone who works in a mine should expect to see and hear. They were using these petty complaints, he said, to bankrupt the union and get rich.

Diane, who didn't understand all the details of Lois and Pat's lawsuit, was dubious of Stan's sincerity. But even if he wasn't telling the truth, she wanted to keep her job; the hardships of being laid off were fresh in her mind. "We were trying to prove that we were tough," she said, "we were trying to stay loyal to the union."

Stan was lining up his ducks. A week earlier, he had paid Marcy Steele a visit in the general foreman's office, where she'd recently taken a salaried job as a scheduling clerk. "Marcy," said Stan, "you should testify for the company. You're nonunion." Marcy got the drift immediately. Her job was no longer protected by the union, so she'd better show some loyalty to the company.

She was livid. "That's when I knew the union was working with the company, and when I called the lawyers," Marcy said. She still refused to testify in court, but she agreed to give Sprenger & Lang an affidavit describing the sexual harassment she had experienced and naming the men who did it. For now at least, Marcy had jumped off the fence. But she was the only one among her close group of friends at the mine, and it strained her friendship with Diane and Joan almost to the breaking point. "The other women went the other way," she said. "I was pretty much alone."

The odd eventuality of the union drumming up support for the company in a case brought against the company by the union's own members had been part of the Oglebay Norton's strategy from the moment

Sprenger & Lang included the union in the women's complaint. As early as 1989, Bob Klasnya and Jay Henningsgard had overcome their initial reluctance and were fully engaged in preparing the company's defense. Klasnya prepared a memo estimating that the company's potential exposure in the case could be as high as $30 million. Then he purposefully left the memo on his desk at a time when he knew Stan Daniels would be coming in, and left his office long enough to give Stan a chance to read it. "It was the most unprivate memo there ever was," Klasnya said. It also sinned by omission; it did not tell the truth, which was that the suit was no threat to the company's financial health. "Once the rumors started, no one did anything to stop them," Klasnya said. "We didn't tell anybody this was going to cost the insurance company, not Eveleth Mines." Klasyna knew that if Stan believed the lawsuit could cost union members their jobs, the union president would do everything he could to oppose it.

A few weeks later, at a union meeting that Lois did not attend, Stan held up a copy of the amended complaint and said that the women were now suing the union and that they would bankrupt the union and the company. Then Stan began a campaign to turn Lois's loyal crew against her. On August 8, 1989, Lois wrote to Jane Lang: "Stan told them that he and the union were working with the company and were going to block the suit. He further said that if we win, women will be given foremen jobs over the men out of seniority and that if this happens, 'it will be Lois's fault.' "

Klasnya had come to appreciate the power of gossip on the Range. "About that time," he recalled, "another group of [managers] passed around the rumor that the women were whores. I defended the women, but once a rumor starts on the Iron Range . . . it's a small place." News of the lawsuit upset the wives of the male miners. "They were wondering what was going on," said Klasnya.

Klasnya paused to marvel at his own complicity in the deception. He had a much better sense than Lois did of the magnitude of the forces arrayed against her. "It took a combination of courage and stupidity for Lois to file suit," he said.

When it became clear that, thanks to Stan Daniels's help, the company planned to call four women as witnesses, Jean Boler deposed Diane Hodge, Joan Hunholz, Michelle Naughton, and Debbie Sersha to get an idea of what their testimony would be. Joan and Diane both sat for their depositions on the same day, May 7, 1991. That morning, they ate breakfast with Stan, who had arranged for the union to pay them $300 in lost wages for the day they took off to attend the deposition. The depositions took place in the same conference room where Ray Erickson had deposed Lois. But Boler spared Diane and Joan the prying personal questions, concentrating instead on their life at work. She treated the women with kid gloves because she knew that some day they might change their minds and become part of the class.

All four women told Boler that they had not been sexually harassed at work, and were not offended by the pin-ups, foul language, and dirty jokes. They also said that they did not believe that Lois spoke for the majority of women at Eveleth Mines. Joan called Lois a "crybaby," who complained about everything. "She didn't like the dirt, didn't like the shift work, and she didn't like the men."

Diane said that she thought Lois was too thin-skinned to work in the mine. Boler asked Diane, "Have you ever told Lois that you thought she should quit?"

"Not to her face. But I have felt it. I feel that not every woman can work in the mines."

"And that's because she is bothered by these kinds of things that are in the complaint?"

"She is more ladylike, or something, than I am. It would be like sticking you out there. You wouldn't make it either."

Boler thought to herself, "She's right. I wouldn't last five minutes out there." The fact that the abuse not only seemed normal to these women, but that some of them appeared to believe that "taking it" was a badge of honor, depressed Boler. "They had to develop a hard exterior, a toughness, to survive," Boler observed. "Lois was the least that way and had the hardest time surviving there. (Although she managed to remain employed there after fifteen years.) Maybe because she was an outsider, maybe because it was just her personality or because she had not been raised to hear bad language and abusive treatment of women, but Lois did not have the same outer toughness as the other women." But Boler also recognized that on some level, Lois was braver, or at least more stubborn, than all the rest of them combined.

Even though Diane had agreed to testify against Lois, she still had a grudging respect for her. On April 20, three weeks before trial, Diane came up to Lois at work. Lois made a note of their conversation in her diary. *Diane: Last night I watched* Silkwood. *It reminded me of you. Everybody knew she was right, but when their jobs were on the line, they turned against her.*

The case was assigned to Federal District Court Judge James M. Rosenbaum, a judge Sprenger had appeared before and thought highly of. In 1985, Sprenger had tried a Burlington Northern gender discrimination class action before him for five months, and considered him to be fair and intelligent. Appointed by President Ronald Reagan, Rosenbaum was known as a hardworking, exceptionally civil judge. He also had a reputation for being a bit of a wild card, an independent thinker.

Rosenbaum's chambers were in the Twin Cities, but Erickson requested that the hearing take place in the federal courthouse in Duluth. Erickson argued that Duluth, which happened to be his hometown, was much closer to Eveleth, where most of the witnesses for both sides lived. Sprenger asked for the case to be heard in the Cities, but Rosenbaum agreed to go to Duluth, which meant that the Sprenger & Lang lawyers would have to transport all their files and trial materials up north.

The purpose of the hearing was to decide two pretrial motions. The first was a request to certify the case as a class action, something that had never been done in a hostile work environment case before.

The legal standards for determining both the question of class certification and of injunctive relief were quite specific. In deciding whether to grant the motion for class certification, Rosenbaum would have to find that the case met the requirements set out in the Federal Rules of Civil Procedure. First, he had to agree that the plaintiffs had demonstrated that a group of female employees at Eveleth Mines had been subjected to the same treatment and practices on the basis of their sex. He also had to find that the same group would be affected by the outcome of the litigation.

Sprenger was going to argue that all the women at Eveleth had been subjected to a hostile work environment, as well as discriminatory hiring and promotion practices, and that they would be affected by the outcome of *Jenson v. Eveleth.*

Rosenbaum also had to determine if there were enough women in the potential class that trying each woman's claim individually would be inefficient. Sprenger would ask that the court certify the class to include all women who had applied for jobs, or who worked at Eveleth Mines since December 1983, approximately one year before Lois filed her administrative complaint. That totaled about 125 women, most of whom were rejected applicants rather than actual employees. Of the remainder, more than 50 percent were salaried workers. If Rosenbaum found that the class should be limited to women who were, like Lois, Kathy, and Pat, hourly workers at Eveleth Mines, the number fell to about 30— still large enough to justify a class, but just barely.

Third, Rosenbaum would have to find that the women's claims contained common questions of law, or fact, that could be proved by the same evidence. Since the women had all been exposed to the same discriminatory environment, Sprenger would argue, the evidence offered would prove each woman's claim to be essentially the same. Oglebay Norton would try to break the claims down into specific, isolated incidents, and argue that each woman's experiences in terms of hiring, promotion, and exposure to sexually offensive incidents were so unique that they could not be established by the same evidence.

Next, Rosenbaum would have to determine that the claims of the named plaintiffs—Lois, Pat, and Kathy—were typical of those of the remainder of the class. And finally, he would have to decide that Lois, Pat, and Kathy were adequate representatives of the class. These last two components would be the most difficult, since the company intended to call other women who would testify that in fact, Lois, Pat, and Kathy were not typical in their reactions to the environment at the mine, nor would they be good representatives of the rest of the women who worked there.

If the plaintiffs failed to meet any one of these criteria, the case would not be certified as a class, and the plaintiffs would have to bring their claims individually. If that happened, the women would lose leverage and would likely be pressured into quick settlements on unfavorable terms.

The second motion before Judge Rosenbaum was a request by the plaintiffs for an injunction—a court order directing Eveleth Mines to adopt a sexual harassment policy and implement procedures for handling sexual harassment complaints. Lois had asked Sprenger and Boler to make this request so that she and the other women could be protected from retaliation in the workplace. Boler also wanted the injunction for strategic reasons. "I was afraid that the mine might make a change voluntarily, like adopt a policy," said Boler. "That could steal some of the plaintiffs' thunder by undermining the immediacy of the claims, because the defendants can say, 'Well, we used to be like that, but we aren't anymore.' "

Sprenger agreed to make the request, but he knew the chances of getting Rosenbaum to issue an injunction at this early stage was unlikely. A preliminary injunction at the motions stage of a case, before any determination of liability has been made, is rare. Courts must find that not issuing the order will result in some irreparable harm, such as bulldozing a historic building or sending assets out of the country, that cannot be undone before the legality of those actions can be determined.

To prevail, the lawyers would have to prove that ongoing harassment was causing irreparable harm to the women at Eveleth Mines, and that the women couldn't wait until after the full trial to be remedied. With some of the women coming in to testify that everything was fine at Eveleth Mines, it was hard to make a case for an injunction. "Irreparable harm is a very high standard," Sprenger said later. "In thirty-five years, I have asked for preliminary injunctions in nearly a hundred cases and have only gotten three."

On the Sunday morning before trial, Lois packed her suitcase. She expected to be in Duluth for two weeks—the duration of the hearing. Sprenger wanted Lois to sit in the courtroom every day to show the judge her commitment to the case. He told Lois that she should dress as if she were going to a funeral. Lois stood in front of her closet and surveyed the three size eight petite dresses she owned. She couldn't decide which one to take, so she packed all three. Pat, who was paralyzed from the waist down and confined to a wheelchair, was scheduled to testify on the second day of the hearing. She would be brought down to Duluth by a Medi-van on Tuesday morning.

Lois had spent the previous day with Sprenger going over questions he would ask her. For the lawyers, the magnitude of the problem at Eveleth Mines was both a blessing and a curse. There was so much material to work with, so many incidents of harassment, examples of graffiti and pornography, that the challenge was to present it in a coherent way that the judge could make some sense of. Lois's acute memory for detail proved to also be a blessing and a curse. She tended to wander from topic to topic, following a strand of logic apparent only to her. To make it more difficult, she had to remember and describe fifteen years' worth of dates, times, places exactly the same way she had in her depositions. Any deviation from her prior statements, no matter how trivial, could be used against her to undermine her credibility.

When Lois arrived at the Radisson Hotel—a round building that looms over the skyline in downtown Duluth—late Sunday afternoon, she and Sprenger spent time going over more questions. Sprenger had been thinking of ways to organize her testimony into a narrative. He tried to focus on short questions, followed by short and precise answers. Sprenger decided to organize the material into categories: unwanted touchings, sexually oriented language, and sexually oriented pictures and graffiti. "How many times did you see pornography on the walls?" "How many times were you touched or did you witness another woman being touched in an unwanted fashion?" Sprenger asked, referring to his hastily typed-up notes. Lois paced up and down the hotel room. "Well, that's a hard question, but I guess I could sit down and count them all, she responded." To Sprenger's amazement, she did.

The other problem was trying to make Lois comfortable about describing what went on at Eveleth Mines, getting over her reluctance to use explicit sexual terms in court. "I kept reminding her that these were not her words, but she still had to get used to using vulgar terms," Sprenger recalled.

He ended the prep session feeling that Lois was in good shape. But late that night in her hotel room, she panicked. She was haunted by memories of her first deposition with Erickson, the shame of having her life dragged through the mud, and not being believed. She couldn't sleep. At 5:00 A.M., she ran to the bathroom and vomited.

When the sun came up, Lois took a shower and chose a dress with a black top and a dark floral-patterned skirt, which fell three inches below her knees. With shaky hands, she pinned her blond, shoulder-length hair up into a bun on the back of her head. She wore no jewelry, and just a light touch of lipstick. As she stepped out of her hotel room, Sprenger was pleased to see that Lois looked more like a librarian than a miner.

Like all courtrooms in America, Rosenbaum's layout was similar to that of a church. The back third of the room was taken up with ten or so pewlike rows of seats for unsequestered witnesses and spectators. A rail divided the back and front of the room, and in its center was a small gate; to the sides sat the lawyers' tables. The table the nearest the empty jury box was the plaintiffs'. The judge of course sat in the front, presiding over the room from his pulpitlike bench.

Boler had arrived earlier with the documents they would need that day, and was setting up the plaintiffs' table when Sprenger and Lois arrived. Otherwise, the courtroom was empty. Lois walked around the room and sat in the witness stand for a moment to get a feel for it. Soon, though, the room began to fill up. Ray Erickson and Scott Higbee, the union's lawyer, came in and sat at the defendant's table, along with Jay Henningsgard and a representative of the company. Behind the railing, a few of the defense side's rows were filled with union members, including Stan Daniels. The women who had supported the case enough to submit affidavits made a show of support that day. Lois noticed Mavie Maki and Connie Saari in the crowd. But Marcy Steele was not there. After going through the process of drafting an affidavit with Boler, Marcy decided at the last minute not to submit it into the court record. She was back on the fence.

Lois sat in the row right behind Boler and Sprenger. Kathy Anderson sat next to George in the back row of the plaintiff's side, wearing a conservative two-piece beige outfit. Pat did not witness the first day of trial. Her failing health meant that she could only come to court for her own testimony.

When Rosenbaum entered the courtroom, everyone rose. His broad-shouldered physique commanded respect. His black hair and olive skin made him look Italian to Lois, who had not encountered many Jewish people on the Range.

After a few preliminary matters, Sprenger stood up to make his opening statement. Many litigators are aggressively macho, particularly in court. Sprenger was his same calm, soft-spoken self. But as he began to speak, a new, forceful quality rose in his voice. He projected the conviction that if someone did not agree with him, it was only because they did not understand him, and he was prepared to patiently explain things to them until they, too, became equally convinced. Sprenger outlined for Rosenbaum the reasons why the women were entitled to bring the case as a class action, and explaining why the judge should issue an injunction.

When Sprenger had finished laying out the plaintiff's case, Ray Erickson rose to make his opening statement on behalf of Eveleth Mines. In court, Erickson's demeanor was more deferential than in depositions. But even here, to Lois, he came across as arrogant and dismissive.

First, Erickson took aim at the discrimination-in-hiring claims, arguing that in fact, the low numbers of women hired by Eveleth Mines from 1981 to the present reflected the downturn in the taconite industry. "Mr. Sprenger can talk about how many females were hired in a ten-year period, but the evidence will show that for a period of six or seven years there was no hiring [of anyone] at all."

Then he turned more generally to the issue of class certification. As expected, he argued that there was no sexually hostile work environment at Eveleth Mines. The only charge Lois Jenson filed, he said, was that "Mr. Povroznik had engaged in improper sexual harassment by way of a series of letters, which, at best I think, show an infatuation. . . . To suggest that there was some widespread vulgarity, that the walls were improperly posted, that there was some denial of employee benefits, there weren't appropriate hires, there weren't appropriate promotions, and the whole list, none of that was done."

"What you're saying," Rosenbaum interjected, "is that Miss Jenson's complaint was an isolated and an individual fact, which is either accurate or inaccurate reporting. And of course if you are correct in that, I wouldn't be able to find that there was any kind of a class issue at all. Two people had a dispute or a problem. Is that accurate?"

"I believe that's correct, Your Honor."

Rosenbaum asked, what if Lois Jenson's claim turned out to be not an isolated incident but one example of a much wider problem? "I could then consider it as a class issue. Is that accurate?"

No, Erickson explained, because even if there was a more pervasive problem at Eveleth Mines, women's reactions to obscene comments and sexually graphic materials are by their nature so different that individual acts of harassment cannot be considered to have a uniform effect on a group of women.

Finally, Erickson argued that an injunction was not necessary, because it had not been established that there was a hostile work environment at Eveleth Mines, and furthermore, the company already had a policy—the wording that was inserted into the collective bargaining agreement in 1987, which said that if the company learned about a sexual harassment claim, it would react to it. Erickson pointed out that even that policy had not done any good: Aside from Lois's complaint about Steve Povroznik, none of the other women had come forward to report any complaints. If women won't come forward and use the policy they have, what would be the point of a revised policy or a complaint process?

When Erickson finished, Sprenger called Lois to the stand. As she stepped up and settled herself into the wooden chair on the witness stand, she realized that she liked being slightly higher than eye-level to the attorney. "It gives me an edge," she thought—looking for any panacea to calm her nerves. Sprenger guided Lois through the history of her experiences at Eveleth, beginning with when she first went to work in 1975. She explained that she had taken the job because the pay was four times what she was receiving at the credit union, and she had a young son to support. She testified about her first day at work, when a man said "You fucking women don't belong here," and how one of her foremen, John Maki, told her that she should be home with her child and that he did not want women on his crew.

Then Sprenger led Lois through the categories of testimony they had worked on the day before. "Over the time that you worked there, about how many instances of physical touching of a sexual nature did you actually observe either that occurred to you personally or that you observed happening to another woman?" Sprenger asked.

"Eighty-one times, sir."

Rosenbaum looked surprised. "Eighty-one?" he repeated.

"Eighty-one."

"Now," Sprenger continued, "about how many of those occurred with the person touching, the male, being a supervisory person?"

"Thirty times."

"How many of those times did you report that physical touching that you found sexually offensive to management, including those that occurred to you that were done by management?"

"Thirty-two, thirty-three times."

Then Sprenger asked her about the number of times she had heard sexually offensive verbal language in the workplace.

"That would be, ah, practically impossible to calculate. I would say probably thousands through the years."

When Sprenger asked her to give examples of the sexually offensive comments that had been directed at her in her fifteen years at Eveleth Mines, Erickson objected on hearsay grounds. Sprenger was not surprised—in fact, he expected it. If Rosenbaum prohibited Lois from repeating in court what she had heard at work, one of the pillars of her case would be knocked out from under her, none of the abusive language or lewd comments that contributed to the hostile environment at Eveleth would be allowed to come in as evidence. But if Sprenger wasn't surprised that Erickson tried to keep the testimony out, he wasn't particularly worried. The hearsay rule prohibits a witness from testifying to the truth of something—say, the color of a car—based on something another person said—"Joe told me the car was red"—rather than something the witness had experienced firsthand. But it does not prevent a witness from testifying about the *experience of hearing* a statement—the same statement can be offered as proof that Joe said the car was red, even if it could not be considered in determining what color the car actually was. Sprenger was asking Lois to testify about what she experienced herself, hearing the statements of her coworkers. If one of them said "Women do not belong in the mines," she could testify that she heard that statement, but it could not be offered as proof that women in fact did not belong in the mines.

But if the line between admissible and inadmissible out-of-court statements is clear in theory, it is not always so evident in practice. Often, to be safe, courts err on the side of excluding what should be admissible evidence. Other times, they themselves get twisted around the rule, and just get it wrong. Fortunately for the women, Judge Rosenbaum overruled Erickson's objection. "Let's see what she has to say."

So Lois was able to testify about Nick Senich repeatedly asking her if she had eaten at the "Y," and if she had "gotten any," and about the frequency with which she heard the word *fuck* at work, as well as myriad other offensive comments directed at her or said in her presence.

Sprenger then turned to the third form of sexual harassment as laid out in the complaint, sexually explicit materials posted in the workplace. In preparation for the trial, Boler put together an exhibit book of images in the workplace that Lois had collected or photographed. Sprenger handed a copy of the black, three-ring binder notebook to Rosenbaum and one to Erickson. Then he turned to Lois and asked her to walk them through the exhibits, explaining where they had been found in the workplace.

The first one, an advertisement for a strip show at a local bar, showed a woman with almost completely exposed size 50F breasts. Lois explained that the exhibit was a smaller version of a two-by-three-foot poster that she found in the repair bay of the concentrator, a central location, in 1988. The second, marked exhibit 32, was a cartoon drawing of a man whose nose was shaped like a penis, and whose mouth was drawn to look like testicles. The caption read "Not all salesmen are assholes." This, Lois testified, was found on a table in a control room in the concentrator, also in 1988.

There were more jokes and cartoons, including a diagram of a woman's body labeled as a fishing map (the vagina, called "beaver dam," was marked as the best place to put in). There were calendar pictures, including full frontal shots of various *Penthouse* Pets of the Year, and pictures of naked or topless women playing with their nipples or rubbing their crotches. Exhibit 47, which Lois identified as having been found in one of the trucks she drove, was simply a close-up of a woman's vagina spread open by female fingers.

Exhibits 51 and 52 showed entire walls covered with pornographic pictures, right next to official company notices. There were also pictures Lois took of graffiti scraped into walls; "I eat cuntz and lots of it" scrawled in huge letters in the Mexico feeder under the surge, drawings of breasts and penises and people fornicating all over the plant.

The testimony was as matter-of-fact as it could be, given the subject matter of the exhibits. Lois seemed to conquer her embarrassment, and her memory served her well. She was able to identify each and every exhibit convincingly and with precision, and Rosenbaum accepted the proffered images into evidence as dryly as he might have received a company's annual report. At exhibit 43—an advertisement for a stripper named Anita Sa'Mour and her "EE-52 bombers," which showed one large picture and four smaller ones of a completely naked woman fondling her enormous breasts—Rosenbaum paused. Now even he seemed slightly red-faced.

Holding it up gingerly, he asked Lois, "Did you observe that in the Eveleth Mines workplace?" He seemed incredulous.

"Yes sir, I did."

"When?"

Once again, Lois was able to be remarkably specific. "I found that hanging in the pellet plant lunchroom over the tables in May of 1990."

The day was unusually hot for Duluth in May, and by mid-afternoon the courtroom was uncomfortably warm. When Judge Rosenbaum suggested a ten-minute break, Sprenger requested permission to interrupt Lois's testimony by calling Kathleen Tessier, Bob Raich's former secretary, to the stand. Sprenger partly wanted to prevent Tessier, who had driven down from Eveleth that morning, from having to return to Duluth the next day. But Sprenger also thought it would not hurt to give Lois a break. She had been testifying for several hours, and he thought she was beginning to tire and lose focus.

Tessier testified that Raich often said that women did not belong in the mines, that they belonged at home, barefoot and pregnant. "He felt that, umm, in his statement, that women were taking jobs away from the men." Milan Lolich, who was Raich's subordinate, made similar comments. When Tessier objected to these statements, Raich and Lolich just laughed. Tessier also testified that Lolich frequently commented on her appearance, and that Raich once pulled her onto his lap at a retirement party.

After Tessier's testimony, Sprenger recalled Lois to the stand. She described the incident when Gene Scaia grabbed her crotch with a greased hand. Then Sprenger walked her through her long, complicated experience with Steve Povroznik. Sprenger concluded by asking, "Miss Jenson, what is it you're attempting to accomplish by your lawsuit?"

"I want the discrimination and harassment to stop at Eveleth Mines. I want the women to be able to report incidences of harassment if they have a problem. I want the men who work for Eveleth Mines to know what sexual harassment is, as well as the women. I want management to handle these cases as they are brought up. I want them to be educated and trained in those matters."

Then Rosenbaum asked Lois how she felt working at Eveleth Mines had affected her.

"Your Honor, I was twenty-seven years old when I started working at Eveleth Mines. I felt I was a confident person. I had done secretarial work and felt competent." But after working a few years at Eveleth Mines, Lois said, "my confidence had gone so low that I no longer took care of myself. I had gone through stages where I stopped dating men because I worked with them all day."

"You stopped dating men?"

"Yes. I had stages where I was bitter. I'm currently in a stage of trying to heal. And I won't be able to do that, Your Honor, until we have a policy. Someone that I can go report these things to that I know is going to listen and to be assured it's going to stop. I would like to be able to go to work without feeling the fear I feel, never knowing what's happening one day to the next. . . . I would like to just get through this and feel that I'm a person again, not to be put down, not to be grabbed, or pinched or patronized."

With that, Lois's direct testimony was over, and Rosenbaum adjourned the hearing for the day. All in all, Sprenger felt good. He thought Lois had proven to be a sympathetic witness; she had come across as sincere and honest. But he was also worried about her. She seemed tired, and he was secretly concerned about her ability to withstand cross-examination.

As they left the courthouse, two television crews were waiting for them outside. Boler steered Lois away, while Sprenger stepped up to the microphones to field questions about the case. That night, KBJR-TV

"News six at six," and WBIO-TV Duluth, "the Northland's source for news and sports and weather," announced that the women at the Eveleth mining company were suing for sexual harassment. The Eveleth Mines sign and stock footage of bulldozers and diggers working in a mine pit were the visuals behind this voice-over: "Some women who work in the Eveleth mining company say they have endured sexual harassment almost daily, from touching and grabbing, even ripping open a woman's shirt, to lewd comments, posters, and graffiti. Some of it is filed in this notebook, material not suited for television."

Then a close-up of Paul Sprenger came onto the screen. He was dressed in a dark blue suit with a pale blue shirt and dark tie. A few strands of his thick, wiry, black hair fell onto his forehead, and his bushy black eyebrows knitted into a frown as he said, "I think that the behavior was . . . barbaric, inhuman, they've been through a lot. They're frightened to death." Sprenger's salacious sound bite ran again on the ten o'clock news and at six the next morning. On the Range, one word that Sprenger said stood out: "barbaric."

Up until now there had been no press coverage of the actual content of Lois's complaint. Now it was all over the airwaves. "I could not give them specifics because this was TV," Sprenger said. "I had to think of a way of describing it without using obscene language. So I said it was barbaric. And it was!"

His sound bite amounted to a declaration of war on the Range. "Paul Sprenger's quotes upset a lot of people," explained one Eveleth miner. "Yes, there were some sick individuals out there, but Sprenger made it sound like it was all of us. There were about twelve people out of a thousand who were harassing the women." A few days later, the local paper in Virginia ran an editorial cartoon of a tourist couple driving through the woods. When they see a road sign of a burly man carrying a club and dragging a naked woman by the hair, the woman in the car says, "Oh look, Larry, we must be near Eveleth Mines!"

Sprenger's comments helped to solidify opposition to the lawsuit among union members. "The biggest strategic error Paul Sprenger made was giving those incendiary statements on the Duluth courthouse steps," said Bob Klasnya. "At the time, the workforce was moderately split. . . . But when Sprenger said that, everyone shifted to being against the women, and it made our [the company's] job a lot easier because the witnesses were more cooperative."

Sprenger was surprised by the reaction. "I always thought it was strange," he said later, "that the people on the Range were offended by my description of the conduct of the miners, which was actually pretty mild, considering, but were not offended by the conduct itself."

The next morning, Sprenger called Pat Kosmach to testify. By May 14, 1991, Pat's wish had not come true. The trial had not arrived early enough for her to be able to walk into the courtroom. Both of her legs had given way, and she was now confined to a wheelchair. Though Lou Gehrig's disease had rendered her immobile, her mind was alert. Pat rolled her wheelchair into position in front of the witness stand, and Jean Boler began the direct examination. Lois overslept that morning and arrived at court half an hour late. As she walked down the aisle of the courtroom, she was struck by the image of Boler looking down at Pat, a third the size of her formerly robust self, gaunt and trembling in her wheelchair. Pat, who had once been so formidable, now looked fragile and weak.

In her matter-of-fact way, Pat told Rosenbaum that she went to work at Eveleth Mines because she was a single mother raising five children on minimum wage. She testified that right after she started working at the mine, one of her foremen grabbed her and kissed her. She described feeling humiliated and angered by the degrading imagery she saw every day at work. She recounted how her male coworkers frequently made comments about her sex life and told her that if she lost weight, she might get herself a husband. And she described an area at work where the men kept their girlie magazines, known as the "porn library."

But the most compelling part of Pat's testimony was her description of how she evolved from being a fiercely loyal union member and officer to being deeply disillusioned with the union and its commitment to its female members. Time and again—when Willie Johnson threatened Diane Hodge, when Don Cummings threw gloves at Michele Mesich's crotch and threatened to kill her for reporting it, when one man masturbated on Judy Jarvela's clothes and another stalked her, when Steve Povroznik harassed and stalked Lois—Pat urged the women to turn to the union for help, and time and again the union failed them. She reluctantly concluded that litigation was the only way to protect the women from an environment she feared was degenerating year by year and would ultimately lead to serious violence against the women.

On cross-examination, Ray Erickson tried to undermine Pat's credibility by painting her as both overly sensitive and hypocritical.

"Now, you have used vulgar language in the workplace, have you not?" he asked.

"On occasion."

"And on occasion you've also used jokes that contained language?"

"Yes, I did."

"On one occasion you recalled, you used a joke that had a word like duck that rhymed with fuck, right?"

"Yes."

"And when I inquired of you, you told me that you hadn't checked with anybody around you to find out if they would be offended by that language before you told it, did you?"

"No, I did not check."

"And when you used the work *fuck* in the workplace, you didn't determine in advance whether or not someone's sensitivities are more acute than yours, did you?"

"No."

Throughout Erickson's questioning, Pat sat in her wheelchair, answering him directly, and sometimes defiantly. "She was a good, fiery witness," said Boler.

Kathy Anderson was as dramatic and theatrical as Pat had been stolid and straightforward. She played to Rosenbaum, vacillating between helpless victim and righteous martyr. When it was Erickson's turn with Kathy, he went to town.

"Now, on occasion you have used what you have described as vulgar language in the workplace?"

"Yes."

"And I take it that the wordage of the language you've used takes all the forms that you've heard in this courtroom up to this point in time?"

"I wouldn't say all."

"Well, on one occasion, ah, you had a discussion with a Mr. Ludy Sampson?"

"Ludy Sampson. It's actually Ludwig."

"And at the close of that conversation you were responding back to him by saying that he should take his fucking club and loincloth and go back to his cave."

"That is correct."

"On another occasion you threatened to kick off the family jewels of another male employee?"

"That is also correct."

"And by that you meant the employee's—"

"Testicles."

But Erickson frequently overplayed his hand, and both Pat and Kathy managed to corroborate Lois's depiction of Eveleth Mines as a workplace inundated with sexually explicit language and images, as well as physical and emotional abuse.

In another exchange with Kathy, Erickson tried to make hay of the fact that she had not complained about some of the incidents that she had testified about.

"Now, you had some testimony as well this morning with respect to what you called a phallus symbol. It's true, is it not, that you do not re-call telling Mr. Stish that you didn't think this phallus symbol was either funny or that you didn't appreciate it?"

"I said nothing."

But Erickson's questions confirmed that the "phallus symbol" inci-dent had indeed occurred. It also echoed the prevalent view at Eveleth Mines that a male worker would have no way of knowing that waving a big red dildo in the face of a female worker might be offensive to her unless she said something about it. Apparently, the "common decency" refrain echoed by Tom Green and other senior management at Oglebay Norton was no longer part of the company's defense strategy.

With Lois, whose language was less salty than some of the other women's, Erickson instead portrayed her as a flirt, or at least as someone who sent mixed messages to her male coworkers. But when Erickson tried to bring up Lois's relationship with Gene Scaia as evidence that she was not offended when he grabbed her crotch with his greasy hand, Rosenbaum drew the line.

"In point of fact," Erickson asked Lois, "you'd had two dates prior to the incident with Mr. Scaia on which you socialized with him?"

"I did socialize with Gene Scaia prior to that."

"And at the time that Mr. Scaia engaged in the activity that you had complained of, you and he had had an intimate relationship?"

"We had slept together once, sir."

At that, Rosenbaum looked pointedly to Erickson. "Counsel, I would like you to tell me what the relevance is of the fact that this woman had been intimate with Mr. Scaia prior to his in the workplace placing his hand on her crotch."

"Your Honor, the issue in each of the sexual harassment incidents is whether or not the conduct is unwanted or is known to be unwanted. I don't know that there is necessarily any cause-and-effect relationship between an intimate relationship and conduct of that sort, but there may well be."

Before Erickson could finish, Rosenbaum ordered that the testimony be stricken from the record. Rosenbaum had equally little patience when Erickson questioned Lois about the propriety of taking pictures in the workplace.

"Let me ask this: The times that you utilized the camera to take photographs of what you regarded to be graffiti occurred during your active work hours?"

"Yes sir."

"And as you would report to a particular area for work, rather than engaging in the work that was assigned to you, you would on occasion take photographs?"

"No sir, I did my work, and if it was on the way to the work, I then took the pictures."

"But during the period you were taking the pictures, you weren't doing your authorized work, right?"

Rosenbaum, clearly annoyed, asked incredulously, "You want to dock her for the time she took taking pictures, counsel?"

Chagrined, Erickson replied, "I don't, Your Honor."

At a break in the middle of her cross-examination, Sprenger called Lois over to the watercooler in the hallway. He was pleased. "You're doing great! You're doing great!" he told her.

The women's testimony offered evidence that a hostile work environment existed at Eveleth Mines. The next step was to show that the company was legally responsible for that environment because it knew or should have known of the harassment and failed to take steps to prevent it. To help make that connection, Sprenger and Boler called Eugene Borgida, a professor of social psychology at the University of Minnesota, to testify. Borgida was an expert on sexual stereotyping in the workplace and its relationship to sexual harassment. He explained in great detail how an environment saturated in sexual imagery that depicts women as sex objects predisposes men to see and treat their female coworkers in that same light. By condoning, or at least tolerating, sexualized images, Borgida argued, a company can contribute to a hostile work environment in two ways. First, the presence of the pictures can encourage male workers to think about women in sexualized terms, and to treat them accordingly. Second, tolerating or condoning sexualized images sends a signal to workers that other forms of harassment will also be tolerated. As Borgida explained, "To the extent that [sexual images are] there, and to the extent that there's no attempt to deal with them, the implicit message is that they're sanctioned. And the effects associated with them are unchecked."

Borgida's theories reflected what Lois and the other women experienced at Eveleth; as time went on, the men grew more rather than less hostile to their female coworkers. When Lois and Pat first arrived at Eveleth, graffiti and verbal abuse were relatively uncommon. But the more women were hired, the more the environment had become sexualized and polarized.

Although Judge Rosenbaum listened intently to Borgida's testimony, he seemed skeptical about whether a "soft" science like social psychology could be of any value in helping him understand what had gone on at Eveleth Mines. He was clearly more disposed to rely on his own common sense to connect the dots between the company's lack of action and the conduct of individual workers, as well as women's reactions to a sexualized workplace. At times, he seemed to almost mock the relevance of Borgida's theories.

At one point, Sprenger asked Borgida whether the fact that a woman did not complain about sexually oriented material in the workplace necessarily meant that she did not find the material offensive. Rosenbaum cut him off, saying, "It strikes me that if you were making a couple bucks an hour and can make six bucks an hour doing a different job, I can draw some conclusions about why you might put up with an unpleasant circumstance."

Rosenbaum seemed equally skeptical of the testimony of another expert Sprenger hired, a woman named Holly Nordquist. Nordquist, the director of the Sexual Harassment Resource Office at the University of Minnesota at Duluth, testified about sexual harassment policies in general and about what kind of policy would be appropriate at a company like Eveleth Mines. Nordquist went into great detail describing the sexual harassment policy she administered at the university, including the procedures for making complaints and ways in which students were made aware of the policy.

On cross-examination, Erickson turned her testimony on its ear. Erickson, it turned out, had sent an investigator to the campus. The investigator took pictures of numerous examples of sexually oriented or offensive graffiti in the carols in the main library, which Erickson showed to Nordquist in court.

"Do you regard what is depicted on these photographs as sexually hostile to female employees of UMD?"

"Absolutely."

"And it is fair to say, is it not, that to the extent that these materials can be found in public study carols in the UMD library, the effectiveness of your sexual harassment program is questioned?"

Nordquist defended her policies, but the damage was done. Either the graffiti had not been reported by students and female employees of the university because they did not find it offensive, which meant that Nordquist was out of touch with what most women believe constitutes sexual harassment. Or the women did find it offensive, but, for whatever reasons, did not avail themselves of the university's elaborate complaint procedures. Either way, Erickson succeeded in showing that the mere presence of a sexual harassment policy does not mean that a workplace will automatically be free of all potentially sexually offensive materials.

After four days of the hearing, the plaintiffs rested their case. Over the next three days, Erickson called Jay Henningsgard, Bob Raich, and Stan Daniels, all of whom testified that they were unaware of the kind of language and materials the women complained about, and that if they had known about it, they would have taken steps to correct the problem. But despite the uniformity of their stories, Sprenger easily decimated their testimony on cross-examination, making them appear to be either lying or stupid and occasionally both. When Henningsgard claimed that all complaints were handled properly, Sprenger pounced.

"Don't you think, sir, that it is true that a number of employees at Eveleth, male employees in particular, don't know what sexual harassment is?"

"I don't know that, sir."

"The truth is that you've seen nude pictures such as some of the pictures that were introduced here in the foremen's offices, haven't you?"

"I can't recall seeing pictures like those that were introduced here in the foremen's offices, sir."

"Sir, in your deposition on July 30 of 1990, at page 127, line 2, do you remember being asked this question and this answer: Question: 'Have you seen pictures of women nude or semi-nude in these offices?' Answer: 'Yes, I would say so. Yes, I would say yes.' Do you remember that, sir?"

"Yes."

"It was true then, wasn't it?"

"My statement there is true."

"And we're talking about foremen's offices, weren't we?"

"Yes sir."

"So, you never did tell the foremen in whose offices you saw these nude pictures to do anything about it, to take them down, right?"

"That's correct."

"And you saw these over the years that you worked there, correct?"

"I saw very few pictures, and none that you had here in court today."

"There were other nude pictures, right?"

"I have seen some calendar art, yes sir. I could not identify what I saw—"

"Okay. I take it that you never reported this material you saw displayed in the foremen's offices to Mr. Raich, right, your boss?"

"That's correct."

"But wasn't it a violation of the sexual harassment policy of the company?"

"I guess I don't know that."

"You don't know what sexual harassment is, do you, sir?"

"Yes sir."

"You don't know whether exhibits 53 and 54 are a violation of the sexual harassment policy?"

"In my estimation they are."

"Okay. But you never reported that to Mr. Raich?"

"I didn't see those pictures, I don't believe."

"You saw pictures just like it, didn't you, sir?"

"Not quite. Not quite as raw as those."

"You never told the general manager either, Mr. Wilson or Mr. Nettell, right?"

"That's correct."

"And you never told Cleveland that there was a problem like that out here, did you?"

"I don't know that there is a problem out here, sir."

"You mean you've been listening to these last four days of testimony about what happened to these women, and photographs and the graffiti and the touching, and the language, and you don't think there's a problem, sir?"

"I don't think there's a problem that hasn't been handled that's been reported."

"That hasn't been handled. Did you handle Lois Jenson's grievance that she filed about this issue in 1984?"

"I had a part to play in that."

"And it's still pending. Nothing's been done, has it?"

"The grievance is still pending."

"Is that what you mean by handled, sir?"

"No sir."

"Maybe it depends on your perception of what is funny and what isn't. In the office, sir, have you seen offensive cartoons, in your office?"

"Yes."

"In fact, you believe that cartoons of a male sticking a Christmas tree in his wife's rectum are funny, don't you?"

"I thought that was kind of funny, yes sir."

Three women who signed the petition—Joan Hunholz, Michelle Naughton, and Debbie Sersha—testified on behalf of the company on the fifth day of the hearing. They were the defense's most powerful tool in challenging Lois, Pat, and Kathy's request for a class action. If the defense could show that Lois, Pat, and Kathy did not speak for a majority of the women at the mine, that most of the women there did not believe they had been discriminated against, then Sprenger would not be able to establish the common occurrence of sexual harassment at the mine required for class certification. And they could severely undermine the chances of getting an injunction if Rosenbaum believed them that everything was fine at Eveleth Mines.

But Sprenger and Boler knew they had to be careful with these witnesses. Both were fully conscious of the fact that, if all went well and the class was certified, these same women could be their clients one day. "I really believed that these women were just being used by the company, that they had been duped," Sprenger said later. "Once they realized that there was nothing in it for them, I believed they might well join us."

Joan Hunholz, looking severe and defiant in a black pantsuit, went first. Lois sat in the front row of the courtroom slumped in her seat, dreading what she was about to hear. She noticed that Joan looked uncomfortable. Her mouth was puckered, her body stiff and awkward. Lois looked over her shoulder and across the aisle, to where Stan Daniels sat with Michelle Naughton and Debbie Sersha six rows back giggling. Lois thought they were acting like children who didn't know how to behave in church. Scott Higbee handled Joan's direct examination.

"Do you feel that you have ever been sexually harassed while an employee at Eveleth Mines?"

"No."

"But do you recall an occasion concerning a foreman Jerry Benz?"

"Yes."

"Would you describe for the Court an incident that occurred between you and Mr. Benz?"

"Jerry Benz was my foreman at the time, and my cigarettes were falling out of my breast pocket, and he helped put them back in."

"And what did you do in response to that?"

"I hollered at him right then and there. Chewed him out. And then brought him down to the superintendent."

"And what is the name of the superintendent?"

"Corky Krollman."

"And what did Mr. Krollman do at that point?"

"He chewed out Jerry for doing that. Asked him if he forgot what he was doing. And asked me, 'What do we do about the problem?' and I felt I was satisfied that he just listened to it and that we had turned him in, and he was aware of it."

"Now, earlier you said you didn't feel that you'd been the subject of sexual harassment at Eveleth Mines. Can you describe for the Court why you don't consider this incident to constitute sexual harassment?"

"I don't think Jerry really realized what he was doing. He just, honestly to Jerry, he thought he was just putting the cigarettes back in my pocket."

"And did you have any further problems with Mr. Benz after this one occasion?"

"No, I never did."

"Now, have you ever been offended by the language that you've heard in the workplace?"

"No, I haven't."

"Have you ever been offended by visual materials you've seen in the workplace? And by that I include writings on the walls or pictures or magazines."

"No, I haven't."

"Have you ever been offended by jokes that you've heard at Eveleth Mines?"

"No."

"Have you ever been offended by cartoons or drawings that you've seen at Eveleth Mines?"

"No."

"And have you ever been offended by comments or statements made to you by coworkers?"

"No, I haven't."

"And have you ever been offended by comments or statements made to you by supervisors?"

"No."

"Do you personally believe that Eveleth Mines is a hostile environment for a woman to work in?"

"No, I don't."

"In general, how would you say you are treated by the male employees of Eveleth Mines?"

"I'm treated very well out there. I very much like my job."

Then Higbee went to the heart of the matter—Lois, Kathy, and Pat's adequacy to represent the other women at the mine.

"Ms. Hunholz, are you familiar with Lois Jenson?"

"Yes."

"Do you believe that Ms. Jenson is an adequate representative of your interests in the Eveleth Mines workplace?"

"No," Joan responded.

"And why is that?"

"I don't think she's qualified at all. She's, umm . . . she makes too much out of nothing all the time. I wouldn't go to her with any of my problems at all."

"Are you familiar with Pat Kosmach?"

"Yes."

"And do you feel that Ms. Kosmach would make an adequate representative of your interests in the workplace?"

"Not anymore."

"Can you describe why that is?"

"Because of her health."

Joan said she did not know Kathy Anderson well because she worked in the pit, but said that Kathy, too, was not in a position to represent Joan and the other women who worked in the mine.

Higbee continued. "Can you tell me what was your intent in signing this petition?"

"It was just to let the guys know that we weren't against 'em."

Joan's testimony was damning. Their only hope was to show that Joan was not telling the truth about what was going on at Eveleth Mines.

Boler, who had been taking copious notes during Joan's direct, rose slowly and crossed the room.

"Now, you testified about your opinion about Lois Jenson, and it's true, isn't it, that you really haven't liked Lois Jenson since back in 1976 when you first met her; is that correct?"

"Well, close around then."

"And as I understand it, the reason that you were angry with her at that time is that you thought she was favored because she had a job that was eliminated as soon as she bid off it; is that right?"

"There was more than just that."

"But that was the first thing that made you dislike her; is that correct?"

"No, it wasn't really the first thing. There was all kinds of things."

"Well, is it true that you thought she got special treatment at that time because of that job?"

"Yeah."

"And you also don't like Kathy O'Brien Anderson; is that correct?"

"I said I really didn't know her that well."

"I thought that you disliked her right off the bat when you met her; is that true?"

"I don't recall if it was right when I met her, or when I got to know her."

"Well, do you recall having your deposition taken a couple of weeks ago, May 7, to be exact?"

"Yes."

"Now, at the time of the deposition, did you think you'd been sexually harassed?"

"No."

"Do you recall at your deposition that I asked you these questions, and you had this answer: Question: 'Do you think that you have experienced sexual harassment at Eveleth Mines of some form?' Answer: 'Yes.' Do you recall that?"

"Yeah."

"And in that you were talking about the incident with Mr. Benz?"

"Yes."

Hunholz admitted that on several occasions she had covered or erased sexually explicit graffiti, and that she had seen sexually explicit photos and calendars at work.

"But your personal opinion is that these kinds of pictures should not be . . . should not be allowed to be posted anywhere. They can be posted some places, but not everywhere?"

"Yeah."

"And the reason for that is that you don't want one in an area where you have to look at it frequently; is that correct?"

Joan nodded and murmured yes. Then Boler turned to the issue of the petition, and the news article that had prompted her to draft it.

"And when you read that article, that made you angry?"

"Yes, it did."

"And I understand that's because you hate the word *sue*?"

"Yes."

"You think that it's just a quick way for people to make a buck?"

"Yes."

"And you thought that the only reason the women were involved is that they wanted to make a buck?"

"Yes."

"Except for Patty Kosmach, whom you weren't too sure about?"

"Right."

"And when you went to work the day that the, umm, article appeared, the guys on your crew started to ask you about it?"

"Yes."

"And you were the only woman on the crew; is that right?"

"Yes."

"And you told them all when they asked that you didn't believe in a lawsuit?"

"Right."

"And at that point in time at least, you never read the complaint?"

"No."

"And to this day you've never read the complaint?"

"No."

"But it was important to you to keep up a steady relationship with the people that you were on a crew with?"

"Right."

"And that's because of safety reasons, right?"

"Yes, and more."

"And you've seen it happen on a crew that if a person is disliked the crew may refuse to work with that person?"

"Yes."

"And then it's very difficult for that person to do their job?"

"Right."

"And now, Mr. Erickson has introduced a petition here, and it's true, isn't it, that the reason that you wrote the petition was because you got tired of the guys all asking which women are for and which women are against the lawsuit?"

"Right."

"And that's the reason that you told the other women that you were making this petition, to let the guys know which women were for and which were against?"

"Right."

"And in the week after that article, and when you prepared the petition, there was a lot of tension at work, wasn't there?"

"Yes."

"And you felt that the men were acting differently toward the women?"

"Well, yeah."

"And, for instance, the men wouldn't ride in the elevators with women?"

"Right."

"And it happened to you more than once that you'd be standing outside of an elevator with a group of guys, and they wouldn't want to get in the elevator with you?"

"Right."

"And then you had to explain to them that you weren't part of the lawsuit so they would feel more comfortable and they would ride in the elevator with you again?"

"Right."

"And so that's when you decided to do the petition to show the guys you were on their side, not on the side of the women that were doing the lawsuit?"

"Right."

"Now, Mrs. Hunholz, you agree, don't you, that it would be in the best interests of women at Eveleth Mines to have a more extensive sexual harassment policy with definitions and procedures?"

Looking defeated, Joan muttered, "It wouldn't hurt."

It was the answer Boler was looking for. Trying not to smile, she crossed back to the table and sat down.

Next, Erickson called Michelle Naughton to the stand. As he had with Joan Hunholz, Erickson led Naughton through a litany of questions about her experience at work—no, she had never been sexually harassed; no, she was not offended by images at work; no, she did not believe in Lois's lawsuit.

Once again, on cross-examination, Boler skillfully dissected her carefully rehearsed testimony. Holding up exhibit after exhibit, she asked Michelle whether the images offended her. Each time, Michelle reluctantly admitted that they did. Then Boler asked, "As a woman working at Eveleth Mines, you believe that you have to put up with pornographic pictures and sexual teasing because it goes along with the job; isn't that correct?"

"To a certain extent. Teasing and . . . it doesn't . . . ."

"And the pornographic pictures?"

"Well, if you don't like 'em you can always take 'em down."

"No, but you personally feel that goes along with the job—"

"It's there. Yes, it's there."

"And something that you accept as part of your job to have to put up with that; is that correct?"

"Yes."

Boler also coaxed Michelle into admitting that she had signed the petition to avoid retaliation from the men on her crew. Then she turned to the most important question.

"Now, you believe that a policy against sexual harassment which would lay out the definitions of sexual harassment, reporting procedures and penalties and appeal rights, that something like that would benefit the people at Eveleth Mines?"

"Oh, yes, I believe it would."

At the end of the hearing, Sprenger renewed his request for an immediate injunction against further harassment at Eveleth Mines, and an order requiring the company to adopt an anti–sexual harassment policy. Pat Kosmach had come down for the last day of the hearing, as did Priscilla Robich, who now supported the lawsuit. Lois, Pat, and Priscilla all sat together holding hands as Sprenger made his request for the injunction. Lois realized that she had not mentioned the hangman's noose in her testimony—whether she had forgotten to mention it, or her lawyer had forgotten to ask, somehow it had been left out. To her, the noose was the most searing image of the retaliation she faced at work. Lois knew that Joan, Debbie, and Michelle's testimony claiming everything at the mine was fine hurt their chances for getting an injunction. But Lois hoped that her own testimony might still be enough to convince Rosenbaum that action needed to be taken now.

"At this moment I have not been presented with sufficient immediate information calling for the invocation of this court's injunctive powers," Rosenbaum announced to the courtroom audience. Lois and Pat let out such a loud gasp that they startled themselves. The courtroom was quiet for a second. Then Rosenbaum continued. "It appears that while it might be wishful thinking for me to consider the total atmosphere as one of ease, comfort, and amity, things seem to be at the moment in stable and operational mode. In light of that . . . I will decline to enter immediate orders touching on relief."

But then Rosenbaum issued a stern warning. "Should there be a momentary change of whatever kind or nature, and I speak to you, Mr. Daniels." Rosenbaum looked Stan Daniels in the eye. "I speak to you Mr. Henningsgard." Rosenbaum then looked at Jay Henningsgard, who was sitting in the front row on the left side of the courtroom. "I speak to you Miss Jenson, as the first amongst your colleagues. I will permit things to remain as they are, but should there be any changes of material nature, I will be available in person or by telephone for such other matters as need to be considered." Until he had time to decide whether to allow the suit to proceed as a class action, Rosenbaum said, "I make no further rulings whatsoever, neither in your favor nor in yours. Okay? . . . We will be in recess."

Lois was devastated. The hearing had been open to the press on most days, and the Duluth paper wrote about her testimony and Kathy's. Now, without the protection of an injunction, Lois dreaded going back to work.

But the lawyers were more optimistic. "It would have been nice to have walked away with something concrete at that early point," said Boler. "But legally, while we thought we had the case for it, and the evidence, it was not a big surprise that we did not get it, especially as an order from the bench." There was still a chance that Rosenbaum might issue an injunction in his written opinion, once he had had a chance to review all of the evidence, but neither Sprenger nor Boler thought it likely. Lois, however, held out hope.

With that, the two-week hearing that had begun on May 13 and ended June 3, was over. Now they would wait for Rosenbaum's ruling on the issue of class certification, which would come in a written opinion. When it would come, no one could tell, but generally, judges take several months at least to issue a written opinion. When the opinion dealt with as complex and novel legal issues as did *Jenson v. Eveleth*, it could be even longer.

The wait for Rosenbaum's decision felt like a lifetime for Lois and Pat. On June 22, 1991, Lois wrote a reminder to herself in her diary: GRACE, DIGNITY, POISE, LABOR OF LOVE. *Had a terror dream about Steve Povroznik—me yelling it's not over yet.* She went back to work at a job she liked in the warehouse, but every day was tense and she felt on display. A chronic rash developed on her hands.

On October 11, 1991, four months after the class certification hearing, the nation's attention focused on a woman named Anita Hill. Testifying in the confirmation hearings for Supreme Court nominee Clarence Thomas, Hill claimed that Thomas had repeatedly sexually harassed her while he was her supervisor at both the Department of Education and the EEOC.

During the Hill hearings, Lois was on layoff, along with 450 others—over half of Eveleth Mines workers—for six weeks. Layoffs were her "saving grace." With unemployment benefits just barely covering her bills, the time off gave Lois a much-needed break from the rumors and accusations that were making her life at work a nightmare. For three days, along with 30 million Americans, Lois sat riveted in front of the television set. She ordered in for pizza rather than miss a minute. She channel surfed, looking for the most balanced commentators. At times, she was so excited that she couldn't sit still. She paced up and down her apartment, and talked back to the TV. During breaks, Lois called Pat, Michele, and her therapist, Claire Bell, to compare notes.

As Hill answered questions from fourteen white male senators, Lois was overcome with a feeling of déjà vu. Like Lois, Hill was embarrassed to describe her allegations of the crude sexual come-ons of her then boss Clarence Thomas—the pubic hair on the Coke can, a porno film starring "Long Dong Silver," Thomas's bragging about the size of his penis. Like Lois, Hill's character and credibility came into question. Hill, too, was prim and proper, raised in a conservative, rural Baptist community, and like Lois, she was easily offended by sexual talk. Hill had even been hospitalized for severe stress-related stomach pains. Lois still nursed a stomach ulcer she contracted after her problems with Gene Scaia.

"I could relate to everything she was going through," said Lois. "I totally believed her. Her eyes said it all. Thomas was not honest and it showed. His anger and body language were so familiar."

The senators reminded Lois of more sophisticated versions of the Eveleth Mines management. Their ignorance and disregard for the issue of sexual harassment, or "this sexual harassment *crap*," as Senator Alan Simpson growled, was eerily familiar. So was the senator's eagerness to slander Hill: "I have all kinds of incriminating stuff coming over the transom," warned Simpson. Flipping open his jacket to show papers in his breast pocket, Simpson said, "I've got faxes, I've got statements from her former law professors, statements from people that know her, statements from Tulsa, Oklahoma, saying 'Watch out for this woman.' "

Anita Hill's life drama mirrored Lois's, except that it was being conducted on prime-time network television. Thanks to Hill, the nation was unwittingly taking a crash course in the nuances of an obscure new workplace phenomena—sexual harassment. "Overnight, as on perhaps no other issue in our history, the entire country made a giant leap of understanding about sexual harassment," Edward Kennedy announced on the Senate floor. "That offensive conduct will never be treated lightly again."

Across town, another woman sat riveted in front of her television set. Diane Hodge watched as Anita Hill never lost her composure or the courage of her convictions. Hodge felt a twinge of conscience, a secret sense of shame. If this woman was brave enough to come forward about such an important man, and risk her reputation and her comfortable, anonymous existence, "If she could do it," thought Diane, "I can do it, too."

CHAPTER ELEVEN

Victories

December 16, 1991

Down the long, cinder-block hallway between the concentrator and the pellet plant was a glass-paned door that opened onto a series of small rooms that made up the plant laboratory. In the large front room, pale green aluminum lockers covered one wall. On an island in the middle of the room, test tubes, plastic tubs, and two sinks formed the command center for testing the taconite purity of pellets in all stages of production. Women tended to bid on lab jobs at Eveleth and keep them. They were the cleanest, quietest jobs at the mine, and Pat had been a fixture there for twelve years before she'd had to stop working. Lois, who bid on a job in the lab earlier in the year, was working the afternoon shift on December 16, 1991, when Pat called her there with the news.

"We got our class!" Pat shouted into the phone. "We got our class. We won!" Lois's heart leapt. "Did we get the injunction?" she asked, remembering that the lawyers had said there was a chance Rosenbaum would issue one in his written decision.

"Oh, the injunction," Pat said, "I forgot to ask."

In her excitement, Pat had hung up the phone on Jean Boler before Boler could tell her the second part of Rosenbaum's ruling. Pat told Lois she would check with Boler and call right back.

Lois waited by the phone. She had always expected that they would get class certification. But what she wanted was a court order forcing the company to establish a sexual harassment policy—she thought it was the only thing that would push the company to make changes at Eveleth. She also believed it was the only thing that would protect her from more harassment and retaliation.

The six months of living and waiting for Rosenbaum's ruling felt interminable. Lois assumed the judge was sincere when he said that she could call him if she had any problems at work. So when she found her time sheet in shreds on the company bulletin board, she called Boler. "Is that enough to call Rosenbaum?" Boler calmly suggested that Lois go back to work. Again, Lois called Boler when her job at the warehouse was suspiciously eliminated. "Do we call him on this?" she asked.

"Lois was always in a crisis about something," Sprenger said later. She kept notes about every conversation she heard at work and sent them to the lawyers. She clipped newspaper articles in the local papers about mines and the steel industry and sent them to the lawyers. She wrote short notes and long letters to the lawyers once a week on average. Buried under a flurry of correspondence, Boler and Sprenger lost track of which of Lois's problems to take seriously.

Lois was now seeing Claire Bell every other week. She watched Deepak Chopra videos, listened to relaxation tapes, practiced deep-breathing exercises, and read self-help books about coping with stress. She talked to Bell about quitting her job, but she could never take the final step to leave—she was too invested in fighting the company, too stubborn. "Lois viewed leaving the job as letting them win," Bell recalled. "I'm not going to let them drive me out of here." Bell tried to help Lois, but the constant tension at the mine made Bell's job of protecting Lois's psychological well-being difficult. "I felt like I was shoveling snow in a blizzard with a teaspoon," she said.

In late October 1991, when it came time to return to work after a six-week layoff, Lois's stress level had shot up. She became paranoid and her ulcer flared. She had nightmares and flashbacks, often about

Steve Povroznik. JoeB had recently moved from Minneapolis to Mexico where he went into the time-share business with his brother. He flew Lois down to Cabo San Lucas for a vacation, and they talked on the phone three times a week, but the physical distance between them started to chip away at their intimacy. Just as she was returning to work, Eveleth Mines reported a 72.4 percent reduction in its net income. Talk of another round of layoffs, and even a shutdown, laced every conversation at the mine and in the bars on the Range. With each bad-news story about the decline of the steel industry, Lois felt increasingly vulnerable.

The phone rang again. Pat was no longer excited.

"We didn't get it. He didn't give us the injunction."

As the information registered, Lois started to feel pressure in her chest. She could hardly breathe. Sitting on a stool next to the counter Lois put her head in her hands and exploded into heaving sobs. "I felt like someone does after they survive a tornado or a hurricane," she said. "You're glad you're alive, but your house is gone and your cat died." Victory without legal protection was the worst of both worlds for Lois. "I needed to hear 'injunction' so I could get on my knees and say thank you," said Lois. "Instead, now it's in writing that we've got the class and everybody's going to know who's in it, but we don't have any protection."

Class certification gave Lois, Pat, Kathy, and any other women who wanted to join them the green light to sue Oglebay Norton. Now the stakes were higher than ever because money would be involved, big money. Lois was scared. If they had threatened her with a noose for just filing the lawsuit, what would she get for winning a class? Her mind raced as she clicked off the different places in the plant that were dangerous to venture into. She called Pat back. "Do I dare walk into the pellet plant again? I don't want to be a member of the turtle club," she told Pat. Members of the turtle club were people who had been struck by hard objects, like hammers, from high places by people who didn't like them.

Sprenger and Boler were disappointed but not surprised by Rosenbaum's decision to deny injunctive relief. After all, the company had not yet been found liable for maintaining a sexually hostile work environment, or having inadequate policies to address employee complaints. It would have been premature to issue an order to enjoin the company from engaging in conduct that it had not yet been found to be engaging in. The purpose of the class hearing had been to decide whether the women could jointly pursue their claims. The determination of liability would have to wait for a hearing on the merits of those claims.

Lois called Boler the morning of December 17. Boler noticed immediately how distraught Lois was, and she worried about her. "I could tell that Lois was getting more and more fragile." Lois also called Sprenger, who was in Washington, D.C. Sprenger was puzzled by their conversation. "When we won the class, Lois was devastated. I really didn't understand it. Lois got a little bit crazy that way. She wanted to be right, but she really didn't know what she wanted." To Paul, Lois did not seem to understand that they had just won a major victory—the right to bring the first class action based on a sexually hostile work environment.

In legal terms, Rosenbaum's ruling was a stunning victory for Sprenger & Lang. "Title VII [of the Civil Rights Act of 1964] does not mandate an employment environment worthy of a Victorian salon. White gloves, crystal, and fine china are neither required nor expected," Rosenbaum wrote. "The Court heard evidence of pervasive offensive conduct. Sexually explicit graffiti and posters were found on the walls and in the lunchroom areas, tool rooms, lockers, desks and offices. . . . Women reported incidents of unwelcome touching, including kissing, pinching and grabbing. Women reported offensive language . . . as well as . . . comments that women did not belong in the mines, kept jobs from men, and belonged home with their children. The Court finds this evidence sufficient to demonstrate that a defined class exists as to plaintiffs' claims for sexual harassment."

Rosenbaum also dismissed Oglebay Norton's assertion that because many of the women had not complained about the sexually explicit materials in the workplace, the company could not be responsible for allowing the materials to be displayed. "Defendants," he wrote, "pointed to no case law recognizing lack of protest as a defense."

Rosenbaum's opinion had set a major national precedent. The significance of the ruling was that for the first time ever, companies that maintained hostile work environments could be liable for damages to an entire class of employees who had been exposed to that environment, rather than to just one individual at a time. "It did not dawn on me that this was a historic case until the class decision was rendered," said Sprenger. "At that point I realized that something special had happened."

Coincidentally, the Rosenbaum decision was made all the more significant by changes to Title VII that were adopted by Congress in the wake of the Hill-Thomas controversy. In late November 1991, Congress amended Title VII to provide compensatory damages for pain and suffering, including emotional distress, in all discrimination cases. The Civil Rights Act of 1991 had the greatest impact on sex discrimination and harassment cases because victims of race-based discrimination had relied in the past on other federal statutes for monetary relief whereas women had no where else within the federal system to go. The new law allowed for women who had been discriminated against to receive up to $300,000 per plaintiff in damages awards. For Lois and the other women the effect was minimal: They were already able to claim damages under Minnesota state law. But now that significant monetary awards were available and sexual harassment class actions were possible, a sea change had just occurred in sexual harassment law.

Immediately in the wake of Anita Hill, the corporate and media worlds took note. On December 18, the *Wall Street Journal* carried the story on the front page of its second section. "The first-ever sexual harassment class action, claiming that all women in a workplace were subjected to a hostile work environment, was approved by a federal judge in Minneapolis," the story began. The article quoted a labor lawyer saying the precedent was a "bad sign for employers." And, in fact, Rosenbaum's decision was the first of many that led Corporate America to begin to take sexual harassment seriously.

Another lawyer told the *Journal*, "It's going to make it easier for plaintiffs emotionally to be part of the class, to become involved in this sort of litigation." The *St. Paul Pioneer Press* ran a banner headline on the front of its business section, "Eveleth women miners' sex bias suit will be class action." The article quoted Sprenger announcing triumphantly, "This represents a major breakthrough that will give all women faced with sexual harassment in the workplace a powerful new tool in future cases."

While the victory caught headlines in papers around the country, the largest paper on the Iron Range, Virginia's *Mesabi Daily News*, buried a short Associated Press story about the ruling on page A17. Bill Hannah, editor of the *Mesabi Daily News*, sent one of his eleven staff reporters to cover the first day of the hearing in Duluth, but from then on, he did not assign a reporter to cover the case. "Once the case was in federal court, its coverage was going to be handled nationally," Hannah said, somewhat unconvincingly. For the next few years, Hannah would make a practice of downplaying this national story that was unfolding in his backyard because, he said, he did not know which side to believe. "This is not condoning what happened, but the men felt that when the case was filed in federal court, there was a broad brush taken to them. They felt slandered because a lot of the behavior cuts both ways. They are men who work hard, earn a living, raise a family. They may not be churchgoers, but they're regular Joes. Now if a woman in the mine flirts with them, or tells them a dirty joke, can they go to their supervisor and complain that they've been sexually harassed?" Hannah's hands-off approach to the *Jenson v. Eveleth* case contributed to keeping people on the Range in the dark. Rumor and innuendo, not the facts, fed the curiosity of Rangers about the case.

But for Lois, obscurity at home was the least of her problems. All she knew was that it had now been more than three years since Sprenger had first filed the federal lawsuit, and so far, all that had happened was that she had been told she could proceed to the next step. Three years might not seem like a lot of time to judges and lawyers, but it seemed like an eternity to Lois.

On the morning of December 18, Marcy Steele called Lois at home, Lois wrote in her diary:

> *Marcy called this morning to congratulate us on the class. She said it was in the Duluth paper that day, and at a meeting with the staff, they announced that we all got our class, that the evidence was sufficient enough. She said everyone was quiet and a couple of the guys asked her how she felt about it. Most thought it was over and done with. Marcy and Diane discussed it and both thought we'd now have a policy.*
>
> *Now guys are talking about suing us for defamation. In the lab Harry Hilliard is getting grief from home [his wife] about the trial. He says he should sue for defamation.*
>
> *About midnight it hit me. This time it might be different. I feel great! Hope it lasts.*

The next day, Connie Saari and Priscilla Robich called to congratulate Lois. Connie said that she was thinking about joining the suit.

"Is Marcy going to join?"

"Honestly, I don't know. You both qualify for the class. All the gals do, but it should be easier for you because you did an affidavit."

When she hung up, Lois called to commiserate with Pat. "Isn't it funny how my phone hasn't rung from Connie or Marcy since the trial, until now? Marcy is like a swinging door. Now she, Connie, and Diane want to be on the winning side. Now that we've won, they've changed their minds."

By December 22, six days after the class certification, Lois's elation over winning certification was once again giving way to her fears of backlash. *Glamour* magazine had published an article about the case in its January issue. The article, featuring a picture of Lois looking distraught and bloated in a white shirt and jacket, carried the headline: "Can a whole company be guilty of sexual harassment?" The first paragraph read: "Anita Hill may be out of the spotlight, but other women across the country are speaking up about sexual harassment. Take Lois Jenson, Patricia Kosmach and Kathleen O'Brien Anderson. On behalf of their fellow female employees at Eveleth Mines, a Minnesota mining company, the three have brought the first class action sexual harassment suit against an employer claiming not just that individual instances of harassment exist but that the entire company sexually harasses its entire female workforce. At press time, a decision was still pending."

The magazine, which Lois picked up at the newsstand at the IGA three days before Rosenbaum's ruling, had not generated much attention. But on the twenty-second multiple copies were posted around the plant, annotated with graffiti. On one, someone wrote the word *BULL-SHIT!* over the words *on behalf of all the women employees,* and the headline was doctored to read: "Can a hole be guilty of sexual harassment?" On another copy, someone drew horns and a mustache on the picture of Lois. Whenever Lois took down the copies, new ones would appear. Two days before Christmas, Lois walked into the lunchroom as a group of men, including some of her own crew members, were passing around copies of the article. When the men noticed Lois, they grew silent, and stared at her until she left the room. Later that night, she took down a copy that had been tacked on the bulletin board. The next day, Christmas Eve, Lois arrived at work to find an enlarged version had taken its place. The retaliation she had feared for so long had begun.

As the New Year of 1992 dawned, the anxiety and depression that plagued Lois on and off ever since the Povroznik incidents in 1984 worsened to the point where she finally snapped. Lois prayed and recited motivational poems in the car on the way to work. Some days, she just cried. "I'd have days when I woke up and felt sick. I would call in sick and two hours later, I'd feel fine because I wasn't stressed about having to go to work." To calm her nerves, she listened to stress-relief hypnosis tapes all night while she slept.

She was often dizzy, and found herself tripping frequently for no apparent reason. At times she had trouble remembering how to do her job. Once, while working as a grinding mill attendant, she couldn't remember what to do, even though she had done the job hundreds of times. When given a hosing assignment, she had to sit down on a bucket because she thought her legs might give out from under her. She had trouble driving her own car. Her sleeping was erratic. She had flashbacks of the hangman's noose, and nightmares about being chased at work. For no apparent reason, she went on crying jags that lasted for hours. She became socially isolated both in and out of work.

Claire Bell had never seen Lois so completely out of control when she came in for an hour and a half session on January 24, 1992. Bell jotted down some notes after Lois left the office. *Uncontrollable crying— fearful—disillusionment: Fought so hard for what? No changes, what was won? Afraid to be at work, isolated, hyper alert, paranoid—sick before work again—dread—feels no support—all alone—flashbacks—full blown PTSD reaction of depression.*

In 1980, psychiatrists treating patients who had experienced all kinds of physical and emotional trauma compared notes with military psychiatrists treating Vietnam veterans for "shell shock." Together they developed a new psychological terminology for an acute anxiety disorder called post-traumatic stress disorder, or PTSD. "The essential feature of this disorder is the development of characteristic symptoms following a psychologically distressing event that is outside the range of usual human experience," wrote the American Psychiatric Association. Lois had the same "characteristic symptoms" as the Vietnam vets and sexual assault victims who visited Bell's office over the past twenty years—flashbacks, blackouts, uncontrolled crying, rage, isolation, and paranoia. Lois had shell shock.

Bell told Lois that she could not return to work that day, or even that week. "This is it, this is the end," she said. Lois needed to take a vacation and seriously consider quitting her job. But Lois resisted. "If I don't go back to work, the company will have won. They've wanted me out from the beginning." Bell recognized Lois's tendencies to put other people's needs before her own. As she put it, Lois was a "caretaker who had difficulty recognizing and respecting her own personal limits." If she had to quit work at Eveleth Mines years earlier, in time to salvage her mental health, "Lois would have had to have been a different person," said Bell.

Bell knew that Lois needed medication. She picked up the phone and called Randall Lakosky in Hibbing. As the only practicing psychiatrist on the Iron Range who could prescribe psychotropic medication, Lakosky was a busy man. He saw a hundred patients a week. Bell made an appointment for Lois to see Lakosky the following week.

Despite Bell's warning, Lois decided to go back to work that afternoon. On the way to the plant, she stopped at the IGA to pick up lunch. When she got to the dairy counter, she became overwhelmed with an urge to hit a woman standing next to her. "I didn't know her. But the urge was so compelling, I ran out of the store." Lois then changed her mind about going to work and decided to follow Dr. Bell's advice.

1/25 called in sick
1/26 called in sick
1/27 called in sick
1/28 called Klasnya for S&A form.

First Lois used up her vacation days. Then she filled out the sickness and accident forms that Bob Klasnya had sent her in order to qualify for disability pay. "It was almost all crying, neck pain, headaches. I was more terrified than ever before." After she had used up the remains of her vacation days, she still hadn't returned to normal, and it dawned on her that she might never go back to work. In February, Lois started taking Pamelor and Klonopin, antidepressant and antianxiety drugs that heavily sedated her. In April, her first disability check arrived in the mail. The benefits totaled $997 a month, about half her salary, and nearly half of that was eaten up by medical bills. Lois could not apply for her pension because Sprenger and Boler didn't want the medical examination required for the pension to become admissible evidence in court.

Her financial situation was getting desperate. Lois could no longer afford to live in her apartment in Gilbert. In May, with the help of her brother Duane, who lived in Minneapolis, and Greg, who was now twenty-four and working in a gold mine in Elko, Nevada, Lois moved into a low-income housing unit for the elderly and disabled in nearby Mountain Iron. Lois's parents had retired to Nevada, where Lois's brother Leland who worked with Greg in the gold mine in Elko, also lived. Lois's sister Marilyn was the only family member who lived geographically closeby. Lois could no longer be trusted to cook or iron for herself. She left food burning on the stove, the iron plugged in. A week of dishes would pile up in the sink of her small kitchenette before Lois could summon the energy to wash them. In just five months, chronic stress had turned Lois into an invalid.

To make matters worse, a month after her move to Mountain Iron, Lois's boyfriend, Joe Bjergo, broke up with her. Their long-distance relationship had lasted almost four years, but for the past year it had become strained. The combination of distance and Lois's declining condition made the relationship more and more remote. Still, Lois relied on JoeB's support over the phone, and they spoke frequently. One night she called him and told him that she loved him. When he didn't return the affection, Lois pleaded, "I need to hear it from you." What Lois heard from Joe when they next saw each other in June was, "The pills have changed you. I think we need to break it off cold turkey."

Lois was not alone in her failing welfare. Kathy Anderson's health had also deteriorated dramatically since the certification hearing. In late December 1991, shortly after the ruling, she experienced an incident that left her severely traumatized. While digging rocks out of the shaft of a jammed crusher, two large rocks fell from a catwalk fifty feet up. If Kathy's partner hadn't seen the rocks and pushed her out of the way, the rocks would have landed on her head. Whether the falling rocks were an accident or the act of someone on the catwalk, Kathy was firmly convinced that someone was trying to kill her—this was the retaliation she had always feared. She also became paranoid and withdrawn, coming home from work, flopping down on the couch and falling asleep for twelve hours. She stopped bathing and started binge-eating. She had a psychotic episode and was hospitalized for five days. In mid-February of 1992, Dr. Lakosky diagnosed Kathy with post-traumatic stress disorder and prescribed tranquilizers. "I was on so much medication, I could barely hold my head up," she recalled. Kathy applied for Social Security disability payments and never went back to work.

On May 13, Marcy Steele, feeling guilty about Lois and Kathy's deteriorating condition, made a peace offering. Marcy knew that the other women were on the verge of changing their minds about Lois, Kathy, and the lawsuit. Marcy wanted to help open the channels of communication between the two groups. A friend of hers sold jewelry in people's houses, so using the jewelry as a nice excuse to get a group of women together, Marcy hosted a jewelry party. She invited Lois and Kathy, as well as Joan Hunholz, Debbie Shersa, Diane Hodge, and Jan Friend. Joan and Debbie had testified against Lois in court, Diane had given a deposition defending the company but had not testified in court, and all of them had signed the petition. None of the women had been on speaking terms with Lois or Kathy for over a year.

The women gathered in her cozy blue-and-white-wallpapered kitchen. After an hour of pleasantries and the trying on of bracelets, earrings, and necklaces, the matter of Lois and Kathy's lawsuit came up. Diane explained that the sexual harassment committee and policy that Stan Daniels had promised a year ago never materialized. Joan Hunholz said she couldn't get Stan to return her phone calls. "We're starting to get a clear picture that we are being used," Marcy confessed. "They are still treating us badly even though we haven't joined the case."

The women stayed up late talking about the frustrations they were experiencing at work. Having only attended the class certification hearing on the day that they each testified, the women still did not know each other's stories. "Every girl told stuff that had happened to them," remembered Diane. "And nobody knew that it had happened to everybody. Each girl kind of thought like me, that the shit I got was because of my personality. Nobody really knew how deep and how many things bothered everybody till we all sat together and told each other."

As the evening came to a close at around 1:00 A.M., Diane Hodge piped up. "Girls, can you say there was no sexual harassment in the mines? Can you say you've never been sexually harassed?" The room fell silent. "Now, can you sit here and tell Lois, 'No, we can't go to court with you?'" By the time everyone had strolled outside into the star-lit night and started up their cars, "we knew we were going to join," said Marcy.

One of the symptoms of Lois's PTSD was the deadening of emotional feeling. Lois appreciated the camaraderie of the evening. She loved being let back into these women's lives after having been shut out for so long. But she couldn't feel excitement or joy. It was almost as if her scrambled brain was protecting her against the possibility of yet another disappointment. And it was a good thing, because as encouraging as the women were that night, none of them called Sprenger & Lang the next day.

Ugly deposition tactics aside, Paul Sprenger thought Ray Erickson was a realist, and that Oglebay Norton would surely settle. After all, the vast majority of cases settle after a class has been certified. Certification changes the dynamics, shifts the balance of power between the parties. The plaintiffs were no longer just three individuals whose claims could be easily bought off. Now the company had to face the fact that its potential exposure extended to all the hourly women who worked in the mine from 1983 to the present. It made no sense financially for the company to keep going when they could end it all before the expense of more discovery and a trial.

Soon after Rosenbaum's ruling, a federal magistrate in Duluth named Patrick J. McNulty retired, and Ray Erickson was appointed to take his place. This, as Sprenger and Boler would see soon enough, was a calamitous turn of events for them.

Whether he had already been fired or was on the verge of being fired by the company because he lost the class motion is unclear. But in any event, when Erickson became federal magistrate, the company declined to continue using the services of his Duluth firm, and instead turned to the high-powered, old-line Minneapolis firm of Faegre & Benson to take over the case.

With more than three hundred lawyers, Faegre & Benson was the second-largest law firm in Minnesota. Established in 1886, it had a long and storied history. Its partnership ranks were filled with prominent Twin Cities citizens; its clients were among the biggest banks and businesses. The firm was housed in the heart of Minneapolis's business district, in the kind of towering steel-and-glass skyscraper that Sprenger had worked so hard to escape. If the firm had one dominant personality characteristic it was its relentless work ethic. When a fire destroyed the firm's offices on Thanksgiving Day 1982, the employees—from partners to clerks—spent the entire holiday weekend salvaging files and materials, and were ready to reopen for business in temporary quarters the following Monday.

The partner assigned to the *Jenson* case was Mary Stumo, a no-nonsense woman with a severe haircut and an equally unsubtle approach to litigation. Stumo was a highly regarded corporate defense lawyer, regularly listed in the annual compilation of the Best Lawyers in America. Her specialty was defending companies against employment discrimination claims, and in challenging plaintiffs' use of expert testimony. Assisting her in the case was an ambitious young associate, a Harvard Law School graduate named David Goldstein, who was just entering his final push for partner at the firm.

Although Sprenger knew of Faegre & Benson, he did not know Stumo. When she took over the case in February 1992, she called Sprenger to ask for time to come up to speed. Out of professional courtesy, Sprenger agreed not to actively pursue the case for two months. He was fairly confident that once she had a chance to review the files, and Rosenbaum's ruling, she would be interested in serious settlement negotiations.

For Boler, the slowdown came at a good time. In January she had given birth to a daughter, Rosie, and began a three-month maternity leave. But she continued to work on the case from home.

In April 1992, Stumo called Sprenger in Washington to say that she was ready for a meeting. Sprenger was in the thick of a race discrimination class action against PEPCO, the largest utility company in the Washington, D.C., area, and he had planned to stay in the capital for a few more days. But he was eager to hear what Stumo had to say, so he arranged to fly back to Minneapolis for the meeting.

When Sprenger arrived at Stumo's office, she listened as he presented the plaintiffs' demands. He told her that they were now willing to settle the entire case for a sexual harassment policy and approximately $1.3 million, including attorneys' fees and costs. At that point, his firm's fees and expenses exceeded $800,000. When Sprenger was finished, he waited for Stumo's counteroffer. But to his surprise she told him that she did not have the authority to settle the case without her client's authorization. Sprenger was furious that she would ask him to fly out to Minneapolis just to hear him make an offer, that she did not have something to put on the table herself. In what Sprenger regarded as a clear breach of professional courtesy, she had apparently set up the meeting to hear his clients' position without having to reveal her own.

Still, Sprenger reminded himself, she did not reject the offer outright. When he got back to his office, he and Boler drafted a formal settlement demand reaffirming the plaintiffs' position, hoping that it might trigger a counteroffer once Stumo had time to consult with her clients.

Stumo's response to the settlement offer was to send to Sprenger & Lang a long, detailed confidentiality agreement in preparation for settlement negotiations. It was five pages long and uncommonly comprehensive—it would have required the plaintiffs to agree not to talk about whatever settlement offers Stumo made and not to talk about the case itself to the press ever again. In a nutshell, it would have required the plaintiffs to agree to a gag order about the case, just so they could hear whatever offer Stumo was prepared to make.

The draft agreement was "ridiculous," Boler said later, and she and Sprenger refused to sign it. Sprenger, less apt to see the dark side of things, was willing to give Stumo the benefit of the doubt, and chalked it up to either inexperience or an abundance of caution. Boler, however, thought it was not only absurd but that it signaled an inflexibility that boded ill for future negotiations. After several weeks of negotiating about the confidentiality agreement, the two sides finally agreed on a one-page version, which would prohibit discussion about the terms of Stumo's offer.

With the agreement signed, Stumo presented her offer to Sprenger & Lang: $300,000 for the entire case, including attorneys' fees and costs. Sprenger and Boler were stunned that Stumo would make them go through the exercise of hammering out such a detailed confidentiality agreement just so she could make such a low-ball offer, one that she knew full well they would not accept. "It was so low, so stupendously inadequate, and her attitude was take it or see you in court," Jean said later. "It was just weird. We had told them what our demand was, and it was nowhere near $300,000, so she had to be nuts to think we would seriously take this."

Sprenger had a different explanation. When he saw the offer, it seemed to him that everything leading up to it had been a delaying tactic to buy more time to prepare for trial. It was his first insight into Mary Stumo's style, and he did not like what he saw. That was the last time Sprenger and Boler ever dealt only with Stumo in settlement negotiations. "From then on, whenever we wanted to talk settlement, we did it with Goldstein or someone who had a potential for reaching a meeting of the minds, or at least having the courtesy to explain their reasons for rejecting an offer," Boler said later. "Stumo did not have the personality for settlement. It requires a give and take, a dialog."

By the end of the summer of 1992, the taconite industry was in real trouble, and Eveleth Mines, as the most cost-inefficient producer of taconite on the Range, was likely to suffer accordingly. In September, Armco Inc., the New Jersey–based steel maker and one of four owners of Eveleth Mines, announced that it planned to buy cheap ore from Brazil instead of from Eveleth. The practice, known as foreign dumping, was gutting the steel market everywhere. A few weeks later, the mine circulated a memo, titled "Eveleth Mines Cost Reduction Program" that stated, "Steel prices have deteriorated to such an extent that steel is presently cheaper than Kleenex or potatoes." To remain competitive, the memo stated, the company would have to cut costs by $10 per ton. In early October, the Duluth *News Tribune* ran an article headlined, "Mine shutdowns make uncertainty a way of life on Iron Range." The story reported that five of the seven taconite companies on the Range had announced layoffs in 1992.

The layoffs began in October and November. Six hundred workers at Eveleth were laid off for a six-week shutdown that many suspected would last longer. Although the economic downturn hurt Lois's case in some ways, heightening tension and fueling hostility toward the women, it also helped.

On November 18, 1992, Marcy hosted another jewelry party and invited the same cast of characters, except this time they had all been laid off. "When they laid us off and told us we were all going home for good, we thought, well, this would be perfect, none of us have to go back," said Diane Hodge. "Things had to change, and three little girls weren't going to do it by themselves." That night, Hodge, Hunholz, Friend, and Robich all agreed that they would testify for the women in the next trial. As much as Lois resented the women for not joining earlier, they did not sense it. "Lois did *a lot* of work [on the suit]," Diane said later. "I felt bad that we snubbed her for so long. But she understood how afraid we were. She knew all along that that's what was keeping us out of it. We had to live here. We've lived here all our life."

———

The case was set for trial before Judge Richard Kyle in the Federal District Court in St. Paul. Kyle, appointed to the bench by President George H. W. Bush in 1992, was relatively new to the bench when he was assigned to the *Jenson* case. A former partner at Briggs and Morgan, a large prestigious Minneapolis firm, Kyle was an imposing, courtly man with silver hair and gentle blue eyes. He was reputed to be exceptionally hardworking: He arrived in his chambers as early as six in the morning, and was often one of the last judges to leave the building at night.

Boler soon had an opportunity to observe Kyle's prodigious work habits firsthand, when he called the lawyers for both sides to his chambers for a pretrial conference, to set deadlines and establish a trial date. Boler immediately noticed that Kyle's desk was covered in the transcripts from the certification hearing, which were festooned with yellow Post-It notes. While many judges rely on their clerks to read the record of earlier proceedings, Boler could tell from Kyle's familiarity with the case that he had already read them himself.

One of the preliminary issues to be decided before the trial started was whether the evidence admitted in the certification hearing, including all the testimony, would be considered part of the record for the next phase of the trial. If not, the witnesses would have to testify all over again to the same things that they testified to at the earlier hearing. Boler, who was worried about Lois's health, was hopeful that she could be spared having to spend so much time on the stand. She was relieved when Kyle told the lawyers that they could call the same witnesses to testify about supplemental facts, including developments since the certification hearing. But he made clear that he did not want any live testimony that repeated what was presented in the certification hearing, particularly since he had already read all of the transcripts from the earlier hearing.

Kyle also responded to a motion by Sprenger & Lang asking that the trial be split into two parts. In the first phase, the only issue would be whether Eveleth Mines had maintained a hostile work environment or otherwise discriminated against its female hourly workers. If the answer were yes, then a second phase of the trial would be held to determine the amount of damages each woman in the class was entitled to. Bifurcation was relatively common in large, complex class actions, where the question of the defendant's liability is applicable to all of the class, but the extent to which each plaintiff had been damaged as a result varied from person to person. It was a more efficient way to handle cases, because time and energy were not expended on the issue of specific damages until the court had found that the defendant was liable in the first place.

It was also, from Sprenger's point of view, preferable for strategic reasons. The issue of liability—did Eveleth Mines maintain a hostile work environment—was relatively straightforward, and the focus was primarily on the behavior of the company. The question of damages would focus almost solely on the women. Sprenger did not want to put the women through that, or expend the resources it would involve—expert medical witnesses, the gathering and production of medical and other records for each woman—unless it was necessary.

Kyle agreed. The first phase of the trial, to determine whether Oglebay Norton was liable for maintaining a hostile work environment discriminating against its female employees, would begin in St. Paul on December 17, 1992—a year after Rosenbaum had issued his certification ruling.

In November, as the trial date neared, Sprenger and Boler decided to try again to breathe life into the possibility of a settlement. But Sprenger found it distracting to talk settlement when he was preparing for trial—for war. While he prepared witness lists and outlines for his direct and cross-examinations, Jane Lang handled the settlement negotiations. Lang had not been actively involved in the case since she'd deposed the Cleveland-based managers of Oglebay Norton in 1990. But she and Sprenger constantly kept each other abreast of their cases, and she was fully aware of what was going on.

Normally, Lang would have gotten in touch with Stumo, but after the debacle with her a few months earlier, Lang decided to approach a senior partner at Faegre & Benson named Jim Samples. Samples was not involved in the case, and Sprenger, who knew him personally, thought he was a reasonable, thoughtful man who would at least listen dispassionately to the plaintiffs' position. Samples did listen, but the talks went nowhere. "I got the feeling that he appreciated the scope of his firm's client's potential exposure, but for some reason he could not get any movement. To this day, I don't know if this is because the client would not move, or he could not get to the client through Stumo," Sprenger said. Whatever the reason, Sprenger and Boler once more began to prepare for battle.

CHAPTER TWELVE

Liability

December 1992

The trial began on December 17, 1992, a warm day by Twin Cities' standards: sixteen degrees with a dusting of snow flurries. It had been almost five years since Lois and Pat first went to see Paul Sprenger. Judge Kyle's courtroom, in the once-modern but now depressingly boxy and bland 1970s-era Warren Burger Building in downtown St. Paul, was filled to the brim. Several of the men went to stores in St. Paul and bought suits to wear in court. "They all cleaned up their acts," said Bob Klasnya. And for the first time, all of the women—Lois, Kathy, Michele Mesich, Diane Hodge, Marcy Steele, Jan Friend, Joan Hunholz, Connie Saari, and Priscilla Robich—were sitting on the same side of the aisle. Even Pat Kosmach, although too sick to testify, had made the trip to the Cities in an ambulance with a nurse attendant so she could show her commitment to the case.

Sprenger, his thick head of black hair showing touches of gray at the temples, his voice confident and measured, made a brief opening statement. He explained something Kyle already knew, that the purpose of this phase of the trial was simply to determine whether Eveleth Mines maintained a hostile work environment and discriminated against women in hiring, promotions, and other job benefits. The plaintiffs, he explained, were not asking for specific damages awards at this stage: If Kyle found Eveleth Mines liable on any of the claims, damages would be tried at the next phase of the trial. But, Sprenger said, the women were asking for Kyle to issue an injunction prohibiting Eveleth Mines from violating the women's civil rights and adopting an anti–sexual harassment policy.

When Sprenger finished, Mary Stumo, wearing a neutral business suit, rose. "Your Honor," she said, "there is no hostile environment at Eveleth Mines. . . . Your Honor, the evidence will show that most of the women prior to coming into the workplace at all had friends or relatives who referred them and in fact worked in the workplace themselves. They were not going into a foreign territory with no friends or relatives. It will also show that many women dated fellow employees, and in fact found some of the sexual overtures by fellow coworkers to be welcome, and in fact married some of the people. They developed close friendships." Stumo went on to say that the few times the company knew of a problem with a particular employee, such as Steve Povroznik, the company effectively and swiftly addressed it. As for the language, the graffiti, the pornography, Stumo said, many of the women did not find it objectionable, and in fact, some of the women told dirtier jokes than the men. All in all, Stumo argued, "there was no pattern or practice of discrimination" at Eveleth Mines.

When Stumo sat down, Sprenger called Lois to the stand. Bob Klasnya sat on the defense side of the courtroom watching the trial unfold with a strange feeling of ambivalence. He had spent months preparing his testimony to defend the company against the charge of sex discrimination in hiring and promotions, and he was convinced the company had not willfully kept women out of higher-paying jobs. Klasnya had the documentation to prove that women tended to pass up promotions and gravitate toward the lower-paying, day-shift jobs. But Klasnya felt differently about the sexual harassment part of the case. He had spent the last three weeks in the Holiday Inn Rivercentre eight blocks from the courthouse watching Mary Stumo and Jay Henningsgard work with Stan

Daniels and a dozen foremen and managers preparing their testimony. The whole scene had made Klasnya uneasy. "I'm sure every one of us went up there and had a very difficult time recalling some of the conversations we had with each other," Klasnya later admitted.

During those Holiday Inn sessions, Klasnya observed the good rapport Stumo had with the men. "She acted like one of the boys." Klasnya liked Stumo. He thought she was competent and warm.

When Lois took the stand for her first day of testimony, Klasnya was shocked to see how much she had changed. Her hands were shaking, her once beautiful face was bloated and blotchy. She looked chubby and disheveled. This was not the poised, self-assured Lois Bob Klasnya remembered seeing in the late eighties and early nineties at company picnics and retirement parties. Klasnya turned to his wife, and said under his breath, "Lois is on *way* too many drugs."

To quell her panic attacks, Lois took 1 milligram of Klonopin three times a day. But on stressful days like today, she doubled her dose. Each day she also took one 75-milligram pill of the antidepressant Pamelor, which helped her transition out of her crying jags. Klasnya noticed that Lois's speech was slow and slightly slurred, and that she had to pause before she answered Sprenger's questions. But despite her tranquilized state, Lois managed to soldier through the direct examination with few flaws.

On cross-examination, Stumo set up a large aerial map of the plant, and handed Lois a stack of red stickers shaped like arrows. Then she showed Lois exhibit 31 from the Rosenbaum hearing, a poster advertising a nearly topless, large-breasted stripper named Bunny Jo. Stumo asked Lois to place an arrow on the aerial map to show where in the plant the poster had been hung. Lois complied, sticking the arrow on a wall in the electrical shop.

"You were rarely in that area, isn't that correct?" asked Stumo.

"I walked by this area every day," Lois answered.

Stumo then asked Lois whether she had complained about the poster, or filed a grievance to have it removed. Lois said no.

Then Stumo handed Lois exhibit 32, the cartoon of a man with a penis for a nose and testicles for a mouth, and asked Lois to place a sticker where that exhibit had been found. Lois placed the sticker on the concentrator control panel. Again, Stumo asked Lois whether that was her work area. "No," Lois answered, "but we were often in there checking on things." And again, Stumo asked Lois whether she had complained or filed a grievance about the cartoon. Again, Lois said no.

One by one, Stumo showed Lois the twenty-eight exhibits from the Rosenbaum trial, and asked her to put stickers where she had seen them in the plant. Again and again, she asked Lois whether the area where she found it was her workplace. Often the answer was no, although Lois pointed out that she had to pass by the areas regularly. And again, Lois had to admit that she had not complained about the exhibits.

At first, Sprenger was not sure what Stumo was trying to accomplish. But soon he realized that her goal was to show that the sexually explicit materials introduced at the Rosenbaum hearing were confined to a relatively small part of the plant, and were not predominantly in areas where Lois was assigned to work. She was also trying to show that the materials could not have bothered Lois very much since she had not complained about them. When Lois finished, Stumo appeared to have made her point. The large white aerial map was only sparsely dotted with red arrows.

As she listened to Lois's testimony, Boler looked over at Sprenger. She saw a familiar gleam in his eyes. After the trial adjourned for the day, Sprenger disappeared for a little while, and then returned to the hotel with a small paper bag. Then he, Boler, and Lois sat down with their own aerial map of the plant.

The next morning, when Stumo had finished questioning Lois, Kyle asked Sprenger if he had any further questions. He rose and walked toward the witness stand. "Yes, I do, Your Honor," he replied.

Then he turned to Lois, with a spring in his stride. "Now, Ms. Jenson, you testified that you observed Plaintiffs' Exhibits 28, 29, and 31 through 59 in various places in the mines."

"Yes."

"Did you observe similar materials at other locations than those which you put little red arrows on Ms. Stumo's photograph and chart?"

"Yes sir, I did."

"Now, I have gone to the great expense of purchasing some little blue stickers. And I want to do this as expeditiously as I possibly can. If I may, I would just put the blue stickers on the photograph. And I would ask you to just tell me where to put them and what you saw there to the extent you can recall it."

"All right."

"It's no secret that I did ask you to do this and you've made a list. Do you need that list?"

"No sir, I don't believe I do."

"Why don't you point where and I will put the stickers on?"

Lois gestured to a blank spot on the map. "In No. 1 thickener. It's a little building inside of a pond."

"What did you see there?"

"There was graffiti and there were magazines in there."

"Go ahead."

Lois methodically went through every inch of the map, pointing out each and every place where she had seen sexually offensive pictures, drawings, or graffiti. Each time she identified a spot, Sprenger added another blue sticker to the map. The more Lois talked, the more she warmed to her task, and the more incidents she remembered.

"In the fine crusher, the elevator had graffiti, c-u-n-t in large letters scratched right into stainless steel. There is a woman's bathroom on the far end of this building, and that had graffiti in it."

"The fine crusher building?"

"Right. It's on what they would call the grade floor, the lower floor. But it was a bathroom. That was also at one time smeared with feces, and it had to be cleaned and repainted."

"The women's bathroom?"

"Yes."

At this point, Mary Stumo rose to her feet, barely able to contain her anger. "Objection, Your Honor. This is going beyond the question and volunteering information."

But Kyle quickly overruled her, and turned back to Lois.

"Go ahead," Sprenger said.

"I think I would be repeating myself to go into where the pictures and the graffiti were in the truck shop."

"You already told Ms. Stumo about that?"

"Yes."

"Go ahead."

"In the concentrator, where we had more employees, the graffiti would be as you came out of the woman's dry area, which would be somewhere in this vicinity. . . . The lunchroom in that area would have on its blackboard some graffiti on different occasions."

"The concentrator area?"

"Concentrator area, main lunchroom. Following the door out, I think we would be repeating part of that, because that's where the sign of sexual harassment will be graded and not reported."

"Where it says office?"

"Between office and concentrator."

"I see Ms. Stumo doesn't have a red mark there, so I will put one right there between office and concentrator."

Lois led Sprenger through the plant, describing graffiti she had seen in the concentrator, the truck shop lunchroom, and on the company bulletin board.

She kept pointing out places, and Sprenger kept adding stickers. By the time Lois finished, the aerial map was blanketed in blue arrows. Stumo's mistake had been to imply that the exhibits in the Rosenbaum trial were the only offensive materials Lois had ever encountered at Eveleth Mines. It was a mistake that Lois's precise memory, even dulled as it was by the medications, was able to capitalize on.

During the rest of the first week, Sprenger called several witnesses from Eveleth Mines, including Leon Erickson, a foreman at the mine.

According to Lois, Erickson had one of the worst attitudes toward women at Eveleth. But Lois at least grudgingly respected him for being willing to openly admit his views. "At least he didn't lie," she said.

He testified, as he had in his deposition, that he did not think women should work in the mines, and that in his opinion, most of the other foremen and managers at Eveleth Mines held the same view. Sprenger also called Jay Henningsgard, who testified that he had been fired two months after the certification hearing, in what he called "a personal vendetta" from Cleveland, but that the company had put him on a retainer to work on the trial.

The remainder of the week was taken up with testimony from women who had either not testified before or had testified for the company at the certification hearing. Marcy Steele went first, describing how she was repeatedly called a "dumb cunt" and a "fucking crybaby" by her supervisors, grabbed in the crotch, exposed to graffiti about men who sucked her "cunt" and her "juicy red lips." When she complained about the graffiti to Stan Daniels, he shrugged and said "Well, it's true, isn't it?" It was, she said, the last time she asked Stan for help.

One by one, the women added their own experiences to the emerging picture of what life was like for women at Eveleth Mines. And one by one, they testified that they needed the protection of a formal sexual harassment policy.

But on cross-examination by David Goldstein, Marcy admitted that she had never complained to any foreman about the graffiti, and that she herself had told off-color jokes and even kept a picture of a "scantily clad" man in her locker. When he asked her whether she thought both men and women sometimes misjudged what other people might find funny, she admitted that she did.

That the women sometimes used coarse language themselves was the least of Sprenger and Boler's problems. If the women's testimony was going to help the plaintiffs' case, they would have to convincingly explain why they originally opposed the lawsuit, and why they had now changed their minds. It was best, Boler thought, to address the question directly, rather than let Stumo and Goldstein have first crack at it. During each of their direct testimonies, Boler asked why they had decided to come forward now. Joan Hunholz explained that she had grown so accustomed to the treatment she was subjected to that she had not known that she was offended by it. Working in the mine had changed her in a way she did not like, made her so tough and so jaded that she was inured to the pain. It took Lois's lawsuit, and then the union's betrayal after the certification hearing, to make her realize that she had been in denial about her own feelings.

"I was very dissatisfied with my union for not writing up a policy," Joan explained. "When I went to them to testify, I had told them that I wanted a policy, and they agreed. They figured that was a good idea. And they never, ever tried to contact the rest of us women again to write anything up."

"When you say 'a policy,'" Jean asked, "do you mean a policy against sexual harassment?"

"Yes."

"Were you told anything else by Mr. Daniels, the president of the union, before you testified?"

"I was led to believe that I was to testify because our union was being sued just for the money, and that the women knew that we had a lot of money and that's all they're going for. I did eventually find out that that's not what it's all about at all."

Diane corroborated Joan's story. "Stan told us that they were suing the union. . . . He told us we could work this out at union meetings and everybody could vote on who they wanted to be in charge of this so-called committee so that men and women had a place to go to complain. And once we did the depositions, there was no more talk of it. Joanie tried a couple of times to get a hold of Stan. And he wouldn't even get back to her. He wouldn't even return her calls."

Jan Friend also testified about pressure from Daniels. "Stan told me, he said, 'Well, you don't want any part of that damn lawsuit,' he goes. 'If you get into that lawsuit,' he said, 'you know, it's going to be six hundred-some guys put out of their jobs.' He never mentioned a woman, but he mentioned all six hundred-some guys at the time. He said, 'Wouldn't that make you feel pretty horseshit?' He said, 'The money is going to be coming out of our pockets.' "

But no matter how the women explained their change of attitude, there was still the problem of credibility. Since their testimony now directly conflicted with their testimony during the certification hearing, Stumo and Goldstein did everything in their power to make the point that either they were lying then, or they were lying now.

During Joan Hunholz's cross-examination, Stumo asked her about the discrepancies between her current and previous testimony. "Isn't it true," Stumo asked, "that you have never been offended by graffiti, posters, magazines, jokes, cartoons, or drawings that you have seen in the workplace?"

"No. I never said never."

"I am going to refer to the hearing testimony again, page 112, starting at line 7. Question: 'Now, have you ever been offended by the language you have heard in the workplace?' Answer: 'No, I haven't.' Question: 'Have you ever been offended by visual materials you have seen in the workplace? By that, I include writings on the walls or pictures or magazines.' Answer: 'No, I haven't.' Question: 'Have you ever been offended by jokes that you've heard at Eveleth Mines?' Answer: 'No.' Question: 'Have you ever been offended by cartoons or drawings that you've seen at Eveleth Mines?' Answer: 'No.' Question: 'Have you ever been offended by comments or statements made to you by coworkers?' Answer: 'No, I haven't.' Question: 'And have you ever been offended by comments or statements made to you by supervisors?' Answer: 'No.' Do you recall those questions and those answers in the certification hearing in 1991?"

"I don't really recall it all."

"Do you recall being under oath at that hearing?"

"Yes."

"In fact, it's your opinion, isn't it, that Eveleth Mines is not a hostile environment to work in?"

"Right."

And on it went, Stumo thoroughly impeaching the women with their previous testimony wherever she could. All Sprenger and Boler could do was to hope that Kyle would believe that the women had lied in the earlier proceeding to protect both their union and themselves, and that they were now, finally, telling the truth.

The following day, the plaintiffs' lawyers called two expert witnesses. The first was Claire Bell, who testified about the various ways that women who are subjected to sexually offensive materials and conduct may react, and why not all women would react the same way, even if they all found the material or conduct offensive. Then Eugene Borgida, the University of Minnesota expert on sexual stereotyping and sexual harassment in the workplace, testified about additional research he had conducted since the certification hearing that corroborated his theory of sexual stereotyping, and the effects of prolonged exposure to sexual materials on the way men perceive and treat women.

Kathy Anderson testified in the middle of the first week. Like Lois, she was heavily medicated, and her testimony was limited to what had happened since the certification hearing. She described the incident with the falling rocks, and her futile efforts to obtain a satellite rest room while working in the pit.

On the afternoon of December 23, after six days of testimony, Kyle announced that the trial was in recess until after Christmas. They would resume on Monday, December 28. Boler couldn't wait for the break. It was Rosie's first Christmas, and Boler was desperate to be at home with her family. On trial days, she would get up at 3:30 or 4:00 in the morning so she could prepare for the day before Rosie woke up around 6:30. Then she would give her daughter breakfast and play with her for an hour before she had to leave for court. It was a backbreaking schedule, but Boler's husband, a professor of business ethics at St. Cloud State University, was on winter break so he was able to help out more than usual, and they had a dependable baby-sitter. With the trial in St. Paul, Boler was also able to sleep in her own bed at night.

The week after Christmas was consumed with testimony from defense witnesses, primarily a number of managers and foremen from the mines whose collective testimony painted a very different picture of the working conditions at Eveleth Mines than did the women's. According to these witnesses, who included Stan Daniels, Bob Klasnya, and Jay Henningsgard, the women rarely complained about anything, and when they did, their complaints were addressed immediately. What minimal graffiti was found on the walls and around the plant was immediately cleaned up. Women and men shared equal opportunities for advancement. Klasnya offered detailed statistical analysis that, he argued, conclusively showed that women were not discriminated against in terms of job upgrades, training, or compensation. No one was ever pressured not to join the suit. No promises to draft a more effective sexual harassment policy were made, and therefore none were broken. Daniels denied that he had rebuffed Joan Hunholz's efforts to contact him. The defense also called an expert witness to testify that, based on two-hour psychological evaluations in 1991, neither Lois nor Kathy suffered from post-traumatic stress disorder.

By New Year's Eve, almost all of the major witnesses had testified except Pat Kosmach. She had contracted pneumonia over Christmas and was on a ventilator in the intensive care ward of the Virginia hospital. Sprenger asked for time to take her deposition, so that her testimony could be presented in writing. Kyle scheduled the final day of the trial for February 2. But on that day, Sprenger reported that Pat's health had deteriorated to the point that even a deposition had become impossible. At the end of the day, Kyle set a briefing schedule for both sides to submit their proposed findings of fact and memorandums of law—essentially, written summaries of their respective views of the evidence and applicable law—and the trial was adjourned.

As the winter began to thaw, the taconite industry warmed up as well, thanks to new duties President Bush placed on foreign steel. Industry experts predicted increasing demand for domestic taconite in 1993. In

March, Eveleth Mines, which had been shut down for three and a half months, called back 519 workers, while keeping 150 workers on permanent layoff. Marcy and Joan returned to work that spring, but Diane had another year still before she would be called back to work.

While waiting for the Kyle ruling, Lois, unable to think about work without panicking, remained on disability. She relied on a $997 monthly check while paying for her own health insurance and expensive medication. She was so broke that she had to sell her bedroom set to pay the bills. Except for visiting her parents for a week in their winter residence, a trailer park on the outskirts of Las Vegas, Lois spent most of her time isolated in her apartment. She slept twelve hours a day and clipped articles in the *Mesabi Daily News* and the Duluth *News Tribune* about the status of the steel industry and sent them to Boler with cover letters written in a shaky chicken scrawl. Lois focused on adjusting her medications and saw Claire Bell every two weeks—she simply couldn't afford to see her more often.

Even on the Iron Range, Minnesota's pocket of social conservatism, a small group of feminist political activists—an attorney, a county commissioner, a public housing advocate, a U.S. senator's aide—had formed their own influential group. They got together frequently over drinks at the Coates Hotel in Virginia to talk and plot. In early April 1993, the women decided it was time to give the Eveleth women miners a show of support. "Something remarkable is going on up here and no one knows about it," Sharon Chadwick told her friends. "It's time to give them a boost." Chadwick, a public defender who shared office space with Claire Bell, spearheaded the group's effort to organize a banquet in the women miners' honor in a private dining room at the Coates Hotel.

Chadwick and her friends sought sponsorship for the event from local organizations like the Minnesota Political Women's Revival, and Range Women's Advocates, Natural Harvest Food Cooperative, and the Unitarian Church. They passed out flyers for the May 13 event calling it a "Sexual Harassment Class Action Recognition Dinner. For $11 a person, a buffet dinner of baron of beef and seafood fettuccini will be served. Come join us for an evening of fun and good food and pay tribute to these special people."

That night, seven tables of ten were crowded with local professional women and a handful of sympathetic men. Chadwick surveyed the room as it filled with more and more people. "This is a really big turnout for the Range," she thought with satisfaction. Helen Rubenstein, feeling regret for abandoning the case, drove up from Minneapolis. So did Jean Boler. Michele Mesich, who felt left out and isolated from the other plaintiffs, also made the four-and-a-half-hour drive from the Cities. Paul Sprenger, unable to attend, sent flowers. Diane Hodge, Marcy Steele, Mavie Maki, and Joan Hunholz all got dressed up and came wearing makeup and jewelry. Not really sure what to expect, they gingerly sat themselves down at one of the tables in the back of the room. The only one missing was Pat Kosmach who was in the hospital, on a ventilator. After the dinner, the women took Sprenger's huge bouquet of flowers and a videotape of the dinner to Pat.

One by one, ten speakers stood behind a podium and paid tribute to the women's struggle, including Karen Hill, a charismatic woman with intelligent eyes and a quick smile, who was a mining pioneer in her own right. Karen Hill grew up in nearby Tower. Her father, grandfather, and great-grandfather all worked in the mines—her grandfather started at the age of thirteen. As a child Karen would visit her father during his lunch break and always dreamed of working there. But when she graduated from high school in 1962, the only options for women on the Range were being a waitress, nurse, or teacher, or getting married. Karen moved to Duluth, where she became the city's first woman taxi driver. Later, she taught school on an Indian reservation.

When she heard that the mines were being forced to hire women, she decided to apply. She knew she could handle the work. She also knew that if she got the job, there was no way the mines could say that women couldn't do the job. "I could drive a railroad spike as well as any man," she said. Karen started at U.S. Steel's Minntac plant in 1974, a year before Lois. Initially, she was assigned to a railroad track gang with seven men and ten women. Then her foreman, saying he wanted to "protect" the women, put them on an all-women crew. Karen filed a complaint, and as a result, the mine was fined $2,000 in punitive damages and could no longer segregate women.

Now a social activist and paralegal at the Legal Aid Service of Northern Minnesota, Karen understood firsthand the courage it had taken for Lois and the other women to come forward and challenge the status quo at Eveleth Mines. After Karen, three women who were part of the Hibbing Seven, who struck at a Hibbing linen factory, stood up and told their tale of adversity. So did Mary Silvestri, the Chisholm teacher who filed a sexual harassment complaint against the school board in the early eighties. Other speakers like Claire Bell, Jean Boler, Helen Rubenstein, and Liz Prebich, the St. Louis county commissioner, thanked Lois and hailed her as a heroine.

For many of the attendees, it was the first time they heard what the lawsuit was about. For some, it was also the first time they understood that it could have much wider implications for the entire community. Lorrie Janatopoulos, a friend of Sharon and Karen's, who had once been married to Eveleth miner Jim Ravnikar, had only been vaguely aware of the details of the lawsuit. That night, listening to the speakers, Lorrie realized that the Jenson case was not just about a few isolated incidents of sexual harassment, but something much more basic. "It's a right-to-work issue." On the Range, Lorrie explained, "men hold all the economic power." There was fear in the community that "letting women work at the mines would start the slippery slope toward giving women their rights."

Some of the honorees were bewildered by the positive attention, so accustomed had they become to the negative kind. Joan found it odd to be in a roomful of women; she was used to being surrounded by men. "We didn't know what the big thing was that we did," said Diane. "People were telling us we were heroes and we just didn't get it. We didn't feel like winners. We didn't understand why people looked up to us. What did we do?"

All night, Michele Mesich had regrets about pulling out as one of the lead plaintiffs on the case. "I felt bad, I felt that I hadn't contributed." Michele's parents had pressured her to keep a low profile on the case. Her father was in a bowling league with union vice president Sam Ricker. Her mother worked in a bookstore in Virginia and was sensitive to the negative comments she heard about the lawsuit from her customers. Michele's parents told her to mind her own business and keep out of trouble. "Why do you want to fight other people's battles?" they pleaded. But tonight, amid the hoopla, Michele regretted her decision. She screwed up her courage and walked to the podium. Choking back tears, Michele gave a halting apology for leaving Lois in the lurch.

For Lois the evening was like a dream. After listening to Bell, Boler, and Rubenstein explain the national significance of the case, she realized once and for all that there was a greater meaning to her struggle. Jean Boler noticed that Lois seemed calmer and happier than she had in a long time. Dressed in a pink shirt, a black floral jacket, and big black hoop earrings, Lois stood up to make the last remarks of the evening. Both loving the attention and embarrassed by it, Lois knew that it would be politic of her to deflect some of the spotlight onto the other women. She paid homage to Pat Kosmach and to Michele Mesich. Then, looking over at the table where Diane, Joan, and Marcy sat, Lois swallowed her pride and in her soft Minnesota drawl said, "These are the bravest women of all. In a way it was harder for them to join after witnessing the retaliation that Pat, Michele, Kathy, and I went through."

By sheer coincidence, the next day a clerk of the court called Sprenger & Lang to say that Kyle had issued his opinion. The clerk did not say how the judge had ruled. Sprenger was in Washington, so Boler, bleary-eyed from her long drive home the night before, jumped in her car and rushed to the courthouse in St. Paul. As she drove, her heart raced. The dinner the night before reinforced how important Kyle's ruling would be, how much it mattered to her clients. And to her. She had butterflies in her stomach as the clerk handed her the long document.

Instead of reading it right away, Boler walked across the street to a bench overlooking the Mississippi River. In the warm sunshine of one of the first real spring days of the year, Boler began to read. It took her awhile to flip through the background of the case, the description of the parties, and the summary of their arguments.

The first part did not look encouraging. Kyle had limited the class to only the hourly workers, found against the women on the hiring, compensation, and training claims. But he did find that Eveleth had discriminated against women in promotions to step-up foreman and foreman. Boler flipped forward to the heart of the opinion, dealing with sexual harassment. There, she found better news.

"Eveleth Mines . . . is a male-dominated environment. . . . In addition to being male-dominated in terms of power and position, Eveleth Mines is male-dominated in terms of the sexualized nature of the workplace. . . . Male-focused references to sex and to women as sexual objects have persisted throughout the time that women have worked at Eveleth Mines. . . ."

So far, so good, Jean thought. She kept reading. "[M]ale employees, . . . (including foremen) felt free to and did exhibit sexually focused materials anywhere they chose." It went on. "Women at Eveleth Mines were subjected to language which derogated them and their sex in general. . . . No female employee should be required to confront sexually suggestive language and noises from male employees, either individually or in groups. . . . Some women were [also] subjected to physical acts that reflected a sexual motive or concern on the part of the perpetrator. These incidents ranged from a male pretending to perform oral sex on a sleeping woman coworker to a man touching a woman . . . to women being presented with various dildos, one of which was named 'Big Red.' " The court concluded that the "materials and conduct constitute acts of sexual harassment."

Kyle also gave considerably more weight to Borgida's testimony on sexual stereotyping and priming than had Rosenbaum, saying it provided "a framework for understanding why consistent and pervasive acts of sexual harassment occur in work environments similar to Eveleth Mines."

Kyle was apparently not troubled by the fact that some of the women were not as offended by some of the materials and language at Eveleth as were others, or that they had changed their positions about the lawsuit. Whatever the women's individual reactions, he wrote, the effect "of the sexualized environment that existed at Eveleth Mines was to inform women that they were perceived primarily as sexual objects and inferior to men, rather than as coworkers, and that these perceptions were an integral part of working at Eveleth Mines."

Nor was he troubled by the fact that a number of the men at Eveleth claimed to be unaware of the graffiti, language, and other forms of harassment. When men are in the majority, "and when they control the avenues of power, and thus are generally immune to unwelcome conduct," they "may fail to observe what a resonable woman perceives on a continual basis."

Kyle also rejected the mine's assertion that it could not be liable for any objectionable conduct by its employees, since the women did not complain about it. The harassment, he wrote, was "too common and continuous to have escaped Eveleth Mines had its management been reasonably alert." And to Eveleth's argument that it had addressed specific incidents of sexual harassment when the women involved filed a formal complaint, Kyle responded that Eveleth had a legal obligation to investigate whether the few complaints it did receive were indicative of a larger problem. "Whatever an employer's responsibility may be . . . it cannot close its eyes when confronted with incidents of sexual harassment; it has the obligation to determine the scope of the problem and take steps to alleviate it."

In sum, Kyle wrote, "Plaintiffs have established that Eveleth Mines engaged in a pattern or practice of maintaining an environment sexually hostile to women." The only question was how much money they should receive as compensation—a question that would be answered in the next phase of the trial.

Finally, Kyle addressed the question of injunctive relief. "An award of injunctive relief is appropriate." However, "simply enjoining Eveleth Mines from engaging in or permitting further sexually harassing behavior likely will not provide the cleansing breeze necessary to eliminate the sexually hostile working environment." The order would also direct the mine to develop a program to educate employees about sexual harassment, and implement procedures for effectively addressing complaints. That would require a complex, specifically tailored order. He directed the plaintiffs to submit a proposed sexual harassment policy and procedure for his consideration within thirty days.

Finally, after five years of federal court litigation, Lois would have her injunction.

And, last but not least, there was good news for Sprenger & Lang's bank account. Kyle ordered that the plaintiffs were entitled to the payment of "reasonable attorneys' fees." A hearing would be held on June 22 to consider the proposed injunctive order, the amount of attorneys' fees, and to establish the schedule and procedures for the damages phase of the trial.

Boler could scarcely believe it. "It was better than I could have written myself," she said later. "It was precedent-setting. It was a brave, intelligent, forward-thinking opinion. There were pages and pages of good law—on the substantive issues, on how to handle a class case, on the use of expert testimony, on sexual stereotyping in the workplace." It was, she realized, "an opinion that would affect how future cases were handled and, ultimately, how companies treated, and allowed other employees to treat, their female workers."

Elated, she put the opinion in her bag and rushed back to the office to announce victory to her anxiously waiting colleagues. Word spread quickly throughout the firm, and soon an impromptu party broke out. As someone popped the cork from a bottle of champagne, Boler picked up the phone to call Lois with the good news.

CHAPTER THIRTEEN

Discovery

May 14, 1993

Lois and Michele Mesich spent two lazy hours over eggs and pancakes on the morning of May 14, still amazed by the warmth they felt at the banquet the night before. When they returned to Lois's apartment, Lois noticed that the red light on her answering machine was blinking. She pushed the play button and heard a woman screaming, "We won! We won!" At first Lois didn't realize that it was Jean Boler. Just the night before, the lawyer's voice had been its usual, flat, measured tone. "This is not typical Jean," Lois said to Michele. "I've never heard Jean so excited."

Her fingers trembling, Lois dialed the number for the Sprenger & Lang office in Minneapolis, which she knew by heart. Boler came on the line and told Lois about the Kyle ruling. Lois handed the phone to Michele so that she, too, could hear the news firsthand. When they hung up, the two old friends, relieved and elated, fell into each other's arms.

"The only thing that would be better is if we heard the news yesterday and could celebrate it together at the dinner," Lois said.

Michele agreed. "The place would have howled."

The two women hopped into Michele's car and drove to the Virginia

Regional Medical Center. Pat's hospital room was still fragrant from the flowers the women had taken to her the night before. They found her dozing in her hospital bed, her labored breathing making loud, rasping sounds. Lois and Michele pulled up chairs to both sides of Pat's bed, held her hands and gently woke her.

"Pat," said Lois. "We won. We won liability. Kyle is going to force the mine to put an anti–sexual harassment policy in place." Pat's milky blue eyes grew alert. "We lost on a few things," Lois explained. "Kyle ruled for the company on the hiring part, and he didn't allow the salaried gals to be part of the class."

When Lois finished, Pat lifted a small device to her neck—during her bout of pneumonia she had had a tracheotomy, and now needed the box to speak. In a mechanical voice that sounded more robot than human, Pat said, "Atta way girls! We beat them!"

For the past year, Lois had visited Pat in her hospital room at least twice a week. Her lungs were starting to fail. "Pat had a death sentence of dying by slow torture and she couldn't do anything about it," her doctor said. She had accepted the inevitable with courage and grace. There was a vulnerability to her personality, and the terrible irony for Lois was that only now could she share her problems and her fears with Pat without worrying about being judged or second-guessed.

The three original plaintiffs spent over an hour together in Pat's hospital room, just like old times, plotting their next move. This time, however, they were savoring victory, too.

By early summer, what appeared to be a concrete victory began to evaporate. On June 22, the lawyers from both sides of the case met with Judge Kyle in St. Paul. The purpose of the hearing was to determine the appropriate scope of the injunction Kyle had promised to issue. In preparation for the hearing, Boler spent several days drafting a proposed order. It would require Eveleth Mines to establish procedures and policies for educating its employees about sexual harassment and to create a mechanism for reporting, investigating, and resolving claims of sexual harassment.

At the hearing, the company argued that such a comprehensive order was unnecessary because the company had now "voluntarily" decided to develop and implement its own action plan for addressing the problem of sexual harassment at the mine. Although the company could not give the court details about its proposed plan—it had not been written yet—the company assured Kyle that they would be adequate to address the problems that he had described in his opinion.

This was what Boler had always feared, that once the company was forced to implement a policy, it would step forward and claim to want to do it "voluntarily." To her it was like the fox asking for permission to guard the hen house.

But she knew that courts do not like to meddle in corporate affairs more than necessary. After listening to the two sides argue, Kyle took the more conservative approach and deferred to the company's promises. He simply ordered Eveleth to "cease and desist" from maintaining a hostile work environment, and to submit to the court its action plan at some future date.

Boler was dismayed and completely perplexed. Kyle's earlier opinion was such a stinging rebuke of Eveleth, yet he was now content to trust the company to make amends of its own accord. Like Rosenbaum before him, Kyle was either naïve about the willingness of the company to clean its own house, or unwilling, for whatever reason, to follow his own findings about conditions at the mine to their logical conclusion. Because federal judges never comment on their rulings, no one but Kyle will ever know why he decided to trust Oglebay Norton's promises.

But a promising turn of events came out of the hearing, or at least it seemed fortuitous at the time. The Federal Rules of Civil Procedure provide that in certain complex cases, a court can appoint a Special Master—often a retired judge, a magistrate, or an accountant—to manage the litigation, hold evidentiary hearings, and make recommendations to the court. The mechanism is often used in cases in which the calculating of damages is likely to be complicated and the hearings time-consuming.

Sprenger and Boler believed that the *Jenson* case fit the bill. Kyle's ruling on the issue of liability established that Eveleth discriminated against its female hourly employees by maintaining a sexually hostile workplace. The issue now before the court was whether, and to what extent, each of their clients had been damaged as a result, and how much money Eveleth Mines would have to pay them to make up for it.

In essence, the damages phase would consist of as many mini-trials as there were class members. Each woman would have to prove that she had been exposed to the hostile work environment at Eveleth Mines, and that she had been harmed in a measurable, and compensatory, way. Logistically, it meant medical records and other documents would have to be produced, depositions would have to be taken, mental health experts from each side would have to evaluate each woman, and testimony would have to be taken regarding each woman's claims. It would be a time-consuming process under any circumstances. Sprenger and Boler believed that a Special Master, who could devote all of his time to the case, would move it more quickly than if it stayed on Kyle's crowded docket.

Because they believed delay tends to favor defendants—on the old theory that justice delayed is justice denied—Sprenger and Boler urged Kyle to turn the job over to a Special Master, and listed five potential candidates, including several magistrate judges from Minneapolis. For the same reasons that Sprenger & Lang wanted a Special Master, Faegre & Benson strongly opposed the request. In the end, Kyle agreed to appoint a Special Master, a victory that Sprenger and Boler would soon regret. Instead of choosing one of Sprenger's recommendations, Kyle appointed Patrick J. McNulty, a retired federal magistrate from Duluth.

McNulty was the magistrate judge who had been replaced by Oglebay Norton's former counsel, Ray Erickson. He was a fighter pilot in World War II, and had graduated summa cum laude from the University of Minnesota Law School in 1949. McNulty was known in the Duluth legal community for his dogged research on cases. Well connected to Duluth's business and political circles, he was a member of the Knights of Columbus and the Northland Country Club, where he played golf with the city's influential citizens.

Sprenger later called the decision to appoint McNulty "a bit of a setup." He had been the federal magistrate judge for many years, but now, at seventy-one, he was considered to be past his prime. "They wanted to replace him with Ray Erickson, so they got him to step down," said Sprenger. Sprenger assumed that Kyle gave McNulty the case to make up for the fact that he had been asked to retire as federal magistrate before he was willing.

Sprenger had another reason to be concerned about McNulty. Several years earlier, when he was in Duluth for the Rosenbaum hearing, a lawyer who had been diagnosed with terminal cancer approached him about taking over some of her employment discrimination cases. In the course of their conversations, the woman told Sprenger that she would not want McNulty on any sexual harassment or discrimination case, because he had made a pass at her while she was trying a case before him. Sprenger had not thought much about it at the time, but when Kyle assigned him Special Master in *Jenson*, he remembered the conversation. If the woman were still alive, he would have asked her for an affidavit he could use to ask Kyle to remove McNulty from the case. Without her testimony, he had no evidence, no proof, and therefore no basis to seek McNulty's removal.

On October 22, 1993, a legal notice appeared in the *Mesabi Daily News*, addressed to "all current and former women employees of Eveleth Mines who worked in hourly jobs at Eveleth Mines at any time since December 30, 1983." It briefly explained that Eveleth Mines was found to be liable "for violations of the Minnesota Human Rights Act and Title VII of the United States Civil Rights Act" on the issues of sexual harassment and denial of promotions to women at Eveleth Mines. The notice also explained that women in the class could be entitled to claim money damages. Anyone wishing to do so had to complete and mail the claim form reproduced in the paper to Sprenger & Lang by November 30, 1993.

Lois was soon deluged with calls from women, many of whom had signed the petition against her lawsuit five years earlier, asking for help in filling out the claim form. Lois suspected that some of them were drawn more by the scent of money than the promise of justice. Still, she helped anyone who asked. "Whatever their motivation," she said, "they had all worked in the same environment in the mine, and who was I to pass judgment on their claims?"

The notice inspired some of her former coworkers to come forward for the first time, but it also pushed some buttons on the Range. A few weeks after it appeared, a letter to the editor about the case appeared in the *Mesabi Daily News*. The letter, written by a woman who worked at Minntac, reflected the hostility that many members of the Range community continued to feel toward the lawsuit and the women who were behind it.

"I've worked at Minntac for two years in both the plant and the pit. Never have I experienced any sexual harassment of any kind from either labor or management," the woman wrote. "Don't let the experiences of three women and the decision of a judge dampen your regard for the hundreds of fathers and sons who labor diligently in our mines."

Lois tried to keep a hands-off approach with everyone, but not when it came to Judy Jarvela. Judy had been laid off in 1984 and did not return to work when she was called back in 1988. "I just said to myself 'I can't go back to that place. There's no way.' It felt dangerous." She had resisted invitations from Lois, Helen Rubenstein, and Boler to join the lawsuit in its earlier stages. A shy and private person, Judy was so humiliated by what had happened to her at the mine that she hadn't even told her husband about the semen on her clothes, let alone the time a miner chased her and threatened to rape her. The only people with whom she had shared this information were Mavie Maki, Lois, and Pat.

Lois called Judy the day before the applications were due. "Judy, we need your help," she pleaded. "Your case is one of the worst stories that happened to any of the gals at the mine."

"I don't think I want to join, Lois. I'm just not comfortable bringing it all out."

Yet Judy wouldn't say she would rule it out. Lois waited an hour and called back.

"Have you made a decision?"

Reluctantly, Judy clipped the notice from the paper and sent it in. She got to the post office ten minutes before it closed, just in time to have her envelope postmarked November 30, 1993.

In the end, eighteen women in addition to Lois, Kathy, and Pat filed claims. There were now twenty-one women in the class, all current or former hourly laborers at Eveleth Mines. As they sorted through the forms, Sprenger and Boler recognized some familiar names. Michele Mesich was back in. Angel Alaspa, Marcy Steele, and Connie Saari had all testified in earlier proceedings. A number of women who signed the petition opposing the case back in 1988 also filed claims, including Joan Hunholz, Diane Hodge, Debbie Sersha, Priscilla Robich, Janice Wollin Friend, and Denise Vesel. There were also several women Boler did not know of, including Shirley Burton, Marge Tolbert, Marilyn Greiner, and Audrey Daniels (Stan Daniels's ex-sister-in-law).

Sprenger & Lang's research, at that time, showed that in individual sexual harassment cases, the average jury award was around $50,000 per claimant, and that in egregious cases, it rose to $250,000 or more. As the lawyers went over the claims, they felt sure that the experiences of the women at Eveleth were as bad or worse than those of women who had filed other sexual harassment cases around the country.

Four days before Christmas, Boler wrote a memo to the class, explaining that over the next six months, "we will work toward preparing for your hearings on the money awards to each of you. We will probably be asking for medical records and some of you will give depositions." She also informed them that Eveleth was now offering to settle the case for $3,000 per claim. None of the women accepted the offer.

A few weeks later, Boler sent the women another memo explaining what they should expect in the coming months. In it, she tried to prepare them for the fact that the damages phase of the trial was likely to be more intrusive than anything they had faced before. "One of the issues we will have to prove for each one of you at trial is how much you were mentally or emotionally hurt by working at Eveleth Mines. In order to give the best possible proof of this type of damage, we will have a psychologist like Claire Bell examine your medical records and talk to you and arrive at an expert opinion as to how you were affected by the environment. The defendants will also have a psychologist of their own choosing examine your records and talk with you about your feelings." Boler concluded by saying, "We will try to protect your privacy as much as possible." But even she could not have predicted the firestorm to come.

The battleground in *Jenson v. Eveleth* had now shifted from the issue of whether the company had maintained a hostile work environment to how much the women who worked there had been damaged as a result. Ever since 1991, both Title VII and Minnesota law had provided that victims of sexual harassment were entitled to damages for mental anguish. The federal law capped such damages at $300,000 per victim, but Minnesota law had no such ceiling. Because *Jenson v. Eveleth* was based on both state and federal law, there was no limit on the amount of damages the plaintiffs could claim based on emotional harm.

But the question was not so much what they could claim but what they could prove. The measure of emotional harm is an issue that the law has consistently struggled with. It is one thing to calculate damages that involve material goods, which can be replaced. If one car rear-ends another, it is easy to determine the replacement value of the rear-ended car, or the cost of repairs, by looking to the market value of the car or the repair services. It is a little more complicated if the driver of the rear-ended car breaks a leg in the accident. The value of physical damages can be gauged by the driver's medical bills and the amount of income the person lost while recuperating.

But the law also allows the driver to collect damages for pain and suffering, which is much less easily quantified. There is no precise mathematical equation for pain and suffering. Still, the average person knows what pain is, has experienced it directly, and so can come to some rough understanding of what the distress caused by a broken leg is "worth."

When the suffering is purely emotional or mental, damages are harder still to calculate. First, a lawyer has to establish that the injury exists in the first place. Emotional and mental injuries do not manifest themselves through lost blood, swelling, or fracture. They cannot be photographed or X-rayed. They cannot even be intuited through common experience, as can physical pain. Mental harm can only be detected through the subjective sciences of psychology and psychiatry, which are not universally understood or even accepted.

Second, even if one can prove that there is mental and emotional harm, it may be impossible to prove the link between the action and the injury. One can prove that but for a car accident, a leg would not be broken. It is much more difficult to establish that but for this action this person would not be depressed, would not be suffering from post-traumatic stress disorder, would not be nervous or paranoid or unable to sleep. Perhaps the person is emotionally distressed for other reasons. Perhaps a child is sick or a husband is abusive or a parent has died. Perhaps this person suffered a horrible trauma years ago that is only now coming to the forefront of the psyche.

And even if one can prove both that the injuries exist and that the action in question caused them, there remains the question of how much they are "worth." What is the market value of an orderly mind, a positive outlook, a good night's rest?

If medical science can only approximate answers to these questions, the law, hampered by the rules of evidence and the relentlessly skeptical minds of many of its practitioners on both sides of the bench, is hopelessly imprecise. In the end, it relies on the unavoidably rough guess of "experts," who do battle with one another armed with little more than their academic backgrounds and their ability to persuade a judge or jury.

This legal swampland was now the battleground in *Jenson v. Eveleth*. The women would try to show, through the testimony of their psychological experts, that they had suffered measurable mental and emotional harm as a result of the hostile work environment to which they had been exposed. Faegre & Benson would try to show that on the contrary, the women were not emotionally harmed by working at the mine, and if they were suffering from any emotional or mental disorders it was due to factors other than their employment at Eveleth. In the process, the women would end up being harmed even more.

As distasteful as it may have been to dredge up the women's pasts to prove their case, Faegre & Benson would have been remiss had it not pursued all available defenses. Even so, there are varying degrees of ruthlessness. How far McNulty and Kyle would permit the firm to go in discrediting the women, and how successful Sprenger & Lang would be at protecting their clients from unnecessary pain, remained to be seen.

It wasn't long before Sprenger & Lang found how aggressively Faegre & Benson intended to dig into the women's personal lives. In mid-January, the company sent lists of questions, called interrogatories, to each of the claimants. The first asked for every name each woman had ever used. The second read, "With respect to each physician, psychiatrist, psychologist, counselor, therapist, chiropractor, osteopath, physical therapist, qualified rehabilitation counselor, hospital, clinic, and other health care professionals who has ever examined or treated you at any time and for any reason, state the person or entity's name and address and the dates and types of all treatments and examinations." Faegre & Benson also asked detailed questions about each woman's background, childhood, social relationships, marriages, and children.

Sprenger & Lang pushed back. The firm only provided the names of health care providers the women consulted during their employment at

Eveleth Mines, and identified the reason for the consultation. They argued that Faegre & Benson's interrogatory was overbroad, unduly burdensome, and unlikely to lead to admissible evidence. They also noted that "the class members do not recall every health professional they have ever seen."

Even limited to the years of employment, the women's collective response ran to sixteen typed pages of garden variety aches and pains, pregnancy, childbirth, abortions, teeth grinding, stomach problems, depression, marriage counseling, CAT scans, arthritis, warts, anxiety attacks, eye exams, and foot problems.

On February 15, 1994, McNulty held a status conference to establish a discovery and trial schedule, and set a trial date for November 1, 1994. He also ordered that all discovery—interrogatories, depositions, production of medical records, and adverse psychological examinations—be completed in only six months, by August 15. It was an unusually aggressive schedule.

McNulty also addressed the issue of medical records, at least obliquely. Since Sprenger & Lang would not respond to their requests for records going back to birth, Faegre & Benson asked McNulty to order the women to sign releases so that Faegre & Benson could get the records themselves directly from the women's medical service providers.

McNulty decided that he did not have the authority to force the women to sign releases, but he did say that it was "obvious" that in a claim for emotional damages, "extensive discovery" is required. He encouraged, but did not order, Sprenger & Lang to provide the records.

When she had not received any response by the February 28 deadline, Stumo sent subpoenas to the health care providers identified by the women, and even to health care facilities in the Range not listed by the women, in a blanket search for all medical and mental health records belonging to the plaintiffs. She gave the doctors one week to come up with the records.

Sprenger and Boler were angered by the direct subpoenas. First, they did not agree that the company was entitled to records dating back to birth. And even if it was, they wanted the records to be produced directly to them, so they could screen them, mark them as confidential, and, if necessary, refuse to produce particular records. They also wanted to be able to go over the records with their clients, and wanted to know what was being produced. "We wanted the women to be able to review every record, so that at any time they could conclude that the litigation was not worth exposing some fact that they wanted to keep private, so they could always say this is where I want to stop," Boler said later.

Citing patient confidentiality, the medical service providers themselves did not believe they could send the records to Faegre & Benson without authorization from each patient. Sprenger & Lang also objected to Stumo's subpoenas on the grounds that Oglebay Norton was not entitled to records dating back to birth.

In response, Faegre & Benson filed a motion asking Kyle, who still retained supervisory jurisdiction over the case, to order the clinics to comply with the subpoenas and to compel production of all of the women's medical and mental health records. In an accompanying affidavit, Stumo argued that the women were seeking damages for emotional distress, which put the subject of their mental health into play.

Boler thought she and Sprenger were on solid ground, at least to the extent that the medical and psychological histories dealt with past sexual activity. As recently as August 1994, Congress had revised the Federal Rules of Evidence to extend the rape-shield protections to civil cases. The amended rule said that evidence of prior sexual activity by an alleged rape or sexual assault victim was not admissible in any civil or criminal proceeding in order to prove that the victim had engaged in other sexual activity.

In a reply brief, Faegre & Benson shot back. "It is well-established that events early in one's life, including (perhaps particularly) events during childhood, profoundly affect one's mental and psychiatric state later in life." When a plaintiff "places her mental or psychological condition at issue, a defendant is entitled to discover the plaintiff's entire medical records," in order to determine "whether other stressful situations" such as "divorce, abuse, the conviction of a child for criminal acts, alcoholism, infertility, death, illness, or preexisting psychiatric disorders" were responsible for any emotional distress, rather than what happened at Eveleth Mines. Any evidence of past sexual activity would be used not to show that the woman had had prior sexual contact, which is what the rape shield law prevented, but to show the *effect* the contact had on her.

It now became perfectly clear that Oglebay Norton was going full guns with the tried-and-true nuts-and-sluts defense. The not-so-subtle message was that if the women did not want their lives examined under a microscope, perhaps they should rethink bringing a claim for damages in a sexual harassment case. At least one of the plaintiffs took this message to heart. Jan Friend, who had a son who had been convicted of murder, dropped out of the case during this period, partly because it was too painful to answer questions about her family.

To help with the crush of work generated by McNulty's six-month discovery schedule, Sprenger & Lang hired Greg Wolsky, a contract lawyer, to work on the case full-time. A former partner in a small medical malpractice firm in South Dakota, Wolsky was affable, hardworking, and experienced in litigating cases involving medical records.

On March 16, just a few weeks after Wolsky's arrival, Sprenger & Lang received word that Kyle had scheduled a hearing in two days, on March 18 on the issue of medical records. Sprenger and Boler were both out of town—Boler was with her family on their first vacation in a year and a half, and Sprenger was in D.C. working on another case. The firm had five major class actions in play, including a huge race discrimination case against Ford Motor Company, and everyone was swamped. It fell to Wolsky to prepare for and argue the motion for the claimants.

On the day of the hearing, the other side, as Wolsky had feared, "came loaded for bear." In Stumo, Wolsky immediately recognized a certain type of high-powered corporate lawyer. "She was a product of her environment, which was all about billing," he said. "You bill, and you bill hard. At every opportunity for a motion, you do it. You don't make anything easy, even for yourself."

Wolsky felt that Kyle was surprised to see a new face on the case. The first words out of Wolsky's mouth were a request for an extension, but Kyle didn't want any more delays. Kyle ruled that the defendants were entitled to request medical records from each plaintiff starting from birth. He also ordered Sprenger & Lang to obtain releases from the women authorizing each health care provider to release the requested records to Sprenger & Lang. Failure to execute the releases could result in dismissal of their claims, he said sternly. He further ordered Sprenger & Lang to turn over any and all records to Faegre & Benson, "save only those records to which a specific objection is made." Kyle made clear that objections should be made sparingly. "If this Court should determine that any noticed objection was improper, without merit, or interposed in bad faith or for purposes of delay, it will not hesitate to levy sanctions" against Sprenger & Lang, including possible dismissal of the claim.

It was a total defeat for Sprenger & Lang and their clients, all the more surprising after Kyle's strong ruling in their favor during the liability phase of the trial. "It was clear that the company was going to rake these women over the coals, no mercy," Boler said. She had a sense of how destructive that process would be to her clients, but she could not yet see the wedge it would drive between the women and their lawyers.

On March 22, Lois, Kathy Anderson, and Audrey Daniels drove together to the Cities to meet with Dr. Carol Novak. Sprenger & Lang had retained Novak, a Minneapolis-based psychiatrist, to evaluate the claimants and determine whether, and to what extent, the women had suffered emotional harm as a result of the harassment they experienced at Eveleth Mines. Novak, a petite blond woman trained in clinical psychiatry at the University of Minnesota, had extensive experience in evaluating and treating victims of sexual abuse, including workplace harassment.

When they arrived, Novak showed the women into her waiting room. One by one, she administered a battery of diagnostic tests, and interviewed each woman at length. In her subsequent report on Lois, Novak wrote, "Ms. Jenson has and is suffering from a large number of severe psychiatric symptoms as a result of the sexual harassment and retaliation experienced at Eveleth Mines. She spent extended periods of time fearing for her personal safety as well as persistent humiliation and ostracism, and she suffers from intrusive and distressing recollections of both the assaults and betrayal by trusted coworkers. At times she has suffered from extreme insomnia and nightmares. She has been jumpy and hypervigilant about her surroundings. She has experienced a largely diminished interest in her previous activities and is greatly estranged from other people. She has experienced irritability and had panic attacks when exposed to reminders of the trauma."

These symptoms, Novak concluded, supported a diagnosis of posttraumatic stress disorder as well as depression. Novak acknowledged that Lois had other stresses in her life, including her relationship with her parents, and her rape. But Novak concluded that prior to the harassment, Lois demonstrated an ability to cope with these sources of anxiety, and had not previously exhibited any symptoms of depression or PTSD.

In sum, Novak wrote, "As a result of the mixed messages, betrayals, assaults, humiliation and other aspects of her sexual harassment," Lois "has suffered a permanent impairment in her ability to trust and build effective or close relationships with people, especially men, on a vocational or personal and social level." Novak noted that Lois's symptoms were likely to be chronic. She expressed a small degree of optimism that with years of therapy, Lois might recover to the point of being able to work on a part-time basis, but predicted that she would never fully regain her past level of income.

Novak reached similar conclusions about Kathy and Audrey. Of Kathy, Novak concluded, "Ms. Anderson has been completely devastated by the sexual harassment and retaliation she received at Eveleth Mines. She has an extremely severe post-traumatic stress disorder solely as a result of these events." The psychiatrist said that while Kathy may have been more emotionally and mentally fragile as a result of the abuse in her previous marriage, the harassment she experienced at the mine intensified her problems so that she was "permanently and totally disabled" from any kind of work in the future. "Paradoxically, her tolerating her [first] husband's abuse may have caused her . . . [to] put up with her work at the mines as long as she did."

A few weeks later, Novak traveled with Greg Wolsky to the Range to meet with Marilyn Greiner, Shirley Burton, and Marge Tolbert at Lois's apartment complex in Mountain Iron. Shirley and Marge came at the appointed time, but Marilyn was so nervous that she vomited in the parking lot and turned around and went home without going inside.

After the evaluations of Shirley Burton and Marge Tolbert, Novak went with Wolsky and Lois to see Pat at the nursing home where she was now living. Wolsky hoped that Novak would be able to evaluate Pat as well, but Novak could tell that Pat was in the advanced stages of ALS, and would not likely live much longer. She told Wolsky that there was no way she could perform a complete evaluation of Pat in this condition, adding that it would be inhumane to even try.

In her interviews with the women she evaluated, Novak was struck by how egregious the harassment they had experienced was. In a report she prepared in April summarizing the cases as a whole, Novak wrote, "although I have evaluated many victims of sexual harassment, the conditions to which these women were exposed goes way beyond the scope of what is generally considered 'sexual harassment.' " It was, she said later, the worst case she had ever seen.

Novak was also struck by how stoic the women were, at least on the surface. "They were all very matter-of-fact about it. Sometimes plaintiffs in cases will overstate their reactions to what happened, because they think it will help their case. But these women, if anything, were the opposite. They were not trying to sell their stories to me." Above all, Novak was impressed by the depth of the women's fear. "A lot of these women were deeply, deeply afraid."

While Novak evaluated the women and prepared her reports, Faegre & Benson launched phase two of its discovery campaign. Now that Stumo and Goldstein had the medical records they were seeking, they sent off interrogatories for each woman asking detailed questions about her life, marriages, children, and other personal matters. "The women were understandably mad about having to respond to questions like 'Relate all the experiences of your marriage relating to your divorce,' " Boler recalled. "Sometimes they would write things in response like 'None of your damned business.' Boler would then have to call and talk to them, explain why the questions had to be answered, and give them the option of not going forward. "I was powerless to protect them after Kyle's ruling. All I could say was, 'You don't have to answer this, but if you don't, you will not be able to pursue your claim.' "

After the interrogatories came the depositions, which were scheduled back to back, nearly one a day from April 11 to May 4, 1993. The women came to Minneapolis in groups of two or three, and stayed in a Comfort Inn Wolsky found on the northern edge of town, selected for its low rates rather than its location. "I tried to schedule it so they could be with their friends," said Wolsky. "They all complained about coming to the Cities, but the truth is, some of them liked it. It was a free trip, and they could visit places like the Mall of America."

But the shopping was hardly a panacea for the degrading grilling that each of them faced from Stumo and Goldstein. Every day Wolsky would drive to the Comfort Inn at the crack of dawn, meet with the day's deponent, drive her to Faegre & Benson's offices, sit through up to eight hours of gruelingly personal, intrusive testimony in a windowless room, drive her back to the motel, and then meet with the next day's deponent for several hours. When one group finished, they would head back to the Range, while a fresh group headed down to the Cities.

The point of the depositions, from the company's perspective, was to find out everything traumatic or disturbing that had ever happened to the women. That meant hours and hours of mind-numbing detailed questions about each woman's life, starting with birth. Wolsky was both horrified and awed by Stumo. "She was a relentless examiner," he said later. The questions went like this: Have you ever been tested for HIV or AIDS? Does your husband have any problems with alcohol or drugs? Do you drink? Has your husband ever been verbally abusive to you? Physically abusive? Does he read *Playboy*? Has he ever been arrested for anything? Have you ever been arrested at any time? Do you and your spouse ever argue? Have you had any financial problems during your marriage? Have you ever been on welfare? Have you ever hit your husband? Have your children ever run away? Has anyone ever abused your children verbally, sexually, or otherwise? Have you ever experienced the death of a close friend? Have any of your brothers or sisters had financial problems? Been involved with the police? Were any of your siblings ever sexually or verbally abused? Given the average life lived on the Iron Range, many of the questions were answered in the affirmative.

At this point, Faegre & Benson had estimated that its total legal costs on the case would be $450,000—a reasonable fee for handling a class action, given Stumo's approach, which Wolsky figured had to involve the work of scores of paralegals and assistants at her firm. It would prove to be a very unrealistic number.

The relentless digging into the women's past lives was humiliating and demeaning, but from a legal standpoint Sprenger & Lang had a bigger hole to plug: how to deal with the fact that some of the women had originally opposed the lawsuit, and their previous testimonies. Kyle, in ruling that Eveleth maintained a hostile work environment, concluded that whether or not these women had been offended, the environment at the mine was so pervasively hostile that a reasonable woman exposed to the conditions there would have been offended. He *did not* rule that these particular women had in fact suffered or been offended by what they had personally experienced there. That was up to the women to prove now in the damages phase, a task made much harder for the women who'd once sworn under oath that they had not been offended. The implication was that at one point, they had lied under oath.

Sprenger believed that it was clear that the women had only testified for the company out of fear of retaliation, and that they had been duped by the company into trusting it. His hope was that McNulty would come to believe that as well.

In Joan Hunholz's deposition, Faegre & Benson zeroed in on this point. After going through each incident that Joan had previously testified didn't offend her, Goldstein asked, "So . . . sitting here today, there is language and behavior that now offends you that would not have offended you ten years ago?"

"Yes."

"What is it that you think has caused that process of change in the way you think about things?"

"I think because I'm older, I have the kids. . . . When I brought the kids out there one day, and I was ashamed of my workplace. . . . And I started thinking, 'That's terrible to be ashamed to bring my children out to my workplace.' . . . And I almost had to put blinders on them. And I had to check and make sure what crew was on before I came out and who was in what department. And I thought this is ridiculous, you know. They had to use the women's bathroom, they're boys, I says, 'You gotta use the women's bathroom.' 'Why, Ma? I ain't going to use the women's bathroom.' . . . I can't have my boys see things written about their mother [on the walls of the men's bathroom], you know."

All in all, Faegre & Benson took forty-one days of deposition testimony from the women, as well as twenty-seven days from the plaintiff's experts, including Novak and Bell. By late spring, the intense demands of discovery were beginning to strain Lois's relationship with her lawyers. Wolsky in particular irked Lois. Because she wasn't working, she was easy to reach on the telephone, and Wolsky would pepper her with questions about the other women. Some, like Marge Tolbert, did not have a phone at all so if Greg had a question for Marge, he would call Lois, who would then have to drive immediately to Eveleth, pick Marge up, and bring her back to her apartment so Greg could talk to her. Then she would have to drive Marge home. "He was always calling me on the weekends and at night whining about how the judge wasn't giving him anything. I had to baby-sit him," Lois said. Lois's fragile emotional health could not withstand the stress of the case. Still taking the drugs Klonopin and Palemor, Lois suffered frequent anxiety attacks, sleeplessness, and paranoia.

She resented the amount of work she was being asked to do for the lawyers and the other women, and felt abandoned by Boler and Sprenger, who seemed preoccupied with other cases, even though Boler was present for each of Lois's depositions. Although she knew that it was irrational, she couldn't help feeling slightly annoyed and jealous that the lawyers were spending so much time on the claims of women who had just joined the case, some of whom didn't always take the case seriously.

Boler's opinion was that Lois's distrust of Wolsky—her irritation with all of her lawyers and the women in the class, for that matter—was related to her illness. "That is part of post-traumatic stress syndrome, when you become paranoid and start to think that even the people who are on your side are not really on your side. And she was getting worse and worse that year." She added that "even in her darkest times, Lois was self-aware enough to say, 'I know I am being paranoid,' or to say later, 'Thank you for sticking with me.' "

As discovery progressed and costs mounted, Sprenger & Lang continued to press for an acceptable settlement. In late summer, Oglebay Norton finally agreed to a mediation session, which took place in Duluth. It lasted for a day and a half, but once again, there was no resolution. The company was now offering $1.5 million, including Sprenger & Lang's fees and costs, which by now had reached $2.3 million. At that time, Oglebay Norton just didn't see its financial exposure on the case; Faegre & Benson was still telling its client that legal fees and expenses were $450,000, although within the year the firm would revise that figure to $1.2 million. To the company, though, it did not matter much, since Faegre & Benson's bills were being paid by their insurance companies.

In Sprenger's mind, Lois and Kathy's claims were worth at least $500,000 each. He once again tried to get Oglebay Norton to separate the award for the women from his firm's fees. They could then either settle his fees separately, or he would seek an award of attorneys' fees in court, after the women's case was over. But Oglebay Norton insisted on packaging his firm's fees with the award for the women. For Sprenger, that made it impossible to settle.

By the end of the summer, Pat Kosmach was nearly paralyzed. The ALS had caused her muscles to deteriorate in her arms, hands, and lungs. Her once robust body was shrunken and emaciated. Her children who still lived on the Iron Range—Brenda, Bonnie, and Susan—held a rotating vigil by her bedside. Sometimes Pat would surprise them with her dark humor. While she was being lifted naked onto a guerney, Pat looked up at Bonnie with a grin on her face and said, "Jesus Christ, just give me a cigarette!"

On August 3, 1994, Mary Stumo addressed a document to Pat, which Sprenger & Lang reluctantly had to show her. It was a list of eighty-three men who worked at the mine that the defense lawyers might consider calling as witnesses to dispute Pat's claims. The names on the list were men Pat had known and worked with for years, men she respected, and whom she thought respected her. Sprenger & Lang needed Pat to tell them who on that list might know something that would sabotage her claims. Although there was no way to know precisely what they would say at trial, Pat took the fact that they might be called by Faegre & Benson to mean that they had agreed to discredit her. Brenda Kosmach helped her mother read the fifteen-page list. "As she read all of the names, some of whom she thought were her friends, the tears started spilling down her face," Brenda said. She took the list away from Pat.

Less than three weeks later Bonnie was married, and she held the ceremony in Pat's hospital room. Bonnie had borne a child out of wedlock, and Pat wanted to see her daughter marry the father of the child before she died. The whole family—Pat's five children and seven grandchildren—gathered for the bittersweet ceremony.

Two days later, on August 24, 1994, Lois received a package from Sprenger & Lang in the mail. It was a set of questions from Stumo and Goldstein for Pat Kosmach. Greg Wolsky had included draft responses. Lois was to take it to Pat, and if she agreed with the proposed responses, Pat was to sign it in front of a notary public. Lois drove to the Virginia Regional Medical Center, and found Pat alone in her room. She sat down next to Pat's bed and pulled the document out of its manila envelope. Without looking at it herself, Lois held the pages so that Pat could read it. By the time Lois flipped to the second page with its list of invasive questions about Pat's medical and sexual history, Pat was sobbing.

Lois held Pat's trembling hand as Pat scratched an X on the signature line in front of a hospital notary. Pat asked Lois to stay with her for the rest of the afternoon. She was scheduled later that day to be hooked up to a respirator so she could breathe more easily. "Pat told me that she knew she was dying, and she was scared. She thought the respirator was her death sentence," said Lois. As the nurses prepared to move Pat downstairs to the intensive care unit, they each paid her a visit to say good-bye. Pat had been a popular patient in the ward where she had stayed, on and off, for two years. Nurses had become accustomed to talking to Pat about their problems and seeking her advice. "It was an endless line of nurses," recalled Lois. "She'd put on a smiley face for them, and they'd all laugh, and when they left, she'd cry." With each good-bye, Pat became more and more emotional.

Pat turned to Lois and asked her to draw up a letter stating that Pat wanted to leave all of her legal documents to Lois. "I'll do that later," Lois assured Pat. "We've got plenty of time." All along, Pat had protected her children from the case. She never told them the details about the sexual harassment she and the other women suffered, and for the most part, Pat's children resented the time spent and emotional suffering caused by Pat's involvement in the case. Pat had written a will that left instructions to divide her portion of the damages award among her children. Although Sprenger had explained to her that under Minnesota law, personal injury claims die with the claimant, he promised Pat that he would try to convince the court that the law did not apply to discrimination cases. Pat still held out hope that Sprenger might be able to pull a rabbit out of a hat for her children.

Lois waited with Bonnie while a doctor performed the surgery to insert feeding and breathing tubes into Pat's throat. That night, after Lois and Bonnie had gone home, Pat aspirated her food. A doctor had to perform emergency surgery to clear her lungs.

"She was awake a couple of times after that, but that was really the end," Lois said. For the next two months, Pat remained in the intensive care unit with only occasional moments of lucidity. Lois felt haunted by the knowledge that Pat had spent her last day of full consciousness under siege from Mary Stumo.

In early October 1994, Sprenger & Lang received notice that Faegre & Benson intended to depose the fathers of Lois's two children. A few days later, Rick Jones, Greg's father, called Sprenger & Lang and spoke to Boler's legal assistant Sandra Riekki. He lived in Indianapolis, and told Riekki that he had been contacted by someone at Faegre & Benson about giving a deposition. He said that the person told him that they were "trying to discredit Lois psychologically and emotionally." Jones wanted to know what the lawsuit was about, and why he had been dragged into it.

Sprenger and Boler were furious. They knew that there was nothing of relevance that Jones, who'd had no contact with Lois for more than twenty-five years, could add to Faegre & Benson's case. The only possible motive they could think of for Stumo threatening to depose Jones was to embarrass Lois and to try to scare her into dropping the lawsuit to prevent Greg from learning who his father was and how he had been conceived. "Their insistence on deposing these men showed the absolute abusiveness of the discovery," Boler said later. "The burden should have been on them to establish the relevance of their testimony, but it wasn't. It was on Lois to show the irrelevance, which she could not do."

Sprenger and Boler immediately filed a motion to prevent the depositions of Jones and James Larson, Tamara's father, from taking place. At the hearing, Stumo argued that she needed it to verify Lois's claim that she was raped. "I would like to know," she told McNulty, "how long Jones has known Lois Jenson. I would like to know if it was close to a single contact, which is the way she tends to describe it. I would like to know if they had a relationship. I would like to know if they had a sexual relationship, if it was ongoing. I would like to know how he characterized how their relationship ended. . . . I think I'm entitled to know the circumstances of their relationship and what impact that might have on her now."

McNulty agreed. Sprenger & Lang immediately appealed to Kyle, arguing in its brief that the relevance of Lois's "relationship" with Jones was "extremely attenuated" and that the involvement of Jones in the case, whom Lois had not seen since 1968, was intended to "annoy, harass, and embarrass" her rather than lead to the discovery of relevant evidence. Once again, they cited the inclusion of civil cases to the rape shield law standards. But Kyle upheld McNulty's ruling, and allowed the depositions to go forward. However, Kyle made it clear that all depositions relating to Lois's rape were to take place under seal and were to remain confidential.

Meanwhile, discovery was still going forward. On October 6, Lois met with Barbara Long, the mental health expert retained by Faegre & Benson to evaluate the women in preparation for trial. Sprenger & Boler were not surprised Faegre & Benson had chosen her. "Long was infamous for finding that victims of sexual harassment and abuse had emotional disorders prior to the harassment," Boler said. In one well-known local case, Long had testified that the psychological problems of a thirteen-year-old boy who was sexually abused by a Catholic priest for eight years were primarily due not to the abuse but to a "borderline personality disorder" the child had before the abuse began.

The interview took place at a conference room at the Holiday Inn in Eveleth. Lois arrived ten minutes early, dressed in faded blue jeans, a white embroidered shirt, and a flowered vest. She was nervous, had not slept the night before, and had taken an extra tranquilizer before the meeting. Knowing that Long was working for the company, that her sole purpose was to find ways to discredit her, Lois took an instant dislike to her. Long was a petite blond woman, well-dressed in soft, feminine clothes. She had positioned herself at the end of the long conference table, surrounded by files; it seemed to Lois that the psychiatrist was in a defensive bunker.

For six hours Long asked Lois detailed questions about her family life, her childhood, her siblings, her parents, her children. She asked about her religion, her medical history, and her family's medical history. She asked about Lois's "social" history, including whom she dated, when and why. She asked Lois about each and every one of her medical records, which she had with her. She also asked detailed questions about her experience with the fathers of her two children. Only tangentially, and somewhat indifferently, Lois thought, did she ask about the harassment Lois had experienced at the mine.

Near the end of the grilling, Long asked what effects she thought the litigation had had on her. "That's a good question," Lois responded. She said she had learned a lot about the legal system, including "how attorneys and courts can be cruel." She said she used to respect Mary Stumo, because she was so thorough, but once she learned that Faegre & Benson intended to call Jones, she thought Stumo was "terribly cruel." "I feel it should be against the law to call Jones," she told Long. "He has nothing to do with it. If they don't think I was damaged [at the mine], let Stumo work there."

Two days later, Pat's daughter Brenda called Lois. Brenda had just received a call from a nurse in Pat's ICU unit. The nurse was alarmed because a woman named Long was in Pat's room, asking Pat questions and asking to see her medical records. The nurses wouldn't let Long look at Pat's records because she did not have a release from Pat's family.

"What should I do?" Brenda asked Lois. Brenda and Bonnie were accustomed to taking time off from work when Pat had to meet with attorneys or therapists for the lawsuit so they could lip-read their mother's responses. Lois immediately called Boler, who told her "let it go." There was nothing she could do from Minneapolis, Boler said, and Lois should not try to do anything either. Lois hung up the phone, furious at Boler, at all her lawyers, at herself, too, for not protecting Pat, for letting things go this far.

Lois sat through her third and fourth depositions with Mary Stumo on October 20 and 27 at the Holiday Inn in Eveleth. A few days later, Sprenger & Lang received a copy of Long's reports on Lois and the other women she evaluated for the case. Long's conclusions were, not surprisingly, almost diametrically opposed to Novak's.

In her report, Long referred to Lois's experiences at the mines as "the alleged harassment." She found Lois to be "a complicated person who qualifies for a number of diagnoses," including depression, although she noted that some of the depressive symptoms, such as weight gain, sadness, and anxiety, could be attributed to her medication. She also concluded that Lois suffered from undifferentiated somatoform disorder, or recurring, unexplained, physical problems.

Long reached dramatically different conclusions about the reasons for Lois's problems than Novak had. According to Long, Lois's most significant problems were the result not of harassment but of the lawsuit, which Long stated Lois was pursuing primarily for financial gain. According to Long, "Lois desires revenge for what she perceives to be the significant and ongoing maltreatment which she has received at the Mines. . . . In pursuing the litigation, she also obtains for herself an explanation for her own life's misfortunes, many of which resulted from her judgment problems rather than problems at the Mines. . . ."

Long also placed most of the blame for Lois's experiences at work on Lois. "Individuals like Ms. Jenson, usually women, are engaging, charming, and manipulative, particularly with the opposite sex. Unconsciously, they engage men in a relationship in which they themselves can be the 'princess,' and the man can be the 'knight in shining armor.' . . ."

As to Povroznik, Long found in his letters evidence that Lois "came on" to him through her "engaging behavior." "As she likely does with most men, she gave Mr. Povroznik mixed messages." The only fault that Long observed in Povroznik's conduct was that "he was a man who was not sophisticated in his pursuits of women."

Long excused the rest of the harassment at the mine as culturally ingrained, and therefore beyond the control of the company or even the male miners themselves. "The culture of the Iron Range is unique. The Iron Range cities consist of about 25,000 people, most of whom are . . . immigrants, whose background reflects traditional, conservative, usually religion-based sexual role dimorphism. . . . To judge yesterday's workplace by today's stricter social standards is unrealistic."

Besides, Long noted, "any of the litigants, including Ms. Jenson, could have left the mines at any time, if they had so chosen. To say that they had no option but to remain, for financial reasons or otherwise, is unrealistic. To have felt the way she did about the workplace, one would have expected Ms. Jenson to quit."

Pat Kosmach died on November 7, 1994. She had lived with Lou Gehrig's disease for five years, two years longer than her doctor's most optimistic expectations. Her daughters attributed her strong will to live to the lawsuit. When Lois got the call from Brenda, she called Jean Boler and then she called Kathy Anderson. Lois was numb with shock and sorrow. She asked Kathy to drive her to the funeral home in Eveleth so she could say good-bye to Pat before they cremated her—a practice that goes against the traditions of the Catholic church. "When I die," Pat had told Lois, "I want to be cremated. I don't want them to look at me, pretending to care. I don't want them looking down on me." Lois found Pat's body alone in a room. Her children were making funeral arrangements in another room. "I wanted a moment alone with her," Lois remembered. "I was surprised by how hard I took Pat's death even though I knew it was coming."

The day of the funeral was sunny and raw. The trees were bare and a cold wind rustled their branches. Pat had had two wishes. She did not want anyone from the union or mine management attending the funeral or sending flowers, and she wanted her ashes scattered over the mine. Pat's family and friends filled the pews of the Church of the Resurrection in Eveleth. Lois took her seat on the aisle next to Michele Mesich and looked out over the faces in the crowded room. Marcy, Joan, and Diane lined up in the pew next to Michele. When Lois spotted Sam Ricker, the union vice president take a seat, she stood up and headed toward him. She intended to ask Ricker to leave, but Michele and Marcy held Lois's arm and forced her to sit down.

Pat's oldest daughter, Bobbie, gave the eulogy. She outlined her mother's struggle: "A divorced mother at twenty-nine with five young children. A strong-willed woman who insisted on not raising her children on welfare, worked three jobs during most of our growing up years. In the middle seventies she landed the job that would make life so much easier . . ." She spoke of Pat's charisma and big heart. "I know that everyone here has been touched by her and her love. She had more love than any person I have ever met."

After the service, Lois accompanied the family to the graveyard in Eveleth, where they buried Pat's ashes under the shadow of the looming Thunderbird Mine building. Pat's daughters had saved a handful of the ashes to be spread over the mine later, when the weather warmed up enough for a friend of theirs to fly his small plane over the site. They buried the rest of Pat's remains in a Catholic ceremony. Bobbie, who lived in Minneapolis, was struck by how Lois had changed over the years. She noticed that Lois's speech was hard to understand because she was so drugged up. She wondered if her mother would have turned out like Lois and Kathy if she hadn't gotten ALS.

Lois had no time to grieve. A week later, on November 17, 1994, Stumo deposed her for the fifth and last time. Deeply depressed about the loss of her closest ally, Lois was now more heavily medicated than usual, with Wellbutrin, Klonopin, and Synthroid. Stumo focused on the flashbacks and nightmares Lois periodically experienced. When did she have them? What did she dream? How long did the dreams last? What did she see in which flashback, and when? Her usually sharp memory muddled by drugs and exhaustion, Lois repeatedly answered "I don't know" and "I don't recall." The deposition lasted from three o'clock in the afternoon to eight-thirty at night. Lois left feeling confused and disoriented, sure that she had made mistakes or contradicted minor details from previous testimony. "My mind was in bad shape," she said. "I was falling into hate. I was so mad at what they did to Pat. But if you hate them, they win." She had discovered that the only way to survive life as a plaintiff is to try to stay neutral with the lawyers and not take their tactics personally, but she was not succeeding in taking her own advice. She also thought that Boler, who had attended all five of Lois's depositions, seemed demoralized and unfocused.

Boler felt the same way about her client as she watched her answer Stumo's questions. "Lois had been deposed so many times, and Mary Stumo was just not finishing with her. Stumo's appetite for detail was matched by Lois's remarkable recall, so between the two of them, things got very drawn out. Lois ultimately suffered in terms of the length of her depositions because of her ability to remember things, because Stumo would always have one more question, and Lois would always have an answer."

The deposition of Rick Jones took place on November 28 at the Airport Holiday Inn in Indianapolis. Mary Stumo and Greg Wolsky attended. Jones had no lawyer of his own. As Sprenger and Boler suspected, he had very little to say. He did not recall Lois, which he attributed in part to the "passage of more than twenty years" since the time he knew her. "And part of it is that my visits to Minneapolis during that era were brief and infrequent. And part of it is because between August of 1965 and December of 1975, I was inebriated." Unable to learn anything useful about Lois from Jones, Stumo then asked whether he had been contacted by Lois's lawyers. He explained that he had called them, after learning that his name had somehow become involved in the case.

"Do you recall telling the person you talked to at the Sprenger & Lang law firm that the person you had talked to at my law firm, Faegre & Benson, was trying to discredit Ms. Jenson psychologically?"

"This is what was told to me by a gentleman from your firm who had spoken to me last spring: He was calling Ms. Jenson's psychological emotional state into question. The [private] investigator who claimed to represent your firm, according to my ex-wife, told her that they were trying to discredit Lois Jenson."

"That's what your ex-wife told you?"

"That's right. I don't have the exact verbiage on that."

With that, Mary Stumo replied, "I don't have any further questions, Mr. Jones."

In the depths of her despair about the case, one good thing had happened to Lois. She had been trying for a year to locate her daughter, Tami, and now the deposition had brought Jim Larson briefly back into her life. After a twenty-three-year silence, Lois spoke to Larson on the phone and they rehashed their short but consequential relationship. After all, if Lois had not gotten pregnant with Larson, and if he hadn't left her, she would never have moved from the Cities to the Range, or worked at the mine. Larson told Lois that he too suffered from PTSD, and that he had been exposed to Agent Orange in Vietnam. Larson's two sons were born with birth defects as a result of the chemical. Larson agreed to sign over his medical information to their daughter, adding urgency to the search Lois had made through the adoption agency.

When Lois first heard Tami's voice on the other end of the phone line, she experienced a profound moment of joy. Tami was now Teresa. She lived in a coal mining town in West Virginia, had a college degree, and worked as a social worker treating victims of child abuse. "She wanted to know what she was like as a baby, and why I gave her up. She felt abandoned." Tami asked Lois to send her birth certificate, and they exchanged photographs of themselves. They spoke on the phone half a dozen times. But even this happiness was short lived. After a while, Tami asked Lois to stop calling.

A few days before Christmas, Boler, tired and dreading the coming trial, sent her clients a deceptively upbeat memo, in hopes of rallying both the women and herself. "Merry Christmas and a Happy New Year!" she wrote. "We know one thing that will be accomplished in 1995 and that is the trial of this case. . . . That means all of you will have a day in court."

For Lois, who was exhausted, isolated, and deeply depressed, it was far from a comforting thought.

CHAPTER FOURTEEN

Cross

January 1995

The damages phase of *Lois E. Jenson v. Eveleth Taconite Co.* began in Duluth two months after Pat's death, on January 17, 1995. The trial was expected to last seven weeks, but because McNulty normally spent the months of March and April in Florida, and Stumo had nonrefundable airline tickets to Hawaii in February, the trial was scheduled in two parts. The first session would last until February 10. Then there would be a break, and it would resume on May 22.

The week before the hearing was to start Faegre & Benson informed Sprenger that Oglebay Norton would be willing to settle the case for $1 million, including legal fees. It was half a million less than what the defendant had offered at the mediation in August, and once again, the offer included Sprenger & Lang's fees and costs. The intense discovery of the preceding year had pushed Sprenger & Lang's fees and expenses over $2.3 million, including more than $800,000 in out-of-pocket costs alone. As long as Oglebay Norton was bundling Sprenger's fees and case expenses with the settlement, the offer amounted to effectively no money for the plaintiffs. Sprenger had no choice but to recommend that the women reject the offer.

Boler, Sprenger, and Wolsky headed to Duluth for trial in mid-

January. As Boler exited Interstate 35 and drove to the Best Western in downtown Duluth, she was struck by how gray, depressing, and miserably cold the city was. Even the snow of a recent storm was grimy-looking, and the roads, icy and deeply rutted, were nearly impassable.

The Best Western was the staging area for what everyone hoped was Sprenger & Lang's last legal assault in this case. They needed rooms for the lawyers, legal assistants, and witnesses; rooms for extra phones and a conference table, a fax and a Xerox machine, and rooms for document storage. The documents, which included the medical records of each woman, every deposition taken in the case, every piece of documentary evidence, and the transcripts of the previous hearings, filled hundreds of boxes, lining the walls of the motel rooms from floor to ceiling.

Ever cost-conscious, Sprenger had been able to negotiate a cheap price for a block of rooms at the motel, and when the lawyers got there, they immediately understood why the rates were so good. Sprenger had found what must have been the seediest accommodations within walking distance of the courthouse. As Boler unpacked, she took stock of the place that would be her home for the next month. The carpets were stained, the ceilings were cracked, and suspicious odors seeped from the thin walls. That night, the lawyers discovered that their rooms were next to the ice machine. Just as they were drifting off to sleep, they were jolted awake by a crash of fresh ice cubes. The motel's rates made it a favorite of operators of junkets to the Black Bear Casino on the nearby Lake Superior Chippewa reservation. Almost every morning around 4:00 A.M., buses would rumble into the parking lot and discharge passengers returning from a long night of gambling, the diesel engines idling loudly. By the time the buses pulled out, Jean Boler could not go back to sleep.

Sprenger spent the first weekend in his room, drafting his opening statement. Boler and Wolsky met with witnesses they planned to call during the first week. They put as much thought into selecting their witness line-ups as baseball managers do selecting batting orders. The strategy was to start strong and finish strong. For a lead witness, they wanted a woman with a powerful story, who was not too vulnerable on cross-examination and had a sympathetic, credible demeanor. While Lois as lead plaintiff might have been the natural candidate, the lawyers were worried about her state of mind.

Ever since Pat's death, Lois's condition had steadily worsened. "It was just so deeply embedded in our lives one way or the other," Lois said of the eleven and a half years she and Pat had lived through the lawsuit together. "Sometimes we relished the little victories we had and enjoyed the fight, but there was so much energy invested, along with emotion. We could pump each other up, burn each other out, but I think we kept each other going. It was so different when she was gone. I lost a strange friendship, a confidante. I missed her."

By December, Lois was depressed, heavily medicated, and unable to concentrate for more than an hour or two at a time. She had become unable to perform even the most basic daily tasks. After Pat died, Lois sat down and wrote out a list entitled "Things I Used to Do. Wash daily, dress daily, brush teeth often, do hair daily, earrings daily, polish and care for nails (did not bite), read two newspapers per day, watch the news, read—books, magazines, regular hours, look at fashion magazines, walk, exercise, hair done, bake, cook, go out eve/dance-dine, kept up with laundry, cleaning (vacuum, dust, as needed), fresh air, crossword puzzles, solitaire."

Lois was no longer doing any of these things on a regular basis. Her hours had become so irregular that she often fell asleep on the couch with the television on at three or four in the morning and would then sleep until the middle of the afternoon. Her sink was filled with unwashed dishes. She kept her blinds closed almost all the time, so her small apartment was dark even in the daytime. She rarely went out, except to walk to the IGA to buy a quart of ice cream that she would bring home and eat in one sitting. She almost never drove her car. Sometimes she did not shower or dress for days at a time. Family members fretted about her health when they dropped by to visit.

Lois also felt more isolated than ever from the other women in the case, and increasingly resentful of her lawyers. In her mind, her lawyers had abandoned her for the other women, and she felt that her interests were not being protected by Sprenger & Lang anymore. Lois called Helen Rubenstein in distress before the hearing started to ask for help looking for new lawyers. "I literally felt like I needed my own attorney because of the things being allowed by McNulty. They didn't tell us what they were doing to fight it. I told Helen I was seriously thinking about getting another lawyer. It was like I was sacrificing my rights for the others. I was burnt out. Helen told me to call Paul and Jean and talk to them, but they were so overwhelmed with paperwork, they didn't have time to talk."

Instead, several weeks after Christmas, when Boler and Wolsky were preparing for the hearing, Lois sat down and wrote the firm an angry, disjointed letter. Titled "Do You Hate Jenson vs. EMs yet?" it began with a rambling narrative about discovery, her driving restrictions because of her unpredictable blackouts, and what she believed to be lies that the other women had told. She wrote:

> *I think we need some common sense and less defense. I KNOW YOU ALL ARE FRUSTRATED & STUMO HAS YOU AFRAID TO TURN AROUND. ANOTHER STUPID BATTLE! Well, welcome to the club of living by Atty's rules, I did it from [19]88 on. AFRAID TO DO & say the wrong thing—Did it really matter in the end? And I'm still trying to live by your rules. To protect the case, to protect the women, to try to be patient and do things right—so we get willing witnesses—not blow it. So you're in the club but you can drive, see who you want, go where you want, do what you want, fight for things that are important—Be part of something other than this lawsuit. I died but I breathe, think— occasionally remember clearly—But I HAVE NO LIFE.*

By now, Sprenger tended just to skim Lois's frequent, disjointed letters. He knew she wanted more attention from him, but he simply did not have time to give it. His experience was that plaintiffs in employment cases, particularly those who had lost their jobs because they had been fired, or, as in Lois's case, become disabled, tended to obsess about their cases. He could spend all his time holding their hands, but in the end, it would not advance their case.

From a strategic point of view, Lois clearly wasn't going to be a strong lead witness; she was not in good enough condition to withstand the cross-examination that they all knew was coming. Although Sprenger and Boler planned to get all of the women's testimony finished by the break, they scheduled Lois last, in the hopes that maybe they wouldn't get to her before the trial's break in February. "We knew that they were going to try to make her seem crazy," Boler recalled later. "By putting her at the end, we thought that by then, in the context of what had already been told, she would be less vulnerable on cross."

They also ruled out the women who had testified for the company at the certification stage, or who had signed the petition against the lawsuit five and a half years earlier. They, too, would be vulnerable on cross-examination. At the liability phase, the fact that Diane Hodge and Joan Hunholz had originally been opposed to the lawsuit was not a serious problem. The issue before Kyle at that juncture was whether or not Eveleth Mines maintained a hostile work environment, not whether Diane, Joan, and the others who signed the petition had or had not been offended by that environment.

At the damages phase, the question was whether each woman was entitled to financial recompense and how much. The fact that Joan, Diane, and the others had once sworn that they had not been offended by what they heard and saw in the mines could now come back to haunt them.

Sprenger, Boler, and Wolsky knew that Stumo and Goldstein would use every shred of evidence they could find to convince McNulty that the women were fabricating their claims in the hope of cashing in. As they had at the liability hearing, Sprenger and Boler would try to convince the judge that the women had in fact been offended at the time, and that they testified otherwise out of fear of retaliation. Still, they knew those women were vulnerable on cross-examination to the charge that their claims of injury were unreliable, if not out and out false.

Sprenger and Boler wanted to begin with witnesses who were most likely to engender sympathy. Before the trial began, the lawyers divvied up the women. Sprenger would handle the testimony of Lois and Judy. Boler took Kathy and the other women with strong claims. And Wolsky got the weakest claims. It was not that the women Wolsky was assigned had not been harassed as badly as the other women, but their responses to the harassment, and their conduct generally, indicated that their sensibilities were less tender than some of the other class members. Given the way damages were assessed in sexual harassment cases, the tougher the women were, the harder it was to prove that they had been harmed by their work environment, and therefore were entitled to significant damages. For example, Denise Vesel had a sailor's mouth and had broken the ribs of a coworker who pestered her once too often. "Vesel was in group three," Wolsky recalled. "Getting her up on the stand and portraying her as this vulnerable woman . . . was hard."

Ultimately, the lawyers settled on Shirley Burton as their first witness. Burton, who started working at Eveleth Mines in 1976, was unknown to Boler and the others until she filed a claim in response to the notice published in the *Mesabi Daily News* after the Kyle ruling. Burton still worked at the mine, and fearful of retaliation from her coworkers, she had come forward very reluctantly. She had spent most of her time at Eveleth Mines working in the pit. Sprenger thought she would make a good lead witness because her experiences had been particularly horrible, and because she had not signed the petition.

On the morning of the first day of the hearing, Duluth awoke to a blinding blizzard. By the time Boler and Burton walked the short distance from their hotel to the courthouse, they were covered in icicles. A few minutes past nine Special Master McNulty, a large, burly man with a florid nose, lumbered to the bench. Sprenger could usually tell whether a judge was liked by the way the courthouse staff greeted him.

He knew a little bit about McNulty and noticed with concern that morning that the clerks and bailiffs did not appear to greet the old judge with enthusiasm.

McNulty signaled for Sprenger to begin his opening remarks. An opening statement in front of a jury is at least part theater. The purpose is to tell a dramatic narrative, to capture the hearts of the jury from the outset. In front of a judge, however, opening statements are more businesslike. So when Sprenger rose, it was without great flourish or flare. The first item on his agenda was to ask for a ruling from McNulty clarifying who had the burden of proof on the issue of causation of emotional harm, whether the women had to prove, or the company had to disprove, that the hostile work environment caused the women to experience emotional or mental anguish. Sprenger argued that, under Minnesota law, now that the women had proved that there was a hostile work environment at Eveleth Mines, all they had to do was show that they had been affected by it in the same way a "reasonable woman" would have been. If they could do that, the law presumed that the hostile work environment was a cause of mental anguish, and the only remaining question was the extent of the damage.

Stumo and Goldstein disagreed. They argued that the women not only had to prove that they had experienced emotional and mental harm, but they also had to prove that the harm they experienced was directly caused by the work environment, and furthermore, that it was not caused by something else. Given the difficulty establishing a precise cause of depression, anxiety, or PTSD, if McNulty ruled that the women had the burden of proof on the issue of causation, it would be difficult for them to prove that they were entitled to damages in the first place, let alone how much.

As the lawyers argued back and forth, McNulty appeared confused. When Sprenger asked for a ruling on the issue, McNulty rolled his eyes toward the ceiling, slowly rocking his head back and forth. "It was extraordinary. As though he did not know how to rule, and perhaps God would tell him," Sprenger said later of the mannerism he would see many times in the weeks ahead. "And, in fact, he did not know how to rule. He was in over his head." Clearly eager to get moving, McNulty declared that he would take the matter under advisement.

Sprenger then turned to the question of damages. How much was each woman entitled to? Sprenger argued that the appropriate amount varied according to the degree to which each woman had been affected by the hostile work environment at Eveleth Mines. But all of them, Sprenger claimed, were entitled to some relief. As a guideline, Sprenger pointed to other cases in which courts had awarded in the range of $100,000 to $500,000 to claimants where the harassment was much less severe and had not lasted for as long a period of time. In this case, the women who claimed to have PTSD as a result of their experiences in the mines were, Sprenger argued, entitled to the most. For them, Sprenger said, "I think the award should be in the neighborhood of 200, 300, 400, half a million dollars for that particular claimant or more."

Before sitting down, Sprenger made one last, ultimately futile, appeal to McNulty. "We just ask that you give these courageous women a fair shake." With that, Sprenger returned to his seat. Stumo declined McNulty's invitation to make an opening statement, so McNulty instructed Sprenger and Boler to call their first witness. Shirley Burton nervously made her way to the witness stand and was sworn in. She had not told anyone at work that she had joined the class, and now they were about to find out.

Under Boler's guidance, Burton testified that she was a divorced mother of four when she and her friend Marilyn Greiner heard that Eveleth Mines was hiring women in 1975. Burton worked part-time at a shirt factory for minimum wage. Both she and Marilyn applied for a job at the mine. Soon after they started work the men began calling them names—"cunt" and "bitch" were favorites. They nicknamed Burton the "Black Lab" and Greiner the "Irish Setter." The two women worked together as conveyor attendants, and routinely found graffiti about them in their work area, particularly images of dogs having sex, labeled with their nicknames. Some of the men also liked to play the "horse bite" joke: A man would ask Burton if she had ever seen a horse bite, then try to grab her crotch before she could get away. Like Lois, Burton once found a noose above her workstation.

In the late 1970s, Burton's foreman was a man named Louie Horoshak. Her first sign of trouble with him came one night when he called her at home and told her he was masturbating. She hung up the phone, horrified. At work, he showed her pictures he had taken of naked women at his hunting shack, telling Burton he was going to take her there. One day, Burton was in a control booth loading the conveyor with her back to the door. Horoshak came in and called to her. When she turned around, he dropped his pants to his ankles, completely exposing himself to her. Burton screamed; the foreman pulled his pants up and walked away.

Burton also testified about a night when she and Marilyn Greiner were working the midnight shift, loading trains. After a train pulled away, Horoshak and another foreman pulled up in a pickup truck and told them to get in. He explained that they had to go to the pit to pick up some equipment and needed extra hands.

Burton and Greiner got in the backseat of the truck. The two men were in the front. But instead of heading toward the pit, the truck veered off down a dark, bumpy road through the woods. Soon, the men stopped the truck.

"And what happened next?" Boler asked.

"They told us to get out of the pickup, that we were going to service . . . Louie said we were going to service them."

"And what did you interpret that to mean?"

"That means that he wanted to have sex."

The men had gotten out of the truck, and Burton and Greiner stayed inside and locked the doors. The keys were in the truck, but Burton and Greiner were afraid that if they drove away, the men would deny what happened and would claim the women had abandoned them and misused the company vehicle. Eventually, when it was time for another train to come by, the men knew that they would all be missed and pleaded to be let into the truck. Reluctantly, Burton and Greiner unlocked the doors and the men drove them all back to work. "What did you think was going to happen when you were out there?" Boler asked.

"I thought they were going to rape us."

"Did you ever report that?"

"No. He was a foreman."

After that night, Burton testified, she began carrying a knife to work in her lunch pail, and would lock the door to her control booth, and then barricade it with a heavy shovel.

Burton also testified that while she and Greiner were working in the conveyer, the nearest bathroom was in the north crusher. It was a long walk, and the bathroom was filled with graffiti. In addition, there was no lock on the door, and men would sometimes come in, inadvertently or intentionally, while they were using it.

After a while, a satellite bathroom was placed near the conveyer, which was a relief to Burton, who hated walking through the cold winter nights to the crusher. But she stopped using the satellite after it was tipped over—twice—while she was in it. Each time, the chemicals in the toilet badly burned her skin. Once, as she crawled out, she saw a man running away, but could not tell who it was.

Burton also testified that another foreman, Hank Brown, would periodically come into her booth and forcibly pull her onto his lap and caress her. Although she struggled to get free, he'd let her go only when he heard someone approaching. When she threatened to report him, he laughed, and told her that he would tell everyone that she was coming on to him. Burton's isolation at work also proved irresistible to another coworker, who would come into her booth during the midnight shifts and try to kiss her. Burton testified that the man said, "Don't worry, I won't rape you. I am only going to get your lips."

When Boler asked Burton what effect her working environment had had on her, Burton replied that she was "panicky," "fearful," and "angry." Boler asked if she suffered any physical symptoms as a result. Burton told her that after she started working at Eveleth, she developed an ulcer and suffered frequent, intense headaches, as well as night-mares and other sleep disturbances.

After a lunch break, on cross-examination, Goldstein tried to make the same two points he and Stumo would make with every one of the women. The first was that Burton must not have been offended by what she had experienced at work, since she had not previously reported the incidents she was now complaining about, with one exception, and in that case, the offending employee received a five-day suspension. As he went through each event and asked whether she had reported them or complained to a supervisor, Goldstein's questions were designed to un-dermine Burton's credibility. Wouldn't a reasonable woman who hon-estly believed she was almost raped by her foreman surely have reported the incident once she returned safely to the plant, fear or no fear? Wouldn't they have driven away as fast as they could, leaving their would-be assailants stranded in the woods? Was it possible, the ques-tions suggested, that Burton was exaggerating or even fabricating inci-dents now, in hopes of cashing in?

Goldstein's other line of questioning focused on possible causes of Burton's anxiety and stress-related physical symptoms. He asked about her two marriages, both of which ended in divorce; an abusive relation-ship with a man who threatened to kill her on several occasions; the deaths of her brother, father, and stepmother; and frequent layoffs or threats of layoffs during the period she was employed at Eveleth Mines. And he asked detailed questions about her hysterectomy and other gy-necological problems.

Some questions bordered on the absurd: Did Shirley have tension headaches in 1957? A sore throat in 1965? Others were more painful.

"Did your brother die in 1982?" Goldstein asked.

"Yes," Burton said.

"Were you upset by his death?" Goldstein wanted to know.

"He was my brother," Burton said.

Finally, at five o'clock, Burton was dismissed, and McNulty ad-journed the hearing for the day. The next morning, Sprenger called Marilyn Greiner, Shirley Burton's close friend. Since Burton and Greiner worked side by side for many years, they encountered many of the same problems, and were harassed by the same men.

On cross-examination, Mary Stumo stood up and strode over to the witness stand.

"Good afternoon, Ms. Greiner. I think you remember me. I took your deposition in May. Ms. Greiner, prior to working at Eveleth Mines, you had very little work experience, isn't that correct?"

"Yes."

"And, in fact, you graduated from Embarrass High School in 1954?"

"Yes."

"You said you worked at Woolworth's. And that was after high school, correct?"

"Yes."

"And you worked at Woolworth's for approximately a year until you found out that you were pregnant, correct?"

"I worked at Woolworth's for . . . yes, for about a year, yeah."

"And you learned that you were pregnant at that time, isn't that correct?"

"Excuse me?"

"You learned that you were pregnant, isn't that correct?"

Boler rose to object to the question as irrelevant, but McNulty overruled her.

"Ms. Greiner, you have to answer the question," said Stumo.

"Oh, I'm sorry. Yes."

"And you weren't married at that time, isn't that correct?"

"Yes."

"And isn't it true that that was very shameful and embarrassing for yourself and your family at that time?"

Greiner said no, but the question carried force. Either she was embarrassed, which would have caused her stress and anxiety, and could possibly have caused psychological harm, or she was not embarrassed, in which case she was shameless.

A little while later, Stumo asked Greiner, "Isn't it true that just before you started at Eveleth Mines you learned that your husband was having an affair with another woman?"

"Yes."

"And you learned about that affair from one of your sons, isn't that correct?"

"Yes."

"And you had four children to support just before you started Eveleth Mines, isn't that correct?"

"Yes."

"You were forced to go on welfare before you started Eveleth Mines, isn't that correct?"

"I was getting child support."

"You were anxious and depressed, isn't that correct?"

"No."

"You were angry and you were distrustful of men after learning about Mr. Pardus having an affair with another woman, isn't that correct?"

Once again, Boler objected, and once again, McNulty overruled her.

"No," Greiner said.

"You didn't even know how to go about getting a job in 1976, did you?"

"Yes, I knew."

"You went with your school friend Shirley Burton to apply for positions, isn't that correct?"

"Yes. I also went by myself."

"And she was also recently divorced and supporting children, isn't that correct?"

But once again, Stumo had accomplished what she wanted. In the first few minutes of her cross-examination, Stumo was able to suggest that Greiner was a disaffected, bitter, immoral woman who was nursing a grudge against men after her husband betrayed her, and who'd weakly followed the lead of Burton, a similarly bitter woman. The unspoken implication was that these two angry women might well fabricate stories together to get back at men and for personal gain.

The rest of the week was much the same. Judy Jarvela testified on Thursday, Mavie Maki and Denise Vesel on Friday. On direct, they told McNulty what they had experienced at Eveleth Mines. Jarvela testified about finding semen on her clothes, Maki about being called an "old cunt" and threatened with rape. Denise Vesel told about being teased and having her breasts and buttocks poked and prodded by the coworker whose ribs she ultimately broke.

On cross-examination, each was subjected to questions about their sex lives, their marriages, their gynecological histories, the deaths of loved ones, childhood abuse, neglect, diseases, injuries. Goldstein asked Jarvela whether her husband ever asked her to perform sex acts that she found unpleasant, and whether she generally liked the smell of semen before someone ejaculated on her clothes at work.

Boler and Wolsky watched in disbelief. Sprenger was not surprised that Stumo and Goldstein could ask such questions. Long before the McNulty trial began, his opinion of them was pretty low. "They were entitled to defend their client, but they were going way beyond what was necessary. Their strategy was obviously to shock and embarrass the women, and make a mockery of the proceedings. It was unbelievably tacky."

What did surprise Sprenger was that McNulty permitted it. "Most judges would not have let them get away with it; in fact, that kind of questioning would have backfired. It would have turned off most judges, made them angry. But McNulty actually seemed to enjoy it."

Finally, at four o'clock on Friday afternoon, the judge adjourned the hearing for the weekend. The first week of testimony was over. As soon as she could, Boler made the two-hour-and-forty-minute drive to Minneapolis. It was her daughter Rosie's third birthday, and Boler hoped to get home in time to play with her. By the time she got there, Rosie was already asleep, and Boler had to spend all day Saturday in the office. On Sunday, she, John, and Rosie shared a rushed birthday cake before Boler made the trek north to Duluth.

The following week was much like the first. Kathy Anderson testified on Monday. In cross-examination, Goldstein was effective in suggesting that many of Kathy's symptoms of mental illness, including her diagnosis of PTSD, were related to a severe reaction she'd had to a medication. He was also devastatingly effective in his evisceration of Kathy's character. Referring to a man Kathy dated, Goldstein asked, "And the two of you had a sexual relationship?"

Boler shot to her feet. "Objection, relevance."

"Is this relevant, Counsel?" McNulty asked Goldstein.

"Your Honor, the claim is being made that Ms. Anderson no longer has any interest in sex as a result of events at the mine. . . . I intend to only establish that she had the relationships and that they were sexual."

Boler interjected. "Your Honor, I'd object. I don't think there's been any testimony that her interest in sex diminished until [much] later. . . . It's not admissible under Rule 412."

"I'll allow you to proceed, Counsel. The objection is overruled."

"Am I correct you had a sexual relationship with [him]?" Goldstein repeated.

"Yes."

"Am I correct that between 1982 and 1984 there were at least three other men with whom you had romantic and sexual relationships?"

Again, Boler stood up. "Your Honor, I register a continuing objection to this line of questioning."

"It will be noted. The objection is overruled. You may answer."

There was nothing left for Boler to do. Somehow, she said later, the trial was no longer about what happened at Eveleth Mines, or what damage the company had caused. "Now, the women were being put on trial."

And it was clearly working. With each day, McNulty was growing appreciably cooler toward the women; more openly hostile to Boler, Sprenger, and Wolsky; and more receptive to Stumo's nearly incessant objections. "He clearly did not believe in the law of sexual harassment and did not like the women," Wolsky recalled. At least that was the impression McNulty gave when he was awake. "Sometimes," Wolsky explained, "he would fall asleep on the bench."

By the end of the second week, Boler knew two things: They were going down in flames, and there was nothing, short of giving up, that she and Sprenger and Wolsky could do to protect their clients from the humiliating invasion McNulty was allowing.

Day after day of watching her clients exposing the most intimate aspects of their lives, simply because they were trying to protect their basic right to work in safety, was deeply depressing for the lawyers. "There were times when I felt like giving up, quitting the practice of law." But Boler found inspiration in her clients. "Marilyn Greiner carried a picture of her granddaughter with her while she was in Duluth, and would look at it and say 'I am doing this for her.' They were heroic," Boler recalled. "Just to get up there and take that questioning from Mary Stumo, it was painful to watch, but also inspiring. I felt like if they could take this, I could take this, I had to take this."

Instead, Boler tried hard not to feel anything at all. "A lot of what I did during the hearing was suppress my own feelings—about the women, the trial, the defense, my family, and my feelings about being away from home. I would tell myself, 'You cannot think about what is going on at home today, or even think ahead to the next day.' "

Sprenger, though, seemed to love the thrill of battle, even when things were not going his way. His energy and optimism were a source of strength for Boler and Wolsky. "I loved litigating with Paul," Boler said later. "He was indefatigable." When she would lament a particular ruling that had gone against them, Sprenger's eyes would brighten, and he would say, "It's *great* that McNulty ruled that way. It was such a horrible ruling that it will be a great issue on appeal." Sprenger also began to realize that Stumo might be her own worst enemy. "Stumo assisted in trying the case to the court of appeals, and so did McNulty. He did stupid things, like always agreeing with Stumo. Stumo would overreach on her objections, would misstate the law, and he would agree with her."

Wolsky also tried to lift everyone's mood. At dinner, in the Greek restaurant near the courthouse that became their regular hangout, Wolsky, a jokester by nature, would regale them with hilarious impressions of McNulty and Stumo. But Sprenger knew his team's spirits were sinking. "When we realized how things were going, and still there were six to eight weeks of trial to go, it got very frustrating," Sprenger recalled. "It's hard to go to work and have your head handed to you day after day."

For the lawyers, the nadir was the third Monday of the trial. Stumo's cross-examination of one of the women who joined the lawsuit reluctantly was so bleakly devastating that they would later refer to that day as Black Monday.

Every one of the woman's fifty-four years had been hard. Her life took a turn for the better in 1993, when she won custody of two small grandchildren, who were being neglected by their mother. She was now fighting to formally adopt the children, and was terrified that what would come out about her past would hurt her chances of keeping them. She did not tell anyone in her family that she had joined the class, or why she was going to Duluth. She told them she was going to Minneapolis for a few days.

On direct, the woman testified that she had been offended by the sexualized environment at Eveleth Mines and that she had been stalked by a coworker. She described a number of incidents of harassment directed at her personally, including once when a coworker slit open her pants she was wearing with a knife. She explained that she had suffered anxiety, humiliation, and physical stress-related symptoms as a result.

On cross-examination, Stumo shifted attention away from Eveleth and focused on the distant past.

Stumo asked, "When you were small you had a lot of responsibility for your two younger brothers, correct?"

"Yes."

"And, in fact, when you were six years old you were left to baby-sit for them?"

"Yes."

"It was in the evening and your parents were both gone, electricity went out?"

"Yes."

Boler objected that the line of questioning was not relevant, but Mc-Nulty overruled her. Stumo continued.

"You were afraid and you took your brothers upstairs and you took a candle with you, correct?"

"Correct."

"And somehow the mattress started on fire?"

"Yes."

"And mother came home and she found out what you had done and she beat the living heck out of you, isn't that correct?"

"Yes."

From there, Stumo methodically led the woman to recite how she had been repeatedly sexually abused by her uncle from the age of six; how she had seen him and her mother having sex. How she married an abusive man who once pointed a shotgun at her five-year-old son and once held a hunting knife so tightly against her neck that it drew blood; how her son was badly burned when he climbed on a stove when she was not looking. How while her son was in the hospital recovering from his burns her husband held a gun to her head and threatened to kill her; how her mother refused to take her and her children in when the woman tried to leave her husband; how she discovered that her husband was stealing and how he shot himself in the head after she turned him in to police.

Stumo was like a machine. She asked the woman about how her older son began to set fires, how he even once tried to set fire to the bed his baby brother was sleeping in. She asked about the woman's second husband, who was even more abusive than the first. Did he, she asked "try to choke you over the kitchen table?" Did he "manipulate you into sex games with other people?" Did he "threaten to beat you if you didn't agree to do it?" Stumo asked her about how her new husband beat her children and sexually abused one of her daughters, and once wrapped their two-year-old in a blanket and stuffed her behind a dresser to make her stop crying. How by the time the woman found the little girl she had lost consciousness. How she periodically sought treatment at the Range Mental Health Clinic for problems not relating to her experiences at work.

It went on all day, Stumo confronting her with every unpleasant or painful thing that had ever happened to her in her life. When it was finally over, she felt like she had been "raped on the stand."

Her objections repeatedly overruled, Boler sat and watched it with awe, disgust, and deep sadness. How, she thought, could any one person have survived so much? Watching her client be forced to recite such painful memories in such a public forum, knowing that each fact would be used to undermine the value of her claim was excruciating. "This woman, and so many of the others, had had a really hard life growing up, a life full of bad things happening, then at the mine," she said. "And then to have this judge, and this lawyer, be so contemptuous of that suffering, and to not be able to do anything about it, was painful to watch." The defense strategy suggested that it did not matter what had happened to women like her at Eveleth, because they were already emotionally damaged by the time they got there. But, Boler thought, the women's "hard lives had made them, if anything, more deserving of protection, not less."

CHAPTER FIFTEEN

The Stand

February 1995

After Black Monday, things got steadily worse for the women. Those who had originally opposed the lawsuit fared as badly on the stand as Sprenger and Boler feared. At one point, Stumo asked Diane Hodge about her deposition testimony in 1991.

"Referring to page 68, line 1 of your May 1991 deposition. Question: 'Have you ever seen pictures of nudes or semi-nudes in a place that you didn't think it was appropriate to have them?' Answer: 'No, any place I've seen them was always someplace I didn't belong in the first place, out of my work area, and there's never been anything put in front of me purposely to make me see it or try and embarrass me.' Do you recall that testimony?"

"Yes, and I lied."

"And you never saw pictures of nude women in lunchrooms, and that includes the pellet plant, the concentrator, and the fine crusher?"

"Nope. I must have lied then, too."

Stumo turned to McNulty. "Ask that the witness answer the question."

"That's not true."

"So you were lying in your deposition in 1991?"

"I wish I could explain this. At that point I was trying to stay out of this lawsuit."

"Answer the question," McNulty instructed Diane. "Do you remember the question?"

"No."

"Were you lying in 1991?"

"On that deposition?"

"Yes."

"Just wasn't telling the truth. I was trying to stay out of the lawsuit."

"So you were lying?"

"Yes."

There wasn't much Sprenger or Boler could do, other than try to make the case that Diane and the other women who initially opposed the lawsuit did so out of fear. But Sprenger realized that it was going to be an uphill battle to convince McNulty that they had been seriously harmed as a result of what they had seen and heard at Eveleth, when they had previously sworn under oath that they had not been offended by any of it.

By the end of the first week in February, Sprenger and Boler realized that they would have to call Lois to the stand before the break. All the other women had testified, and they wanted Lois to testify before the medical experts did, since the experts would be offering opinions about her mental condition. If she had not yet testified, McNulty would have no sense of who they were talking about.

The weekend before the last week of the first phase of the hearing, Lois drove down to Duluth to prepare with Sprenger and Boler. When she arrived, Boler was surprised by her condition. She was taking a powerful cocktail of psychotropic drugs, Wellbutrin, Klonopin, and Pamelor, and her once-impressive memory and concentration were significantly diminished. Lois's medications had also damaged her thyroid and caused her weight to balloon. Emotionally, she seemed fragile and on edge.

Lois took the stand on Monday. For the first day and a half, things went fairly well. She described her experiences at the mines, beginning in 1975. She testified about each incident, as she had in both the certification and liability hearings and the seven depositions in between. Sprenger thought she was holding up pretty well. The second day was about the same as the first. But after an hour on the stand, Lois's mind began to wander, and she was easily distracted. Stumo "would move around" while Sprenger was asking Lois questions, Lois recalled later. "She stood just about the whole time Paul questioned me. She was constantly objecting, and trying to get eye contact. Paul would say two words, and she'd object. I've never seen someone so calm when so angry as Paul. He stood right in front of me to block her view of me."

After lunch on the second day, Sprenger decided it would be a good idea to let Lois have a rest. He sent her back to the motel for a nap. To fill the time, he called Randall Lakosky, Lois's psychiatrist, to the stand. Claire Bell had referred Lois to Lakosky in 1992 when she became convinced that Lois was suffering from "full-blown" PTSD. Lakosky's testimony was vitally important, as he was the one who could best establish that Lois's condition was in fact post-traumatic stress disorder, and that, in his opinion, it had been caused by sexual harassment at Eveleth. Lakosky testified that he diagnosed Lois as having PTSD in February 1992, based on a fifteen-minute consultation and information provided by Bell. He prescribed Pamelor, and a month later, added a dosage of Klonopin, to help manage anxiety. By the end of the year, he had also prescribed Wellbutrin and hydroxyzine. Lakosky testified that he continued to see Lois to monitor her medications, but that no visit lasted for more than a few minutes.

Stumo's cross-examination of the psychiatrist was surgical. She first zeroed in on his ability to attribute Lois's symptoms to any particular source.

"Isn't it true, Lakosky, that you're not aware of any literature supporting a diagnosis of PTSD with job stress being the traumatic event?"

"I can't cite you any specifically, no."

"That's because there aren't any articles on that, is that correct? There's no validated research to support that opinion?"

"I'll have to accept your greater knowledge, yes."

"That's your knowledge though, isn't that correct?"

"Yes. At this point, yes."

"And in order to have a . . . diagnosis of PTSD you have to have a qualifying traumatic event?"

"Or events."

"Pardon?"

"Yes."

"And that event has to be outside the range of usual human experience?"

"Yes."

"And you don't know—you have never identified a traumatic event in making Ms. Jenson's diagnosis, isn't that correct?"

"Only what she reported to me."

"And you don't know the specifics of anything that happened at work?"

"No."

"And you can't tell us as you sit here today what the traumatic event is?"

"Not in a specific sense, no."

"And you can't tell us when it happened?"

"Not the specific dates, no."

"And you can't say anything other than harassment at work, isn't that correct?"

"That's a conclusion based on the few for-instances she gave me, yes."

"That's all you knew on the first day when you made that diagnosis?"

"Yes."

"And that's all you know today?"

"Yes."

Then Stumo got Lakosky to admit that many of the physical symptoms that Lois complained of—dizziness, shakiness, irritability, weight gain, and lack of concentration—could have been caused by the medications, or combination of medications, that she was taking for depression and anxiety. By the time she finished with him, Stumo had completely obliterated the legal import of Lakosky's PTSD diagnosis. Not only could he not assert with any degree of medical certainty that Lois had PTSD as a result of sexual harassment, but he did not even seem reliably certain that what he took to be symptoms of PTSD had not been caused by the medications that he himself had prescribed. Sprenger had been stuck with Lakosky, whose eagerness to overmedicate Lois verged on negligent, and whose knowledge of a known psychological disorder, PTSD, was nil. Lakosky was, after all, Lois's treating psychiatrist—the only one on the Range—and if he had not called him, Faegre & Benson surely would have. All Sprenger could hope was that the other medical experts would do better when it was their turn.

The next morning, Lois once again took the stand. They were coming to the end of her direct testimony. The night before, Sprenger explained to Lois that he was going to ask her about the circumstances surrounding Greg's conception. Sprenger and Boler both believed that testimony about Lois's personal life in 1967 should not be admitted, but they also knew that, given the way McNulty had already ruled on the past sex lives of the other women, there was no way to keep it out. In any case, Sprenger wanted Lois's testimony about the rape to come on direct, where he could lead her through it gently, rather than on cross-examination. When the time came, in keeping with the agreement reached during discovery that all references to Greg's conception would be kept confidential, Sprenger asked that the record be sealed. Stumo agreed. When Lois had briefly explained the circumstances of how she became pregnant with Greg, Sprenger moved on to another subject, and the record was reopened. After a few additional questions, mostly about Tami, and Lois's decision to put her up for adoption, Sprenger ended his direct examination and sat down.

For the rest of the morning Lois was cross-examined by Stumo. Sprenger had originally requested that Lois's testimony be limited to half days, but at the lunch break, she seemed to be holding up to

Stumo's cross well enough that he agreed to let her continue in the afternoon. He did ask that the lunch break be long enough that Lois could take a nap. McNulty granted the request, and asked that they resume at 2:00 P.M. When they returned, Stumo cross-examined Lois for three hours, primarily about Steve Povroznik and the origins of her sexual harassment claim. Stumo showed several inconsistencies in the details of Lois's testimony about Povroznik. For example, Lois testified on direct that when she went into Povroznik's office in February 1984, he "grabbed" both her wrists and pushed her into a chair. But in the written complaint she filed with the personnel department in July of the same year, she said she sat down in his office, the implication being of her own accord, and that he had only "tried" to hold her hand. And why did she now say that Povroznik intentionally touched her buttocks as she was leaving his office, when her complaint to the Minnesota Department of Human Rights said only that he "accidentally" brushed up against her? Why did she now claim to be "terrorized" by the incident, when she once said only that it had made her "furious"?

As the afternoon wore on, Lois became less sure of dates and details, and frequently responded that she did not recall an answer to a question that she had answered many times before in depositions or earlier hearings. Later, Lois recalled, "I felt naked on the stand. The atmosphere in that courtroom was just like being at Eveleth Mines. I felt like a criminal and I was going to be sentenced for something." She also felt that her lawyers were not doing enough to protect her, although she understood that it was at least partly due to McNulty's rulings. "It felt like my attorneys weren't allowed to represent me. McNulty tied their hands so much."

The next day, February 10, was the fourth day of Lois's testimony, and the last day of the first session of the hearing. That morning, the lawyers were relieved, knowing that the ordeal would soon be over, at least for a while. But Sprenger was concerned when he saw Lois at breakfast. She looked as if she hadn't slept at all, and seemed even shakier than she had the previous afternoon.

When Stumo resumed her cross-examination, Sprenger realized that his concerns were justified. Lois had even more trouble following Stumo's questions, and she alternated between losing her concentration and becoming argumentative and irritable. Again under seal, Stumo questioned Lois about what Stumo referred to as "the incident you now characterize as a date rape," getting Lois to admit that she had voluntarily left the party with Jones, and that he "was not a stranger." As the morning wore on, Sprenger and Boler noticed that Lois was losing her train of thought more often, and would frequently pause for an awkwardly long time before responding to Stumo's questions.

A little while later, Stumo asked Lois about an incident with a rubber vagina.

"Now, on direct you testified that Mr. Scaia threw the object in the garbage, do you recall that?"

"Yes, I do."

"But in your deposition you testified that you were so embarrassed, you didn't report it and you threw it in the garbage, isn't that correct?"

Lois instantly realized that she had made a mistake on direct—she knew that she had thrown it in the trash, as she had testified to several times. Stumo continued to ask questions, but Lois kept thinking about the mistake. How had she done that, she wondered? What other mistakes had she made? Her mind began to drift back over her previous testimony. When she realized that Stumo was waiting for an answer, Lois had to ask her to repeat the question.

As he watched, Sprenger grew worried. "There would be these long pauses before she answered a question, or she would give an answer that was totally out of left field, nonresponsive. And then she started sobbing. It was clearly more than just handing her a Kleenex would fix."

Finally, Sprenger rose to request a break. He asked Sandra Riekki to take Lois to the ladies lounge and help her regain her composure. Lois took some Xanax to steady her nerves, but it didn't help. After several minutes, Sandra came out and reported to Sprenger that she did not think Lois could go on.

Sprenger concluded that he had no choice but to request an early recess. He returned to the courtroom and said, "I don't have any good news. I would suggest that we adjourn. Ms. Jenson is disoriented and crying and confused. And I think she's taken some medication. It may be in an hour or so she will be able to proceed, but, frankly, to me it just isn't worth it."

McNulty looked at Stumo, who was clearly annoyed. "Well, obviously I'd like to finish my cross-examination as much as I can, but— I don't know what to say. . . . It's a little tough to insist that she proceed if there's an issue about her ability to proceed."

McNulty, for a change, ruled in Sprenger's favor. "We'll reconvene on May 22 at nine o'clock," he said, adjourning.

And suddenly it was over, for the time being. Boler, Sprenger, Wolsky, and the legal assistants began the process of packing up, organizing what would stay and what would go. Boler felt as if she had been set free: She was going home. With Sprenger and the others, she headed back to the motel to pack up as fast as she could.

Lois had no reason to rush home. She had already checked out of her room, so she sat with Boler while she packed. She was mentally and physically exhausted. Boler suggested that Lois use her room to take a nap before she drove back to Eveleth. Without hesitation, Lois climbed into bed and fell into a deep sleep.

When she awoke several hours later, night had fallen. She checked the other rooms and discovered that everyone else was gone. She still felt groggy and disoriented. Back in Boler's room, Lois looked at the time. It was nearly 10:00 P.M. She turned on the radio. The weather report said that it was going to be a cold night, thirty to forty below. Lois knew that if she did not start her car now, in the morning it would be dead. She didn't have any money to keep the room, or to eat. She had no choice but to drive back to Mountain Iron.

By the time Lois got started, it was nearly midnight. In the middle of the frigid night, Highway 53 was dark and foreboding. Lois had trouble keeping her eyes open. A few times she started to drift off at the wheel but managed to pull herself awake. When she finally arrived at her apartment building, she got out of the car and collapsed into a snowbank. She managed to stagger back to her feet and to the door, but could do nothing but lean against it, shivering, until a neighbor who came to investigate the still running engine, helped her inside.

Back in Minneapolis during the break, the lawyers prepared for the testimony of the expert medical witnesses. At Sprenger's request, McNulty had ordered another round of mediation, this time before a magistrate named Ann Montgomery. But once again, the parties could not agree.

In the spring, Greg Wolsky announced that he was accepting a job offer with another company. Sprenger had recently hired a young, bright associate named Larry Schaefer, who he assigned to take over Wolsky's role in the case. Shaeffer spent most of April and May coming up to speed on the case.

Meanwhile, on the Range, Pat Kosmach's daughters were tending to the scattering of her remaining ashes. "They took my soul," Pat had said. "They might as well have the rest of me." When the first spring thaw arrived, a small biplane climbed into the clear blue sky over Eveleth. Circling low over the pitted, inhospitable landscape, the pilot let Pat's ashes drift quietly down to the place Pat had both hated and loved . . . and had consumed her till her dying day.

By the time the hearing resumed on May 22, spring had come to Duluth. The January snow was gone, the city was slowly turning green, and Boler had convinced Sprenger to change accommodations, setting up shop in the slightly more pleasant Park Inn, which offered a view of Lake Superior.

On the first day of the second session, Stumo resumed her cross-examination of Lois. Her condition had not improved over the break—if anything, it had gotten worse. Lois had spent the break stewing over

Sprenger and Boler's shortcomings. "There were no theatrics, they did not do a lot of objections, they didn't show emotion," she complained. Meanwhile the other women in the class, shell-shocked by their grueling experience on the stand, blamed Lois because she had got them involved in the case. Lois rarely heard from any of the women unless they had a complaint to make about the lawyers.

One of Stumo's objectives was to try to paint Lois as overly invested in her lawsuit, perhaps to suggest to McNulty that Lois would do anything, including make things up, to further her cause. At one point, Stumo asked Jenson whether she viewed the women who testified for the company at the certification stage as having been "against" Lois, or just opposed to the substance of Lois's claims. "I don't know how to separate me from my claims," Lois replied, tellingly.

Throughout the day, Stumo hammered home the idea that Lois was malingering in order to boost her recovery in the lawsuit. She pointed to the fact that immediately after learning that Rosenbaum had granted class certification—when Lois's chance of winning increased dramatically—Lois suddenly became unable to work.

"Ms. Jenson, you understood that you'd get a lot more damages if you weren't working, isn't that correct?"

"Objection," Sprenger started, but Lois responded before McNulty could rule.

"I don't believe I knew that."

"You know that now, don't you?"

"No, I don't. There's no final outcome yet."

"You don't think it affects the amount of money that you can recover in the lawsuit whether or not you're working? . . . You only worked for eighteen days, isn't that correct, after you heard about the decision on December 16, 1991?"

"I didn't count the days so I don't know."

"And you expect to recover millions of dollars in this lawsuit, isn't that correct?"

"I don't know."

"You don't know what you expect in this lawsuit?"

"I don't expect anything. I have not— Let me rephrase it. I have not put my expectations on anything."

"Haven't you told people that you expect to recover millions of dollars?"

"No, I have not."

"Now, although you were having problems going to work and doing your job in '91 and '92, you didn't have any problems posing to have your picture taken for *Glamour* magazine, did you?"

Lois pointed out that she had posed for the *Glamour* article sometime in the spring or summer of 1991, before the certification ruling came out. Stumo plowed ahead.

"In fact, you brought the magazine into the workplace and showed it around, isn't that correct?"

"No, that is not correct."

"You enjoyed the fact that you were getting national publicity, isn't that correct?"

"I didn't like the national publicity," Lois responded.

For the rest of the afternoon, Stumo had Lois on the ropes. One of the most effective moments came when she asked Lois about the incident in the grocery store in 1992, when she suddenly became so violently angry at a total stranger that she had to leave the store.

"You were so upset that although you had started putting groceries in your cart, you just simply left the store and didn't buy anything, isn't that correct?"

"I don't recall that I had started putting groceries in the cart. I think I went in specifically for sandwich meat or milk or something, but I do know I ran from the store, I didn't buy anything."

"You were so upset that you ran out of the store?"

"Yes."

"May I approach the witness, Your Honor?"

"You may," McNulty responded.

"Ms. Jenson, could you describe what that is, please?"

"It's a check written to IGA for $17 dated January 24."

"So you did buy groceries that day, is that correct?"

"Or I put the wrong date on the check."

"You don't recall as you sit here today though, correct?

"As I recall, I ran out of the store."

Lois's suggestion that she had improperly dated the check notwith-standing, Stumo was able to cast doubt on Lois's credibility. When Mc-Nulty adjourned the hearing for the day, Lois left the stand rattled and furious with herself.

Stumo was able to produce the IGA check because, during discovery, Faegre & Benson had requested copies of Lois's canceled checks for the previous three years. The next morning, Stumo returned to the checks, asking Lois to identify the stores and businesses to which she had written checks since she went on disability leave. She started with the "A"s.

"AAA Visa?"

"That's a credit card."

"Ace Hardware?"

"Ace Hardware is a hardware store."

"ADBS Architects and Designers?"

"I believe that's a book club."

"Affordable Cleaners?"

"That's a dry cleaning."

"American Family Insurance?"

"That's insurance for my car."

"American Family Publishers?"

"That would be a periodical magazine."

"Amoco?"

"That's a gas station."

By the time Stumo got to the end of the alphabet ("Zup's, Z-U-P apostrophe S?" "Zup's is a grocery store"), Stumo had painted an entirely different image of Lois's daily life other than the isolated, home-bound existence Lois had testified to on direct. The litany of checks suggested that Lois had a fairly active, normal life.

By lunchtime, Lois was finished, literally and figuratively. In total, she had spent the better part of six days testifying before McNulty, and more than half of the time under cross-examination. Stumo had done everything she could have hoped to do: She cast doubt on whether Lois had been offended by anything at Eveleth Mines, raised serious questions about whether she was even telling the truth about what had happened to her, and elicited testimony that suggested that Lois was not as sick as she claimed to be.

After Lois, Boler turned to the expert witnesses, hoping that Dr. Novak and the other experts would fare better than Lakosky had. They didn't. On direct, Stumo was relentless about objecting, usually successfully, to almost every question Boler or Sprenger would ask. Even getting the experts to recite their background and credentials was an out-and-out battle because of Stumo's storm of objections. Most were barely, if at all, allowed to testify to their opinions about what harm the women had suffered and why.

Not that it mattered much. On cross, Stumo's laserlike ability to deconstruct the testimony of medical experts led each one in turn to admit that there was no scientific proof that sexual harassment caused significant mental anguish of any sort, let alone serious disorders such as PTSD. As for other, lesser diagnoses of mental and emotional disorders, each one in turn was forced to admit that, while it was their opinion that the women had been harmed as a result of sexual harassment at Eveleth Mines, there was no scientifically reliable way to determine which one of several possible causes resulted in a particular symptom or condition.

The second half of the damages hearing was less emotionally draining for Boler than the first session had been, now that the women were not testifying every day. Boler later recalled that "It was a different kind of stress than the first go-round. Then, it was emotional, dealing with the emotional toll of the hearing on the women. But the second time, it was the stress of tactical combat—it was very difficult because of the objections to our expert testimony. McNulty showed real disdain for our experts. And it was so frustrating because we would get our experts up there and he would not let them testify, because Stumo and Goldstein would be making objections to everything they said, and he would sustain the objections. Later, when we would make the same kind of objections to their experts, he would overrule us."

Even before the hearing resumed, Sprenger was certain that McNulty was going to rule against them, and that they were now simply trying the case to the court of appeals. That meant that they had to keep asking the questions they needed in order to develop the record for appeal, regardless of how much Stumo objected, or how McNulty ruled. Other than that, there was not much to do but put witnesses up, ask them their opinion, have Stumo object, and McNulty sustain, and hope that somehow, McNulty would make enough serious mistakes in his rulings to provide some basis for appeal.

Sprenger soon concluded that his time could be better spent elsewhere. His firm had now invested more than $2.5 million in costs and fees in *Jenson v. Eveleth*, without seeing a dime in return, even though they had now gone to trial three times and won twice. It did not make sense to have three lawyers in Duluth asking fruitless questions, so he handed the reins over to Boler and Schaefer, with instructions to keep their eye on the appellate record, and an admonition for Schaefer, who tended to argue with McNulty, to stay calm and focused. "Larry was young and gung-ho and he had a hard time accepting McNulty's stupid rulings."

On Friday of the first week, Sprenger flew to Washington to close the deal on a settlement in a case against the Maytag Company. The case, based on breach of contract and tort claims rising out of a plant closing in West Virginia, had been filed by a young, relatively inexperienced West Virginia lawyer who, once the case gained traction, sought the help of Sprenger & Lang. Once Sprenger got involved, the case settled quickly—for $16.5 million. "The lawyers' fees were $4 million—Paul took two and the other guys took two and everybody was happy and the whole thing probably lasted a month or two," recalled Greg Wolsky, who stayed in close contact with his former employer. "That is the way Paul likes to operate, but he is willing to stand by the cases like *Jenson* that last forever." Maytag, said Sprenger with a smile, "was a model case."

In Duluth, Schaefer and Boler finally finished with their experts, and rested their case. Then it was Faegre & Benson's turn to call witnesses. During the last few days of the hearing, Faegre & Benson called men from the mines to rebut claims made by the women about specific incidents of harassment. Several men came forward to say that Lois had touched them at work, and that she was a bit of a flirt, and a number of others testified that some of the women, including Diane Hodge, Denise Vesel, and Marge Tolbert, regularly used vulgar language at work. Tim Degnan admitted that he once told some of his coworkers that it would take him just three days to get into Lois's pants, but said it was meant as a joke, not a threat. He also admitted that he once came up to Lois from behind and put her in a choke hold, but that, too, was meant as a joke.

John Erspamer, a pellet plant foreman, testified that Michele Mesich had told him that a worker had told Mavie Maki that she needed a "good fuck." But, he said, when he asked Maki about it, she said that it was not a big deal, and she did not want him to pursue the matter. He also testified, as did a number of the men, that they had heard many of the women use bad language at work.

The defense also called Gene Scaia. Lois had testified in February that Gene once grabbed her crotch at work with a greasy glove, leaving a grease-print mark on her yellow pants. In the liability hearing, Kyle had refused to admit testimony about Lois's sexual relationship with him. But McNulty allowed Gene to testify about their affair. He admitted that he had touched her with a greasy glove, but called it a "pat." He denied that he had grabbed her crotch, or that other men had witnessed the incident and laughed about it. He also testified that on the same day Lois had grabbed his testicles as a joke, and that night she made him dinner at her apartment and had not been upset by the incident in the least. He also said that when he broke off their relationship shortly afterward to go back to his wife, Lois was very upset, and even stalked him outside of work for a while.

On cross, Boler confronted him with testimony from his deposition in 1991. At that time, he did not mention that Lois had grabbed his testicles earlier in the day. In fact, he'd testified that she had not touched him intimately at work for several months. He also said in 1991, that after he grabbed Lois, they never dated again, and in fact had nothing more to do with one another from that day on.

When pressed, he explained the discrepancies in his testimony by saying that since his deposition four years earlier, he had "reexamined his conscience."

Don Olin, one of Kathy Anderson's foremen at the pit, admitted that he did not think Anderson would have made a good step-up foreman, because she was "flighty" and a complainer. He said that he thought she should go to the bathroom behind the equipment, as the men did, even though she would have to take off more clothes than the men, and would be more exposed both to the weather and to her coworkers. And he said that once, when Kathy complained about stomach problems, he told her that if she had "female trouble" she should find a different assignment that did not require driving large trucks. But, he said, he was "trying to help her, not hurt her." He also denied having a picture of a naked woman in his office, although he said that he did keep a "real nice" picture of his mother at work.

After the last two witnesses testified on the morning of June 13, 1994, McNulty asked that the lawyers submit their closing arguments in writing. Then he banged his gavel, and the damages hearing was over. McNulty would retreat to review the mountain of evidence and volumes of testimony. Now, once again, after an intense two-year period of frenetic, nonstop action, capped off by six full weeks of trial, all both sides could do was wait.

PART THREE

The Verdicts

1996–1998

CHAPTER SIXTEEN

The Ruling

November 1995

While they waited for McNulty to issue his recommendations on damages, the Sprenger & Lang lawyers turned their attention to two age discrimination class actions. Before the next year was out, the cases against Control Data Corporation and First Union Bank Company would settle for $28.5 million and $58.5 million, respectively.

For Sprenger & Lang, the settlements could not come quickly enough. After eight years, the Jenson case had become a loss leader for the firm. Sprenger & Lang had sunk eight years and more than $2 million into the case, and the likelihood that the case would pay off, at least without significant further investment, seemed slight to Sprenger. But there was no question in his mind that he would see the case to the end. He'd made his reputation, in part, on his commitment to sticking with a case through thick and thin. Clients hired him, and opposing counsel dreaded going up against him, because of his tenacity.

But in the summer and fall of 1995, it looked like Sprenger had met his match. Oglebay Norton had shown a Herculean will to gut it out in court. Most corporations involved in class action suits settle—of Sprenger's opponents, 95 percent had settled. But not Oglebay Norton.

In November 1995, Oglebay Norton fired Faegre & Benson. When the company hired the firm in the winter of 1992 to replace Erickson, Faegre & Benson estimated that its legal fees would be approximately $450,000. The firm revised its estimate in June 1994, projecting that it would cost approximately $900,000 to see the case to the end, assuming it went to trial. Two months later, it again revised its estimate, this time to $1.2 million.

Eleven months later, Oglebay Norton's insurers descended on the offices of the law firm, looking closely into how the case had become so expensive. By the time they finished their audit, in November 1995, they calculated that Faegre & Benson had billed a total of $2.7 million in defense costs, including attorneys' fees and expenses. At the insistence of the insurance companies, Oglebay Norton hired a new firm, Moss & Barnett, to defend the company in the *Jenson* case, and fired Faegre & Benson for "grossly deficient litigation estimates" and "excessive and unreasonable billing practices." Among the practices that the insurers cited as unreasonable were the firm's practice of repeatedly "redeposing witnesses" and the "use of 71 different lawyers, paralegals, and clerks" in connection with the case. Faegre & Benson subsequently sued the insurance companies for payment of its bills; the insurers then countersued the firm for excessive and unreasonable fees.

In the end, the two settled their lawsuit. It was lost on no lawyer connected to *Jenson v. Eveleth* that if Oglebay Norton had simply settled when Lois originally filed her complaint in 1988, the company would have been out less than $500,000 total. "The company could have ended it any time," Sprenger said years later, "by adopting a sexual harassment policy. What would it have cost them?" Instead, by making increasingly smaller settlement offers as the case progressed, which infuriated Sprenger & Lang, "they fueled the fires," he said.

Meanwhile, in the long months it took McNulty to sort out damages, Lois holed up in her apartment, honeycombed with boxes filled with legal documents. She was overcome with anger and paranoia, thinking that she had been deserted for greener pastures. "I read up on why people fire and sue their attorneys," she said. "Most of the time it was because of lack of communication. And we had that big-time."

In Duluth, Lois found self-hypnosis tapes for weight loss and stress release—music with subliminal messages—which she fell asleep to every night. She called 1995 her "year of the couch potato"—it was rock bottom. Her spirit was broken. In May 1995, she wrote the lawyers about her state of mind after the McNulty trial: *Trust of almost everyone is gone, trust of the legal system is gone, trust of the medical system is gone. Trust or faith in God, while still there has changed and that has affected every aspect of my life, friends, family.*

She was more isolated than ever. Lois's family worried that the lawsuit was ruining her life. During the summer, her sister Marilyn took Lois to the Jenson family reunion in Ulen. Every year, on the third Sunday of August, their father, his fifteen siblings, and scores of children and grandchildren got together to eat a meal, have a family picture taken, and put on a talent show. Lois had one topic of conversation: the lawsuit. "She drove people away," Marilyn recalled. Marilyn watched her cousins' eyes glaze over as Lois talked to them. "That was her life. No matter what the topic of conversation was, she would always come back to the lawsuit."

Lois's cousins weren't the only people steering clear of her. Since the McNulty trial, Marcy, Kathy, and Michele were the only women in the class still speaking to her. "The trial had polarized us completely. Very little did I hear from anybody," Lois later recalled. "I felt like I had duped them. I felt responsible. And I'm sure they felt that way."

Then, on March 28, 1996, eight months after the trial's end, Marcy Steele called from work to tell Lois that the mine had posted a notice saying that McNulty had ruled against the women. Lois called Boler immediately. Boler had not gotten anything from McNulty's chambers—common practice dictated that he notify all parties as soon as his ruling was released. Confused, Lois turned on the five o'clock news. The newscast led with the story of McNulty's decision. Lois quickly called Boler back. "I'm looking at the list right now!" she shouted. Sure enough, right there on the screen stood the names of all the women in the class, coupled with the small dollar amounts that McNulty had awarded them. After some scrambling, Boler got a copy of the ruling. She never did find out how or why the company and the media received it first.

The 416-page report was worse than anything they could have imagined, and they had imagined that it would be bad. McNulty came as close as he could to awarding them nothing. The individual amounts ranged from $25,000 for Lois down to $3,000 for two of the women, for a total of $182,500. It was a shockingly low figure, considering that in 1996, women with much weaker sexual harassment claims in other parts of the country were being awarded amounts of $100,000, $200,000, or more.

As the lawyers had feared, McNulty ruled against them on the issue of the burden of proof. The women had to prove that the sexual harassment, not something else, had directly caused them emotional or mental anguish. And he had ruled that all expert testimony on the issue of causation was inherently unreliable, and therefore inadmissible. He had thrown it all out because, he wrote, in the fields of psychiatry and psychology, "experts know no more than judges about what causes mental change—which is to say that they know almost nothing."

The result was a nearly perfect catch-22: The women had the burden of proving that the harassment at the mines caused them mental and emotional harm, but they could not prove that they had been mentally or emotionally harmed because no one, not even an expert in the field, was allowed to tell the court how the harassment had harmed them.

That left only the testimony of the women as evidence that they had suffered mental anguish as a result of the hostile environment at Eveleth Mines. For McNulty, that was not enough. In general, "sexual harassment claimants" he wrote, tend to be "histrionic," to "exaggerate" and to misinterpret "reasonably expectable interpersonal conflicts in sexual terms."

None of the women had convinced him that they had been anything other than temporarily embarrassed or angered by the hostile work environment at Eveleth Mines. None of them had proved that they had suffered any chronic or serious emotional or mental harm. The ones who claimed to have post-traumatic stress disorder, or chronic depression, had failed to prove to him that, if such a condition did exist, it was the result of sexual harassment. Mostly, he was convinced that the women as a group had demonstrated an "inability to get along with others."

None of this was surprising, given McNulty's pretrial rulings and his dismissive, even hostile demeanor during the hearing. What was surprising was the deep, bitter hostility toward the women that oozed from nearly every paragraph of the report. In page after page, McNulty revealed his view that the women were lying, or oversensitive, or both, and simply out to fleece Eveleth's parent company, Oglebay Norton, for all they could.

Lois seemed to offend McNulty the most. Although he found she was entitled to $25,000 for temporary embarrassment and mild mental anguish, she failed to convince him that she had suffered any lasting harm as a result of her experiences at Eveleth Mines. In fact, he seemed to discredit almost everything she had to say. "Generally speaking," he wrote, "Jenson's testimony demonstrates a tendency to exaggerate, towards histrionics and dramatization and to skirt the whole truth." McNulty concluded that Lois was lying about the incident with Gene Scaia. Rather than believe her version that Scaia had grabbed her crotch with a handful of grease, McNulty believed Scaia's version—that he patted her on the rear. Noting that they had slept together the night before, McNulty found that Scaia's testimony "has the ring of truth. . . . This Court concludes that early on we have an illustration of Jenson's misconstruction and carelessness with disclosure of the full truth." Nor did he believe Lois suffered any genuine anxiety from Povroznik's attentions. His letters, McNulty wrote, "cannot be interpreted to be, implicitly or explicitly, threatening, intimidating, coercive or presenting a source of fear." At most, they might be "suggestive of strange quirks."

In sum, McNulty found that Lois's claim "flounders on the shoals of causation. Jenson was obligated to prove, by a preponderance of the evidence, that sexual harassment was not only a possible cause of a mental disorder and symptoms, but that it was a substantial cause." The record, according to McNulty, did not even clearly establish that she had any serious form of emotional or mental disorder—her own psychiatrist, Randall Lakosky, admitted that many of her symptoms could have been caused by medication. But even if she did have some mental or emotional problems, McNulty found that she had not proved that they had not been caused by any number of other possible factors, including her daughter's adoption, "problems with her son," her "break-up with a boyfriend," "financial problems," "difficulties with fellow employees," and her efforts to "engineer damage claims" by the other women.

But for Lois, the worst part of McNulty's report came several pages into his discussion of her claim. When *Jenson v. Eveleth* began, one of Lois's biggest concerns was that the rape would come out, and she would have to tell Greg about his conception. Back in 1988, her lawyers were certain that the information was irrelevant and would not be admissible under the same rationale that underlies the rape shield laws. They assured Lois that the information was unlikely to become public. When Congress in 1994 specifically amended the Federal Rules of Civil Procedure to protect victims of sexual harassment by placing a heavy burden on defendants who wanted to dig into a victim's sexual past, Lois's lawyers became even more confident that the rape would not be discoverable.

But Faegre & Benson convinced McNulty that the women's medical and sexual histories in general, and Lois's rape in particular, were relevant and necessary to their defense. Their original argument was that they were entitled to know whether Lois had suffered trauma in the past that could have caused her emotional or mental problems. That argument was originally premised on an assumption that the rape had occurred—after all, how else could it have been traumatic? But after interviewing Lois, Dr. Long became convinced that the fact that Lois had not reported the rape at the time proved it never happened, despite the fact that rape was routinely underreported in 1967. In her report, Long raised the possibility that Lois was making up the rape, and that it was evidence of her histrionic character and tendency to lie. By the time she went to McNulty for permission to depose Jones, Stumo was arguing both fronts. Either the rape happened and traumatized Lois, or it didn't and she was a serial liar about her relationships with men, despite the fact that Lois had not voluntarily mentioned the rape in the twenty-eight years since it happened.

But even when first McNulty, and then Kyle, permitted the Jones deposition, and when Lois testified about the rape in McNulty's courtroom, her lawyers could still assure her that it would not become public information. As part of McNulty's discovery order, all mention of the rape—in depositions and in trial—was to be under seal. When the subject of the rape came up in court, the courtroom was cleared of any extraneous people, and the testimony was marked as confidential in the transcript. Both parties agreed that the information need never become public.

So no one, not Lois, not Boler, probably not even Stumo, could have expected McNulty to do what he did in his report: discuss the rape openly, publicly, with no acknowledgment that the information was under seal. But there it was, in black and white. And not because McNulty believed it to be true, but because he did not.

"In 1967," he wrote, "Jenson became pregnant by reason of what she now characterizes as rape." He noted that while the "characterization of the event is not particularly important, in and of itself," it nonetheless "has importance as a reflection on credibility." Despite his stated disdain for expert psychological testimony, McNulty lifted wholesale from Dr. Long's report the suggestion that Lois's failure to report the rape proved that Lois was not raped, but engaged in consensual sex. Based on Long's report, McNulty called Lois's testimony about the rape "a long after-the-fact construction of events. . . . In an action in which Jenson's credibility plays a large part, any tendency to put, as they say, a spin on events or occurrences cannot be overlooked."

That it was Oglebay Norton that made Lois's rape an issue in the case—the fact that the rape was originally fair game only because it was presumed to be true—was not mentioned. And so what Lois had always feared would happen if she reported the rape when it occurred, happened to her nearly three decades later, because she did not. Sprenger later said that including the information about Lois's rape despite the confidentiality agreements was "the tackiest thing I ever saw a judge do."

The other women did not fare much better than Lois. Time and again, McNulty believed the men's testimony over the women's, and was thoroughly dismissive of the women's fears of sexual violence. If Shirley Burton and Marilyn Greiner were in fact traumatized by being tricked into getting into a truck, driven deep into the woods, and told to service their foreman and another man, they were simply overreacting to a "proposition." Likewise, Joan Hunholz was either lying or overreacting when she claimed that she became anxious and afraid when a man repeatedly circled her isolated workstation—the same man who several years earlier exposed his penis to her. "This Court," he wrote, "has difficulty understanding why the appearance of a suspected flasher outside the building in which she was working some seven or eight years after a flasher incident would create great fear—of something—in a reasonable woman."

McNulty did at least believe Judy Jarvela's claim that someone had masturbated on her clothes, awarding $20,000 for the embarrassment and humiliation she experienced as a result of "the defilement" of her "wearing apparel," which McNulty described as "egregious" and "dastardly." But he was skeptical of her claim to have been afraid of sexual assault when a coworker who had repeatedly threatened to rape her lunged at her with open arms. McNulty dismissed her concern as a "gigantic leap." Equally as valid, the judge mused, was the conclusion that the man merely intended to say "boo."

McNulty also dismissed Michele Mesich's claim. He did not believe that she had been humiliated when a group of men presented her with a handmade dildo. McNulty pointed out that, according to the testimony of some of the men who were present, "the phallic symbol was greeted with mirth" and everyone, including Michele, joked about it at the time. The men did not dispute that they had, in fact, waved a "phallic symbol" in the face of a female coworker while a group of men watched for her reaction, but this behavior apparently did not strike McNulty as offensive.

McNulty was equally untroubled by comments made by male coworkers suggesting that women belonged home and pregnant, not in the mines. Such statements, he said, were expressions of free speech and were made in the context of the free exchange of ideas. And McNulty clearly believed that Eveleth Mines should not be penalized for what was the cultural norm in the Iron Range. "We must also bear in mind," he wrote, "that for generations the iron mining industry on the Iron Range was dominated by males who were products of a culture which is reflected" in the sexual tensions that gave rise to the lawsuit. A restructuring of the culture, he wrote, could not be expected to happen "overnight." After all, he noted, the Civil Rights Act was only three decades old.

But from the women's point of view, the worst part of the report was not his legal conclusions, or even the low awards, but the gratuitous personal detail McNulty included at every turn. He referred, by name, to one woman's mother, who had a complicated history with men, as "not fully domesticated." He pointed out that the husband of another had "erectile failure." For some reason he felt compelled to note that one of the women had been "the fattest kid in her class." Another, he noted, had gained forty pounds in fifteen years. It was bad enough that they had to testify to such things in a courtroom. But the women simply could not believe—had never even considered the possibility—that all that detail would someday be made public in a published opinion. His reasoning, time after time, was that he was demonstrating that the women were more emotionally damaged by other events in their lives than by anything that occurred in the workplace. And now, every intimate personal detail that they had testified about—their marriages, divorces, abortions, relationships with children and parents, childhood diseases, and past sex partners—was public knowledge, available to anyone with access to the Internet.

"We knew McNulty's ruling would not favor us," Lois said. "What we did not comprehend was that each of us would be so personally attacked. There is no way anyone can read things about themselves in this manner and not be destroyed by it. Criminals get better treatment."

Lois knew, too, that the other women blamed her. To a certain extent, she thought she deserved it. "It was the worst possible outcome, and I am the one who started it all," she said. "They had thought all they had to do was put their names down, tell what happened to them, and they would get compensated."

Lois worried that everything had been for nothing, that they had gone from making good law that benefited working women everywhere to making law that could actually hurt women. If companies knew that they could get away with what McNulty was letting Eveleth get away with, then why *would* they go to the expense and trouble to wipe out sexual harassment in the workplace? McNulty's ruling presented no real repercussions for Eveleth. Worse, if women knew that they would be subject to the same kind of exposure and humiliation that Lois and the other plaintiffs had been, they wouldn't even file suit in the first place.

But Sprenger and Boler were able to see in disaster an opportunity. In their view, McNulty actually had done them a favor by writing such an injudicious opinion. "The level of venom in the report was both extremely disheartening and heartening at the same time, because in it lay the possibility for redemption," Boler recalled.

A few days after the report was issued, Lois received a call from a *Washington Post* reporter named Kirstin Downey Grimsley. She was writing a piece about the women who worked at the Mitsubishi plant in Normal, Illinois, on whose behalf the EEOC had recently filed a sexual harassment suit. The pleadings filed by the EEOC in Mitsubishi relied heavily on *Jenson v. Eveleth* as precedent for the Commission's position that a sexual harassment case based on a hostile work environment could be brought on behalf of many women at the same time, even if their individual damages differed. Intrigued, Grimsley set out to learn more about the *Jenson* case. She was surprised to find that the small, obscure case, which six years earlier had been certified as a class, was still in progress. Grimsley went to Minnesota to find out more about the groundbreaking class action that made the Mitsubishi suit possible.

She interviewed Lois several times and questioned anyone in town who would talk to her. "Most people were amazingly uninterested and uninformed about the case," Grimsley recalled. She also had come to the realization that the term *sexual harassment* was a misnomer. "It should be called gender discrimination. The word *sexual* can imply romance, but there was nothing romantic about what happened at Eveleth."

When the McNulty ruling came out, Grimsley called Lois for her reaction. It was not until Lois realized that the rape was going to be mentioned in the *Washington Post* that it dawned on her how public the information really was. She finally faced the fact that she was going to have to tell Greg.

Greg was twenty-eight years old when Lois sat him down and told him the truth about his conception. It was a conversation Lois had hoped she would never have to have. When Greg was a young child, he often asked "Where's my Daddy?" Lois told him, "He loves you, but he doesn't love me." This time, Lois said, "You've had the chance to experience life, and it's not always easy." She explained to Greg who his father was, how she had met him, how he came to be conceived. She told him that he was a Vietnam vet, and was "carrying a lot of anger and hate and was drinking too much" when they met that night in Minneapolis at a party. Greg didn't respond noticeably to the news.

As soon as they had McNulty's report in hand, the Sprenger & Lang attorneys dove into the appeal process. The first step was to try to convince Judge Kyle to reject McNulty's report. As a Special Master, his findings would not have the force of law until accepted and entered as a legal judgment by Kyle. Working ten hours a day for two weeks, Schaefer and Boler divided up McNulty's opinion, combing through each section looking for legal errors. Fourteen days later, on April 11, 1996, the attorneys filed a brief to Federal District Court, citing eighteen legal errors they believed McNulty made in reaching his conclusions. First and foremost, he misapplied the burden of proof, the lawyers believed. He also failed to consider expert testimony on the issue of causation, and he failed to view the women's experiences in their totality. He misapplied the law of punitive damages, the lawyers charged, undervaluing the women's individual damages.

A few weeks after filing the brief, Boler learned some astonishing news: McNulty had been arrested for shoplifting two packs of Merit Menthol 100s from the Plaza Jubilee convenience store in downtown Duluth. McNulty pleaded not guilty, saying that he had simply forgotten to pay for the cigarettes, but employees at the convenience store told police that they had been keeping an eye on him after watching him do the same thing the week before. Ultimately, the charges were dismissed on the condition that McNulty not be "involved in similar incidents" for a probationary period of six months. But the episode confirmed for Sprenger that the judge was off-balance. "I knew he was eccentric," Sprenger said later. "I had no idea he was that eccentric." Lois gleefully clipped the article about McNulty's shoplifting arrest and saved it for her files. Marcy Steele brought her newspaper clipping into work, where she and the girls shook their heads over the news.

Kyle scheduled a hearing on Sprenger & Lang's objections to McNulty's report to be held in Duluth on July 3. In the days leading up to the hearing, Boler, with Schaefer and Sprenger's help, worked almost around the clock honing her arguments. As she drove back up to Duluth on the morning of the third, it all came flooding back to her—the McNulty hearing, the pain it had caused her clients, the unfairness of it all. As she stood before Kyle, she thought he seemed sympathetic to her arguments. After all, "Kyle had been very careful with the evidence" the first time around, Boler said, "and very brave and bold, making new law." When the Moss & Barnett lawyers, apparently hampered by their unfamiliarity with the case, argued that Special Master McNulty's report should be accepted because it represented so much work on his part, Boler felt bolstered. "Because he *worked so hard?*" she thought incredulously.

At the end of the hearing, Kyle took the matter under advisement. Once again the lawyers found themselves waiting for another ruling.

On October 27, 1996, the *Washington Post* published its story about the *Jenson* case, a two-part series by Grimsley. The first installment, headlined "A Hostile Workplace: Into the Abyss of Sex Harassment at Eveleth Mine," ran on the front page of the paper with a photograph of Pat Kosmach. Grimsley said the precedent-setting case "set the legal framework" for other sexual harassment class actions, including a pending federal suit brought on behalf of hundreds of autoworkers at Mitsubishi. The second installment ran October 28 on the front page with a photograph of Lois. Entitled "In Court, Women Miners Felt Harassed Again," the story offered a detailed description of what the women had experienced throughout the litigation and noted that although the "federal rape shield law prevents such intimate details about sexual assault victims from being revealed in court . . . it does not protect victims of sexual harassment if they are making damages claims." No other newspaper—the local papers on the Range, nor the newspapers in Minneapolis/St. Paul—had reported the details of the *Jenson* case in so much detail, and no other article had made the case for the lawsuit's legal impact so strongly.

A few weeks later, Grimsley and another *Post* reporter, Frank Swoboda, wrote an article about the evolving state of sexual harassment law. They called it one of the "fastest growing" areas of discrimination law in the country. The article noted that because of *Jenson* and other cases, sexual harassment was being taken seriously by corporations and state lawmakers. "At least 14 states have enacted laws dealing" with sexual harassment, including a law passed in Massachusetts requiring all employers to provide sexual harassment training in the workplace and a bill pending in Hawaii that would protect victims of sexual harassment "from overly intrusive investigation into their private lives." Accompanying the article, the *Post* ran a picture of the memo posted on the Eveleth Mines bulletin board: "SEXUAL HARASSMENT IN THIS AREA WILL NOT BE REPORTED. HOWEVER, IT WILL BE GRADED."

After the McNulty ruling, "the women were hateful to me," said Lois. But all that changed after the *Washington Post* article was published. With their story recounted on the front page of a major national newspaper "everyone was so nice. I hated being slapped with kindness." To Lois, in her depressed state of mind, being portrayed sympathetically was confusing. Here was the *Washington Post* "telling us we are heroes when I felt like the scum of the earth."

Kyle's ruling came in mid-November, just two weeks after the *Post* articles. To Boler's dismay, the judge upheld McNulty's report and recommendations in all but one respect. Kyle disagreed with McNulty's view that Diane Hodge's claim was time-barred: She would now receive $7,000 after all. But other than that, McNulty's ruling stood. In retrospect, Sprenger suspected that Kyle, having appointed McNulty to be Special Master on the case, felt some obligation to stand by him. Boler was disgusted. She got the feeling that Kyle wanted to let the U.S. Court of Appeals sort out the mess.

This time, Lois learned about the judge's ruling from her attorneys first. "Jane is sick to her stomach about this," said the legal assistant who called her with the news. "They are already working on the appeal."

Now Sprenger & Lang would have to make its case to the U.S. Court of Appeals for the Eighth Circuit. If the Eighth Circuit ruled against them, they could appeal to the Supreme Court of the United States. But the Supreme Court picks only a handful of cases to hear each year, and there was no guarantee that it would take the case. For all practical purposes, the Eighth Circuit was the last recourse for Sprenger & Lang and its clients. Sprenger & Lang had to deliver nothing less than a brilliant appellate brief. Jane Lang decided to call in an expert, an old friend named Dan Edelman.

Trials are about facts, but appeals are about the law, and writing appellate briefs is considered one of the most intellectual jobs in the legal profession. It requires the ability to spot legal errors committed by the trial court and to craft a persuasive argument that the errors were serious enough to warrant reversal. The attorneys who make their living doing what is known as appellate advocacy are often former law review editors, Supreme Court clerks, and members of their law schools' prestigious Order of the Coif. But the best brief writers—Edelman, a former Supreme Court clerk himself, was one—know how to state the case emotionally, to make it compelling in human and legal terms.

Edelman agreed to help. Once he reviewed the record, he told the Sprenger & Lang lawyers that, in his opinion, McNulty had committed two reversible errors. The judge had placed the burden of proof on the women for the issue of causation, yet he refused to admit the testimony of any of the expert witnesses on the same issue. "Those were the guts of the appeal," Edelman said. "McNulty justified the defendants scorched earth approach to discovery on the grounds that the defendants had the burden of showing that mental anguish and injury had not been caused by the workplace. But when he got around to writing his report, McNulty said it was now the women's burden to parse out what particular symptoms were due to the workplace and what was due to other factors."

With the fifty-page brief filed on March 10, 1997, the lawyers now turned their attention to the oral argument. The court calendar had come out, showing that the argument was scheduled for October 21, 1997. When Sprenger saw the names of the three judges who were assigned to the case, he was elated. "Wow," he thought. "This is fantastic!" Judge Donald Lay had been chief judge of the circuit before he recently took senior status. Lay, a well-respected, liberal judge, had written a strong, pro-plaintiff opinion in another sexual harassment case. Appointed by Lyndon Johnson, Lay was known as an intellectual. Judges Theodore McMillan and Floyd R. Gibson were also Democratic appointees. All three men were "from the old school of Democratic, civil rights–oriented appellate judges who took civil rights issues seriously," Boler said. "So many younger appellate judges now seem to view civil rights cases as less important. These were the old guard, and we were lucky to get them."

The court calendar reflected another interesting fact. The argument would not take place in the federal courthouse. Instead, it would be held at William Mitchell College of Law in St. Paul, where Judge Lay was on the adjunct faculty. When he was chief judge, Judge Lay occasionally scheduled oral arguments at William Mitchell to give law students a chance to observe. Sprenger thought it was a good sign. "Although Lay was no longer chief judge, he still carried a lot of weight, and was close to the new chief judge. I assumed that he said 'I want this case, and I want it at William Mitchell, and I want to use it to teach with.' I don't know if he did, but I assumed he did, and I assumed it was because he thought it was an important case."

But who would argue it? Many trial lawyers will go their entire career without presenting an oral argument before an appellate court. When a lawyer steps into court, he or she is facing a trio of distinguished judges who have already read the brief and have come armed with a battery of questions designed to test the strength of the parties' arguments. The lawyer who presents an oral argument before the Federal Court of Appeals must be able to think on his or her feet and to stay calm and on message under intense pressure.

Edelman had stood before innumerable appellate courts, but he did not know the facts and history of the case well enough. Sprenger, a trial lawyer at heart, never considered presenting the argument himself. He assumed that his wife would make their case in court. Lang had a wealth of appellate experience, and she had engineered the brief with Edelman. But after weeks of talking it over, they both decided that Jean Boler should do it. Although Boler was less experienced at appellate work, she knew the record of the case inside and out. If the judges asked logistical questions—what had happened to whom, when, and where—Boler would be in the best position to answer. "We knew that this panel would not try to trick her into taking a position she did not intend, as some panels sometimes try to do with relatively young lawyers. We knew they would not play any games." And, Sprenger said later, "Jean had earned it. She had put in a lot of dreadful hours in front of McNulty."

Immediately, Boler began to prepare. She went through the transcripts of every hearing, deposition, motion, and brief, and she researched the law. With Schaefer and Sprenger peppering her, Boler tried out every possible question.

In the midst of her preparation, she read that McNulty had died. The seventy-five-year-old judge had become ill with a viral infection during a fishing trip. A Duluth legal journal reported that friends described McNulty as "a fair judge who loved the law passionately."

Ten days before the October 21 argument, Boler flew to Washington to be vetted by Jane Lang and Dan Edelman. They met in Lang's stylish Mission-decorated office overlooking Dupont Circle. "We were like a group of generals preparing for the last battle, prepping their combatant," said Lang. When Boler stood and delivered an unemotional, academic presentation, Lang groaned. It was too dry, too intellectual, too focused on the legal issues; too Minnesota Nice.

"Jean," said Lang, "you're going to have fifteen minutes to get the panel to see the great injustice of this case. Let the emotion come to the surface!"

Boler had told her husband that she'd be in Washington for one night. Instead she stayed a week. She went back to the drawing board on her opening remarks. The firm hired a public-speaking coach, an idea that Boler, the methodical midwesterner, initially viewed with skepticism. But, to her surprise, the coaching worked. "We went through the argument line by line and recast it as an oral argument," Boler said. By the time she left for Minneapolis, she was transformed in at least one key respect: The process had greatly improved her confidence. The coach had shown her how the force of her emotions and convictions could enhance her considerable experience and intelligence. Above all, she felt prepared.

On October 20, the day before the argument, Michele Mesich, who still lived in Minneapolis, drove north to Gilbert to pick up Lois and bring her down to the hearing. Lois was too sick to make the drive herself. Michele found Lois in her apartment surrounded by file boxes, piles of legal papers, and unfinished craft projects. Michele had to pick her way through the clutter to find a place to sit.

Lois's mental state had not improved in two years. In early 1997, Lois, along with her doctors, Randall Lakosky and Claire Bell, had come to the conclusion that the heavy doses of antidepressants and tranquilizers were now part of the problem. Lakosky began to wean Lois off of Klonopin, Pamelor, and Wellbutrin. But with each adjustment in her medication, Lois experienced a series of withdrawal symptoms. She also suffered from hypothyroidism and was thirty pounds overweight.

But Lois had some good news to tell Michele. In September, Lois and Kathy had each received a $32,500 settlement from *Jenson II*. The small side case, which had been percolating over the summer, alleged that the company did nothing to protect the women from retaliation after they first filed suit. *Jenson II* chronicled the lies Stan Daniels had spread about the case, his hostility toward Lois and Kathy, and his efforts to encourage the shunning of the two women. In the wake of McNulty's ruling, Boler pursued *Jenson II* in hopes of providing a small panacea for her two lead plaintiffs. The $32,500—$9,542 of which would pay for her medical expenses—lifted Lois out of poverty. She celebrated by buying a small pearl "win ring" at JC Penny, and she moved back to her old apartment building in Gilbert.

The next morning, Boler arrived at the quiet, leafy campus of William Mitchell Law School and made her way to the front of the auditorium.

Nearly three hundred students packed the seats. The air buzzed with energy and anticipation.

Lois and Michele slipped in and found seats near the back of the room. Dressed in black and wearing her signature scarf, Lois insisted on an aisle seat in case she was overcome with nerves. Medication or no medication, Lois was on edge. Thus far, she realized, *Jenson v. Eveleth Mines* had been a net loss for women—and she took it personally. "If we lost on appeal," Lois said later, "I could be responsible for actually setting women back. We had accomplished a lot to make things easier for women to bring these cases to court. Now it all hung by a thread."

The counsel for Oglebay Norton, Moss & Barnett, arrived. Boler scanned the room for familiar faces from the company. There were none to be seen. Also absent was her old nemesis Mary Stumo. Meanwhile, Lang had taken a seat at counsel's table. Sprenger was back in Washington, working on another case, waiting for the call telling him how it had gone.

Soon, the three judges came in and took their places on the dais. The room fell silent. In the Court of Appeals, the appellant argues first. Boler stood up and approached the lectern that had been positioned directly in front of the dais. The three judges peered down at her. She took a deep breath, and began.

"May it please the Court, my name is Jean Boler, and I represent the appellants in the case of *Jenson v. Eveleth Taconite*."

In the audience, Lang could tell in an instant that Boler's diligence had paid off. "She was wonderful," Lang said. "She was clear and logical and poised, and although not overly dramatic, she did infuse her arguments with a sense of urgency and importance."

Judge Lay, who would write the court's opinion, asked a number of questions that seemed to be sympathetic to the women's argument. He focused in particular on which side had the burden of proof on the issue of causation. "I have looked through the entire record; it seems to me that the defendants" are the ones who sought discovery on that issue, he said. "Don't they have the burden of proof?" he asked Boler.

It was a slow, easy pitch down the middle.

"Yes, Your Honor," she responded.

Lang breathed a sigh of relief. The question indicated that the panel was giving serious weight to the arguments they had made in their brief.

Boler was relieved, too. She was prepared to be barraged with hostile questions. Instead, she said, "I felt like I was almost their straight man."

Once again, the lawyers from Moss & Barnett argued that McNulty had "worked so hard" that it would be inappropriate to second-guess him now. "Well," replied Judge Lay, "who cares how long and hard he worked, if he was wrong?"

As Lois listened, unfamiliar emotions—hope, excitement—flooded through her. For the first time since the nightmare of the discovery process had begun three years earlier, she felt that the momentum was back in their favor. The three judges were asking questions that suggested they understood what had gone wrong in the case.

Michele, too, understood what was happening. "The judges socked it to the mine!" she said with a big grin. After years of hearing the men tell her that she and the other women would get what she deserved, "finally," she said with satisfaction, "the women got what they deserved."

By the time they arrived at the firm's office on Ridgewood Avenue, Lois and Michele and the Sprenger & Lang contingent were walking on air. The place erupted in cheers. They got Sprenger on the phone in Washington and Lang gave him a blow-by-blow briefing on the argument. Boler collapsed in an armchair. As she listened to Lang gleefully recounting how "we got 'em on that one!" and "Jean nailed that," sweet feelings of relief and exhaustion swept over her.

Law students are forever advised not to predict outcomes of appellant arguments based on the judges' questions. Many lawyers have walked out of an argument thinking they had won only to learn they were completely wrong when the written opinion came out. This time, however, the lawyers' predictions were accurate. On December 5, 1997, just three months after the oral argument (near-record time for a decision in such a complicated case), the Eighth Circuit issued its opinion, throwing out the McNulty ruling in its entirety and ordering a new trial on damages, this time before a jury.

"This case has a long, tortured and unfortunate history," the opinion began. First, it acknowledged, as the plaintiffs had argued, that Mc-Nulty "inexplicably" changed his theory on who had the burden of proof on causation of the women's emotional harm. When McNulty allowed Faegre & Benson to delve into the personal lives of the women in discovery, he reasoned that the company had to prove the women's injuries were the result of something other than their exposure to the hostile work environment at Eveleth Mines. But in his final opinion, McNulty flip-flopped, and placed the burden of proof on the women, not the company. The Court of Appeals agreed with Sprenger & Lang's argument that McNulty's discovery rulings and the damages ruling were legally inconsistent. The court also agreed with the women that McNulty was wrong in ruling that expert medical testimony on the issue of causation was inadmissible, but not before pointing out that "ironically, the special master [McNulty] generally accepted the opinions of the expert witnesses produced by the defendants. The imbalance," the court said, "is difficult to explain."

The court chastised McNulty postmortem for allowing the defendant to pursue its "scorched earth" strategy, noting that much of the discovery into the women's pasts "was not relevant or so remote in time that it should not have been allowed" to become part of the record. Finally, the court found that McNulty "erred as a matter of law" on the issue of punitive damages. In doing so, the court shot down his conclusion that Eveleth did not have an affirmative legal obligation to "respect a female employee's right to work in an harassment-free environment" until the Supreme Court's decision in *Meritor* in 1986. In fact, "Title VII has made an employer's discrimination against an employee on the basis of sex an unlawful employment practice since its passage by Congress in

1964." In other words, noncompliance with federal civil rights laws cannot be excused simply because discriminatory traditions die hard.

In its conclusion, the court wrote:

It should be obvious that the callous pattern and practice of sexual harassment engaged in by Eveleth Mines, and the mental anguish of the women was clear. The emotional harm, brought about by this record of human indecency, sought to destroy the human psyche as well as the human spirit of each plaintiff. The humiliation and degradation suffered by these women is irreparable. Although money damage cannot make these women whole or even begin to repair the injury done, it can serve to set a precedent that in the environment of the working place such hostility will not be tolerated.

But the court did not stop there. After ordering the retrial on the issue of damages, the Eighth Circuit took the unusual step of commenting on the overall course of the litigation, and particularly, on the "inordinate delay" encountered by the parties. "This case has been pending for almost ten years. The final chapter has yet to be written." It is simply not possible, the court said, for any of the parties to obtain justice "when a final outcome is issued more than ten years" after the case was filed, and more than fifteen years since the class period began.

After noting that part of the blame fell on the political gridlock over judicial appointments in Washington, D.C., resulting in a shortage of federal judges to hear these cases—hence the stop-gap of a special master—the court also took umbrage with the way the case had been tried. "The lawyers in this case delayed its resolution by exercising senseless and irrelevant discovery, and by making endless objections at trial."

But the court's most pointed criticism was directed at McNulty. "If our goal is to persuade the American people to utilize our courts as little as possible, we have furthered that objective in this case," the judges wrote. "If justice be our quest, citizens must receive better treatment."

For Lois, reading the opinion after so many years of disappointment and frustration was "like walking from the deepest basement into light." Sprenger, in his understated way, described the opinion as "enjoyable to read." But Lang was more effusive. "It was sweet, so sweet, reading that opinion," she said. As it unfurled from her fax machine in Washington, Lang had trouble keeping tears of joy and relief from filling her eyes. "It was the kind of moment you go to law school for," she said. She was particularly surprised and gratified that the court was so frankly critical of the lower courts. "That," she said, "is not common. . . . The tone of the opinion was so passionate at points, it was clear that they cared. It made us feel that after we had been beating our heads against the wall, the court did care about seeing justice done. In the lower courts, it seemed like the case was just an annoyance, like they wished it would just go away."

"It showed," said Boler, "that sometimes you have to go way down, get kicked way low, to rise high, to get major adjustment in the law. McNulty's and Mary Stumo's excesses created a basis for the Eighth Circuit to react. And it reacted not only to the legal principles that McNulty got wrong, but to the parts of the trial transcript that show his bias and unfairness. The Eighth Circuit opinion makes it less likely that that kind of defense will be permitted, or at least that defendants in future cases will realize that that kind of defense can have negative consequences for them."

Immediately, the ripple effects of the decision were felt across the country. The National Organization for Women heralded the opinion as "tremendously rich and valuable," an "important victory" for women's rights. The Eighth Circuit opinion in *Jenson v. Eveleth Mines* would "call a halt to the terribly invasive discovery that's gone on in these sexual harassment cases," Mary Ann Sedey, a prominent plaintiff's lawyer, told *Trial* magazine.

For Lois, the opinion meant pure vindication. "The ruling gave me credibility with the other women," she said. A few days after the opinion came out, Joan Hunholz called her. Joan had not spoken to Lois since the McNulty hearing, but on this day she called to apologize. Joan said she realized now that Lois had been telling the women the truth all along. "You never lied to us once."

"When I put down the phone," Lois said, "I felt at peace for the first time in a very long time."

CHAPTER SEVENTEEN

Settling

December 30, 1998

A year later, on December 30, 1998, Bill Jarvela picked Lois up at her apartment in Gilbert at 4:30 A.M. She found a seat in the back row of the Jarvelas' van next to Kathy Anderson and Marcy Steele. Judy Jarvela, Joan Hunholz, and Mavie Maki sat up front. The temperature held steady at twenty below zero for most of the five-hour drive to the Cities. Lois, weak with pneumonia, had summoned all her energy to make the trip. They were on their way to attend the third settlement meeting in three months.

Oglebay Norton had asked the Eighth Circuit Court of Appeals to reconsider its ruling immediately after it was released. When the court declined, the company filed a Petition for a Writ of Certiorari, asking the U.S. Supreme Court to review the decision. In June 1998, the Court declined to hear the case. That meant that both parties were headed back to court to try the issue of damages again. But as the Eighth Circuit had instructed, this time there would be no special master. Instead, there would be a jury.

From the beginning, this phase of the case was different from all that had passed before. The judge, John R. Tunheim, a young, progressive jurist appointed to the federal bench by President Clinton in 1995, set a trial date of December 8, even before the Supreme Court declined to review the case. One of his first rulings was that anything that had happened in the women's lives more than a year before the class period began in 1983 was not relevant and therefore not discoverable or admissible at trial. That ruling set a tone that carried forward throughout the discovery and pretrial proceedings. The message was clear: This was not going to be a repeat of the McNulty hearing. "It was the discovery order we should have gotten back in 1993," Sprenger said.

Indeed, it was a new world. In September 1996, Oglebay Norton had relinquished its thirty-two-year-long role as the managing agent for Eveleth Mines, and the holding company for the mine was restructured. By December of that year, Oglebay Norton sold its entire ownership interest in the mines to a limited partnership called Eveleth Mines LLC. Tom Green, Oglebay Norton's CEO, and William Ruf, the vice president of industrial relations and personnel, who had presided over Oglebay Norton during most of the Jenson case, both retired in 1997. A new team, with little or no direct experience with Eveleth Mines, had taken over at headquarters in Cleveland.

Much of the lawyers' time was focused on lining up their expert witnesses and obtaining updated psychological reports on the sixteen women who still remained in the class. (Several of the women including Jan Friend and Connie Saari had settled early.) Moss & Barnett did not request any additional depositions of any of the women.

Sprenger & Lang hired a jury consultant, who put together several mock trials designed to help the lawyers hone their trial strategies and help the firm evaluate how much money a jury would likely award each of the women. The mock trials did not precisely replicate trial conditions: the jury pools were not identical; the women's testimony was videotaped instead of live; and Sprenger & Lang lawyers played the roles of Oglebay Norton's defense.

Still, in both mock trials, the juries came back with astoundingly large awards for the women—in the neighborhood of $30 million. It was, to say the least, encouraging. So was the fact that in May, news broke that the EEOC had settled its massive sexual harassment case against Mitsubishi on behalf of 350 female employees for $34 million.

All the while, the Oglebay Norton lawyers and Sprenger & Lang were engaged in settlement negotiations, but they were not even close to an agreement. Sprenger & Lang was asking for $18 million, including $3.1 million for Lois, while Oglebay Norton was offering $1.6 million for the whole case. In that respect, at least, Oglebay Norton still had not changed. Nevertheless, by December, Tunheim was repeatedly urging the parties to try to settle the case. He had pushed the trial date to January 1999, and the delay gave the parties one last chance to reach a settlement. No one believed it would happen. On December 11, the Minneapolis *Star Tribune* quoted Boler saying that a pretrial settlement did not look likely. Scott Herzog, the lead lawyer on the case for Moss & Barnett, was more blunt. He called the chances for a settlement "close to nil."

On December 15, the parties convened in Tunheim's courtroom in the sleek new federal courthouse, a building of teak, glass, and marble, in downtown Minneapolis. It was time for voir dire, the process by which a jury is selected. Sprenger & Lang had learned in the mock trials that they did better with women. But because federal law prohibits striking jurors on the basis of gender, the percentage of men to women on the jury would depend in large part on the ratio of men to women in the overall jury pool. To Boler's dismay, the jury pool that morning happened to be 85 percent male, and after two days of voir dire, they ended up with a jury of ten men and two women. Not only was the jury predominantly male, it was also predominantly blue collar. "They looked like the men in the mines," Boler said. "We were concerned about the women looking over and seeing the same kind of men who were their tormenters."

That evening, Schaefer, Boler, and Sprenger convened in the conference room at Sprenger & Lang's office, the same room where Lois and Pat first met Paul almost eleven years earlier. Boler was worried about the jury. They concluded they needed to change their strategy in light of the jury composition, and emphasize the management's culpability, rather than the miners', to be less threatening to the working-class men on the jury.

But the jury was not the only thing Jean and Paul were worried about. They had split the plaintiffs up into two groups; those who had suffered too much emotional damage to be able to work again, and those who were still functional. Lois, Kathy, Judy Jarvela, and Angel Alaspa had all been diagnosed with PTSD, and as a result, they were expected to get much higher awards than the other eleven, more stable women. But Lois and Kathy had broken down during the five-minute videos they had prepared for the mock jury, and Angel, who was in and out of mental hospitals, could not testify at all. Lois worried that she would no longer be able to remember everything. She told Boler that her memory was like a person carrying stacks of paper files, spilling them and putting them all back in the wrong place. "I'll remember things I haven't remembered for years at the strangest time," she said. "And I used to have such a good memory." Increasingly unpredictable and heavily medicated, Kathy was in worse shape than ever. During an early settlement meeting, she burst into giggle fits at inappropriate moments. "We were worried they would not make it through their testimony," Boler said. "We were concerned about getting out the details we needed in their fragile state."

In a positive turn of events for the women, on December 17, Tunheim ruled that in addition to the damages they were already claiming, the plaintiffs were also entitled to recover damages for the stress caused by ten years of litigation. This significantly increased the potential for damages. As even Dr. Long had found in some of her reports, the protracted litigation had contributed to the medical condition of Lois and some of the other women.

Boler and Schaefer spent the days before and after Christmas preparing their witness outlines, and reviewing medical records. For Boler, it was the fourth Christmas in seven years that she'd given over to *Jenson v. Eveleth Mines*. Back in Washington, Lang spent eight hours on

Christmas Day putting the final touches on Sprenger's opening statement.

One more round of settlement negotiations remained before the trial started on January 5. At Tunheim's orders, the parties would attend a last-ditch mediation session on December 30 under the guidance of Minneapolis mediator Brian Short. Short had been involved in the case for several months, helping the parties try to reach common ground. But this time Tunheim had taken the unusual step of instructing Fireman's Fund, Oglebay Norton's lead insurer and now the lead negotiator for the defense, to send a new representative to the mediation session. The insurance company's local representative had annoyed Tunheim by repeatedly asserting that future negotiations were futile. When the man said that he would not be available on December 30, Tunheim ordered Fireman's Fund to produce an alternate and specified that it be someone from senior corporate management with the authority to settle the case.

Paul Sprenger and Jane Lang flew into Minneapolis on December 29. Lang was ostensibly there to help her husband prepare for trial. But he had also asked her to come along just in case settlement talks got serious. He knew from experience that if the talks were going to go anywhere, the eve of the trial was when it was most likely to happen.

Sprenger also knew that his frame of mind at that moment was to do battle, not compromise. Lang, on the other hand, excelled at negotiation. She was also better than Sprenger at helping clients make the emotional and mental adjustments required for settlement. A large part of it involved helping clients recast their sense of themselves. "When you litigate a case, you become stuck in the past, stuck in the role of victim," Lang said. "You have a sense that life is a battle. It can be hard to see when it is time to move on." Lang knew that Lois especially fell into this category. "Sometimes, when litigation has been the centerpiece of your life, settling can feel like giving up. But settling is not about caving, it's about saying, 'All right, now I can let go.'" She saw her role as helping clients evaluate offers and to keep an open mind. "I will never say, 'Take this or don't take this.' If I think an offer is too low, I will tell them I think they can do better, and if it is a good offer, I will tell them it seems pretty fair. But the decision has to be up to them."

The lawyers met their clients at Short's office a little after 10:00 A.M. on December 30, 1998. As the women sat down in the blue wool chairs around a large conference table, Short, with slicked-back brown hair and a ruddy complexion, snapped his purple suspenders and explained that the nature of settlement is closure, not justice. "If you're here expecting justice," he said, "you're not going to get it."

Lang, who had not seen Lois in over a year, was shocked by how visibly her health had deteriorated. She realized that for Lois in particular it would be healthier to let go of the case and move on with her life. The women—Judy Jarvela, Kathy Anderson, Marcy Steele, Mavie Maki, Joan Hunholz, and Lois—all seemed to vacillate between wanting the case to settle and being afraid that if it did, the people in the Range would accuse them of being in it only for the money.

Lois had urged the rest of the women in the class—they were now down to fifteen—to come to this meeting, but they refused. Instead, they'd given Boler the authority to settle if, by some miracle, an agreement was reached. Boler had driven up to Eveleth to secure the power of attorney after the first settlement meeting, when hardly any of the women showed up. No one at all showed for the second one. Shirley Burton and Marilyn Greiner, so disgusted by the process, had told Boler they would settle for almost nothing.

The women's expectations about the upcoming trial were high, having been raised by the mock jury awards and their lawyers' constant pep talks. But now that the jury had been chosen, the lawyers were not as confident about the trial as they had been earlier in the month. They worried about the jury makeup and the fragility of some of the most important witnesses—Lois, Kathy, and Angel. They also knew that even if the women won, Oglebay Norton would appeal, and the case would go on for several more years at the very least.

The one thing the lawyers and their clients had in common that day was that no one expected the case to settle. They had all been through way too many settlement conferences to think this would end any differently from the others. Short met with the women and their lawyers first, then went to another room and talked to the other side. While Boler worked with Kathy, Schaefer strategized with Lois, and Lang rewrote Sprenger's opening statement on her laptop. The new representative for Fireman's Fund, a senior vice president, happened to be a woman. Whether it was her presence, Lang's, or the combination of the two, the two sides suddenly began moving toward each other. In a matter of hours, Fireman's Fund was abandoning positions that Oglebay Norton had defended for more than a decade. By lunchtime, the two sides were beginning to approach numbers that Sprenger & Lang thought could represent a fair resolution of the case.

Very soon, it became clear that this day would be different. For one thing, the company agreed to take the lawyers' fees out of the equation, and let Sprenger & Lang petition the court for an award of attorneys' fees under Title VII and Minnesota state law. That cleared the way for serious negotiations. Once it became obvious that there was going to be real progress, Lang, Schaefer, and Boler put aside their laptops and witness outlines and began to focus on the task at hand.

All of a sudden, the women began to settle in waves. The third and second tier plaintiffs who did not suffer from PTSD settled for sums ranging from $50,000 to $150,000. For a while, it looked possible that they would settle all but the biggest claims—Lois, Kathy, Judy, and Angel Alaspa—and still go to court on those. Schaefer seemed to want to go to court, eager to litigate. He and Lois had been working on their outline all morning. When he heard that the first eleven had settled, Schaefer said to Lois, "Good! Let's go to court!" Judy Jarvela stopped Lois before she went into the separate conference room to talk about her settlement offer. "You know, Lois, if you decide not to settle, I'll go to trial with you because I'm not afraid. I think we're strong enough to do it." But Judy was aware that Lois was sick with pneumonia, and tired.

Lois went into the conference room, where Boler, Schaefer, Sprenger, Lang, and Short presented her with an offer. She could not tell

whether her lawyers thought she should take it. They showed her the offer and said it wasn't bad. What did she think? Lois returned the question: "What do you think? You all have spent ten years of your lives on
this case, too." The lawyers did not respond—this had to be her call.
Lois tried to read them. Schaefer seemed flustered, Boler looked pained,
and Sprenger was poker-faced. Only Jane Lang spoke. She repeated
something she had told Lois earlier that day, "You look like you're ready
to get on with your life." Confused about which way to turn, Lois said
later, "I felt like I needed my own lawyer. . . . It was really uncomfortable. I didn't like it at all."

The offer was just shy of one million dollars. It was less than the
$3.1 million Sprenger & Lang had been floating, but also a far cry from
the $25,000 that McNulty had awarded her. The lawyers knew that a
jury might have come closer to the higher figure, but it might not, and
even if it did, it could be years before Lois saw any of that money. And
despite the big settlements in the news at the time, the fact was, it was a
lot of money for a single sexual harassment claim. Most sexual harassment claims were brought under federal law, which capped damages at
$300,000 per person. Even the $34 million Mitsubishi settlement, when
divided by the 350 claimants, resulted in less than $100,000 per
woman. Here, Fireman's Fund was offering to pay a lump sum of about
$3.5 million for all fifteen remaining *Jenson v. Eveleth* plaintiffs, which
averaged out to more than $233,000 per person.

Lois may have felt unsupported by her lawyers, but the firm had no
incentive to sell Lois and the other women out, not at this late stage of
the game. They had already spent more than $6 million and ten years on
the case—a few weeks more was not going to matter. If Sprenger & Lang
really thought the case would likely bring in a $30 million verdict and
that that verdict would stand, the firm had every incentive to stick with
it and take a third of the award, as it was entitled to do under its retainer
agreement. But the combination of ten men sitting on the jury and their
star witnesses' failing health convinced the lawyers that this was the

best moment for the women to extricate themselves from the case, with good law intact and at least a decent amount of money in their pockets.

If Paul Sprenger had told Lois the day she walked into his offices in 1988 that she would receive more than three quarters of a million dollars, instead of the $5,000 she was then asking, she would not have believed him. But then again, she never would have believed that she would have to go through what she did to get it. Then, she had been a healthy woman with a high-paying job. Now, the money would be all she had. Exhausted from the long car ride and the ten hours of negotiations, and feverish with pneumonia, Lois looked at her options: with the other women out, it was now down to Kathy, Judy, Angel, and herself. Kathy and Angel were way too sick to make it through another trial. Now that they had come so far as a group, Lois did not want to go it alone, or even just with Judy. She dreaded the prospect of taking the stand again for a fourth time. Her memory was shot, and she could no longer remember the details of events that happened twenty-five years ago. She knew that Oglebay Norton would appeal if the women won large sums in damages, and it could take years longer to resolve the case.

After weighing her options, she reluctantly concluded that it was time to give up the fight and accept the offer. "I realized that we weren't going to see justice if we settled, but we may not have seen it if we had gone to trial. Quite frankly, one of the reasons why I settled was because I don't know if I could have remembered everything if there had been a trial." Kathy and Judy, who had been presented slightly less than Lois, followed her lead. "I was the last to hold out," said Judy, "but I didn't have a choice, I didn't feel I could go to trial alone." On behalf of Angel Alaspa, Sprenger accepted a large six-figure sum that amounted to about half of Lois's settlement.

As a condition of settlement, Oglebay Norton required that the women agree not to disclose the amounts they received to anyone, not even each other, before they received their checks on January 15, 1999, under penalty of a $10,000 fine. But they already knew how much money they had each received. The only woman whose settlement was a mystery was Angel Alaspa's. The women mistakenly believed that Sprenger had wrangled $1 million for Angel.

In the conference room afterward, Mavie Maki jumped for joy. "I got my silver car! I got my silver car!" she shouted. Mavie had always said that she wanted a brand-new silver Ford Crown Victoria to replace her fourteen-year-old car. "We went to Minneapolis for three settlement meetings, and every time I'd see a silver car going past us, I'd say, 'That's what I want. When I get my silver car, I'll be satisfied.'" Maki's good cheer gave the rest of the stunned and bedraggled group something to laugh about. "She should have gotten ten silver cars for what she went through," Marcy said later.

Lawyers are used to turning on a dime. Settlements on the courthouse steps are not only common, they are expected, particularly in the case of jury trials. But for Boler, it was a bittersweet moment. When the finality of it all began to sink in, she felt vaguely disappointed. For one thing, she had just spent an entire year gearing up for a jury trial, and now it would not happen. Lois was right—part of Boler really wanted to get this case before a jury. Despite the risks, she wanted the women to be able to tell their stories in their own voices, if only because doing so would be cathartic in a way that a secret settlement agreement never could be. Boler also felt frustrated with the system for causing the women, at least Lois and Kathy, to get worse instead of better. "It is supposed to help them, not hurt them. Class actions work well for creating systemic change, for setting standards, but this case shows that there is a human cost to achieving that change." Later, Boler reflected that the women probably could have managed the stress of the job. "If they had kept their heads down, they would probably still have their jobs, be able to work. Maybe not, but I think they would probably have gone through less stress by not speaking out than they did by standing up for what was right."

But later the next evening, at a New Year's Eve party with her husband, Boler realized that she would still be at the office if the trial had gone forward. She had just gotten her life back, and it would take some getting used to.

For Paul Sprenger and Jane Lang, it was not over. They still had not gotten paid a dime and would now have to petition the court for their fees. Unlike the women, they had no idea how the case would come out for them financially. The firm's out-of-pocket expenses came to $960,353, plus the 24,790 billable hours that attorneys and support staff had spent on the case, totaling $5,597,956. But Sprenger and Lang were heartened by the fact that they had made good law. "It was an important case," Sprenger reflected later. "If it were not for the toll it took on the women and on Jean, it would have been a great case."

They had won a precedent-setting decision on certification, won convincingly on liability, and won a stunning victory on appeal. Lloyd Zimmerman, head of the federal EEOC office in Minnesota, called *Jenson v. Eveleth Mines* the "seminal sexual harassment case." He listed its many achievements: "It was the first to be certified as a class, the first class action to go to trial on the issue of emotional distress, the first to win on liability, the first to be affirmed on appeal." Sprenger & Lang, he says, deserves credit. "These lawyers have done more to enforce employment discrimination law in this country than anyone else. How many people are willing to work for ten years without pay?" The impact of the case, he said, is enormous. "It is a lesson to employers that if you have a problem, fix it, and fix it early. And it is a lesson to plaintiffs and their lawyers to persevere." It also "puts the breaks on intrusive discovery in other cases. More than any other case, this case will make bringing harassment cases less costly for victims." *Jenson v. Eveleth Mines* had made the legal system a safer place for future sexual harassment victims to venture.

For the women, the settlement was more complicated. That night in the Cities, they piled into the Jarvelas' van, and Bill drove them back home.

The group in the van had made three trips to Minneapolis together. After years of antagonism, breakups, and makeups, they had found a way to be friends. It had been fourteen years since Lois had filed charges against Eveleth Mines with the Minnesota Department of Human Rights. As the truth that their struggle had ended began to sink in, Joan Hunholz turned to Lois and thanked her. "If it weren't for you, we would never have gotten this far."

But as the bleak scenery of a northern Minnesota winter passed by outside their windows, the women also began to share their doubts. They realized that they wanted something more than money could buy. They wanted an apology from the company. They wanted credibility in a community that did not trust them. They wanted to be believed. Now they felt that they had sold themselves out. They felt unsatisfied, and for many of them, it had nothing to do with the amount of money they received. "We had always said they'll pay us when hell freezes over," said Marcy, "and it did."

On January 15, 1999, when the blue Express Mail envelopes arrived at each woman's house, they discovered that they had to sign a draconian confidentiality agreement as a condition of cashing their settlement checks. In another blow, the women also learned that the settlement money would not be exempt from federal income tax. Damages for physical injuries from settlements or judgments are not considered income under the Internal Revenue Code. In 1996, Congress amended the tax laws to limit the exemption to physical injuries. Since the women's settlements were based on mental and emotional harm, they were considered taxable income.

The secrecy of the settlement amounts allowed rumors to flow and jealousies to linger. Was it true that Angel Alaspa got $1 million? Once the false rumor started, no one could stop it. The secrecy of the settlement meant that people on the Range thought that the women got much more money than they actually did. "Would I still be working here if I had gotten $300,000?" Marcy would tell her curious coworkers at the mine. Pat Kosmach's children were bitter because they mistakenly believed that the women were now millionaires. Why, in that case, had they not shared some of the spoils of the case with the Kosmach children? Under threat of being sued by their nemesis, Oglebay Norton, the women could not defend themselves.

Lois's pneumonia dragged on through the month of January. One icy, cold afternoon Joan and Marcy paid Lois a visit. They felt a need to talk about everything that had happened. "We were feeling that maybe we shouldn't have settled," Marcy recalled. "When we settled, people thought that it proved that all we wanted was money. Settling was like saying the money is more important than justice, that's how it got twisted up here [on the Range]." Lois agreed. The settlement still wasn't sitting right with her. "Even if my check was for $5 million, I don't know if I'd feel good about it," she said. Most of all, Lois realized, she had wanted an apology from the company, because it would have made her feel vindicated in a way the court system did not. "We never got a chance to set the record straight," Lois said. Echoed Marcy, "We just wanted to be believed."

Epilogue

"The nature of social change is that we make martyrs out of pioneers. We have yet to figure out how to make social change without sacrificing people along the way."

—Laura J. Cooper, labor law professor at the University of Minnesota, as quoted by the Minneapolis *Star Tribune* in reference to *Jenson v. Eveleth Mines*

Sprenger and Lang

On September 1, 1999, Judge Tunheim awarded Sprenger & Lang attorneys' fees and costs for *Jenson v. Eveleth Mines* in the amount of $6.28 million. In the end, they had just barely broken even for almost eleven years and 22,254 hours of work—not Paul Sprenger's ideal rate of return. But he had no regrets, at least not for himself or his firm. "It was worth it. The case didn't make us rich. In fact, we could have probably made more money during that time doing something else. But we made some good law. It was an interesting case, and I think an important case." He is less sure how his clients feel. "It was hard on them. I don't know whether they think it was worth it."

Shortly after the judge awarded Sprenger & Lang their fees, Sprenger and Lang announced that they were going to reduce their day-to-day involvement in class action litigation and devote more time to philanthropy. With an initial $7 million investment, the couple founded the Sprenger Lang Foundation to fund the performing arts, and arts education for disadvantaged youth. Sprenger and Lang turned over the management of the firm to Larry Schaeffer and Michael Lieder, but they kept their offices in the DuPont Circle building, and still control the firm's budget and personnel.

But Sprenger could not give up the practice of law completely. In 2001, a large group of middle-aged Hollywood screenwriters convinced the sixty-year-old lawyer to represent them in what may be the biggest age discrimination suit ever against fifty-one TV networks, studios, production companies, and talent agencies.

Jean Boler

Jean Boler left Sprenger & Lang in 1999. She devoted 5,636 hours to the *Jenson* case, which spanned her entire career at the firm. Boler moved to Seattle where her husband took a teaching job. She works part-time for the Seattle City Attorney's Office and writes fiction.

Mary Stumo

Faegre & Benson's website lists McNulty's damages award in *Jenson, et al. v. Eveleth Mines, et al.*, as one of Mary Stumo's professional accomplishments. The website does not mention that the decision was reversed by the U.S. Court of Appeals for the Eighth Circuit.

The Company

Oglebay Norton sold its interest in Eveleth Mines in 1996 and is now under completely new management. *Jenson v. Eveleth Mines* cost Oglebay Norton and its insurers more than $15 million.

The Case

Jenson v. Eveleth set many important precedents. Judge Kyle's opinion establishing the liability of Eveleth Mines for maintaining a hostile work environment sent a clear signal to employers that they could no longer look the other way when their employees were being sexually harassed. The Eighth Circuit's influential opinion is routinely cited by courts, lawyers, and legal commentators as precedent for limiting abusive discovery in sexual harassment cases. Collectively, the decisions make both the workplace and the courtroom safer for victims of sexual harassment.

But the most important precedent established by *Jenson v. Eveleth* was also the first: Judge Rosenbaum's decision certifying the case as a class action. That decision elevated sexual harassment from an individual complaint by one, usually a powerless person against another, more powerful one—a complaint that could easily be ignored or swept under the rug—to a significant civil rights issue. By putting the principles of collective bargaining to work in the context of the courtroom, it gave formerly voiceless working women a megaphone with which to demand change and the leverage with which to achieve it.

It now seems inevitable that sooner or later, a sexual harassment suit would eventually be certified as a class action; that employers would have to start taking the civil rights of working women seriously; that companies would have to pay a significant price for failing to do so. But in 1988, when Lois Jenson and Pat Kosmach first walked into Paul Sprenger's office, it was anything but. With Lois and Pat's determination and courage, and Sprenger & Lang's vision and commitment, they turned the unheard-of into the ordinary, and by so doing, improved the daily lives of millions of working women.

Jenson v. Eveleth did not eradicate sexual harassment in the workplace. But it made corporate America take real note of it for the first time, and established once and for all that women who are subjected to a hostile work environment need never stand alone again.

The Men

Kent Erickson, Lois's old friend on crew four, speaks for many of the men at the mine: "A lot of good people's images have been hurt because we were all grouped together in this case as being animals. There were only a select few that treated the women that way but we all got the rap for it."

Stan Daniels works in the United Steelworkers' Minneapolis office as a lobbyist.

Bob Raich retired in 1990 and spends the winter months in Arizona.

The Women

Marcy Steele, Joan Hunholz, Denise Vesel, and Jan Friend still work at the mine. Diane Hodge stopped working at the mine in 2001 due to a back injury. Joan Hunholz spoke for herself and her friends when she voiced her regret about her role in the case. "I wish I had gotten wiser earlier. There were a lot of names that we didn't reveal because they were union and friends. We told just what we had to tell and we left a lot out. If we did it again, we would have named more names and more people would have been fired."

Although threats of a shutdown loom constantly, conditions for women at Eveleth have improved. All Eveleth employees are required to take sensitivity training courses, and a woman was made foreman in 1999.

The national Steelworkers' Union now has a committee called Women of Steel, which encourages women union members to organize and protect their rights. In August 2002, the group hosted a conference in Pittsburgh with the theme Sisters in Solidarity.

Mavie Maki bought a new silver Ford Crown Victoria with her settlement money.

Judy Jarvela never returned to work. She still suffers from post-traumatic stress and only leaves her house on Thursdays to go grocery shopping.

Kathy Anderson never returned to work. She lives in Virginia with her husband, George, and continues to take medication for her PTSD symptoms.

Pat Kosmach's children did not receive a penny from *Jenson v. Eveleth*. After their mother's death, they learned more about the seriousness of the sexual harassment the women experienced at the mine, and are now proud of the role Pat played in the case.

Lois Jenson

Her son, Greg, a truck driver, became a father in 1997. Holding and caring for the baby boy brought Lois back to life. "He helped me feel again," she said. Lois stopped taking medication and is slowly regaining her strength and stability. The PTSD has caused irreparable damage, and Lois functions at a level that is a fraction of what it used to be. She moved to Babbitt to be closer to her sister and aging parents, and farther away from the mine.

On September 30, 1999, Sprenger & Lang celebrated the firm's tenth anniversary. Lois and the other *Jenson* plaintiffs were all invited to attend the firm's open house in Minneapolis. Unable to convince anyone else to join her, Lois drove down to the Cities by herself. She had some unfinished business to take care of. Her brother Duane and his wife, who live in Minneapolis, accompanied her to the party. That morning, Lois sent Sprenger & Lang flowers—a $75 bouquet—with a note that said, "Thanks for sticking with us."

When she walked into the front hall of 325 Ridgewood Avenue, Lois was proud to see her flower arrangement prominently displayed next to the front door. The Sprenger & Lang office was packed with local lawyers, and plaintiffs—none of whom Lois knew. Lois found Boler,

Sprenger, and Lang in the crowd. It was the first time she had seen them since the New Year's Eve settlement meeting nine months earlier. She wanted them to know that she was getting better, that she had survived. Lois told the three lawyers that she was at peace with the end result of the case. "Thank you," she added. "I am grateful to you for representing us."

It didn't take long for perfect strangers to discover who Lois was and come up to congratulate her. Lloyd Zimmerman of the local EEOC office made his way across the crowded room to introduce himself. To Lois's surprise, this powerful man seemed to know every detail of her case. He showered Lois with praise. He could not say enough about her courage, her perseverance. Another lawyer kept dragging people through the crush to meet Lois. It was unreal—like waking up in someone else's life. One lawyer from Duluth shook Lois's hand and said, "Do you know how many women you've helped?" The truth was, she didn't. Despair was what she knew, and she had held steadfastly to it. For fifteen years, she had been buried by the fight, unable to see the greater significance of what she, and the women who stood by her, had started. There, in the midst of the party chatter, she let it sink in. *Jenson v. Eveleth Mines* would always bear her name, but now it had a life of its own. And so did she.

Notes on Sources

Class Action spans twenty-five years and three trials. The foundations of this book rest in the legal record left behind by *Jenson v. Eveleth*. Thousands of pages of court documents—trial transcripts, depositions, exhibits, and judicial opinions—provided the brick and mortar of this narrative. Innumerable interviews with the plaintiffs, their families, and their lawyers, made it possible for us to understand the people and the values of the Iron Range of Northern Minnesota.

In 1999 and 2000, Clara Bingham made nine trips to the Iron Range. She interviewed community leaders, the women miners involved in the case, and their families. Lois Jenson had kept detailed notes and journals chronicling her experience both at Eveleth Mines and as the lead plaintiff in *Jenson v. Eveleth*. Lois generously shared these personal records with us and spent more than one hundred hours sitting for interviews with Bingham. Paul Sprenger, Jane Lang, and Jean Boler also patiently answered our questions in regular interviews over the course of two years. Laura Gansler interviewed the other lawyers and legal assistants at Sprenger & Lang who were involved in the lawsuit, as well as expert witnesses, and independent legal experts familiar with the case, both in Minneapolis and Washington, D.C.

Most of the former and current male miners at Eveleth whom we contacted, refused requests for an interview. Nevertheless, Bingham found several men, both in management and from the rank and file, with important firsthand experience who agreed to be interviewed both on and off the record. Meanwhile, Oglebay Norton's former managers, Bill Ruf and Tom Green, as well as the company's current management team declined to be interviewed, as did their lawyers in the case, Ray Erickson, Mary Stumo, and David Goldstein. Stan Daniels, the former president of the union, met our requests with a cold shoulder; so did the current management of Eveleth Mines. We were denied an official tour of Eveleth's taconite plant, and Bingham had to visit the facility as a private guest of one of the miners.

From the start, our goal has been to tell a fair, balanced story. The company's freeze on any information that would tell their version of events made our job harder. In the end we could only help the reader hear the voice of the company, as well as the voices of the men at the mine, by depending on our interviews with some key players, as well as depositions, trial testimony, and other legal records and exhibits.

Most of the dialogue in the book comes directly from trial transcripts. The rest has been gleaned from interviews with one or more people who were present at the scene. When scenes were recreated, we consulted several sources. For example, when Lois and Steve Povroznik had a scuffle in his office, we took Steve's version of what happened from his depositions, Lois's version from her trial testimony and her interviews for this book, as well as the version Lois told her therapist Claire Bell, which was recorded in Bell's notes. With each of these subtle variations of a twenty-minute-long event, we constructed the story that seemed the most believable and consistent with all of the versions that had been told over the course of nearly fifteen years.

Class Action is the only publication that attempts to tell the full story of these people and this trial. We relied on a surprisingly slim number of secondary sources. For coverage of the lawsuit, we read articles published in the *Washington Post, Wall Street Journal, St. Paul Pioneer Press, Minneapolis Star Tribune, Duluth News-Tribune,* and *Mesabi Daily News.*

For information about the history of the Iron Range and the iron ore industry, we relied on the following books and publications:

Margaret Culkin Banning, *Mesabi: A Novel.* New York: Harper & Row, 1969.

James Howard Bridge, *The Inside History of the Carnegie Steel Company.* Pittsburgh: The University of Pittsburgh Press, 1991.

Ron Chernow, *Titan: The Life of John D. Rockefeller Sr.* New York: Random House, 1998.

Clifford E. Clark Jr., editor, *Minnesota in a Century of Change: The State and Its People Since 1900.* St. Paul: Minnesota Historical Society Press, 1989.

E. W. Davis, *Pioneering with Taconite.* St. Paul: Minnesota Historical Society, 1964.

Robert F. Harney, "Tuteshi: Understanding the Historical Evolution of Iron Rangers," *Entrepreneurs and Immigrants: Life on the Industrial Frontier of Northeastern Minnesota.* Iron Range Resources and Rehabilitation Board, 1991.

Barbara Lamppa, "Women on the Iron Range," *Range History,* a Quarterly Publication of the Iron Range Historical Society, June 1978.

Marvin Lamppa, "Iron Country," Minnesota Public Television documentary series, 2000.

Paul H. Landis, *The Iron Mining Towns: A Study in Cultural Change.* Ann Arbor: Edwards Brothers, Inc., 1938.

William E. Lass, *Minnesota: A History.* New York: W. W. Norton, 1998.

Dana Miller, "Did Taconite Save the Iron Range?" and "Iron Range Communities in Transition," published in *The Iron Range in Transition: Roots for People Discovering Minnesota's History.* St. Paul: The Minnesota Historical Society, Vol. 17, No. 3, Spring 1989.

Minnesota, A State Guide by the Federal Writer's Project of the Works Progress Administration. New York: Viking Press, 1939.

Frank L. Palmer, *Spies of Steel: An Expose of Industrial War.* The Labor Press, 1928.

Robert Shelton, *No Direction Home: A Life and Music of Bob Dylan.* New York: Shelton Da Capo Press, 1997.

Frederick Stonehouse, *The Wreck of the Edmund Fitzgerald.* Gwinn, Michigan: Avery Color Studios, 1977.

John Syrjamaki, *Mesabi Communities: A Study of Their Development,* a dissertation presented to the Faculty of the Graduate School of Yale University in Candidacy for the Degree of Doctor of Philosophy, June 1940.

David A. Walker, *Iron Frontier: The Discovery and Early Development of Minnesota's Three Ranges.* St. Paul: Minnesota Historical Society Press, 1979.

We also consulted *Skillings Mining Review,* Duluth, Minnesota, and the Annual Report of the Inspector of Mines, St. Louis County, Minnesota, 1946, 1975, 1979, 1980, 1983, 1984, 1985, 1986, and several years of the Oglebay Norton annual report.

For information on the history of sexual harassment law, we referred to:

Catharine A. MacKinnon, *Sexual Harassment of Working Women.* New Haven: Yale University Press, 1979.

Gwendolyn Mink, *Hostile Environment: The Political Betrayal of Sexually Harassed Women.* Ithica: Cornell University Press, 2000.

Ruth Rosen, *The World Split Open: How the Modern Women's Movement Changed America,* New York: Viking, 2000.

Vicki Schultz, "Recapturing Sexual Harassment," 107 Yale L.J. 1683. April 1998.

Laura W. Stein, editor, *Sexual Harassment in America: A Documentary History.* Westport, Connecticut: Greenwood Press, 1999.

—Clara Bingham and
Laura Leedy Gansler

Acknowledgments

When we first proposed to write the story of *Jenson v. Eveleth*, we knew that we couldn't tell an in-depth, personal narrative without the cooperation of the plaintiffs and their lawyers. First we met with Paul Sprenger, who agreed not only to spend many hours over the course of three years answering our questions, but also to give us access to the complete court record of the case. Jean Boler and Jane Lang were also generous with their time. We are in debt to Jean, Paul, and Jane for putting their trust in us.

Paul introduced us to the plaintiffs. At a meeting in a Minneapolis hotel room, a group of women sized us up and decided, with some trepidation, to let us into their lives. Resurrecting the humiliations of the three trials and the events at the mine that caused the case to happen in the first place was not a pleasant task for these women who wanted nothing more than to put the whole nightmare behind them. Their courage to come forward yet again, in the face of potential retaliation and more disapproval from their neighbors and community was admirable—a leap of faith.

We also want to thank the Rangers who welcomed us, showed us the ropes, helped us meet key sources, and entertained us with their wit and warmth: Karen Hill, Lisa Radosevich Pattni, Lorrie Janatopoulos, and

Sharon Chadwick. Two Minnesota exiles, David Johnson and Tom Nides, made important early introductions to the region.

Elizabeth Perkins, meanwhile, never took no for an answer. Her tireless research at the Minneapolis Historical Society, the Iron Range Research Center, and the Library of Congress, helped to shape the book's historical perspective. We want to thank the Sprenger & Lang staff, and especially Doug Olson, for locating obscure legal documents. We are also grateful to Sydney Brooks, Lorrie Janatopoulos, Tracy Kolker, and Sarah Abruzzese for their research and logistical assistance.

A few dedicated friends read the manuscript and gave us valuable suggestions. Many thanks to David Michaelis, James Chace, Jean Leedy, Jennifer Maguire, and Steve Fogg.

Lisa Chase, a friend and talented editor, took on the manuscript in its infancy and pushed us to write a much-improved second, and then third draft. Her dedication enhanced almost every sentence in the book.

Several editors at Doubleday helped bring this book to life. Betsy Lerner was the first to believe in the concept of the book. Amy Scheibe skillfully guided us from first to final draft. Deborah Futter, with the able help of Anne Merrow, published the book with her customary excellence.

We are also indebted to our agent, Esther Newberg, for her constant encouragement, enthusiasm, and loyalty to the project.

Our mothers, Jean Leedy and Joan Bingham, gave us inspiration and provided crucial child care help, while Bill Leedy gave unflagging encouragement. We also have our husbands, Doug Gansler and David Michaelis, to thank for their love and support—while we closed ourselves up in our offices on weekends and traveled far away from home on frequent research trips. Our five children, to whom the book is dedicated, gave up precious time with their mothers so that we could tell this important story.

Above all, we are grateful to Lois Jenson. Her sharp memory, meticulous record keeping, and willingness to give of her trust and time, allowed us to chronicle twenty-five years of her life as accurately as possible.